# The American Talleyrand

# THE
# *AMERICAN*
# TALLEYRAND

---

The *Career* and *Contemporaries* of

MARTIN VAN BUREN, *Eighth President*

---

By

Holmes Alexander

*Good Lord! What is Van? For though simple he looks,*
*'Tis a task to unravel his looks and his crooks;*
*With his depths and his shallows, his good and his evil,*
*All in all he's a riddle must puzzle the Devil.*
                    —DAVY CROCKETT

---

NEW YORK / RUSSELL & RUSSELL

COPYRIGHT, 1935, BY HARPER & BROS.

COPYRIGHT © 1962 BY HOLMES ALEXANDER

REISSUED, 1968, BY RUSSELL & RUSSELL

A DIVISION OF ATHENEUM HOUSE, INC.

BY ARRANGEMENT WITH HOLMES ALEXANDER

L.C. CATALOG CARD NO: 68-10899

PRINTED IN THE UNITED STATES OF AMERICA

FOR THREE:

AND THEY KNOW WHY

# THE CAST

## MARTIN VAN BUREN—The Little Magician

### Supported by:

JOHN QUINCY ADAMS—*a nudist*
AARON BURR—*a man about town*
NICHOLAS BIDDLE—*a rugged individualist*
HENRY CLAY ⎱
DANIEL WEBSTER ⎰ *Les Misérables*
JOHN C. CALHOUN ⎰
WILLIAM H. CRAWFORD—*the lost heir*
DE WITT CLINTON—*a ditch-digger*
DAVY CROCKETT—*himself*
PEGGY EATON—*a woman of some importance*
ALBERT GALLATIN—*an immigrant*
ALEXANDER HAMILTON—*another immigrant*
WILLIAM HENRY HARRISON—*the clodhopper*
WASHINGTON IRVING—*a gentle skeptic*

ANDREW JACKSON—*none but the brave*
THOMAS JEFFERSON—*a plain man*
EDWARD LIVINGSTON—*a refugee*
ABRAHAM LINCOLN—*a passing stranger*
WILLIAM L. MARCY—*a realist*
DOLLY MADISON—*a laughing lady*
JAMES MADISON—*Dolly's husband*
JAMES MONROE—*a Virginian*
JOHN MARSHALL—*a notary*
JOHN RANDOLPH—*a damaged soul*
DANIEL D. TOMPKINS—*a natural*
M. DE TALLEYRAND—*a linguist*
THURLOW WEED—*the Nemesis*

### and

| THE ARMY | THE NAVY | THE PRESS | THE THRONE |
|---|---|---|---|
| GEORGE CLINTON | OLD IRONSIDES | DUFF GREEN | WILLIAM OF ENG- |
| SAM HOUSTON | | HORACE GREELEY | LAND |
| WINFIELD SCOTT | | WILLIAM LLOYD | WILLIAM OF HOL- |
| ZACHARY TAYLOR | | GARRISON | LAND |
| THE VAN RENSSE- | | IKE HILL | JAMES K. POLK |
| LAERS | | AMOS KENDALL | MILLARD FILLMORE |
| | | FRANK BLAIR | FRANKLIN PIERCE |
| | | WATSON WEBB | JAMES BUCHANAN |
| | | | JOHN TYLER |

Ensemble by: ⎰ The N. Y. Legislature
The U. S. Senate
The Albany Regency
The Kitchen Cabinet
The Sons of Tammany
The Court of St. James's

### and others

# Table of Contents

# ILLUSTRATIONS

*The illustrations, grouped in a separate section, will be found following page 430.*

# ILLUSTRATIONS

*BOOK I*

# A Founding Father

DARKNESS lay over the Hudson, enshrouding the slim steeples of Kinderhook village, but two miles down a dusty road that runs between ripening crops, there were lamp-lights burning in an upper chamber. From a big sleigh-bed against the wall came feeble wheezings of an old man dying of asthma. A doctor, hastily summoned from New York, crouched over him; his three middle-aged sons loitered anxiously about the house. When midnight came it was the 24th of July, 1862, and the Eighth President of the United States was breathing his last.

Before sunrise he was dead. Next day they laid him in a rosewood casket and carried him downstairs to the large reception room where thirteen years earlier he had entertained old Henry Clay, where almost forty years before that young Washington Irving had written his Knickerbocker's History. On the 29th, the day of the funeral, eighty-one carriages trailed the hearse up the dusty road to town. In the first rode the Governor of New York, followed by that containing Samuel J. Tilden, who almost went to the White House. At the end of the procession tramped a delegation from Tammany, headed by Grand Sachem Elijah F. Prudy, who almost went to jail.

Stranahan's Hotel, as they passed it, was draped in mourning; the shops along the street had their doors closed, and over the pulpit at church was an American flag, festooned with crêpe. Mounted there, the parson eulogised for "about three-quarters of an hour," the village choir sang "God our help in ages past"; the red-shirted Kinderhook Fire Department, Company No. 2, shouldered the coffin and carried it to the cemetery. Down in Washington the Chief Justice adjourned the Supreme Court, and the Chief Magistrate ordered presidential salutes for the deceased. But the chances are that Abraham Lincoln gave little thought to his predecessor this day. He was wondering whether McClellan would ever take Richmond.

2

Martin Van Buren was nearly eighty years old when he died and, despite the cavalcade that followed him to the graveyard, he had been a forgotten man for more than a decade before they buried him. There is food for much melancholy philosophising here—*sic transit gloria*—for all adult Americans living at the time were bound to have been reminded by his death that here was a man who had literally run the gauntlet of public office and honor. He had been President, Vice President, Secretary of State, United States Senator, Ambassador to England, the Governor and Attorney General of New York. Nor is this to mention the several local and minor offices he had held, or that he had been Grand Sachem of Tammany Hall, czar of the infamous Albany Regency that mulcted New York and the nation for over a quarter-century, and acquaintance, enemy or adviser to all but one of the 15 Presidents from John Adams down through Abraham Lincoln.

But that his own time should have neglected the little Kinderhooker is not half so wondrous as that posterity has done the same thing. To date only one biography of him has graced the Twentieth Century, and of the 13 published in the Nineteenth only 2 were written after his death, the rest being political propaganda for use during his several campaigns for office. Yet, obscure as he is, it is hard to see how any one man has been more significant in the growth and development of American statecraft. The heritage he

4 ]

left his country was proved more durable than anything bequeathed by the Signers of '76, the Law-Givers of '87 or even by the sainted Father of the Nation. Surely it is no cynicism to say that the Declaration of Independence, the Constitution, the Farewell Address have become mere fossils of their pristine selves. The ink had been dry less than thirty years on the consent-of-the-governed clause when its very author, Thomas Jefferson, bought without benefit of plebiscite, the several thousands of souls who lived in the Louisiana Territory. The freedom-of-speech manifesto was aged hardly a decade ere John Adams clapped on the Sedition Law to silence press criticism against his administration. And Washington's plea for non-partisan leadership was scarcely given to the world before his own cabinet ministers were girding their loins for party warfare.

This is not to say that the idealism of the early founding fathers was not intrinsically worthy, but only that its actual value has proved totally mythical. Their names are remembered; their precepts ignored. But just the reverse is true of Van Buren. Few Americans recall his name, yet who does not know that American politics, no matter how charitably judged, is nine-tenths a concoction of cant, farce, corruption and sham?

Martin Van Buren, more than any one man, was responsible for this. It was he who conceived and constructed the gigantic patronage system which directly caused the death of two Presidents, nearly drove Lincoln insane and caused Cleveland to cry out, "It makes me feel like resigning and hell is to pay." It was he who mainly visualized and brought to pass the National Conventions where a people's choice can be conveniently nominated by a conclave of political job-holders. The adjective "vanburenish"—once in wide circulation—was coined as a synonym for vapid non-committalism, and Van Buren it was who set the style for candidates who agilely straddle the issues, who, no matter how much wire-pulling there has been back-stage, always declare themselves astonished and overcome at the honor of being "called" by the People. Possibly no man in high office ever enjoyed

[ 5

less popular affection or attained more nominal honors by sheer craftiness, yet Van Buren was faithful to his professional hypocrisies even after death. In his unfinished *Autobiography*, which he intended should be published posthumously, he still maintains the pose of a reluctant Cincinnatus urged from his furrows to serve the Republic. That was his story and he stuck to it. And so have his host of spiritual heirs unto the third and fourth generation—though many of them never heard his name.

In his day men called him the Little Magician. It was with the wave of his wand that statesmanship vanished from the American scene and politics remained in its stead. He stands in the pivotal position between the sublime and the ridiculous. He lived through the administrations of fifteen Presidents. Of the seven who preceded him to the chief magistracy—Washington, the Adamses, Jefferson, Madison, Monroe, Jackson—at least six can be called statesmen by world standards. Of the seven who followed—Harrison, Tyler, Polk, Taylor, Fillmore, Pierce, Buchanan—the best hardly scales the knoll of mediocrity. Before Martin Van Buren had his will of the body politic, it was quality of mind and intensity of purpose that made a man First Citizen. Afterwards, it was availability, subservience and party regularity. The Little Magician brought the presidency down within reach of the Average Man.

3

All this Martin Van Buren did for his countrymen, and they have not even remembered to damn him. Is it because his conduct smacks of treachery that he has been banished to Limbo? But Aaron Burr did service against his people and is remembered. Is it because America abhors bossism? But Boss Tweed's memory is still green. Is it because Van Buren ultimately died in failure? But who has forgotten John C. Calhoun?

No, none of this has reacted against the Little Magician. It is simply that to historians and life-writers he seems to

A Founding Father

lack color. After all, Aaron Burr bred bastards; Boss Tweed
plundered a city; Calhoun engineered a bloody revolution.
No such high adventures ever befell Martin Van Buren. He
left illegitimate heirs to his shame, but they are spiritual
ones. He undid a nation's honor, but no one cares about
that. He steered the country through an economic depression, but no one believes that a real depression could have
happened in those distant days.

No wonder biographers have left him alone. He can
neither be debunked nor exalted, much less defended or
exposed. Search his memoirs, his correspondence, the com-
ments of his contemporaries—there is little to justify either
the leer of the scandal-monger or the tender tear of the sob-
sister. True, he was accused of being the natural son of
Aaron Burr, but there is nothing to it. True, he exploited
a woman in the process of making his way to the White
House, but there is no reason to suppose he ever laid carnal
hands upon her. Once he became President, he served wisely
and with sacrificial nobility, but so outrageous had been his
previous record that it was too late then to live down his
reputation.

Put to it to vitalize the man, his one modern commentator
has attempted to plant deep and tender emotions under the
vanburenish surface of suave indifference. His early poverty,
says this Boswell, gave the Little Magician a profound and
heart-felt sympathy for the suffering masses, compared to
which Lincoln's humanity seems little better than mere sniv-
elling cant. Wasn't Van Buren instrumental in abolishing
the Debtor's Prison? Didn't he defend the common folk
against the machinations of robber baron, banker and loan
shark? Yes, but if, until President, he ever did more than a
single thing which cannot be authentically traced to political expediency; if he ever, till then, took an unqualified
stand save with his back to the wall, then the proof that he
did has perished with his bones.

And as his public life appears to lack stuff to make it
colorful, so also does his private one. There are hints, but
no evidence, of irregularity. Where, for instance, did he

[ 7

make his money? Martin Van Buren began the struggle for
life not only penniless but in debt. He carried on a desultory
law practice until middle life, when he suddenly retired,
bought himself an estate, travelled abroad, entertained lav-
ishly, dressed extravagantly, and partially supported three
married sons with families. Other men of his time reaped a
fortune by political collusion; some of them were exposed to
public disgrace and several were his henchmen. But he who
was called the Careful Dutchman took no chances. In a day
when duels were as common as fist-fights, he was challenged
twice but never faced an opponent. In a day when it was the
part of gentlemen to play the cards and the races, he gambled only on elections—but since he arranged most of these,
it will hardly endear him to a sporting public.

## 4

Casually considered, then, the soul of Martin Van Buren
seems one it were best to let lie. For though a man be historically important and have not color, his life-tale lacks
even the empty pleasantry of a sounding brass or tinkling
cymbal. But that is the paradox of the little fellow. Because
he is vague he is fascinating. No one ever solved the enigma
of him, because he intended that no one ever should. In an
age when men like Webster, Calhoun and Clay were wise,
Van Buren was merely clever. Yet while these were gnashing
their teeth in the Senate Chamber, Van Buren ascended to
the White House. What he lacked in genius he made up in
ingenuity, and he took a whimsical pride in being the man
he was. Once a Senator accepted a bet that he could trap
Van Buren into committing himself to some positive belief.

"Matt," he said, "it's been rumored that the sun rises in
the East. Do you believe it?"

"Well, Senator, I understand that's the common acceptance, but as I never get up till after dawn I can't really
say."

Another time two newspaper men saw him leaning against

the railing of a Hudson River steamboat and one of them accepted the same wager.

"Fine day, isn't it, Mr. Van Buren?"

"Now that depends on what you mean by a fine day. There are all sorts of fine days. This particular one ——"

These, at least, are two legendary anecdotes about him, and unquestionably they are essentially if not literally true. The first one he quotes in his *Autobiography*, and lives up to his name by declining to say whether or not it actually happened. Doubtless it did and many incidents like it, for they are the things that reveal the man whom Randolph of Roanoke was moved to call one who habitually "rowed to his object with muffled oars."

What was his honest opinion on most of the important issues of the day, no one was ever sure. And probably the reason was that he *had* few opinions. About the art of political chicanery he knew aplenty, but about the business of government next to nothing at all. Throughout his first twenty years in public harness he remained abysmally ignorant on outstanding problems. In a pinch he could cram his head full of facts and figures like a college sophomore, and bluff his way through. He did it again and again.

"Much adroitness," he confesses posthumously, "was often necessary to avoid appearing in debate until I had made myself master of the subject under discussion."

Adroitness—that was always his forte. It was truly a magical feat he performed in bringing the presidency down to his own level. He could not go up the mountain, so he brought the mountain down to him. This he did because to be President, as he admitted in an unguarded moment, had always been "my most earnest desire." That does not mean he was truly ambitious. Vanity he had, but no more real ambition than he had real genius. He aspired to the White House only because it happened to be the peak of a public career. He had no intention of doing anything more than enjoying himself there. Arriving, he found himself engulfed in the maelstrom of a financial panic, and labored gallantly and cool-headedly against it, steering the country through at his own political peril. But this claim of greatness, thus thrust upon him, was no part of his plan. All he asked was to serve the honorable period of two terms, then retire to his acres and pose as a patriarch—like Jefferson at Monticello, like Jackson at the Hermitage.

And to attain this comfortable eminence Martin Van Buren gave all that was in him. Having only a modicum of brain-power and being opposed by half a dozen men who had it abundantly, he was forced to resort to trickery. Craftiness became not second nature to him, but his ruling passion. What Davy Crockett says of him—"If he could gain an object as well by openness as intrigue, he would choose the latter."—seems to have been a solemn fact. Not for nothing was he called the Red Fox of Kinderhook. No trail he laid ever went straight to his destination, and many a time the pack yapping at his traces was left barking up the wrong tree. When he decided to be Secretary of State, he confounded his rivals by resigning from the Senate and running for Governor of New York. When he deemed it time to make himself Vice President, he feinted off in another direction by resigning the State Department and becoming Ambassador to England. He was Governor ten weeks of a two-year term, Ambassador less than five months, and when the pursuers finally caught up to him, he was calmly sunning himself in the position he had originally chosen.

As a political strategist Martin Van Buren never had an equal in America, and because his type no longer exists, he never will have a rival. On the day following his death the New York *Times* editorially linked his name to Machiavelli and Mephistopheles. Before that, and since, he has been called the American Talleyrand. He was not a boss, but a courtier. Had he been born into a monarchy, the palace, the drawing-room and the privy council would have been his scene of action, but even in a republic his dealings were always with the princes and lordlings of the governmental power. A dandy in dress and in mannerisms, his methods were immaculately free from the sordid crassness that characterizes political leadership in the United States. With infinite delicacy and the politest of deceit, he performed his atrocities. Almost all the great and the near-great of his time bit the dust before the Little Magician. John Quincy Adams he manoeuvred out of office. Clay he side-tracked. Calhoun he banished. Clinton he ambushed. Jackson he utilized. Randolph he slew. Webster he waylaid. With such an array of scalps at his belt, it is no wonder that the conqueror had few friends and a legion of enemies. Yet the suavity of his personal charm and a disarming smile saved him from any intense and unrelenting hatred. Men with a sense of humor surreptitiously admired him; those without it glumly despised him. Adams, Calhoun and Webster were barely civil, but Clay and Randolph good-naturedly licked their wounds and made merry in the tent of the victor. The byplay and repartee of these three friendly enemies was for many years the small talk of Washington. Once when Van Buren, as Secretary of State, rather gruesomely consigned the warm-blooded and consumptive Virginian to a winter in Petrograd, Randolph subtly retaliated by sending him an unbroken saddle horse which Van Buren dared not refuse to ride for fear of a duelist's wrath. Once, as President, he was receiving at a White House levee when Clay sidled up and banteringly whispered that it must be pleasant to be surrounded by so many friends.

"Well, the weather is very fine," returned the President.

## 5

The tale of Martin Van Buren, however, is no success story. To be sure, he started at the bottom and reached the top by his own efforts. To be sure, by telling half the tale he can be pictured as something of a champion—an under-sized David triumphant in a veritable den of Goliaths. But his ultimate goal he never attained. When he quitted the White House, it was not at the end of a second term but a first. It was not voluntarily but in rout. And Lindenwald, instead of being a Monticello or a Hermitage, became an

Elba from which he made frantic and repeated efforts to escape.

Nor was he ever, though he cheerfully tried to act out the fiction, a martyred exile. No pilgrimage led to his door. Henry Clay came there, but Clay by this time was no more than a battered old soldier from the hostile camp. Sammy Tilden dropped in, but Tilden was only a youngish hopeful who came less to serve than to learn. When the Little Magician's hand lost its cunning, the tame rabbits jumped out of his hat and ran to new fields of clover. When his ship finally went down, few of the crew remained on deck with their captain. Three times after his Inauguration he was defeated candidate for the presidency, and the third time he showed the unmistakable symptoms of a politician *in extremis*. Jilted by his own Party, he ran on a third ticket. After that he was finished. Fourteen more years he lived, but the world scarcely knew it. The Red Fox of Kinderhook had gone to earth.

There is irony in the tale, but it is comic irony. There is pathos, but it draws no tears. Martin Van Buren was a man too clever for his own good. As he outwitted others, so he ended by outwitting himself. Like the fabled Dr. Frankenstein, he fashioned an organism after the human image and then lost control of it. The political system which Van Buren built up was his own undoing. America learned too well, and turned his engines against him. He who had devised methods with which to beat such stout fellows as Calhoun, Webster and Clay, lived to fall by the same methods before such political pigmies as Harrison, Polk and Taylor.

But the irony does not stop here. Whether the tale of Martin Van Buren is tragedy or farce, it is his country's too, and the telling of it is the telling of her back-stage history. Of political America he was the Founding Father; as he, so was she, finally victimized by the system. There are epic qualities to the story. Like Odysseus, he represents a race of men who set out to pillage a fair nation. Like Aeneas, he sailed through many happenings and conflicts to establish an empire for his heirs to inherit. Figures greater than himself he constantly encountered and, where he lacked strength to deal with them, he used trickery—hoodwinking the gods, blinding the giants and dragging more than a few victims at his chariot wheels.

To be a real epic his story lacks only the nobility of a high and happy ending, and that is perhaps because the true ending is not reached at his death. His System marched on, and who can write *finis* to the travesty of American politics?

CHAPTER II

# A President Is Born and Reared

## (1782–1796)

---

HARDLY ever has History arranged anything so artistically as when she contrived that America's first real politician should have been literally born at the polls. In his father's tavern at Kinderhook-by-the-Hudson, Martin Van Buren entered the nation he was to rule and to baffle. The nation itself was at the time not much older than he, for this was December 5th, 1782, and little more than a year earlier Cornwallis had been cornered at Yorktown and the Declaration of Independence became an accomplished fact. Kinderhook's newest-born was the first son of his father and the 360th lineal descendant of the peasant ancestor who had been shipped out of Amsterdam 151 years before in a cargo of indentured servants, all bound for the estate of the rich diamond-merchant, Kiliaen van Rensselaer.

The American forebears of the Little Magician seem to have been remarkable for one thing—consistency. None of them ever amounted to much, and all of them show a bovine, cud-chewing contentment with the *status quo*. In a land fairly teeming with opportunity, they never rose above the humble caste of small and impoverished land-owners. In a land embattled for its own freedom, their names are missing from the rolls of regiments. In a land whose frontier beckoned to the ambitious and adventurous, they preferred to stay where a frivolous fate had dropped them. So far as the

14 ]

record exists—and all six generations are accounted for—no Van Buren till Martin ever ventured to plant a homestead more than a few miles from the River. Apparently only two of them ever bore arms—and these both in self-defense against the Indians. Apparently only one of them ever did anything worth mentioning—and this was a prehistoric bootlegger who is known to have invested most of his available capital in firewater, evidently for forbidden traffic among the redskins.

Far from being the industrious, intelligent fellows that tradition likes to make of colonial Dutchmen, these early ancestors of the Eighth President were as inert, unimaginative and uninteresting as the soil which they half-heartedly tilled. Other families beside which they worked as bondsmen to the Patroon rose to wealth, prominence and power, but the Van Burens, once they had passed out of mere serfdom, went no further. So slovenly were they, indeed, that they never learned either to speak the language of their adopted land or to write that of their native one. Whatever fell into their hands they seized, but to reach out for more seems to have been too much of a tax on their phlegmatic energies.

Even the name by which they have come down to modern times was wholly an accident. When Marten Cornelissen van Buurmalsen found himself possessed of nine children and half of a small island in the River near Albany, he deemed it time to draw up his will. But when he called on his lawyer he could not for the life of him remember how to pronounce his name, much less how to spell it. Apparently what they did was take down a map of Holland and locate a small village called Buren. It was neither geographically nor phonetically the town of his ancestor's birthplace, but it was close enough. "Van Buren" was the name beside which he finally scrawled his X mark, and the heirs who acquired the land did not quibble over the title. No more did their most distinguished descendant when, years later, a King of Holland embraced him as a cousin, declaring that Count Buren was one of his own royal titles. The little diplomat only bowed and smiled, returning one of his characteristic answers that neither denied nor affirmed the kinship. He had no intention of snubbing a monarch, but neither did he forget that within a few months he would be going before the People as a candidate for the vice-presidency. Any implication of royalism, he knew, would be hard to explain to that ferocious king-hater, Andrew Jackson, his running-mate—not to mention the great American public.

But when the last election was over and lost, the ex-President quietly returned to the King of Holland, claimed the relationship and procured himself a dazzling coat-of-arms to hang on the wall at Lindenwald.

2

The village of Kinderhook, which in the year of Martin's birth contained seven families of Van Burens, was in a strategic position to catch whatever gossip, political or otherwise, might be circulating about the State. It was not only on the post-road from New York to Albany, but on the water-route as well, being the only town on the east bank of any importance north of Poughkeepsie, then the State capital.

And Abraham Van Buren's tavern was the social heart of the village. It was a long, low clapboard affair, topped with a sharply pitched roof and supplemented with a small wooden annex which served as kitchen and overflow sleeping-chamber for the patrons of the inn. The tavern, established by Abraham's father, had been doing business for about a quarter-century, and this thin layer of tradition gave it the dignity of respectability. Here once every year (and twice in congressional years) came the voters to cast their ballots. Here in the yard the coach horses were changed, the mail unloaded and the traveller dismounted for a few minutes' respite from the bumpy journey. Here in the taproom gathered the townsfolk of an evening, puffing their three-foot clay pipes, sipping their schiedam and settling the affairs of the new nation.

In the back room the quality of the town took its ease, not mingling—save around election time—with the lower orders. Upper New York in the late eighteenth century was no less of a feudal domain than was Virginia. There was a three-level social system. The aristocracy, consisting of the old patroon families and a few others who had come into dignity by their own efforts; the yeomanry, consisting of tenant farmers, poor white trash and shop-keepers; and finally the slaves, who were not to be freed for another forty-five years.

It seems to have been fortunate for Abraham Van Buren that his father passed down to him a going concern which maintained its momentum without much help from the proprietor. Mine Host was an improvident soul, a ne'er-do-well and a dreamer. When he had money he lent it without much hope of recovery, and when he had none he borrowed with as little hope of return. Moreover, Father Abraham occupied many of his waking hours by building up great schemes that had nothing to do with his tavern. They were mainly founded on the airy indignations of Messrs. Locke, Rousseau and Jefferson, and though the good man could not possibly have read or heard these gentlemen in the original, he did come into a second-hand knowledge by listening to what was being said about the inn. To these gleanings he added a few drops of his own peevish philosophy about the difficulty of getting on in life, and the result was that he became something of a mellow and engaging misanthrope. During the Revolution he was a Whig when nearly everyone else in the neighborhood was a Tory, and after the Revolution he was a Republican when everyone that mattered was a Federalist. News of this bold fellow reached General George Clinton, the State's Irish and fire-eating Governor, and he mailed Abraham a captain's commission. Mine Host was truly embarrassed. Bark he could, but he could not bite. *He* go out and fight for his principles? *He* risk shot and shell to promote the rights of man? Not while he could snooze by his fire-side and think of them.

So he returned the commission, and lapsed back to his dreaming. He had more and more time for it as the years rolled on, for his eccentricities of thought began to tell on the business, and though his tavern remained the focal point of the village for a long time after his son's birth, some of his old customers were drifting into Quackenbush's place down the street a bit. And more were to drift later.

In the midst of his Whiggism, and at the thoroughly un-romantic age of thirty-nine, poor Abraham became enam-oured of a pious, though penniless, widow with three grow-ing children and a ten-year advantage on him in youth. Whether the widow Van Alen was comely cannot be said, for the reputation she left among her townsfolk was mainly for piety. To pray was the one thing she could do superbly and tirelessly. When a hard war-winter depleted the food supply she chanted the *Geloof* over an empty larder. When she mar-ried Abe and produced him two successive daughters, she recited *Het Onze Vater* over the empty crib. And she rejoiced and was justified to find her supplications answered. The spring would come, and the cupboard was no longer bare. A few winters slid by, and a baby boy kicked in the cradle.

3

These two helpless, harmless, laughable, lovable, middle-aged misfits bred the Little Magician. It would be pleasant and doubtless profitable to invoke psychology here, and to show that Martin Van Buren was in some shape or form a psychic chip off this pair of old blocks. But the fact seems to be that he owes as little to his immediate ancestors as he does to his distant ones. If just one time in his subsequent career the son of Mary and Abraham turned over the puz-zles of life to the will of a watching Providence—if just one time he betrayed a philosophic concern for the destiny of the race—it would be highly enlightening. But if there is one single, outstanding trait in the Red Fox's make-up it is that he never left anything to chance, much less to God. Only two sacred quotations appear in the mass of his corre-spondence, one a brief line and the other Acts 23, 6-10, where Paul artfully escapes the wrath of a mingled crowd of Sadducees and Pharisees by turning their wrath against each other. And as for philosophic concern for the rights of the governed, this expressed eagerness for enlarging the Spoils System shows the state of his mind on the occasion of his entry into the national government.

"The Post Office Department is one of the most interesting departments of the Government, and instead of wasting our time on small matters, I am for taking the bull by the horns at once."

Whatever inner heritage Van Buren owes to his parents is purely a sentimental one, and since he was never known to let sentiment stand in the way of his public or private dealings, these emotions—such as they are—are of small value to his historian. That he loved and venerated the old folks is beyond question. He was the stay and support of their declining years. As soon as he could afford it, he brought old Abe out of the tavern and set him up as a country squire. After he moved to Hudson, and later to Albany, he never let a spring or winter go by without a trip through the floods and the snow to visit them. But neither in their life or death did his parents mark him. It was he who did the influencing, not they. And that was as it should be. Mary's weepy petitions turned to hymns of praise and she lauded the Lord for having blessed her with such a famous and dutiful son. Abe puffed pridefully about town, no longer the gloomy iconoclast but the triumphant prophet whose eyes had seen the glory. Their Matty, his parents knew, would live to be President.

It was unquestionably the obvious discrepancy between the man and his sources which fostered the spicy rumor that America's pet scapegoat, Aaron Burr, was father of Martin Van Buren. There was, too, some circumstantial evidence against the accused. Throughout the year just prior to Martin's birth, Burr seems to have been a constant frequenter of the Kinderhook tavern. He had just been invalided out of the Army and was actively engaged in building up for himself an itinerant law-practice along with the reputation of being a gay and careless man of the world. Actually he lived in Albany, but business naturally brought him to the seat of Columbia County and, besides, the Van Nesses, who owned Kleirood, the estate which was later to be Lindenwald, were his boon companions. Often he visited them and freely he caroused about the country-side.

Moreover the resemblance between Burr and Van Buren in their mature years was unmistakably striking. Physically and in mannerisms they were much alike. Both were small, slender, obsequious, quick-witted and crafty. True, there were some significant differences, mainly in temperament, but Christian minds, intent on believing the worst, could easily be persuaded that these were outweighed by the likeness. Certainly the rumor had its day, and even so proper a Puritan as John Quincy Adams could gloatingly record the insinuation in the privacy of his Diary—which he knew perfectly well would be published after his death.

That the report could reasonably have been true, however, is too much to believe. For one thing Mary Van Buren was hardly the one to stir passion in the urbane and fastidious Aaron Burr. The record is silent on her beauty, but we know she was thirty-five at the time and already the mother of five. It may be argued, since Burr married a widow of exactly Mary's years, that he had a weakness for seasoned romances, but further observation compels the opinion that Theodosia Prevost's appeal was not that of the flesh, but of the mind. She was the polished product of drawing-room and salon; Mary was a hewer of fire-wood, a drawer of wellwater, as near as anyone can say the typical God-fearing, child-bearing hausfrau of a country village. But the crowning destruction of the rumor is this—that it did not originate in Kinderhook at or around the time of Martin's birth, but forty years later when he began making his first manoeuvres toward the White House.

4

His obscurity cheats Martin of a presidential childhood. No legend shows him hacking a traditional cherry tree or adorably reading the Good Book by his father's fireside. We

20 ]

have vague pictures of the yellow-haired, smiling boy doing odd jobs around the house and tavern, running errands to the neighbors and trudging off to the village school. With him sometimes trudged two other tow-heads who were to matter a little in his later life. One was Billy Van Ness, a friend who became an enemy. And the other Hanna Hoes, a cousin who became his wife. Of the school itself we have a vivid and lovable memoir, for this was the very one where Washington Irving was to find his Ichabod Crane. Like most other buildings in the vicinity it was of clapboard, with a high-peaked roof to shed the winter snows. Lighting and heat were missing, so was any variety of text-books, and so was any inspired instructorship on the part of the pedagogue.

Small wonder if the last were true, for the master, poor devil, tormented by teaching conditions that would have tried the patience of a missionary, was, in addition, under the paradoxical obligation of working his way through his own school. That an able-bodied man should be good for nothing but to wield a hickory stick and to drum sums into helpless children was too much for thrifty communities like Kinderhook, and the teacher was usually compelled to justify his existence by manual labor in the fields and barns of the neighborhood. Classes, therefore, were spasmodically held. Winter blizzards, spring ploughing, autumn harvests—any of these periodic emergencies might cancel a day's work.

For little Matty the situation was still further complicated in that he could not always be spared from home. Father Abraham's life by the time his eldest son came of school age was indeed an unwieldy affair. He seems always to have been inheriting things, and these things, which to a man of different temperament might have been blessings, were only so many burdens to him. Besides the tavern, he undertook to run a farm; besides five heirs to his own line, he had the three step-children, and on top of it all, someone had left him six huge, hungry slaves.

The problem of clothing and feeding this multitude, which included all ages and sexes, nearly prostrated the philosophic host. Until entering his fortieth year he had

[ 21

been a bachelor, dreamily free of the realities of life, and now when they fell thick and fast upon him, his reaction was to become increasingly frenzied. The many hands might have made light work of the jobs to be done, but under Abe's management, disorder ran rampant. Mary did her best to see that her brood got a fair share in the good things of childhood. She skimped and saved and prayed for a windfall, and but for her brave efforts Matty would certainly have had less education than he did. Actually he had very little. He attended the village school so irregularly that he outgrew it before he ever completed its haphazard set of courses. After that, she managed to enroll him at the Kinderhook Academy, where he suffered much the same difficulties: lack of funds and time to spend on his studies. Mary's hope was that he might eventually go to Columbia College along with Billy Van Ness, but the hope was a vain one. At thirteen he was withdrawn from the Academy and put to work in Francis Silvester's law office.

It might be surmised from Mary's anxiety to educate the boy that he showed more than a usual aptitude for his studies. After all, there was no imperative reason for an innkeeper's son to go to college. There may be something, too, in the fact that he was put to office work when there was a hostelry and a farm in the family. In the natural course of events the eldest son would take over these establishments and plug along in his father's footsteps. Just how much Matty made of his sorry opportunities at school cannot be positively said, for evidence and rumor offer conflicting conclusions. There is a vague and unfounded statement in one of his biographies that the teacher told Mary her boy could read and write English better than anyone in the class. Even if the teacher said this, it may not have been true, and even if true, certain it is that the pupil never followed up his advantages. He says of himself that he read only fitfully, and then "for amusement," and until deep in his fifties, his handwriting was worse than Shakespeare's. To his dying day he never mastered the simple rules of rhetoric, and though he could camouflage this weakness in his spoken speeches, it constantly betrayed him in his writings. He was State Senator when De Witt Clinton said of one of his letters, "It is equally offensive to grammar and truth." He was Vice President when a Speaker of the House had to ask him to decipher a note he had written. His career made it necessary for Van Buren to become a voluminous writer of pamphlets, reports and public statements, but he soon learned never to release them till they had been thoroughly edited by his friends for spelling, punctuation and grammar.

His lack of a formal education, however, was more of an embarrassment than a disadvantage. He did not need culture to be the Little Magician, and his practical knowledge of wiles and guile could not have been learned from books. Congressional Washington, when he went there, was a highly snobbish community where, culturally speaking, the goats were ignobly herded from the sheep. Most of the Westerners were, of course, ignorant, forthright fellows, but from New England and the South came men not only educated but scholarly. And neither were they unconscious of the fact. When John Quincy Adams could find nothing worse to say of his *bête noir*, Andrew Jackson, it was that "the barbarian . . . could not write a sentence of grammar." When a Senator like Randolph of Roanoke took the floor, his speech was a veritable shower of classic lore and literary quotations. Latin tags and Greek epigrams were the despair of the unfortunate clerks whose job it was to record all addresses, and once when Randolph undertook to insult a pair of his colleagues by likening them to Blifil and Black George—two characters out of Fielding's *Tom Jones*—half the Senators rightly predicted a duel within a week and the other half wondered what the insane Virginian was talking about.

A man of Van Buren's foppish tastes naturally yearned for intellectual ease among these savants, but he never attained it. His attempt to become a patron of letters by appointing Irving, Paulding, Bancroft and Hawthorne to government sinecures earned him only the jeers of the intelligentsia, and his few essays at injecting learned allusions into his speeches had such graceless results that he soon abandoned the effort.

Nor was he cheered by the fact that at his own game he could make blockheads out of these Magi. Five years from his death he was still idly bemoaning his own ignorance and declaring that, if he could start life over again, he would "have first acquired a sound education."

### 5

It was not at school or in his home life that the child became father to the man. It was in the tap-room of the tavern. Working there in the evenings as pot-boy he learned to hold his own against the banter of tipsy customers and to follow something of their conversations among each other. How much of American history has been written in alcohol has never been told. Already the era was beginning when the city saloon and town tavern were to be the hatching-places of political policy and plot. It is an old parable which tells how one day a man came running into the board-room of a city hall crying, "Mr. Alderman, your saloon is afire!"— and a moment later stood in a room whence all but he had fled. By the time Martin Van Buren came to die the record would show that something like two-thirds of New York's polls were in saloons, and there never was to be a time in the Republic's life when liquor, either the consumption or the discussion of it, would not hold a high place in the councils of state. So it is not without symbolic significance that the founding father of politics should have matriculated in a school not of hard knocks but hard drinks.

And while he grew up, America was coming to know herself. The country was being drenched in the pamphleteering craze that was the beginning of her political self-consciousness. These journals were not as yet newspapers, for they dealt more with issues than events, and were, for the most part, venomous and one-sided diatribes aimed at personalities who represented the current problems of the day. Hardly ever did they praise any one directly, for the common mode of defending a man, or an idea, was simply to vilify their opponents. The result of these vigorous and exciting methods was a wide popularizing of political knowledge. Even people interested only in hearing the latest slander, accidentally imbibed much information concerning matters of state, and in taking sides with their favorites, found themselves heatedly defending their favorites' doctrines.

Moreover these pamphlets usually carried with them the double enchantment of intimacy and mystery. Frequently they were published in the form of an open letter to the victim of the attack and nearly always they were signed by an obviously fictitious name, such as "Cato," "Aristides," "Caesar" or "Brutus." The signature, however, was more a custom of the time than any timorous attempt to disguise the writer, and the game of guessing the authorship was only difficult enough to be intriguing. Freedom of speech being among the most luxurious of the new liberties, it was considered a high privilege, for instance, to address the exalted George Washington in person and to call him (as often happened) "a crocodile," "a hyena," "a traitor."

Whether such pamphlets were among the things that Matty read "for amusement" can only be guessed, but there can be little doubt that they found their way into the tavern, and that he heard them debated. Now and then he must have heard discussions from the lips of venerated authority, for not only Aaron Burr frequented the tap-room during this period, but also there came two very serious-minded gentlemen, one old and one young, called respectively, Mr. Jay and Mr. Hamilton. With the gossip that surrounded these men and others of equal, though more distant, greatness Matty was at close quarters. He heard how Mr. Jay, having won the governorship from General Clinton, had been cheated out of it, mainly by the machinations of Mr. Burr and much to the wrath of Mr. Hamilton. Thrilling it was to hear how Mr. Jay had been burned in effigy and Mr. Hamilton stoned from a platform and how "ten thousand people in the streets of Philadelphia threatened to drag Washington from his house." He came to understand why the "great little Madison" hated Mr. Hamilton; why an obscure young Senator named Monroe had accused the same gentleman of adultery;

why the new capital was going to be situated in a wilderness on the Potomac; why the arrival of Ambassador Gênet so delighted Mr. Jefferson and at the same time caused Mr. Washington to cry out, "By God, I would rather be in my grave than in this present situation!"

War, heard Matty, was menacing every day, first with England, then with France; a group of grown-up men in New York were playing children's games by dressing like Indians and calling themselves sons of Big Chief Tammany; an impudent Senator had nicknamed the Vice President "His Rotundity"; Lady Washington had called Mr. Jefferson's followers "filthy democrats"; Mr. Jefferson had retaliated by calling Mr. Hamilton's followers "monarchists"—and it was a question which was the greater insult.

If Matty were given to pondering, he must have thought these were queer pastimes for men who were supposed to be leaders in a new and noble Republic. He could not know that out of this chaos of slander, scandal and bile was coming the stuff to make his own life's drama. He, like his amused but bewildered country, could not understand that these were not premature death-pangs she was undergoing, but merely the birth-agonies of party feeling. Organized party politics, in its modern sense, was not yet, but the makings of it were there. And so were the makings of the Little Magician. The man, Martin Van Buren, was no offspring of Mary and Abraham. He outgrew that. The Red Fox of Kinderhook no more had congenital ancestors than he had an indigenous background. The heredity and environment that made him what he was were both political. Ere he was twelve years old, and America only a year older, her statesmen had learned the art of stooping to conquer; and in these ungainly and often hilarious postures they became his true ancestors, the ones from whom he took the real foundation of his character, traits and methods.

Around the smiling little pot-boy an heritage and a destiny were forming, and events were coming to pass that would set the scene for his entrance. Perhaps as he sat there listening to the tap-room chatter, he heard names that gave him vi-

sionary glimpses of what was to come, of some of the characters who would stalk the stage with him. Could he know,
for instance, that Andrew Jackson had already been made a
Congressman and John Quincy Adams an Ambassador; that
De Witt Clinton had graduated from Columbia with her
first diploma, William Henry Harrison left Hampton-Sidney
without one, and Daniel Webster was soon to be debating
grandly at Dartmouth; that Randolph of Roanoke was quite
sure he was impotent and Peggy Eaton's father quite sure
he was not; that John C. Calhoun was reading fat books on
philosophy in South Carolina and Henry Clay learning to
overcome his stammer by haranguing the cattle and pigs he
was herding in Virginia?

It would take a biographer wiser than this one to say all
that, but at least we have it from the chronicles that when
men talked politics at Abe's place, Matty would sit silently
and solemnly among them, his blue eyes wide, his yellow-
crowned head cocked to listen, as if he were fondly conscious
of the great drama that was gathering itself about him.

# CHAPTER III

# A Politician Learns His Ropes

## (1796–1800)

THE poet who boasted that in childhood he "lisped in numbers and the numbers came" had nothing on the Little Magician. Matty, of course, had yet to perfect his technique, but all the essential instincts seem to have been his from the start. Until his heyday most men who attained importance in governmental affairs were what Brander Matthews was to call "polygonats." They—for instance, Washington, the Clintons, Franklin, Jefferson, Jackson—had other interests save politics. They were country gentlemen, lawyers, writers, soldiers, dabblers in the arts and sciences, to whom statecraft was a public duty, but never a profession. Martin Van Buren was all of one piece. He was a politician, almost pure and far from simple, but a politician to the mysterious marrow of his bones. Before he came to cast his first ballot he would have given evidence of every talent that earned him his niche in history. He would have masterfully evaded some issues, have sought and accepted a public trust, have elected a candidate of his own choosing, and have cunningly deployed himself into a position where the moving tide of men and events would bear him upward and on.

He was, even in his nonage, the Red Fox. Already and somehow he had become "one who rowed to his object with muffled oars." Matty was thirteen when he left the Academy to go to work, and in less than four years he had slid slyly into his first political office. The office, to be sure, was a purely nominal one with not much authority or responsibility, but it happened to be the only one within legal reach of a minor, and Matty sought and took it with the same purposeful aplomb he was to show for every stepping-stone on his way to the White House. He never did anything without forethought, and he rarely did anything where his real objective was his apparent one. Matty wanted to go to New York, and the way he went about it was to run for a local office in Kinderhook. To New York he went ostensibly to learn the law, but what he actually succeeded in learning was something else.

He did not need to go much further than his own front door to demonstrate his happy faculty for evading embarrassing issues. Politics in Kinderhook was an almost perfect model of the caste system. The aristocrats, save for a few *nouveau riche* families like the Van Nesses and the Van Schaacks, were all Federalists, while the yeomanry were all Republicans. It could scarcely have been otherwise, for Mr. Hamilton had said in so many words that "Your People, sir, your People is a great beast!"; while Mr. Jefferson, fresh from the French Revolution, had been no less explicit in declaring that all men were "free and equal." Matty Van Buren, being scion of a tavern-keeper, had Republicanism socially forced upon him, and even if he had attempted, as yet, to rise above his sources there was always the uncompromising volubility of Father Abraham about his neck. Moreover, it was difficult even to disguise one's political identity, for all good Republicans proudly attired themselves after the fashion of Citizen Jefferson—wearing staid hues in breeches and waistcoats, laces at the shoes instead of buckles and short hair instead of long.

This flagrant flying of his colors was the first problem that confronted Martin Van Buren when he set out to make his way in the world. For his job was that of law-clerk to Francis Silvester, and the Silvesters, amiable folk that they were, were nevertheless Federalists. Plainly, then, when Matty, garbed in the homespun of one of Lady Washington's "filthy

[ 29

democrats," appeared that day at the office, affairs were brought to something of a humorous impasse. It would be making too much of a good story to say that young Francis (he was just out of Columbia) was any more than mildly amused at the situation, but we know that he noted the incongruity and pleasantly jibed Matty about it. To Francis it could have made little difference what theories of government his clerk espoused or represented, for the boy's connection with the firm was only a menial one—his duties consisting of sweeping the floor, cleaning the pen quills and copying some of the chancery cases. Still, if the situation was funny to Francis, it was not so to Matty. To a less observant youngster than he, it must have been apparent that his chances of rising in the firm were greatly diminished by belonging to the wrong party. Therefore one day he vanished, and when he returned, Francis knew that he had hired no numskull. The little apprentice had borrowed money, gone to Albany and outfitted himself—no doubt despite the outraged protests of Abe—in the sartorial grandeur of a Federalist: triangular hat, bright breeches and silvery shoe buckles.

Childish as the pantomime was, its very simplicity reveals the making of the man. It seems no coincidence that 1797, a banner year for the Federalists and the Silvesters, was also the year Matty decided to change his colors. John Adams had trounced Mr. Jefferson for the presidency; Francis' father became State Senator; Francis' cousin, Stephen Van Rensselaer, became Lieutenant-Governor; Francis' friend and idol, the austere Mr. Jay, had finally managed to unhorse George Clinton and become Governor. In view of all this, Matty doubtless reasoned, why not be one thing at the tavern and something else at the office?

Because the Federalists were momentarily in the saddle did not mean that they were the popular party. This same John Jay had drawn the New York Constitution back in '77 and carefully disenfranchised as many of the lower orders as he conveniently could. No one not possessed of a hundred-pound freehold could vote for the Governor or State

Senators, and only those worth twenty pounds in property, or paying forty shillings in rent, could vote even for the local Assemblymen. This ruling did not work so stringently in rural districts as in the cities, but it was effective enough to make the elections of Columbia County close contests, and a neat manoeuvre by Mr. Hamilton had given his party the vantage. Hamilton, after much breast-beating (something of which he was rarely guilty), had persuaded the Legislature that it was un-American, un-Christian and nonsensical to keep War Tories from having their vote in the Land of the Free. He did not carry his argument to its logical conclusion, namely that it was also un-American to disenfranchise his pet aversion, the People, but if his logic was incomplete, his success was not. Tories, naturally, were Federalists; the result at the polls spoke for itself, and Matty would have been no embryo of the American Talleyrand if he had missed this initial opportunity to play the weathervane for moving events.

Nor could he have been otherwise than encouraged in his duplicity to find that it brought him rewards. Had he, poor Cinderella of a Republican, been left behind to do the chores while his betters fared forth to the courts? Not now! Instead of a broom, his badge of service became the briefcase of his employer, and where Francis went, went Matty. It is a timid biographer who will not say here, and despite the lack of documentary evidence, that the result followed the cause. No proof is extant that Matty ceased to be office drudge simply because he ceased to wear Republican raiment, but the happenings exist almost side by side, and if the causation is not to be proved, then let it be abruptly surmised. Off to the courts he went, and, by a further surmise, in a high and exultant humor.

For to escape enjoying himself a-carrying Francis's papers, Matty would needs have been not an infant prodigy but a problem child. Law practice around the Dutch counties was as primitive a process as it was diverting. Court for the most part was held in taverns where the enlivening presence of liquor, and the general character of the natives, made even

the dullest cases an entertainment and an education. The
drinking bar was the bar of justice, "and the party," says a
lawyer of the day, "who should be so wanting in good sense
or generosity as to forget or refuse to enlighten the minds
of the jury by a good substantial drink . . . would be very
likely to lose his cause." Upon each counsel's table there
stood a bottle of rum "to be used as the trial progressed,
whenever it should be necessary to solve an intricate problem." On one such occasion, it seems, a noted drinker and
hard fighter was haled into court and, while the Justice in
broken English arraigned him, the defendant pulled out a
filthy pack of cards and shuffled them nonchalantly under
His Honor's nose. Having finished the arraign, the bench
addressed the accused, and the following conversation ensued:

"Well, Mr. C, what do you say to dat?"

"What do I say to that?" roared the bad man. "I say you're
a damned old fool."

"Oh, tut, tut," rejoined His Honor. "Dat may be very
well, Mr. C, but what has dat to do with this case?"

Whereupon "the defendant knocked down the constable,
threw the cards in the Justice's face, kicked over the table
and cleared out."

There comes down, too, another incident which throws
some light upon court procedure. This time a Justice found
himself on a case where honesty forced him to give a decision
which did not at all win popular approval. Throughout the
hearing an audience had sat in sinister silence, drinking
copiously but not moving. Having pronounced the verdict,
His Honor put on his coat and started homeward through
the dusk, but just outside the tavern he was surrounded by
a crowd which "commenced urinating on him from every
direction."

Matty seems to have fitted pretty well into the scheme of
things, for he remained Francis Silvester's porter only a
little longer than he did his janitor. Attorneys in Kinderhook and the vicinity, being mostly aristocrats who could
afford an education, did not function any too smoothly with

juries, especially on cases that involved action against representatives of the common folk. Any firm that could produce
a lawyer with his family roots and his sympathy in the soil
would be so much to the good, but such men were hard to
find. Silvester and his associates, however, nursed an idea in
the back of their minds, and at the first opportunity they
determined to try it out. The opportunity came one day on
a minor case heard at a village about two miles from Kinderhook. One Aaron Gardinier was in charge, and when he
had finished with the evidence he turned to the little clerk
who sat beside him.

"Here, Matt, you sum up."

When he came to tell the story more than half a century
later, Van Buren says, of course, that he spoke extempore,
and anyone may believe it who can. It is barely possible that
this is the truth, and there is nothing but skepticism to dis-
prove it. It seems largely improbable that any attorney would
entrust a case, no matter how simple, to a child of fifteen
who was not only untried but unprepared. And it seems far
more characteristic and creditable to Matty that he quietly
rehearsed this speech and brought it off with satisfying success. A boy of his manly good sense would scarcely have allowed himself to be caught without preparation for a crisis,
and a man of his boyish vanity would scarcely admit it, even
if he were. But prepared or not, Matty covered himself with
glory. The jury gave him a verdict, and his employer gave
him a big shiny half-dollar.

After that Abe's Boy became the Boy Lawyer. Silvester
used him exclusively in cases where the court's heart needed
to be touched or its humor prodded by the sight of an attractive, handsome man-child pleading the cause of justice.
It is unlikely that the Boy Lawyer treated his juries to anything very wonderful in the way of eloquence or logic. Unless he got worse instead of better as he grew up, Martin
Van Buren was never much of an elocutionist, though oratory was one of his special conceits. The *Autobiography* tells
how "the Congress-going ladies whose name was legion,"

[ 33

used to flock to the galleries when he took the floor, but evidently all was not admiration above decks.

"I can see the eye-brows of the fashionable raised at his false pronunciation," testifies John Randolph. "He always says 'conthiderable' for 'considerable', etc."

The lisp and the pretty Dutch accent probably added much to his childish appeal, but in manhood they were impediments which he never bothered to overcome. For oratory, as for every other serious business he essayed, the Little Magician had no genius. Much more to his credit, he merely had talents which he made to serve the purpose. Both in conversation and public-speaking his were the fascinating gifts of sophistry and easy persuasiveness. Undertaking (as he frequently did) to prove black to be white, he resorted not to the rhapsody or bombast of a Clay or Webster, but to the beguiling intimacy of a heart-to-heart talk which seldom failed to disarm and captivate an audience, even unto the United States Senate and the Supreme Court.

The importance, and possibly the misfortune, of these early conquests was that they taught the boy how easily he could substitute the counterfeit for the genuine, how handily he could turn to account the charm of his personality and the nimbleness of his wit. It was well for his progress, but bad for his fame, that he learned so soon that the race is not always to the swift nor the battle to the strong. To cajole an audience and ambush an opponent were things he learned before he was out of his teens; how Francis Silvester and his engaging little helpmate rode from triumph to triumph became Kinderhook lore. And when, at the tender age of seventeen, he won a case from the renowned Elisha Williams, many years his senior and recognized champion of Columbia County bar, the Boy Lawyer became the Boy Wonder. He was the toast of the taverns, the darling of the Dutch peasantry who claimed him as their own, and it is not remarkable if his self-esteem grew with his reputation.

"Poor little Matty!" sneered the disgruntled Williams. "What a blessing it is for one to think himself the greatest little fellow in the world! . . . Inflated with pride, flattered for his pertness, caressed for his impudence and praised for his importance, it is not to be wondered that . . . he should think himself great."

Before long Matty came to see that Silvester was getting much the better of the bargain. As apprentice the boy could not charge for his services, and until he was of age he could not go out on his own. The intensity of social and political feelings made it unlikely that he would ever rise to much responsibility with the Silvester firm. What he needed, he saw, was a patron—a rich Republican lawyer to whom to article himself and with whom he would be in line for an eventual partnership. There was no such person in Kinderhook, but there was his schoolmate, Billy Van Ness, who had just graduated from Columbia and was setting himself up in New York. Billy's family was every bit as wealthy as the Silvesters, moreover they were rabid Republicans, and yet again Billy had valuable connections in the City through his association with Senator Aaron Burr and Congressman Edward Livingston, in whose office he now worked. His best chance of advancement, deemed Matty, was to go to New York and tie himself up with Billy.

But to go to the City one needed money, and one needed the certainty of employment once arrived there. Billy, for the time being, was only a clerk himself, but in a year or so he would be hanging out a shingle, and time was at hand for making some plans. Matty kept his own council and his eye open for opportunity. In the spring of '98, when the Federalists won reëlection, the Silvesters made him a proposition. Why not come over to their side? The inference was clear that to do so would further his chances in the firm, and Matty was not one to turn down such an offer point-blank. There is no telling how long he might have dallied over this, his first major temptation in life, had not Cornelius Silvester, younger brother to Francis, cornered the Boy Lawyer one night in his bedroom and demanded a flat answer.

"I replied calmly," reported Matty, "that I appreciated thoroughly the kindness of his feelings and was well satisfied

[ 35

with the purity of his motives, but that my course had been settled after much reflection and could not be changed."

When old Abe heard the news he was hugely elated. His son's vacillation had disturbed Mine Host. Sell out to the aristocrats? Matty was no son of his if he did that! But now he was proud of the boy! And Abe would have been much prouder had he understood that Matty was laying plans that would far surpass being a subordinate in a rural law office. The opportunity he had sought was coming toward him, and characteristically enough he met it more than half way. Characteristically, too, the opportunity he chose was one that depended less on his own efforts than on his life-long talent for hitching his wagon to the nearest rising star. It was a method that would eventually land him in the White House, and already the adolescent hand of the Little Magician was reaching out for the strings of circumstance. The object was still to go to New York, and now he was ready to map out a campaign.

2

Talk had been going around Kinderhook for more than a year that John Van Ness, Billy's elder brother, and black sheep of the family, was contemplating a turn of life. Two very staid and certainly respectable moves he was consider-ing—running for Congress and marrying an heiress. But un-fortunately for John these two ambitions were tantalizingly enmeshed. To win the girl and her fortune he first had to win the office, for so she had stipulated. And to win the office he needed—so he thought—money. Old Peter Van Ness had further complicated matters by cutting off the young scamp's allowance until he should prove himself of some use in the world and, faced with these problems, the candidate found himself in a position of stalemate.

Matty was well aware of the situation, and the more in-volved it became the better it suited his purposes. Finally, when things had come to a complete stand-still, he approached John and, as well as the evidence can be pieced together, offered the following solution.

Of gold and silver, said Matty, I have none, but nevertheless I have something that will help you more than either. You know, of course, that before you are eligible for election you must be nominated by the Republican State Convention. That means you must tour the several counties that make up the Eighth Congressional District and persuade the leaders that you are the best candidate. For this you need money, both for travelling expenses and for standing treats at all the taverns you visit. And even if you had unlimited means you might run into difficulties, might you not?

He might indeed, granted John.

Now, Matty continued, I, as Boy Lawyer, am constantly journeying about the District. Already I have more acquaintances among the influential Republicans than you have. Therefore let me do the campaigning. Let me stand for a delegateship to the Convention, and, if successful, I will put you in nomination and do my best to see that you win. All this I will do on two conditions.

And those?

These: First, that you, having won the election and subsequently your lady and her fortune, will advance me enough money to live in New York for two years. And second, that when I arrive in the City, Billy will either get or give me a job.

The bargain, said John, was accepted.

Thus it happened that before he could vote, Martin Van Buren undertook not only to run for an office himself, but to elect a candidate of his own picking and to profiteer on the deal to boot. Nor does that complete the picture. Articled to a Federalist law-firm and wearing, in effect, its uniform, he was utilizing his business hours in campaigning for a Republican ticket. If that jealous mistress, the Law, suffered from neglect during this period, she would have to get used to it, for from now on Martin Van Buren's first professional love was politics. He won appointment to his delegateship without much trouble and, elated with the news, he sought out John and excitedly suggested that they take seats on the coach and be off to Troy, where the Convention was to be held. John found it necessary to remind his young manager that funds were low with the heir to the Van Ness estate, but Matty was not to be foiled by trifles. He borrowed the money to see them both through the meeting, as well as a pair of horses to carry them there, and when he stood on the table to make the nominating speech, he was greeted with loud and probably drunken huzzas. John polled a majority on the first ballot, and the man who has been called America's first Easy Boss had nominated his first candidate.

Back to Kinderhook they rode next morning, John and Matty, the one exultant, the other expectant. For Matty knew his task was only half done. It was one thing to nominate a candidate, something else to elect him. Only one event, he was quite aware, could swing the Republican ticket in his District. That was for the whole State to landslide for Mr. Jefferson in the nearing presidential election. At home Mother Mary was ready to pray for success, but Matty was already too much of a realist to believe his fate in the lap of the gods. His fate, like Mr. Jefferson's, was, he knew full well, in the hands of that very capable and resourceful strategist, Mr. Aaron Burr.

3

With the dawn of a day in 1800 Mr. Aaron Burr rose from bed in his fine, white-columned house on Richmond Hill. And this was a most extraordinary event. Many were the dawns that found Mr. Burr, now a gay and wealthy widower, climbing into his bed, but when he climbed out of it at such an unholy hour, there was bound to be something afoot. Emerging from his own gateway he strode across the meadows that separated Greenwich Village from the City proper, and planted himself inconspicuously at the gateway of No. 52 Cedar Street.

This was even more extraordinary, for No. 52 was the residence of Mr. Alexander Hamilton, and though these two had been long acquainted, they were, at the moment, not quite enemies and not quite friends. Together they had served on General Washington's staff, and together they had won fame and Burr had won fortune at the New York bar. Once, indeed, Hamilton had gone so far as to invite Burr into a partnership, which the latter had graciously declined, but all that was before politics had them both in thrall. It was before Hamilton became what Thomas Jefferson spitefully called the "prime minister" of the first President's cabinet, and before Burr became what Tammany's first Grand Sachem called "our Chief" of the Society. Much had happened since then, and some of it explained why Aaron Burr was loitering around Alexander Hamilton's front door at this unfrequented hour of the morning.

He had not been there long before he espied just what he hoped to espy. He saw a small boy coming toward No. 52 with a parcel under his arm. Mr. Burr stepped forward.

"What have you there, my lad?"

"Pamphlets for General Hamilton."

Mr. Burr took one.

Here, if anywhere, is the real and successful beginning of foul-play politics. This is not forgetting that the past few years of the waning century had seen some rather ungentlemanly tactics among men who sat in the seats of the mighty. The first presidential Cabinet, which contained Hamilton and Jefferson; the first National Congress, which contained Madison and Monroe, had unquestionably distinguished themselves for unseemly behavior, and statesmen had already mutually agreed that all's fair in parliamentary war. But if methods had been low, motives were high. Both great leaders sincerely believed themselves ordained of the Lord to rescue the Republic from each other. There was nothing selfish about the squabbling of Hamilton and Jefferson, and furthermore if all had not been ethical, at least all had been legal. Slander, scandal and a little polite blackmail had been present, but nothing worse. It remained for Aaron Burr to start the ball rolling towards more high-handed procedures, and when he stole one of Alexander Hamilton's pamphlets this morning, he was performing a deed of far-reaching, historical importance.

For the pamphlets were not, or were not intended to be, public property. Mr. Hamilton had written "The Public Conduct and Career of John Adams" wholly for private circulation, and had chosen this form of communication as the easiest and most reliable method of corresponding with his party lieutenants who were scattered up and down the Atlantic seaboard. What the pamphlet said was that though President Adams, Federalist candidate for reëlection, had made a frightful botch of his administration, though he was something of a dunderhead and considerable of a dunce, still he was better than Mr. Jefferson who, along with a villainous upstart called Burr, would head the Republican ticket.

Why Mr. Hamilton preferred these opinions to go only to a few selected friends is evident enough, and when he awoke a few days after Burr's coup and read them in the cold print of several Republican papers, his rage equalled only the rage of the man in the new White House. The best John Adams could do was to call Mr. Hamilton "the bastard brat of a Scotch pedlar," and Mr. Hamilton could only shake his handsome, sandy-haired head and declare Mr. Burr a man of "no principles, public or private."

Doubtless when the news found its way up the River to Kinderhook, Matty Van Buren was joyfully and profoundly impressed. His visions of a trip to the great city, which had already increased its size three-fold since his birth, began to materialize into reality; and along with the rise of his hopes he was, consciously or not, imbibing the soundest sort of education in practical politics. A few more coups like this and the Republicans would have New York State by the heels. Trust Mr. Burr. To Mr. Burr there were more things in heaven and earth than had ever been dreamed of in political philosophy.

Two years before, as a member of the Legislature, he had laid the ground-work. One of the perennial plagues of yellow fever had been sweeping the City which he represented, and the altruistic Assemblyman offered a bill which, he convincingly explained, would be a godsend to the stricken people. He proposed that the lawgivers should grant a charter to the Manhattan Company, which should supply the City with pure, up-country water. On the face of it, this was a humane and worthy piece of legislation, but apparently no one saw what it actually amounted to. Tucked into the bill was what later came to be termed "a joker," for the Manhattan Company was no other than a subsidiary of the nefarious Tammany Society; and the charter was, in effect, not a water bill, but a bank bill. Five years earlier the Federalists under Hamilton had chartered the Bank of New York, which had served them handily. Now, thanks to Mr. Burr's subterfuge, the Republicans had the Bank of Manhattan, and though citizens were still drinking water out of the same polluted wells, no one could deny that Tammany was on a sound fiscal footing.

With this task behind him and the presidential campaign in sight, Mr. Burr turned to the more immediate problem of guiding enough right-minded voters to the polls. In those days presidential electors were chosen not directly by the People, but by the Legislature, so that the matter resolved itself into getting a party majority in the local Assembly and State Senate. Hamilton had already picked a Federalist slate made up entirely of reliable nonentities who would vote exactly as they were told, but Mr. Burr, in order to thwart him, instituted what was soon to be known as the traditional scheme of "perfuming the ticket." New York State's two wartime heroes and best-beloved citizens were Generals Horatio Gates, conqueror of Burgoyne; and the five-time governor, George Clinton. Both were elderly men, laden with public honor and now retired to private life, but Aaron Burr had the superb audacity to call on them and invite them to be candidates for humble seats in the Legislature. Both indignantly refused, but their suitor would not take "No" for an answer. He spent the better part of a month wearing them down with grandiose arguments on public duty and finally, by telling each that the other had accepted, he wrote their names on the ballot, along with the names of ten other prominent citizens.

That, he decided, would take care of the up-State vote, but there still remained the City—a far sterner problem, since under the suffrage clause of the Jay Constitution no more than ten percent of white male citizens could vote. To meet this emergency Mr. Burr evolved yet another system which has come down to posterity—the method known as "colonizing" or the use of "floaters."

Most of the homeless, transients and down-and-outers who happened into the growing City soon became members of the hospitable Society of Tammany. Its headquarters—or so-called Tammanial Hall—was the Long Room of Brom Martling's tavern on Spruce and Nassau Streets. The meeting place, however, did not quite live up to all the elegant pageantry that surrounded its name, for it was a small two-storied shack, generally so strewn with drunkards and so miserably tended that its colloquial name about town was the Pig Pen. It is not to be wondered that the fastidious Mr. Burr, who kept the grandest house in the most exclusive suburb; who entertained such gentry as the Princes Talleyrand, Louis Philippe and Jerome Bonaparte; whose tastes ran to gold snuff-boxes and gilded sets of Voltaire and Lord Chesterfield—did not grace the Pig Pen with his presence. So far as is known he never set foot in the place, and never joined the Society, but for all that, he was its guiding light as long as he lived, and when he was gone the Sachems began naming their sons after him. He now gathered together a few of its leaders, including Grand Sachem Mathew L. Davis, who was to be his first biographer, and Billy Van Ness, who was to be his second in a rather famous duel, and explained his latest inspiration.

It was amazingly simple. Let the Society divide its members into groups ranging from thirty to seventy souls, and let each of these groups club together in renting or buying some empty houses. There they would register as property-holders, and from there they would sally forth to the polls. Money? Ah, that was his next problem. Meanwhile let them draw out of the Society's funds. He'd have the money when the time came. And he did.

For his solution of the money problem was the last though not least of Mr. Burr's innovations for this unique campaign. The idea of asking voters to contribute to the election expenses of their law-givers as well as to pay their salaries, was not only completely unheard-of, but must have been even unguessed. The prevalent notion was that the honor of serving the Republic made wages no more than an embarrassing, if necessary, compensation to men who consented to leave home and fireside for a sacred duty. But Aaron Burr was never embarrassed by the lack of a precedent. These contributions, he argued, were equivalent to a war-time tax. The country must be saved from the vandalism of Federalism. He made a card-index of every Republican in town, noted the temperament, gullibility, generosity of each; checked off those who were to be solicited for money, who for service in herding voters to the polls, who merely for moral and balloting support.

Long before the actual election, tidings reached Abe's Tavern that the Federalists were scuttled. Doubt was no longer in Matty's mind that his man was headed for Congress and he himself for the City. What could he have felt but admiration and affection for the one who had wrought these wonders? How could he fail to bless the preceptor who had taught him the ins and outs of a new system? And all was not yet. When the returns of the Electoral College arrived, none in Kinderhook could have foretold the results. Jefferson elected? No, indeed. Adams? Not at all. Who then? Why Mr. Jefferson and his running-mate, Mr. Burr, had drawn a tie vote for the presidency!

Matty and many another besides him must have gasped at this intelligence. Here was magic indeed. It was, of course, mathematically possible that the tie could be a coincidence, but the chance was too remote to make it credible. Why, if it were only an accident, did not Mr. Burr prove it by withdrawing his name from the presidential nomination and accepting the second office? Why did the House of Representatives have to sit for seven days, casting ballot after ballot to unravel the tie? And, when Mr. Hamilton at last unlocked the dead-lock by manipulating his Federalist votes, why did Mr. Burr, smiling so sourly, take to his garden and begin practicing up his pistol shots?

Questions like this went round the tavern of an evening, and the one person there who could probably have answered them sensibly chose to be silent. Matty was only eighteen by the calendar, but in the one sense that mattered he had already come of age.

*BOOK II*

# CHAPTER I

## He Boards the Band Wagon

(1801–1804)

---

BY EIGHTEEN, too, Matt had come to his full physical stature. He was five feet six that morning when he climbed into the south-bound stage coach at the tavern door, and he never grew taller. He was trim and slender, and not till he was nearly sixty did he put on enough weight to lose his figure. The suspicion around Washington was that in these later days he wore a corset, thus preserving his trimness long after it was gone, but this, like most of his personal secrets, remains part of his mystery. The modish, still rudimentary, side-burns that came down to the points of his jaw were yellow as a field of Columbia County dandelions, and in time the hair, like the dandelions, would turn to a blown and fluffy white. For the rest, Matt's appearance was to change as little as his character did. He retained always the same disarming smile, the guileless blue eyes, the courtly mannerisms and stylish tastes.

It was, he knew, good-bye to Kinderhook for more than two years. And if he succeeded at his work, it would be to return a full-fledged lawyer and in a man's estate. Great hopes went with him as the coach rolled off from the tavern porch. Probably Father Abraham was flagging him farewell with a big red paw, Mother Mary weeping into her apron, his brothers and sisters grinning enviously, and no doubt, apart from the group, stood little Hannah Hoes, with whom he had exchanged secret and sacred vows. Matt never kept a diary, and though no writing of his recounts his feelings of departure, it is not much of a guess to suppose that there was a fullness in his throat and a thrill furrowing its way up his back-bone as he turned for a final look at the tavern. Behind him now were home, kin and his sweetheart; ahead was the opportunity he had made with his own cunning— the chance to learn about life in the third largest city on the continent.

As for the City itself, it offered him all the shocks and surprises a country boy could ask. Billy Van Ness found him a miserable little lodging in Catherine Street, and from it Matt sauntered forth to see the sights. John Adams, passing through on his way to and from his Inauguration, reports that New York streets were "vastly more regular and elegant than those in Boston and the houses all more grand as well as neat," though it was "not half the size of Philadelphia, nor in any way to be compared with it for elegance." But that must have been because he either meant to damn it with faint praise or because he visited only one part of town. In its two extremes of poverty and wealth, the City, when Matt first saw it, surpassed both Boston at its worst and Philadelphia at its best.

In the Richmond Hill and Bowling Green districts the Boy Lawyer found fine country estates, set far back off the streets, with rolled, sloping lawns in front and gardens behind that reached down to the shining River. But this, he soon learned, was only how one-half of the world lived. Squalor, disorder, and penury seemed to have made their mark in the other parts of town. Sewers were gutters down the middle of the crooked, narrow streets that had once been lanes of the Dutch village. Butchers drove herds of cattle and sheep through town, by way of advertisement; the bleats and the lowing mingling with the shouts of pedlars, the tunes of the street-singers, the whine of the innumerable beggars. Domestic pigs, chickens and cows roamed the Broad Way and scurried to the indifferent safety of the muddy sidewalks as the carriages of the grandees swept by; immigrant families squatted on empty lots; the stench of garbage dumps, sewage and animal refuse joined with the moral and very real stink of the three adjoining dungeons which served respectively as Alms House, Debtor's Prison and Gaol.

It was here before the Debtor's Prison—if anyone cares to believe the Eighth President's most gullible biographer—that the boy paused long enough to utter a soliloquy in which he pledged himself to undo this frightful wrong to human unfortunates. It is certain beyond all reasonable speculation that he did nothing of the sort, that the anecdote is inspired by the similar one which portrays another President-to-be standing in a slave market and taking a like vow to crush the infamous thing. Neither of these men of destiny were of the kind given to oral and spontaneous moralising, and though the idea ties up convincingly enough with Lincoln's subsequent history, only the afterthought of a Boswell could have put such an expression into the mouth or mind of the Little Magician.

It is true, of course, that as State Senator Martin Van Buren did offer several bills to do away with imprisonment for debt, but the very fact that none of them passed suggests that possibly he was indifferent that they should. He who ruled the Regency would have had little trouble pushing through such a measure had he not preferred to use it for what politicians learned to call a "bell-ringer." It was good publicity to show an affectionate interest in the People, but both as lawyer and candidate, he made the Bankruptcy Laws work to his own advantage. Many of his cases were suits over debt settlement, and until he graduated from the State Senate to the national one, persons without property had no vote. It is not without significance that once suffrage restrictions were removed, Mr. Van Buren promptly helped sponsor a bill that abolished the Debtor's Prison. But though he took credit and made campaign capital out of the passage, he was not author of the measure—and frequently wished that he were.

Of entertainment, Matt found, the City offered an ample store for those who had money to buy it. The New Theatre, just off the Broad Way and in sight of the dungeons, played to packed houses, especially when some English troupe was in town to give productions of Shakespeare, Sheridan or Goldsmith. Except for crude vaudeville and melodrama, the American theatre was yet unborn, but there were open-air arenas about the City where native spectacles were staged. Public executions were still in vogue and attracted huge audiences; bear-baiting, cock-fighting and horse-racing drew enthusiastic crowds, and when the River and the many ponds were frozen, so did skating-contests and an improvised form of ice hockey.

For the gentler forms of amusement one could visit the Columbia Gardens at the Broad Way and Prince Street. Here of a summer evening were outdoor concerts by the military band and dance orchestras. Colored lamps twinkled among the trees; fountains played sparklingly over the marble-bodied Cupids, Dianas and Venuses, and in secluded grottos were rope swings with seats just wide enough for two. Surrounding the Gardens were circular buildings with intimate little dining rooms and open boxes, looking down on the midway, from which one could beckon to the gaily-dressed girls who served as vendors for refreshments of ice cream, fried oysters and hot cross buns. And now and then there came to the nearby Park travelling shows of wild animals from the West or overseas, and wax figures of gruesome scenes such as the beheading of King Louis XVI or Marie Antoinette.

Down toward the Battery Matt found the social elements of this queer City most equally mixed. Here dandies, ruffled and sworded, walked for the air, rubbing elbows with jobless immigrants and well-to-do sisters of shame. Over on Wall Street business was booming. The three banks, the several real estate firms, the one insurance company were making men rich. Jewish money-lenders stood in the doorways beckoning in customers; Dutch shop-keepers stood there reflectively smoking their long pipes; fur traders, wine-sellers, blacksmiths, wheelwrights, sail-makers, builders, lawyers, journalists—all seemed prosperous.

## He Boards the Band Wagon

During his first year in town Matt discovered that, so far as it interfered with his work in Billy's office, he could spend nearly all of every day seeing the sights. Billy's clientele was mostly hypothetical, but rather than worrying Matt's young employer, the fact seemed a very convenient excuse for enjoying the pleasantries of leisure. Everything, Billy felt, would turn out all right, and meanwhile there was his allowance to be spent as boisterously as possible. Somewhat resentfully Matt was to remember that Billy never offered him anything in the way of money. And the congressional brother, despite his preëlection vows, was proving a niggardly patron.

"By God, my friend," he wrote from Washington, "cash is out of my power. . . ."

Several times during the first winter Matt appealed for help and received each time only a pittance or a promise. Had it not been for his own half-brother, James I. Van Alen, the Boy Lawyer's return to Kinderhook might have been both premature and inglorious. Van Alen was not rich, but at Matt's request he agreed to "let you have the amount of thirty or forty dollars out of the proceeds of my wheat." Much was to be made in the campaign pamphlets thirty years later of the hunger and hardship Matt endured while in the City, but most of it was without foundation. He was unquestionably hard up, but with frequent touches on friend and family he never went hungry. It was, perhaps, something of a hardship that he could not always attend Billy on the latter's incessant tour of gaming-house, dance hall and theatre, but all pity for the gallant young starveling can safely stop here. Matt enjoyed himself hugely in the City, applied himself sufficiently to the law, and in off-hours was never at a loss for gay company and an instructive education in matters closer to his heart.

For to Richmond Hill, the splendid mansion where George Washington had made his headquarters in '76 and where John Adams had lived as Vice President, Matt went repeatedly, and the reputed father of his existence "treated me with much attention." It was the beginning of an intimacy and preceptorship that would last for many years, but Matt could scarcely have guessed that in times to come he would be sheltering a homeless, friendless Mr. Burr under his own roof. It does not fit in very well with the villainous caricature history would make of the man to know that Mr. Burr's greatest delight was in young company, that his wife's dowry of stepchildren was the only visible incentive for an otherwise inexplicable match. Richmond Hill, when Matt came there, was the Mecca of New York's Young Intelligentsia, for Mr. Burr, besides being a gracious and open-handed host, was very much a dilettante of the arts and letters—something rare in this raw, adolescent City. The artist, John Vanderlyn, was a protégé of his; Washington Irving was writing the Jonathan Old Style essays in Burr's *Morning Chronicle*, and scarcely a week went by but argosies from Europe brought some literary treasure. The *Edinburgh Review*, to which he subscribed, was publishing a series of poems by a man named Walter Scott; a London book-store, where Mr. Burr kept an account had sent over a Gibbon's *History*, volume by volume; the works of Chesterfield, Rousseau, Voltaire, Mackenzie and Jeremy Bentham stood side by side in the paneled library with the polite little novels of Fanny Burney.

Indeed but for the Little Band—for so his clique of young associates liked to be called—the Vice President would have been insufferably lonely during the congressional recesses he spent at home. The two Prevost boys, whose education he had greedily undertaken, had grown up and departed, and—worst of all—the beloved Theodosia, his one legitimate child, had married and moved off to the hinterlands of South Carolina. Why, Matt may have heard her father grumbling as he often did, hadn't the girl taken one of her host of suitors around New York? Hadn't she had the pick of the town? Theodosia certainly had a wide selection, for if one could believe her father and the gossip (which one positively should not) such rising young fellows as De Witt Clinton, Irving, Vanderlyn, and a score of others, were still nursing their aching hearts.

Aaron Burr nursed one, too, but events were in the saddle

which would help him forget. The brief calm that followed his presidential sortie was but a lull in the storm; black clouds of vengeance were gathering about his restless head. Though Mr. Burr did not know it, there was only one element of greatness he lacked, and that was luck. He was a man born about half a generation before his time. Had he been the spiritual brother or son of Martin Van Buren, instead of the father, there is no gainsaying that he must have gone far. The day in politics was to come when both his talents and his shortcomings would have served him toward the same end, but it was his misfortune to have shown them to the world too soon.

His ascension to the vice-presidency was a Pyrrhic victory for Mr. Burr. It cost him more than it gained. It showed an interested and horrified country that here was a man, a creature of their faith, who had risen to loftiness without a single motive but his own selfishness. Aaron Burr to date had been Attorney General, Assemblyman, Senator, Vice President, and in none of his positions had he proved he had anything but a likeable personality and a sleight-of-hand ability for getting his own way. That was not enough for the age which had known so much true high-mindedness. It will not do to argue that human nature was any more capable or appreciative of altruism then than ever, but it is plain history that the *mores* of the times would not tolerate any laying of unworthy hands on the machinery of government. Its government was the nation's soul, and too many persons were living who could remember what painful labor and birth-pangs had wrought her existence. Before long America would learn to endure political trickery as either inevitable or diverting, but that had not happened yet. Politics was still an expression of patriotism, and the nation's attitude of mind was emphatically that public office was a public trust.

There were those of the Little Band who knew along with their Leader that his marshalling of the Tammany forces and his purloining of Mr. Hamilton's pamphlet were not the sum of his efforts in the past election. Dreadfully they hoped that the rest of the story would never come out, and faith-

[ 53

fully they vowed that, even if it did, they would not falter. Mr. Burr was only 45; the presidency, the prize for which he strove, was well within sight. He was never to reach that final goal, but failing, he did not fail wholly in vain, because he taught a man after his own image how it might be won. Martin Van Buren was learning, and learning as much by his master's mistakes as by his methods.

To judge by the standards of a coming day, Aaron Burr's single sin was in being found out. And Matt was on hand to take the lesson to heart. Being found out was something that never happened to the Little Magician.

2

It was James Cheetham, vindictive and enterprising editor of the *American Citizen*, who bared Mr. Burr's scarlet secret. Ever since the election of 1800, Cheetham had been nibbling away at the Vice President's reputation with a series of carnivorous editorials that made much bad blood around town, but his "A View of the Political Conduct of Aaron Burr, Esq.," and several companion volumes exposed as consummate a political intrigue as America will ever know. It seems, according to Cheetham, that in the pre-election year the Republicans at Congress met in caucus and agreed that since the Chief Magistracy was going to Virginia, New York should have the vice-presidency. That left the choice of a candidate up to the Republican leaders at Albany, and behind closed doors they considered three names: General Clinton, Chancellor Livingston and Assemblyman Burr. The last two were quickly eliminated, Livingston's because he was deemed too old, too deaf and too blind for the duties; Burr's because he was considered not quite worthy of the honor. A letter was drafted petitioning the Congressional Caucus to name Clinton, and a Mr. Nickolson was despatched with it to Philadelphia. But before leaving New York he encountered Mr. Burr, to whom he confided his mission. Just what methods of persuasion were used on the messenger is not clear, but the result was (so Cheetham said) that Mr. Burr

caused the name of George Clinton to be erased and his own
inserted. The Republicans at Washington promptly nominated him for Mr. Jefferson's running-mate, and Mr. Burr as
promptly accepted.

When the report of this atrocity reached the public there
arose an indignation that had scarcely been equalled since
the Stamp Act. Staying not to weigh how much truth and
half-truth might be in the accusation, the country recoiled
with horror. Not only in New York but everywhere, righteous editors, Federalist and Republican alike, joined in the
clamor, and ere many moons the name of Aaron Burr was
well on its way to become a by-word for chicanery and treason. And Cheetham laid on the fuel. Burr, he said, besides
having done this, had spent "little less than one year's
salary" trying to buy himself the presidency! The nation
frothed at the mouth. Here was scheming against two of her
war-time heroes! Her profoundest philosopher of the People's Rights, Thomas Jefferson! One of her bravest soldiers,
George Clinton! It was unspeakable. And when Mr. Burr
appealed to the President to scotch the rumors, and Mr.
Jefferson refused, the guilt ceased to be a matter of speculation. From that day forward Aaron Burr was damned.

Louder and louder rose the wails of wrath, but loudest of
all they came from those two clannish families, the Clintons
and the Livingstons, who represented New York's political
aristocracy. The Livingstons were to the manor born, being
scions of the proud Scottish house of Callender; the Clintons
had attained the purple by works of the heart and hand.
When they considered how noble old George had been
hoodwinked out of the vice-presidency, how he had actually
been traduced into giving aid and comfort to the enemy by
running for the lowly legislature, their rage was positively
Homeric. A joint meeting of the families was called, and
venerable heads were put together to fix some plan for undoing this suave little scamp who had so neatly trussed them.
Ironic it seems that this gathering, convened in the name of
good government and fair play, should have initiated what
is by all odds the most pernicious of all political abuses. Yet

[ 55

so it turned out, for to insure a complete renouncing of this Devil Burr and all his works, the Clinton-Livingston combine stumbled upon a scheme that became the forerunner of the Spoils or Patronage System.

The plan, as De Witt Clinton, nephew of General George, explained it to the assembled patriarchs, seemed logical enough. John Jay, the Governor, was the only man who had ever approached Uncle George for popularity at the polls. Jay was not a candidate for reëlection, therefore let the General stand for the governorship and, having won it, let him appoint Edward Livingston the Mayor of the City. Between them they could control a host of appointive positions which included everything from the justices of the State's supreme bench to the humblest sheriff of an up-state county. In that way all Burrites and anti-Jeffersonians could be summarily eradicated, and as for Lord Aaron himself, as soon as his term expired, the General should have the coveted vice-presidency.

The only flaw in the plan was that it stood in direct contradiction to Jeffersonian principles, which called for a frugal and unbiased administration of governmental services. The many appointive offices had been kept out of elections in the very hope that they would be filled with the best of men, regardless of party. Between them the last two Presidents had dismissed only 17 job-holders without assigned cause, and Governor Jay had bent over backward in an attempt to be upright in the matter. Despite their ethical qualms, however, the conspirators adopted the plan, and it worked out to perfection. George Clinton galloped through the election and chose Edward Livingston to be Mayor, and together they assumed the responsibility for turning the State into a Utopia. To make sure it was stainless of Burrism, they instigated a great turnover of office holders; and to be certain that the new incumbents were the best of all possible men, they appointed only members of their own family to the higher posts. For the next few years the roll-call of the New York officialdom read like a Clinton-Livingston family album:

The Governor
    George . . .

The U. S. Senator

The Mayor
    De Witt . . .
    and

The Congressman
    George, Jr. . . .

Constitutional Committeeman
    Charles . . .

Member of Assembly
    James . . .

The District Attorney
    William Stewart
    Brother-in-law of George

The Attorney General
    Ambrose Spencer
    Brother-in-law of
    DeWitt . . .

**CLINTON**

The Chancellor
    Robert . . .

The Mayor
    and

U. S. District Attorney
    Edward . . .

The Supreme Court Justice
    Smith W. Thompson
    Brother-in-law of Edward . . .

The Supreme Court Justice
    Brockholst . . .

The Recorder of the City
    Maturin . . .

The Auctioneer of the City
    Schuyler . . .

The Surrogate of Dutchess
    County
    Gilbert . . .

The Clerk of Dutchess County
    Robert Henry . . .

The Chief Justice
    Morgan Lewis
    Brother-in-law of Edward . . .

The Secretary of State
    Thomas Tillotson
    Brother-in-law of Edward . . .

The Supreme Court Justice
    and

The Mayor
    John Armstrong
    Brother-in-law of Robert . . .

**LIVINGSTON**

Feeling ran high among the Little Band as the significance of these manoeuvres began to take shape. Their Leader had been cut down from behind, and it demanded desperate remedies. Two of the group, the Swartwout brothers, John and Robert, decided upon absolute measures, and they called De Witt Clinton and Richard Riker, his lieutenant, to the field of honor. Robert winged his man, but John came home feet first with two flesh wounds in his leg. Meanwhile another Burrite, George Eacker, deciding that their old enemies, the Federalists, were at the bottom of the brewing trouble, had done his share by challenging a pair of them.

His first victim he missed, but the other, young Philip Hamilton, returned from the engagement to die in his father's arms.

Billy Van Ness had his blood up. He crowed loudly over Phil Hamilton's death. So perish all foes of the Leader! But Billy, when he entered the fray himself, chose a less perilous weapon, the pen. Over the pseudonym of "Aristides" he essayed a defense of his hero in the time-honored way of castigating the opponents. He printed an 80-page pamphlet that dripped vitriol in its depiction of the Clinton-Livingstons. He named names and he spared not the rod. The Governor was "an instrument"; the Mayor "an object of derision and disgust," all of whose doings were "finished examples of profligacy and corruption." The Secretary of State was " a contemptible, shuffling apothecary"; the District Attorney, "an imbecile and obsequious pettifogger"; the Attorney General, "an offspring of treachery and fraud."

So pertly was the diatribe written and so penetrating were its thrusts that Billy, all unknowing, found himself famous. His pamphlet was favorably compared to the best barb-throwing of Jonathan Swift and M. Voltaire, but it was a renown that Billy did not care to embrace. No sooner was his missive abroad than his courage began to ooze. It was customary in that period that when a man offended a family's fair name, its members, one by one, would challenge until the offender paid with his life. Young blades among the allies swore to bring this scandalizer to his death, and Billy hovered fearfully behind the nom-de-plume. Only one person knew he was the author, and Billy implored Matt never to tell. Matt swore that he never did, but years later when the secret leaked out it caused a lasting breach in their friendship.

Verily Matt, posing through it all as an innocent bystander, resembled the young Napoleon watching the mob storm the Tuileries. In a few years he would be levelling his own cannon, but here was a preview of the havoc in store. Bloodshed, rancor and commotion were not all that ushered in this first trial of the Spoils System. Close behind stalked corruption. They were honorable men, these allies, but it is a truism of politics that none can dig dung and not get dirty. The Clinton-Livingstons did not steal, but their henchmen did. In order to control up-State support against Burr, they appointed one Silvester Miller to serve as Surrogate for New York City, for which he accepted a round salary; he continued to reside a hundred miles away and never came near the scene of his duties. In order to allow Edward Livingston to be Mayor and U. S. District Attorney as well, much of his work was turned over to subordinates, who promptly looted the Government of $100,000, and caused Livingston to flee to New Orleans in disgrace.

This last fiasco almost upset the allied apple-carts. New York was not yet schooled to its subsequent apathy toward wholesale thievery, and the first cry of "Turn the rascals out!" came with a real vigor. Hastily the Clinton-Livingstons met in conference. Richard Riker, now retained as advisory strategist, had a solution. Let the impeccable De Witt resign from the Senate, and accept his uncle's appointment as Mayor. And let John Armstrong, a Livingston in-law, be sent to Washington for the unexpired term. The deed was done, and the storm blew over.

It was inevitable that Matt should be fundamentally influenced and inspired by the tactics he was witnessing. This shifting of personnel from one office to another was something at which he became marvellously adept in the days he ruled the Regency. And the Spoils System, now in its rudimentary stages, was to be his greatest gift to the country. What the Clinton-Livingstons had done accidentally, he would do by design. What they had done in miniature, he would do on a canvas that eventually became the size of a continent. Their works would fade; his would remain to the everlasting glory of the nation.

Moreover he was now about to see tested an axiom which he learned never to ignore—that no politician is stronger than the organization behind him. Mr. Burr, coming home from Washington to run for the governorship in hope of restoring his vanishing prestige, would have on his side the emotional loyalty of the Little Band and of the Sons of Tammany. Against him would be aligned a state-wide organization whose fidelities were cemented not with sentiment, but with money and jobs. The election would be further significant in that now for the first time was a campaign with no issues. Hitherto political fights had been little more than embattled arguments between two clear-cut philosophies of government—Federalism and Republicanism, rule by the classes against rule by the masses. But the schism among the New York Republicans was no schism of faith. Both sides were loudly proclaiming their abiding belief in the sacred doctrines of Mr. Jefferson. And still more important was the fact that the campaign was no longer a contest between Right and Wrong. If Mr. Burr had been apprehended in trickery, then the allies had been tarred with corruption, and honors were even. Lord Aaron gathered his cohorts at Tontine's Coffee House for the formality of a nomination; the allies sent George Clinton after the vacated vice-presidency and selected for the governorship a suitable Livingston in-law in Morgan Lewis. The combat was on—a test-case for Organized Politics—and a test on his first semester's work for Martin Van Buren. If he had learned anything during these two hectic years in the City, now was his chance to prove it.

### 3

Cakes and ale. Matt was back at the home tavern. Father Abraham dusted off some of his best bottles, and Mother Mary produced heaping plates of her far-famed olie-koekjes, which Matt, completely Americanized, called cookies. The long clerkship was over, the bar examinations were passed and the Boy Lawyer, now a legal-aged man, was qualified to set up his own practice and to cast his first vote.

These to Matt were twin privileges. Politics and law-practice could be made to work in double harness, and he was determined that they should do him energetic service. He was deeply in debt to Brother James and prodigiously in love with pretty Hannah. The two matters demanded attention so, with his usual despatch, Matt cleared decks for action. In imitation of Mr. Burr's "floater" policy he persuaded Abe to register the tavern in his name that he might comply with the suffrage regulations of owning property. And that he might pay off the debt and ready himself for marriage, he entered into partnership with Brother James, who ran a meagre law-business in conjunction with his farm. On the face of it he might have done better for himself, for James's law firm only deserved the dignity of that name by courtesy. But he had plans, had Matt, that Van Alen-Van Buren should prosper, and his first move toward that end was that Brother James should run for the House of Delegates under his junior partner's management.

Matt's return to Kinderhook and to an interest in local politics came at a propitious moment, coinciding exactly with the opening of the Burr-Lewis campaign for the governorship. It was deemed fortunate by Billy Van Ness and other knowing members of the Little Band that the precocious Boy Lawyer should be situated in Columbia county for the great effort. Mr. Burr, arriving in New York from Washington, had cast a practiced eye over the situation, and perceived that the rural vote was going to tell the tale. With Tammany's aid he might hold his own in the City even against Mayor Clinton's moneyed retainers, but the allies' greatest strength was in the outlying counties.

For a while Mr. Burr had had hopes of cancelling this disadvantage by joining forces with the Federalists who, putting up no candidate of their own, were undecided which of the two Republicans to back. The Federalist leaders held an executive meeting at an Albany tavern, voting at first to support Mr. Burr, but Mr. Hamilton would hear none of it. He took the occasion of this supposed privacy to relieve his mind of considerable venom on the subject of his suave little tormentor, and the two Burrites hiding under the bed in the next room dutifully relayed his words to their waiting chieftain. Mr. Burr had all but forgotten the old grudge about the pamphlets but, being reminded, he retired to his garden again to quicken up his shooting eye, and became all

[ 61

the more aware that without the Federalist alliance there would be hard going to carry the county votes. If he thought of Matt at all during this anxious period, it must have been with the assurance that he had at least one industrious worker in the Dutch districts.

Mr. Burr's many friends around Kinderhook thought so too, but when word went round that Abe's boy had taken the hustings against the Little Band, astonishment knew no bounds. Hadn't Mr. Burr befriended Matt in the City? Wasn't he one of the Little Band himself? Wasn't he Billy Van Ness's close friend? All this, assuredly, was true, but those who felt surprised that Matt had turned traitor to his sentimental loyalties, did not take into account that the Boy Lawyer, full-fledged politician now, had put away such childish things as sentiment. So well had Matt learned his lessons in the City that he had no illusions about Mr. Burr's chances to beat the Clinton-Livingston organization. And he was too wise in his new knowledge to back a loser. He saw that picking a winner under the new-fangled patronage system offered more than the mere satisfaction of a vicarious victory. He judged that with Morgan Lewis Governor there would be another apportioning of local offices, and that it would be strange if Van Alen-Van Buren were not remembered on the day of rewards and punishments. Therefore he nominated Brother James on the Clinton-Livingston ticket, stumping the length and breadth of the county for the allied cause.

It was an eminently practical thing Matt had done in betraying the friendship, but it was anything but popular. Most of his friends around Kinderhook were friends also to Mr. Burr, and they violently resented the presence of a turn-coat in their midst. Billy Van Ness wrote him a curt and injured letter saying he "should be gratified to be informed of the principles upon which your decision has been made." Matt, with a glibness of explanation which would some day make him famous, replied that he felt a "pure and disinterested affection" for Billy and Mr. Burr, hoped they would credit "the purity of my motives" and that "a difference of opinion on this subject will not affect the friendly relations which have hitherto existed between us."

Billy scorned to answer such weaselling words, but the congressional brother, coming to town to do his share of electioneering, gave Matt a thorough snubbing in the presence of a goodly crowd. Nor were the slurs visited upon him only by his own generation. At twenty-one, Matt had become a recognized figure of importance. On election day lordly old Peter Van Ness and old Peter Van Schaack, his peer in station and age, took the trouble to wait at the tap-room until Abe's boy came in to cast his ballot, whereupon they stepped up and challenged his vote, the most humiliating of political gestures.

All this scorn and displeasure Matt bore with the cheerful fortitude of one who knows that his reward awaits him. Mr. Burr, as expected, carried the City but lost the State, and among the first orders which Governor Morgan Lewis signed was the appointment of Assemblyman James I. Van Alen as Surrogate Judge of Columbia county. After that anyone who wondered why so much official business suddenly came pouring into the Van Alen-Van Buren office simply did not understand the new system of politics. But Martin Van Buren did. In his first year of manhood he had shown every promise of the future that would be his. He had evinced a pragmatic and truly political scorn for anything so impractical as friendship; had elected another chosen candidate, had produced some professional plunder, and effectively boarded his first band-wagon.

# CHAPTER II

## *He Runs for Office*

I NDEED, the boarding of band-wagons, the manoeuvring of himself into positions where he could utilize other energies than his own, may be called the essence of the Little Magician's artistry. Having, most of his public life, neither the taste nor the talents for wide-spread popularity, he was forced to rely on other modes of locomotion. Martin Van Buren never pushed himself into any of the many offices he held. He was pulled into them by forces outside, above and beyond him—even when, as often enough, he invented the forces. His ability for attaching a tow-line to such forward-moving vehicles as the Clinton-Livingston combine (and for knowing when to cast loose) became so proverbial that at the peak of his career the stars could scarcely stir in their courses but some poetaster or pamphleteer would have out his pen to blame or credit the Little Magician.

Viewed from the distance of another century, some of the many allegations against him are too remote from possibility to be considered, and others are too scandalous to dovetail with his character. By selecting and emphasizing a few it were possible to offer an exaggerated caricature of the man, to deck him with the horns and cloven feet of a Mephistopheles. But exaggeration in the case of Martin Van Buren is entirely unnecessary. The truth about him is far stranger than any fiction. Despite all his high soarings, he was never more than a mediocre man. His inordinate cleverness, carefully dissected, proves to be nothing but average intelligence, industriously applied; and his public and private morals, far

64 ]

from being Machiavellian, were bourgeois to the last degree.
Considered for what he was, a professional politician, his
career is as the lily compared to those of the bosses and political shysters who flourished during his middle and late years.
The very fact that he was never even suspected of owning
money he had not earned sets him apart from the lowest of
his colleagues, just as the very fact that he rarely attempted
true statesmanship sets him apart from the highest.

It is worth the emphasis of repetition that his very mediocrity is the most fascinating and remarkable thing about
Martin Van Buren. To know him to be no better, no wiser,
no worse than an average American adds glamor to his success. Many an ordinary man has risen from low beginnings
either on the wings of fate or by dint of strenuous labors.
But the Eighth President was neither lucky nor obviously la-
borious. Luck, as such, played small part in his progress, and
what most men call hard work played less. At twenty-one,
and without having done a day's work to deserve it, he was
a political power in his community, and was building up a
thriving practice. At forty-five, and with the same ease, he
had held six high offices and, on the side, made enough
money at law to retire from it for the rest of his days. His
is the story of a man who constantly took thought for some
labor-saving device to make his wheels go round. It is the
story of one who was always in port for the flood-tide. Circumstance was his trade-wind, and such was the effortless skill
of his seamanship that, amid lull and storm, he moved perpetually forward while others drifted from the course or
crashed upon the rocks. Somehow he managed that his sails
should always be filled, and events, apparently remote, kept
wafting him on.

## 2

### (July 11, 1804)

Mr. Burr was up early again. John Swartwout, limping a
little from the wounds Mayor Clinton had put in his leg,
came into the panelled library at dawn this morning of July

11, 1804, and found the Vice President, in shirt-sleeves and stockinged-feet, sleeping soundly on the couch. Roused from his slumber, Mr. Burr attired himself briefly for the day's work. Less than a fortnight ago he had read in the *Chronicle* how an English girl, shot in the breast, had been saved by the ball's striking a silk handkerchief carried in her bodice. It was, he must have known, a mere freak of science, but if it had saved her life—why might it not his own? Therefore Mr. Burr put on a bombazine coat, woofed in wool and said to have been ordered for the occasion. On the library desk lay his Last Will and Testament and a pair of letters written in the dead of night to Theodosia and her husband. One dealt almost exclusively with the matter of settling his estate, providing an honorarium for faithful servants and mistresses; the other said—

"If it should be my lot to fall, yet I live in you and in your son."

Billy Van Ness arrived, and then Mathew Davis and a few others, who along with Swartwout would remain behind as messengers to spread the first tidings, glad or otherwise, among the anxious Sons of Tammany and the Little Band. With Billy and Davis, Mr. Burr walked down the hill to his private wharf and stepped into the waiting barge, manned with black oarsmen. In one hand Billy carried a brace of pistols; in the other, and though the day promised to be clear, he bore an umbrella.

New Jersey's shore, despite the nascent town of Hoboken, was a high wall of summer-green woodlands, broken here and there by the verdant roll of a lawn that came down to the river-front. Three miles diagonally up-stream from Mr. Burr's wharf reared the craggy heights of Weehawken. Only at low tide could a boat find landing-space among the rocks at its base, and now as their prow grounded in the sand, Billy raised his umbrella and covered his hero's head. New Jersey's laws, like New York's, forbade duelling, and it was a polite hypocrisy of the day that gentlemen should go covered to their crime. Not that the law was ever enforced, but in case it became necessary to go through the motions of an

66 ]

inquiry, the umbrella helped honest men to swear on the witness stand that the principals of the encounter could not be recognized.

It was just six-thirty, the men remembered, when they dis-embarked and began toiling up the nearly perpendicular path. Twenty feet above the water-line was the field of honor —a narrow shelf of level land, hemmed in on three sides by rocks and canopied from above by over-hanging foliage and wild-flowers. The men occupied themselves in trampling down the underbrush to clear a space for the activities, and though two of them heated by the climb and the labor found it necessary to remove their coats, Mr. Burr kept his on. They talked in hushed tones, lest they should disturb one whom they called "the Captain"—a kindly old hermit who owned the mount and dwelt in a cottage at its summit. It greatly harassed this good man that his retreat should have been made a communal slaughter-ground, and more than a few times he had upset the stilted dignity of such affairs by planting himself between the opponents and scolding them off the premises, whereupon all would repair to the tavern half-a-mile down the shore and regale themselves into maud-lin friendship by aid of the landlord's wine. But the Cap-tain's sleep was not disturbed this morning. It lacked a few minutes of seven o'clock when the men beheld another barge coming toward them over the water.

### 3

### (July 11, 1804)

For the last time in his life, Mr. Alexander Hamilton reached into his coat pocket, drew forth his gold-rimmed spectacles and hitched them solemnly to the crown of his straight and aristocratic nose. He squinted into the sun that now, a little past seven o'clock, just reached the level of his eyes. Having won at the drawing of lots, Mr. Hamilton had chosen to face eastward and down-stream, though his second had protested that it would spoil his aim. He saw at ten paces a dapper little man with a suave mocking smile, which even in tense moments was said never to leave his lips. He saw at half-a-dozen miles, down the gleaming reach of the River and plainly visible under the blue arch of the sky, the City which had honored him above any man alive. Distance lent enchantment to the view; not long before an English poet had written of a similar scene:

> Never did sun more beautifully steep
> In his first splendor, valley, rock, or hill;
> Ne'er saw I, never felt a calm so deep!
> The river glideth at its own sweet will:
> Dear God! the very houses seem asleep;
> And all that mighty heart is lying still!

Mr. Hamilton stared. There under those roof-tops slept his seven children, their mother and a posse of creditors who would sell the house over his family's head unless he lived to come home to breakfast. Here under his feet was the very ground to which his other child, Phillip, had fallen with a bullet through his bowel.

Mr. Hamilton heard the second's warning and cocked his pistol.

Not the first time, this, that Mr. Hamilton had faced gun-fire, nor the first time either that his somewhat hair-triggered temper had brought him to the brink of disaster. Since that day thirty-two years ago when he had landed in Boston from his native island of Nevis, both these experiences had been his oftener than he now had the leisure to count. As a sophomore at King's—later Columbia—College, he had organized his own company, the Hearts of Oak, and led it into action at the two early battles of Long Island and Harlem Heights. Soon afterwards he was transferred to George Washington's staff, and since the General himself was possessed of an impetuous tongue, the course of their friendship had rarely run smoothly. Six years of pushing a pen quill over the General's ledger, of wheedling the General's funds out of a reluctant Congress, of running the General's errands, of scolding the General's officers had not tended to soothe young Hamilton's natural irascibility.

For what he had longed for in these days of his teens was to taste the fiery elixir of heroism. What he craved was fame. Often enough he had dashed about carrying dispatches where the fire was thickest, and once Lady Washington in admiration had named a favored tom-cat after him—a remarkable creature it was, too, with thirteen yellow stripes on its brindled tail to represent the embattled colonies. But neither of these distinctions satisfied the young Colonel's restless soul, and one day when the General called him down for keeping a tardy engagement, Hamilton resigned his commission on the spot and left camp. But for the intervention of the amiable M. de LaFayette, Mr. Hamilton's shortness of temper might have ended his military career, just as it was eventually to end his mortal existence. LaFayette took him into his own division and made him a General, and as a result Mr. Hamilton managed for once to see an ambition of his unqualifiedly fulfilled. At Yorktown he led a column with such headlong and spectacular fury that he was first over the enemy ramparts and took one of Cornwallis' two redoubts with the naked sword and without losing a man.

Mr. Hamilton heard the second's voice again. He lifted his right arm.

So long since that heyday at Yorktown. So much had happened. Returning to Albany after the battle he found himself in no position to take the warrior's proverbial ease at the fireside. His wife, the "blessed Eliza" to whom as a young calf he had written those mawkish little love-poems, was at her father's house and heavy with child. He himself was homeless, jobless and penurious. Twenty-five was not old for being a retired General, but it was over-ripe to be seeking a new profession without prospects or equipment and with a family to support. Proudly he renounced of Congress "all claim to the compensation attached to my military service," and with borrowed money he rented part of a house and set about learning the law. On the side he partially

[ 69

supported himself by writing a case-book, by tutoring other law-students, and within a year he was admitted to the bar.

Then politics. The Confederation—a union without unity —a government without funds. Fourteen petty powers, jealous of their separate rights, squabbling among each other, keeping their best men home and sending their third-raters to sit in a farce of a Congress that was without the essential law-giving or tax-making authority. Foreign debtors on the national doorstep; veterans of America's first war howling for money, marching through the streets, threatening, if Washington would lead them, to overthrow the Republic and make him king, and in the midst of it a letter from Robert Morris, asking him to accept a governmental appointment and to lend a hand. His refusal because "time is too precious." The insistence of Morris and of others. His final acceptance, and with this first plunge into statecraft, the rest of a lifetime devoted to little else.

Not all had been pleasant, but always it was thrilling. Days in the Legislature fighting old shaggy-browed George Clinton and his inane ideas about People's Rights and State Sovereignty. Days in the Congress fighting inertia, stupidity and the folly of doing "what will *please*, not what will *benefit* the People." Writing the Federalist papers with Madison and Jay. Building a new Party that called for a government ruled by the ruling classes. Battling for the Constitution and, with success, the Roman triumph of that day when the City turned out to honor him as not even Washington had ever been honored. A parade two miles long, in which every guild and society in town was represented with floats and costumed marchers. And the feature of the whole celebration—a 27-foot frigate, fully manned, armed and rigged, drawn along the Broad Way by ten beribboned horses and bearing across its prow the single word—*Hamilton*. Forgot that day was the indignity of the tom-cat.

And letters to Mount Vernon brow-beating the General into quitting his estate and taking up the new office of President. And Thomas Jefferson coming home from France because the government could no longer pay his bills. And cabinet meetings where more than once he and the man

from Monticello nearly came to blows. And the Bank Bill—
the Assumption Bill—the Reynolds woman—the new Capital City. Quarreling with everyone—with Jefferson, of course,
—with the "great, little Madison"—with dour, earnest Monroe—with fat, fussy John Adams—with smooth, cunning
Burr. Losing his temper and losing his cabinet seat; losing
his temper and losing elections. Twenty-two years since
Yorktown; twelve of them spent in and out of public office;
the last ten no less actively spent as manager of his fading
Federalist Party.

Well, if he went, his work would remain. The Constitution was there, and the ruling classes would continue to rule
for all the Jeffersonian twaddle about the People. His City
would grow into a metropolis; his country into an empire.
That was his dream—it would come true.

Mr. Hamilton pulled the trigger, and as he did a hot pain
went burrowing into his right side, just below the nipple.
His own shot went skyward, clipping a branch overhead, and
a broken twig fell at the feet of Aaron Burr. Slowly Mr.
Hamilton rose on his toes, slowly he twisted and, turning his
back on the gleaming sunlight—on his enemy—on his City,
he sank rhythmically to the ground.

And the spectacles slid from his nose.

## 4

(1804–1808)

Billy's umbrella proved no shelter from the storm that
fell. The City was no sooner home from the ornate funeral
at Trinity Church, it had not even put off its official mourning, than grief for the dead turned to wrath for the living.
While Mr. Hamilton lingered through the rest of his last
day and night, the Tammany Wigwam put on a celebration,
swilling down toasts to the conquering chief. But on the
sobering morn:

Brothers: Your attendance is earnestly requested at an extra
meeting of the tribes, at the Great Wigwam precisely at the

setting of the sun this evening, to make arrangements for the joining of our fellow-citizens and soldiers in a procession, in order to pay the last tribute of national respect, due to the manes of our departed fellow-citizen and soldier, General Alexander Hamilton. By order of the Grand Sachem.

James B. Bisset, Secretary.

Season of fruits, in the Year of Discovery Three Hundred and Twelve and of the Institution the Fifteenth, July the 13th.

Mr. Burr, too, expressed his sorrow, but even that failed to appease the popular ire. A coroner's jury pronounced him guilty of murder and his companions accomplices before the fact. A grand jury met to get out an indictment. Mr. Burr took to his barge in the dead of night, escaped to Perth Amboy and thence to the South. Mathew Davis, unhelped by the umbrella alibi, was clapped into jail. Billy Van Ness, a fugitive from justice, hid in his father's house, and sent for the best lawyer in Kinderhook. Matt tramped down the dusty road, and agreed to handle the case. It was to drag on for years, but in the end Billy's attorney pulled enough political strings to have him not only restored to citizenship but graced with the ermine of a federal judgeship. His harrowing experiences in the ranks of Mr. Burr thoroughly tamed Billy. Henceforth he eschewed the furor of party warfare, and even his flaming pen found its only expression in turning out dull books about law.

The historic duel did more for Matt than simply to bring him in an attorney's fee. It offers a typical example of the way he constantly managed to make events with which he had only the vaguest, if any, connection, serve his purpose. It would require a far-fetched argument to prove that the moment of Mr. Hamilton's agony was also the turning-point of Martin Van Buren's career. Yet there is something to be said for the case. Alexander Hamilton's death caused the dramatic removal of Aaron Burr from the scene of New York politics, and his removal was somewhat second-handedly the cause of Martin Van Buren's alliance with Tammany—an alliance which was to be his greatest strength for the next thirty years. Whether the little tactician would have found other means to effect the merger, or whether he would have gone just as far without it, need not be debated, for as it happened the tragedy of Weehawken turned out to be a vital chapter in his life-story. With Burr gone there was a re-shuffling of the forces that ruled the State, and Matt was not one to miss a chance of bettering himself. God, Matt knew, in politics as in war, was likely to be found on the side of the largest battalions. And where God was, there would Matt be also.

Hardly had Burr and Hamilton done with hunting each other's blood before it was a case of dog eat dog with the Clinton-Livingstons. That grateful in-law, Morgan Lewis, was no sooner Governor than he found himself confronted with the thoroughly domestic problem of choosing between his friends and his relatives. There were any number of minor jobs within his gift, and these he bestowed with an open hand. But of the more important positions there were comparatively few—much fewer than were Clinton-Living-stons. Therefore when he made his wife's brother, Maturin, Recorder of New York City, there was an outraged howl from the Clinton family. The City, they argued, was their own to do with as they pleased. Hadn't De Witt nobly left the Senate to pull Edward Livingston's chestnuts out of the fire? Wasn't he Mayor? Didn't he deserve to have his own way in his own province?

But the Governor stood firm on the appointment and an open breach cleft the friendship of the two families. They did not know, perhaps, that in this quarreling over the spoils of office they were inaugurating a new American custom, which bosses, from Presidents down to ward-heelers, would carry on for them unto, possibly, the end of time. The Liv-ingstons having struck the first blow, the Clintons responded in kind. No appointment under his jurisdiction, resolved the Mayor, should go to a Livingstonian. It was a resolution that had teeth in it. For, as Mayor, De Witt Clinton was also magistrate of the criminal courts, chief of police, clerk of the five City markets, and president of the Common Council —attributes that carried with them the control of hundreds of petty jobs and the licensing of all public services such as tavern-keeping, dray-driving, baggage-transfer, street-peddling and many others.

Faced with the problem of distributing this multitude of favors, the Mayor remembered his own predicament. His mayoralty itself was an appointment of the Governor's, and if the Livingstons won another gubernatorial election, they would surely make one of their own clan Mayor. Therefore it behooved Mr. Clinton to prepare against the coming election day, and with this in mind he performed a clandestine meeting with no other than his lamed adversary, John Swartwout. Now that Burr was out of the picture, Mr. Clinton was ready to admit the respectability of Tammany, for the Society, even in defeat, had proved itself master of the City. Later, in the back room of Dyde's tavern, representatives of the Mayor and the Sachems met to work out an agreement whereby the Braves would have their share of the City patronage, in return for which the Wigwam would lend its valuable assistance against the Livingstons.

At news of this treaty Martin Van Buren lost no time in aligning himself with the latest coalition. Three years ago he had worked for Lewis. A year ago he had further added to his prestige by sending Brother James to Congress on an anti-Tammany ticket, but as the wind veered, so did his affiliations. Business was good, he was rapidly paying off the debt, and he longed to have the fair Hannah in holy wedlock. This was his chance.

The Tammany-Clintonians nominated a Daniel D. Tompkins as their choice to beat Morgan Lewis. It was a strange pair of contestants. Lewis was elderly, scholarly and dignified. Tompkins was young, handsome, good-natured, possessed of but one outstanding quality, and that one not hitherto considered a prerequisite of statesmanship. This was an astonishing gift for tireless affability, coupled with a knack of remembering the names and personal affairs of literally thousands of voters. On the authority of contemporary records it is possible to put down Dan Tompkins as the first of the long line of back-slapping, baby-kissing politicians whom the Republic would soon come to know and to cherish.

Happy Dan's affability was no pose. He truly loved people —loved above all a group of cronies gathered about the flowing bowl. He hailed from Fox Meadows, Westchester County, but as law clerk in New York he had served Burr and the Wigwam by dwelling in the same house of "floaters" with Billy Van Ness and thirty-eight others. His leaders dubbed him the "farmer's son" candidate, and pointed with pride to the fact that he was not related to either of the royal families. The Livingstons rejoined stoutly in defense of Lewis that there was no stigma attached to marrying into their clan; the Clintonians expressed some doubt about it —and that became the sole issue of the campaign.

Bravely Matt swung round his circuit in Columbia County, calling out votes for the Farmer's Son. It was during this canvass of 1807 that he seems to have developed another reputation with which he was extraordinarily pleased —and to all reports, justly so. The reference here is to his capacity for imbibing enormous amounts of intoxicants without the usual result, and for which he later earned the proud title of Blue Whiskey Van. In the Tompkins campaign this quality stood him in good stead, for most of the electioneering was done in the tap-rooms. The system of standing drinks in the Dutch counties was to gather at the bar over a large loving-cup compounded with schiedam, and to pass it right to left down the line. Then, also from right to left, each man would replenish the cup until each had both bought and drunk a full one.

Considering that Matt covered as many as a dozen taverns a day, his capacity seems to have been all that was said of it, and for that alone he unquestionably deserved his brother's vacated office of Surrogate Judge, an appointment that came to him shortly after Tompkins ascended to the governorship at New Year, 1808.

It was an elevation welcome both for its dignity and its income, and Matt was counting heavily on the latter. For one day early in the campaign he and Hannah had slipped off to Catskill, and come back man and wife.

5

\(1811–1812\)

Guests and retainers of that local dignitary, General Jacob Rutsen Van Rensselaer, three lawyers at Claverack were eating a Sunday dinner. The wine flowed free and the food was good, but there was no joy among this company today. Glumly Mr. Elisha Williams considered his stolen thunder, and glumly his two compatriots, Tom Grosvenor and young John Sudam, considered it with him. Nor was their host much merrier, for if they had lost a law-suit, he had lost not only some irreplaceable prestige, but a sizable piece of his fortune. When they spoke it was frequently of one whom they designated harshly, and if they named him by name, they called him Martin Van Buren.

It was, General Van Rensselaer might have reflected, almost three years ago since the erstwhile Boy Lawyer, now a husband and father, had moved from Kinderhook to Hudson, the new county seat, there to take up his duties as Surrogate and to form a partnership with the local attorney, Sylvanus Miller. The General could well have remembered the date, for it marked signicantly the beginning of his present woe. Shortly after Martin's arrival, there appeared in the Hudson *Advocate* a series of anonymous letters, obviously of the same authorship, and obviously, too, of provocative intent. For nearly two hundred years, said these epistles in substance, the Van Rensselaers, along with their kinsmen, an up-country branch of the Livingston family, had been shamelessly defrauding their neighbors. Back in the seventeenth century the heirs of Kiliaen Van Rensselaer had accepted land from the Dutch King's charter, but by the aid of scoundrelly surveyors and unscrupulous lawyers they had claimed far more than their rightful share, and the rest of

76 ]

the inhabitants had been paying rent and purchase money for it ever since.

Except for the implication of fraud, there was nothing original in the statement. Since 1772 the Manor Lands case had been in and out of the courts, but with such indecisive results that both sides had informally called a truce. The appearance of these letters caused a re-opening of hostilities between the patroon families and the Tenants, so-called. These last were mostly the peasantry to which the elder Van Burens belonged, too ignorant and easy-going to have much knowledge or sustained interest in their technical rights. But among them were other families, including the Van Nesses and Van Schaacks, now richer than their former masters and, like all men who made their own fortunes, highly interested in making some more. Old Peter Van Schaack himself had for years attempted to act as counsel for the Tenants' claims, but he was now nearing his dotage, and in calling new blood to the fray he quite naturally selected the enterprising firm of Miller-Van Buren.

That Martin himself was author of these unsigned publications, the General and many others firmly believed, but they, like Martin's historian, would have found it difficult to prove. What the young Surrogate needed on arriving in Hudson to set up housekeeping and raise a family was the opportunity to improve the hand-to-mouth livelihood he was making in the spare time between his duties on the bench and his incessant campaigning. He needed a case with some respectable amount of money attached. If the case also combined some political value, so much the better, and if it did not come to him in the natural course of events then Martin Van Buren was just the man to go after it.

It seems fairly probable that go after it he did. He was accused of having written the letters, both at the time of their printing and as long as twenty years afterwards, when his biographies began to appear. Little faith can be put in the latter, but in his *Autobiography* Martin offers a veiled reference to it with the covert excuse that right was on his side and his own family were involved. Moreover the use of

[ 77

anonymous writings was something he is known for certain to have cultivated and admitted in other instances. If he had subsequently proved himself above such things, if the tale did not correspond so convincingly with several known examples of his methods, if indeed he had dealt more openly with the accusation, it might be readily dismissed. But as it stands, it smacks suspiciously of the truth, and even with appropriate reservations it belongs to his legend.

But what he did next, the General and his guests could testify, was by no means legendary. Engaged during 1810-11 in this, his first big-monied suit, Martin was also making his first run for office, and illustrating in it nearly all of the artfulness that was to grace his later years. Especially was this true of the two characteristic poses that are inseparable from his name and fame. Martin Van Buren was always the unwilling, unseeking candidate, "forced" as he repeatedly explained it, into accepting his honors from the People. And nearly always he was the "martyr" candidate, discovering at this early stage the now-familiar proverb that the great American public loveth a martyr only a little less than it does a hero.

With his eye on an opening in the State Senate for 1812, the Surrogate had need of all the cunning he could muster. Columbia County, back-boned by the feudalism of the patroon system and by the Jay Constitution, was still basically Federalist, and doubly so in its representatives to the exclusive State Senate, membership to which was safeguarded by a property clause. Theoretically Martin could claim eligibility, since Abe had indulgently registered the tavern in his son's name, but the chance of any young commoner's attaining the office was extremely remote. So long had the senatorship from the Middle District been in the hands of the landed aristocracy that they and the whole community had come to regard it as part of the feudal prerogative. The Van Rensselaers, the Livingstons, the Silvesters, the Schuylers—lords of the Manor—simply alternated in the office with little or no competition from outside their own clique.

But the vigor, nay impudence, with which Lawyer Van

Buren handled the Manor Lands case was having a purgative effect on the stuffy acceptance of the whole patrician system. No one before had dared the *lèse majesté* of questioning the personal integrity of these autocrats. Peter Van Schaack had conducted the case from a gentlemanly and highly technical angle, but Martin in the court-room was a Daniel come to judgment, levelling against the bewildered patriarchs charge after charge of collusion and fraud. He did more than that. He brought the case out of its cloister of legal terminology, and gave it a political flavor. At public meetings, in hand-bills, through the newspapers, he used the Manor Lands suit as a spring-board from which to fly at the throat of Federalism, denouncing the members of the patroon coterie as examples of baronial tyranny, calling upon the yeomanry to renounce them now and forever.

For the first time in his life Martin was gaining a State-wide publicity. He drew the Federalist fire upon himself, and then struck the attitude, in speech and publication, of being a much-abused victim who patiently bore the cross of martyrdom for the sake of a holy cause. It became rather a difficult pose when a Federalist journal quoted a letter of his wherein he proposed delaying the case throughout the elections in hope of "gaining some kindred votes in the Manor towns." But even this charge of playing politics with his client's case and the People's rights was turned to his own advantage when Martin posted a bet of $500 that no one could prove him guilty. No one could, for Martin took care the original letter was never found, and his stock rose higher. De Witt Clinton, now Lieutenant Governor as well as Mayor, heard of him; so did Richard Riker, field marshal of the Clintonian forces, and that was important because as yet Riker had picked no senatorial candidate for the Middle District.

On the final day of the trial, foregoing his usual glibness of manner, Martin surpassed himself in wormwood and gall. Summing up the case, he turned loose such a flood of invective, innuendo and bald accusation of dishonor that Elisha Williams, chief counsel for the Van Rensselaers, con-

signed himself once more to defeat by the despised Boy
Lawyer. Resentfully, but with resignation, he heard his
client's reputation ripped into shreds. Martin being entitled
to the closing speech, there could be no rebuttal, but if Mr.
Williams was willing to endure the humiliation, not so his
young assistant, John Sudam. Sudam, a stranger to the Boy
Lawyer's local privileges, was fired with indignation that any
young upstart should presume to scandalize the exalted Van
Rensselaers. Several times he interrupted the address with
tart rejoinders, only to be painfully impaled when Martin
occasionally turned the sword-hand of his wit against the
mocker.

That had been on Friday; on Saturday the case went to
the jury, and at dinner on Sunday the General and his aids
wondered only how large would be the judgment against
them. Smarting under the lash of defeat and from the thongs
laid across his own back, Sudam gave unstinted attention
to the wine before him, and as the evening wore on his emotions attained the scope of a righteous, uncontrollable passion. In this state of grace he accosted Tom Grosvenor, and
commanded him to take the Boy Lawyer a challenge.

It rings of the paradox that the same *code duello* which
finished off the blazing careers of Hamilton and Burr should
have given the career of Martin Van Buren the needed im-
petus for a start. No fighting man was Martin, but between
the dawn and dusk of two days he was both challenged and
challenger, and without facing gun-fire, so contrived that the
affairs, instead of bringing him to the field of honor, made
him an Honorable—a holder of the People's franchise. At
court on Monday morning, he was approached by Grosvenor, who apologetically delivered the message. He was
sorry, said Tom, to be bearing such a mission, for Sudam
had been far from his sober self last night. Still when one
gentleman asks another to wait upon a third, there is no
choice under the Code but to obey. Martin solemnly agreed,
and Tom as solemnly bowed himself away.

The message, reluctantly delivered, was received in the
same spirit. Martin had never seen Sudam until the Manor

trial; bore him no grudge, and certainly had no lust for his blood. From the point of view of his own safety he claims to have been less frightened than annoyed. Accept the challenge he must, yet on this November 25, 1811, that was the last thing on earth he wanted to do. His future was opening before him, Hannah was his helpmate, two babes crowed in the cradle, and "no one entertains a more contemptuous opinion of the bravery of the duel field than myself." But save by showing the white feather there was no way out. He called in his friend, George Morell, and sent him to Sudam to make the arrangements.

Had the duel actually come off, it would certainly have been a matter of no importance to American history. Whether Martin had killed Sudam or lost his own life, whether they had both come through it alive, would have mattered to none but the persons involved. But as it happened the meeting failed to materialize, thereby creating a situation farcical to the untrained eye, but to such an opportunist as the embryonic Little Magician, one pregnant with welcome possibilities. For just as the casual passerby looks blindly at the flower which inspires a poet's rhapsody, so a multitude of men could have ignored a circumstance in which Martin found a tide for his own advancement.

Morell, after waiting upon Grosvenor as Sudam's designated second, returned to inform his principal that Tom, having delivered the message, would have nothing more to do with the affair. The Code now demanded of Martin that he send his own challenge directly to Sudam, which he did in writing. Here all serious aspects of the quarrel came to an end, for the fire-brand of Sunday night had awaked the next morning much the worse for wear and in no health for further heroics. Languishing in pain at the hotel, he told Morell that since Tom Grosvenor refused to act as second, there would be no duel.

Now it was that Martin took personal charge of his destiny. A hesitant foe he might have been while his rival showed signs of aggressiveness, anxious to live, bound down by moral scruples, mindful of his family duties; but with the enemy in full flight, this peace-lover became a demon enraged. Sounding again his favorite keynote of martyrdom, he enacted the part of a saint come to the end of his patience. Long enough had he borne the snobbery and animosity of these scheming aristocrats! Long enough had he, a friend of the People, been maltreated by these enemies of Democracy and Justice! Seizing a quill he scratched out a note branding the suffering Sudam as a spineless craven, and rushed across the street to post it at the hotel.

It is not among Martin's confessions that, before crossing the street, he noted the presence of enough witnesses to grant him an audience and also the presence of the town marshal to insure him a safe return. It may have been mere chance that his gesture of posting the notice and his accompanying remarks concerning his martyrdom were given to an appreciative crowd, and that the officer of the peace was on hand to prevent Sudam and the Surrogate from destroying each other then and there. That, apparently, was what happened, and it would be scant appreciation of the Little Magician's showmanship to assume that it happened by accident.

More, it would do him no justice to suppose that he did not foresee the general result in terms of political publicity. Republican papers, already full of the Manor trial, seized upon this highly colorful dénouement, carrying Martin's name the length and breadth of the State, interpreting the affair as still another example of the aristocrats to crush this patient but theatrical champion. De Witt Clinton broke silence to send Martin a word of praise; Richard Riker wrote him a letter commending his actions. The tide was swelling; again Martin prepared himself for an onward journey.

While the affair was still hot in the minds of all, he announced his candidacy for the State Senate, modestly declaring he had "no desire to be a candidate," but that he was "forced into that position by circumstances." There were several other and older aspirants for the Clintonian nomination, but another letter from Riker endorsing Martin gave him a majority at the District Convention.

## He Runs for Office

A veteran campaigner and not yet thirty, Martin swung around the circuit, this time in his own behalf. On the face of it he seemed to have drawn a well-nigh impossible assignment. He was operating in a Federalist stronghold. No man so young as he had ever been State Senator. The disgruntled aspirants for his nomination had withdrawn to a rump convention, agreeing to support the Federalist candidate, E. P. Livingston. But again he had chosen a tide that was running in his direction. It was a presidential year when local prejudices would be outweighed by larger matters, and both outstanding issues of the national election were in his favor —the question of declaring war on England and the matter of re-chartering Hamilton's Bank of America. The Republicans were pledged to the first and against the second. To prove the Bank a creature of corrupt, city-bred aristocrats was not too difficult in the rural Middle District, while as for flag-waving and foreigner-damning, when was there a campaigner who did not revel in it? Needless to say Martin made the most of his chances, but on the day after election it seemed that the best of his efforts had been in vain. The early reports that came into the tavern where he had confronted Sudam showed Livingston well out in front and gaining steadily.

Late in the day, conceding defeat, he packed his bag for a trip to New York, where the upper court was sitting. Luggage in hand, he passed out of his front door and started for the dock, noting gloomily that some of the celebrating Federalists at the tavern "appeared on the piazza and shed upon me, at parting, the light of their beaming countenances." His last hope vanished on the boat when he encountered a lawyer from up the River who confirmed reports that the Federalists were still holding their own. But two hours later, as his vessel passed Catskill, Martin noticed the tall, familiar figure of Moses Cantine, his brother-in-law, signalling strenuously and pointing toward a skiff that was putting out from the shore.

The smaller craft drew up alongside, and a packet ad-

dressed to him was tossed aboard. Trembling Martin broke
the seal. The letter showed that an unreported county had
overcome the Federalist lead, that in the final count he had
won a constituency of 40,000 by less than 200 votes.

And so the man who would not know a major setback for
nearly thirty years to come had gained his first law-giving
office by the proverbial skin of his teeth.

# CHAPTER III

## *He Holds Office*

THE original proposition here advanced—that Martin Van Buren stands historically as the Founding Father of American Politics—seems to totter a bit with the listing of events and personalities that shared his early years. That Aaron Burr organized Tammany and concocted the several stratagems of organized vote-getting; that De Witt Clinton utilized patronage as a means toward an end, seem obvious rebuttals to the theory of the little Kinderhooker's importance.

But the discrepancy is less real than apparent. It is part of the Van Buren mediocrity that he was not an inventor, but a promoter; part of his character that he soared to the heights on borrowed wings. He had neither the creative genius of Aaron Burr nor the rugged leadership of De Witt Clinton, yet he went further than either of these, and by plans which they had suggested. Martin Van Buren no more discovered the powers secreted in Democratic Government than Robert Fulton discovered steam. But both devised methods for domesticating these forces, and both surpassed all predecessors in the very fact that they managed, where others had failed, to harness untamed energies to sound, successful and permanent usage.

Neither Burr nor Clinton contrived to add his system to American Culture. The first was too luckless; the second too scrupulous. Burr met with defeat and banishment in the very flower of his prime, leaving behind an unfinished work. From his passing, until the rise of Fernando Wood forty years later, the Wigwam was as a house half-built, no more than a subsidy to Martin Van Buren's state-wide Regency. He became lastingly what Burr had been temporarily, the recognized strategist of her lumbering strength. He restored her to power in the City, guided her through some of her palmiest years, and was withal more responsible than Burr for her continued existence as a model for the efficient harvesting of votes.

As for Clinton's works, he himself renounced them. His patronage system was never, properly speaking, a spoils system. In the short-lived Clinton-Livingston era, it was purely a defensive measure, and only accidentally a corrupt one. In the even shorter-lived Clinton-Swartwout period, it gave promise of becoming permanent; except that Clinton revolted and retched at the thought, it would have endured. That very squeamishness of his was the basic reason why his alliance with Tammany barely lasted through one election. Learning what was expected of him, the Mayor (he was now simultaneously State Senator) forthwith cancelled the bargain, and became the Wigwam's most evangelical enemy; later, as Governor, his first act was to announce that there would be no general removals.

It remained for the man from Kinderhook to take up the torch where Burr and Clinton had dropped it. Until he assumed command, political trickery, though existent, was a spurious, haphazard practice. He standardized it. Until he developed its possibilities, the use of patronage was localized, loose-jointed and slap-dash. He nationalized it.

And the importance of the Little Magician lies deeper than that. It was through him and his example that the moral code of politics was re-written. Before he became an influence, a man in public life was assumed to be sincere and upright until proved otherwise. Afterwards and forevermore, the commonest plea for a candidate's election was being called "frank, honest, courageous," words never missing from any campaign and qualities taken for granted in any other profession. So great was the Little Magician's metamorphic powers that it has finally been judged downright impossible for a person to be ordinarily decent and still a successful politician. That very name entered American dictionaries as a term for degradation and contempt.

Almost single-handed Martin Van Buren accomplished these wonders. Beginning his first term as State Senator, he immediately established himself as the outstanding apostle of a New Era. His gospel soon captivated the home State, and before long encompassed the rest of the Union. In 1832 William L. Marcy, a member of the Van Buren Regency, stood on the Senate floor at Washington and enunciated a creed that could with more truth than blasphemy be inscribed on the very temple of State. Said Marcy:

"It may be that the politicians of New York are not so fastidious as some gentlemen are. They boldly preach what they practice. When they are contending for victory, they avow their intention of enjoying the fruit of it. If they fail, they will not murmur. If they win, they expect to reap all the advantages. They see nothing wrong with the rule that TO THE VICTOR BELONG THE SPOILS OF THE ENEMY."

It is not surprising that the messiah of such a faith should have fallen considerably short of being a statesman. A lawgiver over a period of nearly three decades, he took but scant interest in the mere matter of legislation. During his score of years in national office, he was responsible for just one measure important enough to be recorded: the establishment of a Sub-Treasury, which came after he had attained the presidency. During his ten-year reign at Albany, he sponsored exactly three measures worth mentioning. First was his series of bills to abolish the Debtor's Prison— and it is certain beyond all reasonable doubt that he never wanted them to pass. The second is like unto the first, his sham-battle against the rightly-named Banking Mania. Even granting the sincerity in his early assaults on wildcat banking, what is there to be said of the fact that when Governor Clinton proposed an investigation to protect the public, Senator Van Buren blocked it to protect some of his hench-

men who were involved and one of whom was his law-
partner?

The third and most important of his measures at Albany
was one promoting the aggressive conduct of the War. For
this he was hailed as the noblest of patriots, and doubtless
he was so long as patriotism could be practiced at a safe distance from the smoke of battle. He doted on calling the affair
of 1812 the "Second War of Independence" and one of his
published speeches "the Second Declaration of Independence." But though he devoutly served the cause by drafting
a bill for compulsory enlistment, he himself never smelt
gun-powder. When the State he so professed to love was
invaded, nearly everyone of consequence rushed to join the
colors. There still existed at that time the now-obsolete
theory of *noblesse oblige*, that men who rule a country are
the ones to protect her in emergency, but the Red Fox was
a man too much ahead of his time to be influenced by any
such trumpery. His own brother donned a uniform, the
Governor, the Mayor, the Adjutant General, the Patroon,
flocks of Senators and Assemblymen, three future Presidents
and a dozen future candidates—family men all—but not
Martin, though he dutifully spent his sessions cheering on
the combatants and his recesses scouring the landscape for
new recruits. Mr. Monroe, Secretary of War, so mistook the
Kinderhooker's zeal as to offer him an Army commission,
but Martin, like his father before him, preferred to express
himself only in words. Not the least of his examples to posterity was this salutary mode of enacting patriotism. After
his day there would never be an American War which was
fought by the same men who encouraged it.

Yet it is grossly unfair to judge a man save by his own
standards. Obviously neither soldier nor statesman, there is
no point in measuring Martin Van Buren as such. At the
State Senate he made his first bow in formal statecraft, showing himself as a tactician of campaign, a ring-master of parliamentary encounter, an ever-striving careerist whose
shrouded designs made every new objective a winning post.

Here, by his dandyism of dress, his beguiling graciousness of manner, his subtlety of intrigue, he begins to take shape as the best and last of American courtiers. With the rise of bossism during the next thirty years, the shillelagh supplanted the rapier as the most effective of political weapons, but the Little Magician held to the latter and wielded it with such delicate grace that even men whom he ran through the vitals had difficulty in hating him for it. Always the princeliest of good fellows, a schemer of infinite charm, his personality, as well as his sword-point, touched the hearts of his victims. When Henry Clay said of him—"An acquaintanceship with him of more than twenty years duration has inspired me with a respect for the man, although . . . I detest the magistrate."—he was putting words into the mouths of many others who felt the same way.

His capture of the senatorship gave Martin Van Buren another and a larger chance to illustrate his unfailing aptitude for opportunity. So quietly did he glide into advantageous positions that fate itself seemed to conspire for his benefit. A War is fought, and without glimpsing a battle field, Martin becomes a national figure. A hero rises, and without risking a hair Martin begins to rise with him.

Men and events, they were the media he worked in. The Little Magician moved his wand, and they became soundless tides that bore him ever forward and on.

2

(June 1812–November 1812)

The square-jawed, rugged countenance of Mr. De Witt Clinton showed this day of June, 1812, a russet glow of rage. The Magnus Apollo was furious, and he had good reason for it. Not that he necessarily demanded any specific cause, for this state of temper had been his almost perpetually since his return to State politics in '03. First there had been Burr, then the Livingstons, then Swartwout, and always there was Tammany to stir his wrath. But none of these was the present cause of his ill-temper. Mr. Clinton had lost a bet.

In his papers, under a date of four years back, was the notation that he had wagered his friend and publisher, James Cheetham, the price of a beaver hat that "there would be no War with England." On the 18th of this month the wager had fallen due, for the House, under the lash of War Hawks Clay and Calhoun, had passed the resolution, and the Senate by a majority of six votes had concurred.

The price of the hat Mr. Clinton could afford, but not the consequences that went with it. In May, when death was about to remove the embarrassing rivalry of Uncle George, the nephew had accepted the nomination of the New York and New England Legislatures to oppose James Madison for the presidency. For a while the chances of success seemed remarkably strong. The country had reacted not unfavorably to Mr. Clinton's democratic tirades against the Virginia Dynasty; neither Mr. Madison's cloistered personality nor his foreign and domestic policies struck the popular fancy. Moreover Mr. Clinton, already calling himself the "Peace President" and the "People's Candidate," had promised to keep the nation out of War.

But now he saw that circumstance, personified by Congressmen Clay and Calhoun, had forestalled him. Once war was definitely declared, his support began to dwindle. It was his patriotic duty, everyone was saying, to drop his candidacy and back the Administration. Mr. Clinton did not see it that way. A delegation from New England came to say that if he would resign it now, he should positively have the nomination four years hence. Experience, replied the Magnus Apollo, had taught him that political bargains were ignoble affairs. Judge Ambrose Spencer, twice married to Clinton sisters, dropped in at the house at No. 9 Cherry Street and attempted to reason with its master. The Judge was told to mind his own business. Others came with the same message and departed with the same result.

They should have known better. Anyone acquainted with Mr. Clinton must have been aware that taking advice and changing his mind were not among his manifold attributes. Already he had taken steps to found the public school system, the Academy of Fine Arts, the Literary and Philosophical Society, the New York Historical Society, a hospital for the care of the insane, and some people were even beginning to believe that there was some sense in that project of his for joining the Great Lakes to the Hudson by an Erie Canal. Besides being simultaneously Mayor and Lieutenant Governor, he was an authoritative writer on science, medicine and aboriginal history, and he wielded a popular pen that was the scourge of Tammany. It was no idle boast when he declared himself the People's candidate, for classes and masses would have been justly proud to seat him in the Palace on Pennsylvania Avenue, except that war-time was no time for a Peace President.

This, however, Mr. Clinton refused to admit. To him the War was no less absurd now it was actually declared than beforehand. Supposed to be a contest for Free Trade and Sailors' Rights, it was truthfully, saw Mr. Clinton, nothing of the sort. The very states with mercantile and maritime interests were against it. The New York and New England delegations in Congress had violently opposed a declaration, only to be out-voted by a combination of the South and West. Mr. Clay's Kentucky, for instance, had not a single sea-port, and Mr. Calhoun's South Carolina had but one. Clearly, urged Mr. Clinton, it was not a defensive war, but one of aggression and hence an abomination to American principles. Southern statesmen yearned to add the British-protected, Spanish-possessed Floridas to their domain. Western spell-binders pictured an empire rolling through the British-protected Indian lands as far north as, and including, Canada. Jefferson's bungling Embargo, he argued, and Madison's equally preposterous Non-Intercourse Act had brought about the diplomatic impasse which resulted in hostilities. For if freedom of the seas were at stake, why not pick on Napoleon? He, too, was guilty.

But despite the evident logic of his arguments, Mr. Clinton knew himself to be losing steadily as the summer wore on. His points bounced as unimpressively off the public consciousness as British cannon balls were soon to be bouncing off the flanks of Old Ironsides. By early November, when the law-givers were assembling at Albany for the special session when the presidential electors would be chosen, Mr. Clinton had come to realize that his chance for an outright win had gone, that the best he could hope for was a good enough showing to earn renomination in 1816. Even this seemed an impossibility, for he discovered himself in a fair way to experience the insufferable humiliation of losing his own State. A check-up of the incoming Legislature revealed a Federalist majority in the House and enough Madisonians in the Senate to force some compromise concerning the electoral votes. It was a situation that called for inspirational measures, and about this time Mr. Clinton beheld at various public places around Albany a dashing little figure in a green coat, buff breeches and white-topped boots, looking, someone remarked, "much more like a sportsman than a legislator."

Unlike his friend and faithful retainer, Governor Dan Tompkins, Mr. Clinton was not blessed with the affable talent of remembering names and faces. Preoccupied, doubtless, with loftier thoughts, his absent-mindedness frequently gave as much offense in his neighborly City as did his violent spasms of temper and his more quiescent moods of unbending hauteur. Probably he did not remember the name of the Middle District's new Senator-elect, for they had never met on any intimate terms, but being reminded, Mr. Clinton recalled some remarkable things he had heard about the man. The more of these things he recalled, the more Mr. Clinton's mind centered upon a plan. One day, shortly before the Legislature convened, he put on his tall beaver hat, strode to the hotel, and sent up his card to Mr. Martin Van Buren.

It argues well for the reputation Martin brought with him to Albany that Mr. Clinton should have deigned to pay such a call. So far as either of the men seem to remember it was the first time they had ever faced one another, and since it was also one of the few times they ever met as political friends, neither of them ever forgot it.

"I hear," said Mr. Clinton, when they were alone, "that you despair of my election."

"I had," admitted Martin, somewhat abashed by the great presence, "made the observation . . . but —— "

He got not much further with his explanation when the Magnus Apollo impressively produced from his pocket a table of calculations "made by a noted politician" and showing the Clintonian chances to be "very favorable." Here again is evidence to show how well-known must have been Martin's preference for the winning side, and though the calculations "did not change my opinion" concerning the Peace President's odds, Mr. Clinton's next suggestion went home.

Would Mr. Van Buren, the Magnus Apollo wanted to know, consent to act as his floor-leader at the special session and the Republican Caucus which preceded it?

Martin hesitated. It was a flattering proposal to a man still in his twenties and who had yet to take the oath of office. Many an older head might have been chosen. Still there were several considerations. In the first place he knew that the Lieutenant Governor had practically no chance of displacing Mr. Madison. What was more, to back a peace candidate only a few months after having ridden into office on a war platform might require some intricate explanation to the voters who had elected him. And yet, again, the useful Sons of Tammany had endorsed the War as "a just and necessary" enterprise.

But on the other hand, Mr. Clinton was not one to be offended. He would not be President this time, but he was a distinct probability for 1816. As Lieutenant Governor, as Mayor, as Dan Tompkins' sponsor and creator, he held mighty power over many appointments. As leader of the Republican party of the State, he was one whose influence was worth courting.

He would, replied Martin, be delighted to accept the offer.

Whatever were Mr. Clinton's first impressions of this exceedingly polite and foppishly handsome young man, he must have been overjoyed a few days later to see with what confident breeziness the neophyte appeared at the State House to take over the unaccustomed duties of floor-leader. It was a tradition, which still exists, that a maiden legislator is expected to be seen and not heard at his opening session. But the custom, Mr. Clinton perceived with pleasure, did not in the least inhibit his protégé. On that electoral Tuesday in November, the Republican Caucus had scarcely been rapped to order and the roll called, when Martin leaped to his feet and commanded the floor. It is befitting that his first formal utterance as an American law-giver should have been an example of masked strategy. His motion burst like a bomb-shell among the assembled Republicans.

He nominated for the chairman of the Caucus the venerable Senator Taylor, a notorious Madisonian.

A flurry of amazed apprehension went over the anxious Clintonians. They had their orders to follow the new Senator's leadership, but this had all the appearance of treachery. At the joint session of House and Senate which would follow immediately, the Republicans would hold only a slight majority over the Federalists, 74 to 67, too close for comfort when it was remembered that 26 of the Republicans were avowedly for Madison. With the Federalists offering up no candidate, there was little knowing how they would divide, and it seemed either stupid or seditious of young Van Buren to be giving the War Wing the decided advantage of having their own chairman. Mystified as they were, the Clintonians voted to order, and if the floor-leader's first motion had caused the repercussions of a bomb-shell, his next drew forth a full-batteried bombardment.

He moved, Mr. Chairman, that the entire vote of this great and patriotic State go to that stalwart citizen, the Honorable De Witt Clinton.

This time it was the Madisonians whose ox was gored, and they gave tongue to their indignation with loud wails of protestation. Over the din of the banging gavel, they sprang collectively to their feet and opened fire on the fair-haired

Columbian. Didn't the gentleman know that now War was declared the State was heartily behind the President? Wasn't he aware that Republican principles demanded that they hearken to the voice of the People? A fair division of electoral votes they might accept, but no such high-handed arrangement as this.

Throughout the whole storm, Martin stood with folded arms and an unflinching smile. Rave they might, but he had the votes. True, this application of the majority lash was unprecedented, but it would, he knew, work. Even back in the days when Hamilton on this same floor had opposed George Clinton over the vital question of the Constitution, the fighting Federalists had been granted a minority representation at the all-important Convention. Days of political chivalry those, but not these that were dawning. Chairman Taylor's flaying gavel finally restored order, and he beckoned the floor-leader to the rostrum. Did the Senator from Columbia really intend to press his motion?

"Certainly," Martin says that he said.

This was too much for the old-school gentleman in the chair. As presiding officer he had no choice under parliamentary rules but to put the Columbian's question to a vote, and this he would not do. Seizing his hat, he stamped down the rostrum steps, down the chamber aisle, roaring for his servant to bring up the sleigh and take him home. The rules still gave Martin the floor, and unperturbed as ever he sent a Clintonian to the empty chair, moved the previous question and, amid renewed clamor, voted it through. No matter what the Federalists did now, the entire bloc of New York's electoral votes were bound to Mr. Clinton, and no one was responsible but Martin Van Buren. On his first day in the parliamentary lists he had come through a baptism of fire and scored a rousing victory.

Gala occasion as it was for Martin, it behooves his biographer not to pass it by lightly. Martin, besides winning the encounter, established a reputation that was to remain with him the rest of his days in Albany. From then on his associates at the State House never quite fathomed this wavy-haired, soft-spoken little gentleman whom the majority found as impossible to admire as to despise. Even the oft-offered analogy of Aaron Burr was of negligible aid. Burr, suave and courteous in repose, carried the proverbial chip on his shoulder for anyone who called himself an enemy. Burr was a fighting man, a potential killer, quick to anger and provocative in debate. But the Kinderhooker's words were honeyed; his explanations (when he made them) had a well-nigh unanswerable plausibility. Above all he became, as he improved with practice, a past-master in the art of sophistry. Once at Albany he persuaded the Senate, which was trying a Regency ex-Governor for a $110,000 shortage of accounts, not only to cancel the obligation but to award the accused (who was unquestionably responsible) the amount of nearly $12,000 in damages and a vote of thanks. Once at Washington, called upon by the upright Andrew Jackson to justify the Spoils System, he so convincingly ennobled it as the democratic principle of "rotation in office" that Jackson was completely persuaded and became an enthusiastic devotee.

It is necessary thus to reach into his future to show Martin at his practised best as a sophist, but even on this first official day in Albany he was no bungler. Hardly had the special session adjourned when he was flitting about the corridors patching up strained relations with soft words. And before they went home, men who had come as Madisonians were not sure but that Mr. Van Buren had done them a great favor in sparing them the iniquity of turning the State against her favorite son.

As for the favorite son himself, Mr. Clinton was far too elated to look past the patent fact that the amazing little tactician had rescued him from certain disaster. To be sure he subsequently lost the Electoral College to Mr. Madison by the count of 89 to 128, but nevertheless the fat was out of the fire. His own State he had carried, New Jersey, Delaware, all of New England except Vermont, and he had penetrated the South's borderland by taking five votes from Maryland. All he need do was remain in the public eye and good

96 ]

graces until the next presidential year, when, the South and New England both having had Presidents, New York would assuredly be given a chance to name hers. Certain now that the country was behind the War, Mr. Clinton understood his duty, applied to the Governor for a commission and prepared to be off to the front. Service under arms, he felt, would soon restore him to popular favor, and his absence from the political firing line need not interfere with his hopes. His lieutenant-governorship had another year to run; on February 4th, 1813, a few months hence, he would be up for renomination to another three-year term, which period would bring him very conveniently to the significant year of 1816. Best of all, the gifted Mr. Van Buren had practically agreed to be his floor-leader again—in itself a soothing augury of success.

A happy and expectant man was Mr. Clinton when he departed from Albany to join his wife and eight children at home. Undoubtedly he blessed the day when he had first laid eyes on Martin Van Buren. But he would live most heartily to rue it.

### 3

### (December 1812–February 1813)

For the first time in his blissful and praiseworthy existence, Happy Dan Tompkins could look into his soul and see it infected with an unfamiliar malady. Never before had he known what it meant to be plagued with the germ of ambition or with the poisonous unrest that goes with it. Till now the Farmer's Son had coasted rather than striven his way through life. Like many another country boy he had left the old homestead to make his way in the City and, arriving there to learn the law, he had found both solace for his homesickness and companionship for his jovial spirits in the Long Room of Brom Martling's tavern. Into politics he had drifted, not plunged. At Martling's he had met Billy Van Ness, through Billy he had met Mr. Burr, and joining up with the Little Band, had lent whatever assistance was asked of him to further the cause of his friends. Unlike Billy and others, Dan failed to get excited about the ups-and-downs of the game. It was not in him to hate a man merely because he happened to belong to opposing cliques. His dozens of acquaintances grew into hundreds of friendships, overlapped party lines, and wherever good fellows were gathered together, they were like to find Dan Tompkins in their midst.

If his pursuit of happiness interfered with Dan's legal possibilities, it was not to be seen in the results. Columbia '92, he had graduated at the top of his class, substituting hard periods of concentration for a lack of brilliance. Admitted to the bar, he showed a clear enough mind to attain a comfortable standing and income, and having put poverty behind him, he had no urge to aspire higher. Hard-headedly honest, sufficiently diligent and eternally good-natured, his character was a bridge that served to span the gap between the Clintonians and the Wigwam immediately after the departure of Burr. When the new coalition wanted a congressional candidate acceptable to both sides, a natural sequence of thought led them to decide upon Dan Tompkins. Later, when an opening appeared among the New York judgeships, he was again drafted, and still again, when the Clintonians needed a man of the People to oust Morgan Lewis, Happy Dan was brought to the fore.

As Governor he had put forth sincere and strenuous efforts to fill the office that such great men as George Clinton and John Jay had held before him. He could not give the People the transcending leadership his predecessors had, but to Dan Tompkins there was nothing complicated about justice and honesty. A thing was either right or it was wrong, and if a particularly intricate problem turned up, there was always his friend, Mr. Clinton, at his elbow to lend scholarly advice. When the War came, Dan's simple powers of perception understood only that an invader threatened his native shore. He could not follow Mr. Clinton's subtle side-lights on the subject, and though he respected the latter's viewpoint, Dan was immeasurably relieved to find that, with

98 ]

Madison re-elected, Mr. Clinton was ready and eager to do a patriot's duty. Glad was Dan to be receiving a series of letters from his friend, the Mayor—asking for a commission, suggesting that the Narrows at the mouth of the harbor be fortified, that the city be barricaded with earth-works against possible attack, that the City and State lend the bankrupt Government enough funds to carry on centralized operations. And though the correspondence remained for some time unanswered on the Governor's desk, it was not because he was either uninterested or unduly slothful. The truth was that these particular days found Dan in an unusually distracted state of mind. Finally, when several persons questioned him on the delay, Dan confessed his reasons. Mrs. Tompkins, he said, was in the process of making him a father, and that expectation kept him from his office during many business hours. He promised to get after the correspondence as soon as he could.

In this confession honest Dan stooped to a half-truth. For a fact his lady *was* in an interesting condition, but Dan's own mind was also pregnant of a new idea. Where he had picked it up he could not say for certain, but someone (and later Dan had reasons to remember that it was someone from Columbia County) must have whispered it to him. Dan knew, as did everyone else concerned with politics, that in 1816 a New Yorker would almost surely be chosen President. Logically the candidate would be Mr. Clinton, and Dan wished him well. But somehow and from somewhere, between the time of the special session in November and the regular one in January, a report had come to him that he, Dan Tompkins, was just as good a man as De Witt Clinton— would, in fact, make a better Chief Magistrate and the People were all for him.

Moreover, and from the same direction, came other suggestions. If he wanted to answer the People's call four years hence, he had better watch this Clinton. Clinton was a snake-in-the-grass. Clinton was a schemer. He had betrayed the country's honor by trying to keep her out of a "just and necessary" War; he was now trying to usurp Governor Dan's rightful leadership and to ingratiate himself into the People's favor. Give Clinton a command, accept his plans, sign his loans, and the first thing Dan knew the fellow would have made a hero of himself. How would Governor Dan like to be President Dan when Madison was finished?

Come to think of it, Dan decided, he would like it mighty well. The Tammany boys—the Bucktails as they were coming to be called—thought well of it too, and most delighted of all—at least the one who smiled most knowingly when the subject came up for mention—was a friendly little Senator whom the Bucktails admiringly called Matty Van. Columbia's Senator, being a non-resident of the City, was only unofficially a member of the Bucktails, but he was on familiar terms with them all, sat in on their conferences and frequent banquets, and was soon to be taken into the brotherhood by becoming honorary Grand Sachem of the Eagle Tribe. Strange, it must have been thought around Albany, that Matty Van could be simultaneously so friendly with both the Bucktails and with their hated enemy, the Magnus Apollo; stranger still that the blond Columbian should be smiling on Happy Dan's secret hopes, for until recently most of his sunny beams had been shed on Mr. Clinton.

Mr. Clinton, as the weeks went by, was also thinking it strange—the whole business. Governor Tompkins, instead of giving him command of the militia, had taken it himself; instead of authorizing him as Mayor to entrench the City, had endorsed a resolution of Tammany Hall to do the same thing; instead of allowing the Mayor credit for negotiating the loans, took it himself and basked in the forthcoming praise. Already newspapers were coupling Dan's name with the most envious of adjectives—"the Patriotic Tompkins." Decked in a gorgeous buff-and-white uniform, he cut a splendid figure prancing about town on a high-stepping charger, and later on when news came that he had led his troops in a smashing surprise attack that re-captured Fort Erie from the British, Dan's popularity was boundless.

But strangest of all to Mr. Clinton was the averted face of his late coadjutor from the Middle District. New Year's passed; the time for the Caucus drew nigh, and still the Senator was inexplicably formal. Mr. Clinton consulted with friends. Evidently Mr. Van Buren had been offended, but how?

They told him. Back in August death had left a vacancy in the attorney-generalship. Matty Van, not then acquainted with Mr. Clinton, had audaciously applied for the opening by a letter to Richard Riker. He had hoped that the new title, added to the two he already possessed—Senator and Surrogate—would greatly enhance his dignity among the brethren of the Law, not to mention his income, for Hannah in the fourth year of their marriage had produced a third son. Failing to get the appointment (it went to a man twenty years his senior), Martin had accepted the disappointment philosophically until he heard it noised about that Mr. Clinton himself had prevented it. Had Mr. Clinton, reasoned Martin, done so because "he thought I was too young," it was understandable, but rumor had it that the appointment was made for political purposes—and Martin had no humble estimate of his own importance on those grounds.

When he heard this explanation from his friends, Mr. Clinton moved quickly to make amends. As presiding officer of the Senate, he appointed Martin chairman of the committee to draft an answer to the Governor's message—an unheard of honor to a maiden Senator. And about that time he sent Martin an invitation for tea.

Arriving, Martin was surprised to find himself the only guest, a trifle more surprised when Mr. Clinton locked the door of his lodgings behind them and left orders with the servant to admit no callers. Immediately they were alone the host began a lengthy and apologetic discourse to prove that all rumors concerning his hand in the attorney-generalship appointment were "entirely unfounded." Here was the Lieutenant Governor, the Mayor of New York, the State's most noted citizen and a presidential candidate, actually cajoling for the favoritism of a mere political stripling, when by all reason it should have been the other way round. Entirely aware of the situation, Martin found in it a balm for his hurt feelings, and parted with Mr. Clinton less convinced by his assurances than flattered by the attentions.

Had De Witt Clinton managed to stay on the good side of this little dandy a short while longer, the list of American Presidents might very conceivably have included another name. But unfortunately, just two days before the meeting of the February Caucus, he found Mr. Van Buren once more uncomfortably cold to his salutations. Inquiring the reasons, he was told them. It appeared that, again, it was a matter of political preferment. Martin, at the end of his first month in regular session, had embarked upon another of his courses —that of becoming a party manager. United States Senators were then chosen by the Legislature, and there being an opening, he had decided to assist Tammany in electing one of her Bucktails, Mr. John W. Wilkin. At the last moment the rumor came (it was later corroborated) that Mr. Clinton was secretly using his followers to elect a much more worthy man, Rufus King, who happened nevertheless to be a Federalist. Again the proud Apollo came to the sulking Achilles with denials, but when King was elected by what looked like connivance, Martin's soft manners for once evaporated.

"I hope you no longer entertain the suspicion you spoke of," said the Lieutenant Governor as they left the Senate Chamber.

"No," sneered Martin. "My suspicions have become convictions. I know!"

How he could have known so surely on what was supposed to be a secret ballot does not appear, but Mr. Clinton's haughty spirit bowed lower under this displeasure of a man thirteen years his junior. For two days they did not speak, then, on the day of the Caucus, Mr. Clinton made another advance to find Martin expansively—almost ominously— cordial.

What did Mr. Van Buren think would happen in the Caucus?

Well, to tell the truth there was some talk of nominating Senator Tayler for Mr. Clinton's place as Lieutenant-Governor?

And in that case what would Mr. Van Buren do?

Why, Mr. Van Buren would keep his agreement to nominate Mr. Clinton, *"if he did not object."*

"If he did not object?" That was a queer qualification, Mr. Clinton must have thought. Why should he object? Still there was a foreboding tone to the phrase, and Mr. Clinton's confidence was somewhat shaken when he left the Senate Chamber. He waited at a distance to hear what the Caucus would do. And when he did hear, he must have wished either himself or Martin Van Buren deep in the grave with Uncle George.

For Martin, as soon as the Bucktails had offered their ticket of Tompkins and Tayler, solemnly rose and, with no ghost of a smile, began a speech that set the Bucktails to rubbing their hands in glee. He moved, in effect, Mr. Chairman, the nomination of a traitor; of a man who had but recently betrayed the great Republican Party, and from whom there was no guarantee but that he would do so again. Yet it was "expedient" that Mr. Clinton's name be brought before this Caucus. Both the country and Mr. Clinton deserved to know just what the Party thought of him now. "Powerful" was the Party and it was "magnanimous," too. Would it take back to its bosom this treason-hatcher? Would it endorse a man whom the nation had just finished repudiating? The patriotic Tompkins was against him, but that did not matter. The noble Madison was against him, but that made no difference. Let the Caucus vote as it felt in the matter, and Mr. Van Buren's sentiments would be expressed in the voice of the majority.

So adeptly had Martin turned his phrases, so sugared had been his tone of delivery that the man who rose to second this burlesque of a motion actually thought the Columbian had made it seriously and "applauded the grounds upon which I had proposed the nomination." It is a misfortune to the Van Buren student that this speech does not exist in complete manuscript form, but even handed down piecemeal it shows a master at work. He had discharged his promise to Clinton; had not openly maligned him; had left a loop-hole in case the

Caucus by any chance stampeded; had effectively crucified an opponent, though no one had actually seen his hand driving the nails.

And nails they were, too, in Mr. Clinton's presidential coffin. His defeat for the nomination retired him temporarily to obscurity and when New York came to put up her candidate in 1816 it was not Mr. Clinton, but (and who till Martin's arrival could have guessed it?) Dan Tompkins. That Dan was rejected by the national Caucus and tendered the sop of the vice-presidency only proved to whomever was interested that the chief magistracy was not yet open to second-rate men. Both Clinton and Tompkins died before they quite realized what the future would unfold—that when the first New Yorker did finally achieve the White House, he would be no other than this smiling little trickster who held the whip-hand over both their lives.

4

(August 1814–October 1814)

It was no White House this August morning—that Palace on Pennsylvania Avenue—but a charred and smoking ruin. A murky symbol of the country whose hope and pride it represented, only the emptiness of its outer walls remained; inside it was gutted of its simple grandeur and despoiled of its beauty. Capitol Hill and the rest of the official city completed the scene of desolation and defeat. Only two of the public buildings remained, the Post and Patent Offices, these spared lest they should contain something of value to the world at large.

Not even a Nero had stayed to fiddle among the flames. At the eleventh hour Mr. Madison, with Secretaries Monroe and Armstrong, had gone to take command of the Army's last stand at Bladensburg, six miles away, but shot and shell were not for Jemmy:

> " 'Fly, Armstrong, fly; run, Monroe, run!'
> Were the last words of Madison."

Just before giving them he had penciled a similar warning to his wife, who was at home keeping his dinner for him. Both had fled, Jemmy to wander about like an unthroned King Lear in the stormy forests of Virginia; Dolly, disguised as a gypsy, to trundle to safety in a pony cart accompanied by a soldier and a servant, likewise in costume. Once she had sought refuge by trotting upstairs and preparing to go to bed in a roadside farm-house, only to be trailed by a furious housewife who thus expressed her Virginia hospitality:

"Mrs. Madison, if that's you come down and get out! Your husband's got mine out fighting, and damn you, you sha'n't stay in my house. So get out!"

Most of Washington had hardly waited for the First Citizen's example. For weeks families, like little Peggy O'Neil's, had disobeyed city ordinances by keeping horses in the cellar to facilitate a quick escape. Several days before the battle Mr. Monroe had moved the portfolios of his State Department over the Potomac to his home at Leesburg; banks were shipping out specie; hundreds of residents had their silverware buried and their trunks packed, ready to vanish at the first sound of a cannon. Only a few invalids, too sick to be moved; a few optimists, who hoped too long for the best; a few fatalists, who neither hoped nor cared, were on hand to receive the veterans of the Peninsula campaign when, on the evening of the 24th, they marched into town, red coats against the red of a setting sun.

Admiral Cockburn tramped up the steps of the deserted Capitol, seated himself in the Speaker's chair and heaved his spurred heels to the desk where Mr. Clay's gavel had so often rapped a House to order.

"Shall this harbor of Yankee democracy be burned?" he is said to have bawled. "All for it will say 'Aye.'"

The "ayes" had it. Flame where before there had been nothing hotter than the War Hawks' oratory. Mounting, the pillager cantered down the Avenue to the White House, stalked muddily over Dolly's carpets and sat down to devour Jemmy's waiting dinner before ordering the torch applied.

Over night the redcoats remained, commandeering the

several hotels and many boarding houses for their comfort. Then on the second day a tornado fell upon the City, carrying away chimneys, dousing the flames that otherwise might have levelled off the whole town and taking a heavy toll of damage as price for the mercy of nature. Off marched the marauders to see what could be done with Baltimore. Fort McHenry turned them back, and a young lawyer named Francis Scott Key glorified the occasion by writing a national anthem to the tune of an English drinking song.

Painfully a humiliated country wrenched its gaze from the pillage of its Capital City and looked northward, for the British were now massing their forces along Lake Champlain. "Albany," wrote the Army's commanding General, "became the watch tower of the nation." If Albany fell, New York would fall and then there would be nothing to do but accept the shameful terms of peace which Great Britain had offered to the Commission of Ghent—surrender all of Wisconsin and Michigan, most of Illinois and a third of Ohio. Everyone, it seemed, had forgotten about a pious sailorman named Thomas McDonough until one day in September he knelt on his deck with a gamecock for a mascot, prayed for good luck or life everlasting, and led his few gun-boats out of Plattsburg bay to smash the British fleet and send the land forces scurrying temporarily back into Canada. Again the country rejoiced, this time in words adapted to a Scotch love-lyric.

> "O, Johnny Bull, my Jo, John,
>   Behold on Lake Champlain,
> With more than equal force, John,
>   You tried your fist again;
> But the cock saw how 'twas going, John,
>   And cried, 'Cock-adoddle-do!'
> And McDonough was victorious, John,
>   O, Johnny Bull, my Jo."

Well it was for America that she was able to find solace in minor victories and defensive counter-attacks, for the War of 1812 offered little real cause for pride. The War Hawks' boast that Canada could be annexed in six weeks had turned boomerang. For all the resounding feats of Old Ironsides and her sister ships, the coast was blockaded from Portsmouth to New Orleans; Free Trade and Sailors' Rights were represented by harborfuls of vessels with tar-barrels—called Madison Night Caps—draped over their mastheads to prevent rotting. Despite the able cooperation of Perry and Harrison in clearing out the Lake Erie country, the North West had been invaded and could be invaded again. Despite the belated glory of Fort McHenry, the nation's Capital lay in ashes and the confidence of her leaders in much the same condition. England, having disposed of Napoleon temporarily, was sending over the flower of her Army and Navy, and, as a finishing blow, a convention of New England states was about to meet at Hartford to consider seceding from the Union and making a separate peace.

It was at the most dismal moment of chaos that there arose before the disheveled Administration a dim figure of hope. Just prior to McDonough's welcome victory and when all eyes were on Albany, there appeared against the darkened horizon a dapper little man who moved with unexpected precision and force. The Wigwam's Matty Van had served but half his first term as State Senator, had become the Bucktails' acknowledged champion, but even they were surprised to see him suddenly blossom forth as the key man of the Madison Administration and the white hope of a cringing nation.

For by this time it was only too evident that no matter how many minor victories were won, the one way out of the national crisis was to mass an impregnable bulwark of manpower against the invasion. The Army had failed, the Militia had failed, the volunteer system, rife with desertion, was proving wholly inadequate to fill up the ranks. Mr. Madison was confessedly at his wits' end; Henry Clay, most oratorical of the War Hawks, had given up and gone abroad to dicker for peace, and this was the crucial moment that Martin Van Buren chose to bring forward his plan of compulsory enlistment.

The idea of herding out citizens to fight a politicians' war was no new one. Many a European sergeant had led his re-

cruiting squad about darkened city streets, cracked a few
lads over the head and clapped them in uniform. But Martin
Van Buren stands as the first American law-giver to conceive
and carry out the plan of legalising such methods. In it he
admits he was aided by Aaron Burr, who had returned to
Albany after a long exile abroad, was living with Martin and
may have procured the germ of the notion from his reading
of Voltaire. For Candide, it will be remembered, was a victim of military impressment.

Be that as it may, when Senator Van Buren offered his
Classification or Conscription Bill at the special session of
September '14 he became overnight a figure of national importance. The Bill provided that the population of the State
should be divided into classes, each required to supply its
quota of soldiery under pain of having the men seized
forcibly if it did not. The fact that under the voting qualifications, only a small percentage of the population was entitled to the prime privilege of citizenship, did not exclude
the rest of them from its responsibilities. The common cause
was in peril, the Bill argued, and the country's leaders had
no choice but to call out the People in her defense.

A doubtful nation watched curiously to see if such a morti-
fication of personal liberty could possibly be voted through
a legislative body. Mr. Monroe, now Secretary of War, sent
for a copy and privately resolved that if the Bill passed at
Albany, he would present it to Congress. Mr. Madison, sensing a happy issue out of all his afflictions, could only hope
against all apparent probability that this unknown young
Dutchman would make good his local reputation as a master
parliamentarian.

His conduct in connection with the Classification Bill is
one of the two oases in the Van Buren career where he gave
real promise of fulfilling his potentialities of true greatness
and vision. Whatever may be said of the democratic heresies
in his Bill; however much fun may be poked at the arm-
chair patriotism which orders other men into the firing line,
there is no gainsaying the naked fact that conscription, and
conscription alone, loomed as the one respectable way to save

108 ]

the nation. Nor can it be denied that Martin on his own initiative had undertaken a project which no politician would have envied him. He knew, and usually he sedulously practiced the axiom, that the way to thrive in politics is not on controversy but compromise. While the statesmen at Washington and the People at large were all for him, his own electorate most emphatically were not. He was reviled by tongue and pen, the length and breadth of his State. Editors publicly advised their readers to snub him at sight, and Elisha Williams stopped him on the street one day to say "he had always regarded me as a man of too much sense to get into such a scrape."

But in the teeth of a vehement opposition Martin persisted in his efforts to push through what a historian of the period was to call "the most energetic war measure ever adopted in this country." The many who thought that the Bill had no chance of passage had calculated less closely than Martin. He was far too sapient a pioneer to push into a wilderness he had not charted beforehand. Until the third year of the War the Federalists and the Peace Republicans had held enough seats at the Assembly to block every militant measure that was introduced. But at the Spring elections of '14 the War Wing had gained a clear majority, and though not all were pledged to anything so drastic as the Classification Bill, Martin knew that he commanded enough support to give him a working nucleus.

With that as a beginning he supplied the rest. He took to the stump, drumming up enthusiasm and enlisting recruits. He wrote a spirited address, steeped in the glories of the nation's past and in ghostly apprehensions for her future. After a more scholarly hand than his had smoothed off the rough edges it was given to the public as an Appeal to the People from the Republican Party. He helped Dan Tompkins write his Message to the special session, and as chairman again of the senatorial committee to draft the reply, saw to it that the two documents were in perfect accord. He discovered Winfield Scott in town recuperating from a wound, and pressed him into service as what later came to be called

[ 109

a lobbyist. Long before the Bill ever came to the floor, Scott was besieging the State House, cornering delegates and urging on them the imperative necessity of conscription. Near the end of October a majority was mustered, the Bill went through, and Martin Van Buren stood on the brink of statesmanship.

That eminence, however, was never to be his. It was not written that the Little Magician should be a statesman, but that he should go forward to found a far different type of dynasty. Almost, a cross-current of the War had taken him off the course, but before that happened the main tide of men and events had caught him again and saved him for his fated destination.

One day, earlier in the year, he was walking down the street and encountered Winfield Scott, who explained joyfully that he had just been made a Major General.

"General," exclaimed the Senator extending his hand, "we must celebrate this happy event. Come to my house this evening; I'll invite a few friends and we'll have a glass of wine and a few oysters together."

Scott came, and found one of the other guests to be Aaron Burr, whom he had last seen in Richmond on trial for treason. Wine and oysters were followed by a game of whist, and between rubbers as they fell to talking politics and War, Mr. Burr blurted out:

"There's a man in Tennessee to whom Jimmy Madison will not give a commission because he is a friend of mine, but he is equal to any service. I mean Andrew Jackson."

5

(January 8, 1815)

A weary man with his back to a weary city stood on a hump of dirt and stared anxiously into the milky dawn before him. There was little he could see even through his telescope, but against his sunken and sallow cheeks he could feel the wet clamminess of a drifting fog. The man shifted heavily from

one foot to the other. He was tired, and the fog did not
soothe his anxiety.

Two different kinds of weariness were his and the city's
behind him. His was the fatigue of depletion and spent
strength; hers of surfeit and the agony of a long and fearsome
waiting. For nearly two years now had proud and excitable
New Orleans grovelled within the encircling blockade. Her
warehouses were crammed to bursting with gold-gaining
produce she could not sell; her business was at a standstill;
her citizenry in a jabbering, trilingual frenzy, for every one
of these seven hundred-odd mornings she had waked in the
expectation of seeing the dreaded British Armada sweeping
into her bayou.

Vainly all that while had Governor Claiborne tried to calm
his people by assuring them that the danger of attack was
"too chimerical" to worry about; vainly had he attempted to
scoff down the well-founded rumors that spies were among
them inciting the slaves to revolt and arming them for the
purpose. No use, at least, to deny what the whole town knew
—that England had spent a million pounds sterling to out-
fit the great fleet of fifty ships and a thousand guns, still
biding its time in Negril Bay, Jamaica; that General Sir
Henry Pakenham, kinsman to the mighty Wellington, had
sailed from Europe to take command; that Admiral Sir
Alexander Cochran had vowed to eat Christmas dinner in
town; that officers were whetting their men with promises of
"Booty and Beauty" as soon as the pillage was done. The
threat of this dire slogan struck the deepest terror. Merchants moaned over their accumulated stock; ladies carried
shiny daggers under their hoops to emulate Lucrece in defense of their honor; officials wrote frantic despatches to *le
president Madison*, imploring him to send forth a General
to save them.

And then on December first—just a jump ahead of the
enemy—the General had come. Not in plumes and finery as
they had expected, but in dress that a contemporary has
described as "simple and nearly threadbare." He wore a
back-woodsman's leather cap pulled defiantly down over his

spiky gray hair and large bony nose; a short blue cloak wrapped Indian-fashion about his gaunt body; a pair of over-sized dragoon boots, "innocent of polish," crusted with horse-sweat and frowsy with the dust of many a hard-ridden mile. Gloweringly he had clumped through the crowd to the Governor's piazza, listened painfully to the ornate speech of welcome, and briefly told the assembled multitude through interpreters that he would "protect the city . . . drive the enemy into the sea or perish in the attempt."

There was something, New Orleans remembered, in the "fierce glare of his bright and hawk-like eye" that made men believe him. A loud huzza went up at his words, but he seemed not to notice it. Graciously he declined the fine feast prepared in his honor, gobbled up a bowl of hominy and, preparatory to a tour of inspection, retired to his newly-selected headquarters at 106 Royal Street for a ten-minute rest.

He needed it. Already Andrew Jackson was Old Hickory to the militiamen who had followed him to the starvation on the bluffs of Natchez and to the gory victory of Horseshoe Bend. They had seen him eat acorns when rations were low, had seen him stalk the snows of a freezing night when the rest were hovering at the campfires, had seen him give up his horses to the sick and wounded, while, sicker and worse wounded than many, he had tramped thirty miles a day at the head of infantry.

But even hickory will bend, and sometimes it will break. At forty-seven that long useful body, shifting restlessly on the mound, was dented within and without by enough axe-scars to fell a whole forest of taller trees than himself. Over one eye was a sword gash he had suffered at thirteen for refusing to shine an Englishman's boots. In one breast was a duellist's bullet too close to the heart to be removed. In one shoulder was a volley of pistol-shot that had let out enough blood, according to Mrs. Jackson, to soak through two mattresses. The rigors of border warfare had left him a perpetual indigestion that was starving him into a shadow, a case of chronic diarrhoea that all but disemboweled him, a paralytic rheumatism that so disabled what he designated in writing as "my rist" that he could barely scrawl his reports. And the vanguard of tuberculosis was just finding its way into his lungs.

Not all of Andrew Jackson's multitudinous infirmities were garnered on the fields of battle and honor. That "glare of his bright and hawk-like eye" was an internal fire that of itself almost consumed him. It required but the mildest incentive to kindle his wrath, and the lava of profanity that came from his lips to express it was unrivalled even after the able-tongued Davy Crockett joined his regiment. Were Jackson alive at this hour it would require a bolder hand than this to record the plain fact that he had married Mrs. Rachel Robards and lived with her for two years before she was legally divorced. Once His Excellency, the Governor of Tennessee, had made that mistake and only lived to tell the tale because a bullet went wild and nicked an innocent bystander in the crowd. Once another gentleman who erred likewise, was called out to a duel, allowed to shoot Jackson in the breast and then killed with an empty pistol in his hand. Slurs upon Rachel's honor were only among a miscellany of provocations that Andrew Jackson regarded as insults. Such natively pacific pursuits as politics, law-practice, and horse-racing were matters of brimstone and bloodshed to him. He killed one man and caned another over a racing bet; he challenged and duelled a lawyer who sarcastically rebutted one of his arguments in court; he swelled with such venom over the every-day routine of parliamentary quarrels that Jefferson remarked:

"When I was President of the Senate and he was a Senator, he could never speak on account of the rashness of his feelings. I have seen him attempt it repeatedly and as often choke with rage."

Indeed Old Hickory, or more probably his Rachel, seemingly realized that public life was burning out his vitals, for he had already made a definite attempt to leave it. At thirty-five he had been Solicitor, District Attorney, Congressman, Senator, Federal Judge, General of the Militia, and had achieved near-bankruptcy as a country store-keeper. He set it all behind him, sold his splendid estate, Hunter's Hill, closed his accounts, and removed to a log cabin and waste-land which he significantly called the Hermitage. Farming, horse-breeding and slave-trading were to be his livelihood from then on. His own marriage being sterile, he adopted two children, rebuilt the Hermitage and settled down long enough to supply future biographers with several affecting pictures of his home life: Sitting with Rachel while she read the Bible of a winter's evening, a child on one of his knees, a lamb rescued from the snows on the other, or walking his acres, patting his horses, endearing himself as the traditional Old Massa to his slaves.

But such things could not be for long. War came and his "rist" rounded out letters to Washington asking for an assignment against the British on any or all of the fronts, designating the War Department as "unfit to be a granny" when none was forthcoming. Not until May, 1814, shortly after General Scott had attended Senator Van Buren's whist party, did Secretary Monroe accept advice and appoint this wild man of the West to take up the defense of New Orleans.

From the first it had seemed that Mr. Monroe had made no mistake. The so-called Battle of New Orleans was in reality no battle at all but a long-drawn campaign of nine months wherein both commanders shuttled and shifted their forces in true checker-board warfare, so manoeuvring that the crucial engagement would not be so much an outright test of strength as the result of a well-played game. That a raw Indian fighter, leading a batch of backwoodsmen, could successfully match wits with a schooled European tactician seemed unbelievable, but as the summer and autumn wore on, Old Hickory continued to hold his own. For eight months neither of the main forces came within a hundred miles of each other, but sparred for openings with advance guards. In July the British seized the port of Pensacola, which happened to be in neutral Spanish territory, and Jackson seized it back. In September the British sent five ships to experiment with the idea of making a base at Mobile, and

Jackson sent a small detachment to displace them. In November, not knowing whether the next drive would be again at Mobile or directly at New Orleans, he placed a portion of his Army at each point and a troop of fast-moving cavalry midway between. So far so good, but in December the British finally out-guessed him by circling New Orleans through the lakes to the north and west, landing the bulk of their forces there. Reverting momentarily to his Indian tactics, Old Hickory fell upon them shouting:

"By the Eternal, they shall not sleep on our soil!"

But they did. They slept there on Christmas Eve, and a week after New Year's they were still there—ten thousand of them against half that number of defenders. From his stand on the darkling mound Old Hickory could hear the invaders mobilizing for attack behind the curtain of mist. Well, if Mr. Monroe had really made a mistake the whole world would soon know it. Dawn—what there was of it—was just beginning to find its way over the frosty stubble. By noon the tale would be told, and no one knew better than Andrew Jackson that unless the mist lifted it would have to be told in mournful numbers to Americans. For what chance would his men have against twice their number of veterans whose bayonets had served Wellington so well in the Peninsular War?

No chance at all, Old Hickory had already deduced. No chance at all, if those bayonets ever reached the American ramparts. But between the entrenched forces was a six-hundred-yard stretch of open ground, and Andrew Jackson, who hated retreating as he hated Hell, had dropped back to the very outskirts of the city so as to place that open plain in front instead of behind him.

From his position now he could look down into the trenches which his men had so strenuously objected to building. They'd come to fight, they snarled, not dig. If the General wanted digging let him bring up some niggers from town. But the scowl that had already sentenced seven men to death for mutiny brought the woodland warriors back to discipline, and when the trenches were finished they were further insulted by being commanded to level off a stoop just shoulder-high along the forward wall. It afforded them, they found, both shelter from British snipers and a perfect rest for their long-barreled rifles—if only there were something to aim at through the fog.

Old Hickory stiffened. A rocket raced through the murkiness before him. He spoke to an aide:

"That is their signal to advance, I believe."

He needed no imagination to picture the sight he could not see. Red columns, sixty men wide, each with a white cross-plate over his chest, would be moving through the mist. Between the columns would be splendid red officers galloping grandly to and fro; behind would be the reserves, correctly deployed to the rear. Almost upon them by now would be a bristling thorn-thicket of bayonets, glistening in the sun —if only there were a sun.

A whippy gust of breeze that seemed to have come out of nowhere struck upon Old Hickory's cheek. He stared. He was no praying man, though he had listened tenderly to Rachael's Bible, but he nearly believed in divine miracles at what he saw. Not Noah's dove returning to the Ark was more welcome than the sight that met his eye. Not Elijah's chariot had risen more majestically from the earth than that curtain of mist as the wind took it, revealing the red columns and the bristling bayonets just coming into rifle range. Andrew Jackson could not know that the rising curtain was a curtain on the main act of his life's drama—and on that of a man whom he had never seen.

Old Hickory glanced down at his waiting woodsmen, and barked a command.

6

(February 1815)

So did Dolly Madison bark one when she learned wherefore "a coach and four foaming steeds" came clattering down to the corner of New York Avenue and 18th Street, plunging to a stop before the Octagon House where she and

Jemmy had dwelt since their Palace was burned. "Peace!
Peace! Peace!" people were shouting in the streets. Men
were parading, guns booming, bells tolling the glad tidings
that the Commission of Ghent had come to honorable terms.

"Serve wine," sang out Dolly, "without stint."

Ten days ago she would have liked to give the same
command, for on February 4th had come news from New
Orleans that "put the Administration on stilts" and convinced Dolly that nothing would do but she must have a
party. Ever since Mr. Jefferson, a widower, became First
Citizen, Dolly had been official hostess and First Lady of
the Land, reigning through his and her husband's terms
with the happy-hearted grace and gentility of a true aristocrat who knows neither snobbery nor pretension. Seventeen
years younger than Jemmy, she was light-headed and tender-
hearted without being either frivolous or silly, and her gay
undefeated spirit had been about the only ray of light in
Washington during its dark days. Till the rude and unin-
vited appearance of Admiral Cockburn, the giving of parties
had been Dolly's chief contribution to the cause, so hearing
that a man called Andrew Jackson had laid low 2,492 redcoats including three Major Generals and over fourscore of
officers, she began bustling about to prepare a celebration.

But Jemmy's academic preciseness had somewhat damped
her vim. After all, knew Jemmy, General Jackson had not
quite accomplished his objective, to "drive the enemy into
the sea." The British were still entrenched on Louisiana soil,
still technically besieging the city with superior forces. The
wildman had indeed ordered out a sortie to dislodge them,
but with the anti-climatic result of being repulsed and losing
three times the men he had lost in the successful defense.
Moreover, later despatches were still less reassuring. The
British fleet had struck back by seizing Fort Bowyer in Mobile Bay; the Legislature of Louisiana was in open revolt
against Jackson's martial law; a plague of swamp fever, which
would eventually carry off 500 fighting men, was threatening
to accomplish what the British bayonets had not. And though
the War Department found it tactful and more overwhelm-

ing to do what popular historians were to do ever after, namely, to announce the trifling number of 13 Americans who were killed or wounded in the main assault, actually 333 had paid for the victory with their lives.

The news of the 14th, though, cancelled all restraint. Jackson's triumph had not won the War but it had made the War a victorious one. It is the common fallacy of undiligent historians to say that the engagement of New Orleans came after the War was over, but that is not true. The proclamation from the British Foreign office read that "it is understood that hostilities will cease as soon as it [the Treaty] shall be ratified by the President of the United States." The document never saw Mr. Madison's signature until 37 days after Jackson had turned back the invaders. That, however, was time enough to make Dolly's postponed party a prodigious success. On the night of the Glorious Fourteenth she held a preliminary reception when, according to one of the guests, she shone "in the meridian of life and queenly beauty," spreading a "radiance of joy which lighted up her countenance and diffused its beams about."

And a few days later came the real function. Hearing of peace, timorous law-givers, diplomats and social butterflies flocked back to the pillaged city for the grand musicale whereat Signor Pucci charmed one and all with his renditions of such patriotic compositions as "Jackson's March" and "Decatur's Favorite" on a "much admired and fashionable King David's harp." The concert and its ensuing ball marked the opening of the famous Peace Winter, the golden year of Capital Society, and Dolly, in her element, reigned like the queen she was.

The rest of the country which was neither on Dolly's invitation list nor in Jemmy's confidence had not waited for any news beyond the confirmation that Old Hickory had done for more than two thousand enemies of the Republic. It was enough for them to know that a hero had risen among their own class and proved himself a better man than the peerage of England, a better man than all the minions of Mr. Jefferson's vaunted Virginia Dynasty. The Dynasty's diplomacy and generalship had got the country into the War, and dragged it through years of calamity and disgrace; but it had taken a man of the People to restore the nation's lost glory. No tribute was too fine for this unlettered son of the soil; no comparison too far-fetched to exalt him. Congress struck him off a gold medal and gave him a sword; legislatures, city councils, secret brotherhoods, colleges, schools, clubs, societies and ordinary mass meetings vied with one another to find adjectives and honorary titles with which to bedeck him. Country parsons, bishops and cardinals called down the blessing of heaven on the head of this deliverer. Authors and orators compared him to the military genius of all age. He surpassed Napoleon, he eclipsed Caesar, he put Hannibal in the shade. New Orleans built him a triumphal arch, and the Creole beauties threw away their daggers to strew flowers in his path. Philadelphia declared a public holiday at his coming and New York moulded him a key to the City. When he passed through Virginia, Mr. Jefferson descended from his mountain refuge and rode sixty miles through the dead of winter to meet him en route. When he came to Washington he was the President's guest, and Dolly gave a special ball at the Octagon House in his honor. Not a town in the country where his name was not shouted in the market place; hardly a gathering from the Great Lakes to the Gulf where it was not mingled with the toasts of triumph and the prayers of thanksgiving.

But there were at least two men among America's millions to whom this sudden change of affairs was a threatened setback to their careers. One was Assemblyman Harrison Gray Otis; the other State Senator Martin Van Buren, and it is not unprofitable to note how each reacted to the shock. Assemblyman Otis is important to history largely as the leader of the seditious Hartford Convention. Long had it affected his New England conscience and the income of his constituents' shipping and textile business that New England was playing the butt of Liberty's paradox. Wherever majority rule prevails someone is bound to hold the short end of the stick, and doing so did not please the Puritans who half a century

later were to be so horrified when the Cavaliers of the southland revolted under the same provocation. Hence Otis and
others had organized the Hartford Convention by way of
protest. And at the very time Jackson's couriers were spurring northward with joyful dispatches Otis and two associates were coaching toward Washington to present the President with resolutions enunciating New England's right to
abandon the War, if it pleased them, and make a separate
peace. Throughout their journey this grim trio had been
looked upon with awe and apprehension, but at Baltimore
they collided head-on with the reports from New Orleans
which laid them under a cloud, and at Washington they met
the good news from Ghent which caused them to be all but
laughed out of town. Dourly Mr. Otis retraced his steps, and
arrived at his Massachusetts Legislature in time to praise
God, through a resolution, for the triumph of American
arms. He did not mention Andrew Jackson.

But Martin Van Buren did. It is not too disconnected a
clew to find his first foot-print toward the White House in a
resolution offered in his name lauding "Major General Jackson, his gallant officers and troops, for their wonderful and
heroic victory." It required a long toss of his tow-line to hitch
his wagon to the rising star of Old Hickory, and though the
line would not be taut for several years, it was securely
fastened. Martin saw and rightly translated the writing on
the wall to read "the People." In 1815 only 6 of the 22 states
had anything approaching universal white man suffrage, but
voteless as they were, the People were not voiceless, and loud
rose their demands for recognition. It is vital to note that
the louder they screamed and the closer came their day, the
closer glided Martin Van Buren to the convenient coat-tails
of Andrew Jackson.

Had Martin allowed it to be so, the Jackson ascendancy
and the sudden cessation of hostilities could have inconvenienced him no less than it did Assemblyman Otis. The
coming of peace, of course, nullified the Classification Bill,
all of his work and prestige connected with it. Had Jackson's
victory been less complete, had the War been fought out to a
finish, there is every probability that Martin's plan would

have had a decided effect upon the outcome. Given a few
months more New York State alone could have conscripted
enough man-power to engulf any of the puny expeditions
that periodically descended from Canada; and had the law
finally been pressed through Congress, such a horde could
have been rushed over the border as to swamp the whole
Dominion under the Stars and Stripes.

Fate, then, had thwarted the Little Magician's earliest
effort at statesmanship. On the Classification Bill, he had
shown every sign of large possibilities. He had looked past
externals into the heart of a problem, diagnosed the ailment
and prescribed a practical cure. He had met and overcome
the reactionary opposition that always hinders a new departure in government. He had proved himself able to lead men
and to forward ideas, had dared to be unpopular for the sake
of a cause. According to all accepted authority on moral rewards and punishments, one of two things should have been
the result of his unselfish devotion. Either Martin should have
been forthwith acclaimed and promoted by a grateful country, henceforward renouncing all but the true, the good and
the just in politics. Or else he should have been churlishly
thrust into exile, hurt but happy in the knowledge that he
was a patriot spurned.

As it happened neither alternative became a reality. His
patriotism neither sank nor sanctified him, and his first adventure into altruism could have taught him but one thing—
that in the end it availeth nothing. So long as he had relied
on political scheming, he had prospered; so soon as he
aspired to higher matters, he only risked losing what he had
already won. Consciously or not, he seems to have taken the
lesson to heart, for never again, until he reached the top,
did he try anything so impractical as visionary, unselfish
statecraft. And when he did try it again, he learned the same
lesson—too late.

The end of the War saw the beginning of a new phase in
the Van Buren career. So far he had depended more or less
upon the natural elements of wind and tide to assist his
progress. Now he became a product of the budding Machine
Age. He set about inventing an engine to tug him along.

# CHAPTER IV

# He Builds the Regency

THAT profound but fading philosopher, Mr. H. L. Mencken, once drew the aptest of contrasts between courtier and boss. Theirs, he points out, is an identical process, and the means employed differ more in mode than in morals. For both are engaged in flattering and befooling the ruling power, and doing so without ethical restraint. The contrast is that the courtier, serving a King, deals with an entity which is at least his social equal and usually his superior; while the boss, serving the People, must fawn, flatter and prevaricate in the presence of a being which is infinitely beneath him.

Martin Van Buren never stooped to this latter indignity. He did, upon occasion, gush forth no small amount of cant about the rights of the masses, but at least he did it from a wholesome distance and with the air of one who may be for the multitude but not of it. Even when he might have done so with profit he never capitalised the humbleness of his birthplace and of his parental origins. Dearly he loved and almost childishly he nurtured the vanity of playing the high-born, dandified gentleman. It was very necessary to profess a blind faith in Mr. Jefferson's somewhat theoretical creed of equality, but so far as mortal man can deduce from the garbled, non-committal record of his utterances, the Little Magician's opinion of the masses was not very different from that of Alexander Hamilton. The People, Mr. Van Buren apparently felt, were, if not a "great beast," then a brainless, blundering carnivore whose teeth must be drawn for its own protection. Often he tossed the brute tasty morsels of lip-service to assuage its temper; often he actually, though incidentally, befriended it; but never did he so demean his calling as to fling brotherly arms about the shaggy neck.

On the contrary the Little Magician's whole mature career comprises a series of intrigues in high places. He would not find unlimited opportunity until he came into national politics at Washington, but at Albany he definitely showed his leanings toward courtiership. On his first day as State Senator he had undertaken to manage the affairs of a presidential candidate, De Witt Clinton; in his first regular session he was whispering strange suggestions in the ear of a Governor, Dan Tompkins; half-way through his first term, he had made himself useful to a President and a Prime Minister, James Madison and James Monroe. Always it was among the upper strata that he worked. Even his lowliest henchmen bore the democratic title of Honorable. At first these were legislators of his own Assembly, then petty officials of the Federal Government, and when he reached Washington he would have Congressmen, Senators, Cabinet Ministers and Ambassadors running his errands.

So also with the Regency he built. It is essential to an understanding of the Eighth President to know that this vehicle of his was in its original conception a forerunner but not a counterpart of the modern political Machine. Nominally, at least, a Machine belongs to the People. Voters are the pistons, ward-heelers the cogs, universal suffrage the wheels, and the boss in the driver's seat can choose his road only because the People supinely allow him to do so.

But the Regency was different. Its integral parts were not humble vote-casters, but officials of the State. Under the system then in force, the People were not only almost voteless, but their candidates were hand-picked by a party caucus before the names ever went on the ballot. Again, practically all the administrative offices were appointive: that is, the entire State House staff, including the Treasurer, the Comptroller, the Attorney General; the Mayors of all cities; the sheriffs of all counties; the judges of all courts high and low. Thus to control the Caucus and the Council of Appointment (it was composed of the Governor and four State Senators elected by the House) was to be uncrowned king of the Empire State.

That, exactly, was what Martin Van Buren became. In constructing his Regency he manoeuvred so as to capture Caucus and Council, then filled up every available office with his sworn retainers, saving a few of the choice places for himself and his family. The idea is easy enough to explain, and certainly required of Martin no great amount of brain power to conceive. But to carry it out demanded rare deftness. History is replete with evidence that becoming the benevolent tyrant over a thorough-going democracy is simplicity itself compared to becoming one over an oligarchy where the opposition of jealousy, ambition and righteous indignation are concentrated into a solid, never-lagging force, intelligently directed. Let it be remembered to the Little Magician's credit that the antagonists he was constantly unhorsing were no dullards, but the most sensible men of their day; and furthermore that he was not only operating in an oligarchy but in one that, ironically enough, professed democratic creeds. Thus Martin, as the Regency manager, was beset by the personal enmity of the peers on his own level and by the savage disapproval of the masses beneath.

That such a contest could be one-sided is too much to expect even of the Little Magician. Not until he had been President and abandoned most of his wiles did Martin Van Buren ever taste ultimate defeat, but the Red Fox's hairbreadth and ingenious escapes came to make up a large part of his saga. It adds to his lustre that he never showed to better advantage than when called upon to rise from the very dust of defeat and smite down an adversary whose blade was already poised for the death blow. At the peak of his Albany career Martin owned every office that emanated from the State House, and intermittently held four titles himself. At his lowest point he was bereft of everything, and seemingly about to vanish into the shades of private citizenship, when by a sudden foray he recouped all and went on to higher places.

It was during this period of building the Regency that he started earning his reputation for vanburenism. On two lively issues of the day—Slavery and Universal Suffrage—he was simultaneously on both sides and yet on neither. For years to come both the adherents and opponents of each question claimed him for their own. One day he voted to memorialize Congress to admit no more Slave States, but less than a week later he refused to risk signing a petition doing the same thing and mysteriously vanished from town when he was expected to address a meeting to forward the cause. At the Convention called to amend the State Constitution so as to remove voting restrictions, he made a full-day speech which was so purposely ambiguous that one commentator hailed him as a proponent of "government of all by all"; another understood him to be for "rational liberty," and still a third, who took notes on the address, recorded him as saying that he was "decidedly against the amendment and against universal suffrage" because it was "cheapening," and "would drive from the polls all sober-minded people."

Indifference or inconsistency regarding important matters of state is, of course, equally characteristic of courtier and boss, but there is one detail whereby Martin Van Buren belongs to neither category. It cannot be stressed too often that he was utterly uninterested in enriching himself by his scheming. Once he had made a start at the law, he kept it divorced from his politics, so much so that even his contemporaries wondered how he earned a livelihood that allowed him to retire at 45 with what was then considered the sizable fortune of $200,000.

Partly he accomplished it by some rather astute speculation in real estate and by owning (later on) the Albany *Argus*, which was said to have netted him $10,000 a year. But for the most part he earned his money in open competition before the bar, where he frequently encountered and overcame such redoubtables as Aaron Burr, Thomas A. Emmett, Daniel Webster, Abraham Van Vechten, Samuel A. Talcott and Elisha Williams. So many were his social and political engagements, and so casual his attitude toward work, that the several Van Buren biographers have either ignored or eluded the question of when he found time to do it. Only by accident was it possible for the present one to discover what appears to be a clew. While in Albany the Senator employed an office boy who obligingly kept a journal.

"I rose," relates the boy, "at half-past four, and at five in came Mr. Van Buren, ready for the business of the day." And again: "I rise early and what is more provoking Mr. Van Buren some mornings back has risen at half-past four."

But even in possession of such evidence it remains difficult to believe that Martin Van Buren was in any real sense an inveterate hard worker. He had his spurts of energy, but in the law as in politics his chief ability was for finding ways of avoiding any strenuous endeavor. At Albany he took himself an able associate in Benjamin Franklin Butler, who lived to be Jackson's Attorney General, and around Butler he built up a staff of ghost-writers whose duty was to comb through the technicalities of a case and turn their findings over to the senior partner. He who had been the Boy Lawyer knew how to make a little knowledge go a long way, yet Butler, writing to a friend, could exclaim:

"If I were Van Buren I would let politics alone. . . . This morning I heard him open a case before the Supreme Court in the most able, eloquent and exact fashion I almost ever heard. He could be the Erskine of the State."

Probably Martin Van Buren could never have been anything of the sort, but undoubtedly there were fleeting moments when he heartily wished he *could* "let politics alone." Well enough he understood what this game was doing to him, and several times he made half-hearted efforts to wrench himself away from its influence. At least twice he attempted to assuage his thirst for high titles by gaining a place on the Supreme Bench—once of the State, once of the United States. On another occasion he had positively decided to quit politics when Aaron Burr looked him in the eye, and said with tender cynicism:

"You have gone too far to retreat. The only alternative left to you is to kick or be kicked; and as you are not fool enough to prefer the latter you will not resign."

Indeed, much as a man may do to politics, the game invariably does more to him. Aaron Burr knew that, and Martin Van Buren was just finding it out. Something had gone into his blood, and would not be denied. Something had got hold of him, and could not be shaken off. Much as he joyed in conquest and exalted titles, he had as yet no goading desire for place and no sleepless devotion to a cause that bound him to politics. Nor greed, nor ambition, nor evangelism, nor even vanity kept him in harness, but a thing stronger and stranger and more devastating than any of these. No psychiatrist has ever analyzed that invincible urge which sets men, otherwise sensible, to dabbling in and then dying for politics. But no one who has lived very long in a Republic will deny that it is as real and captivating a passion as the one which drives men, otherwise sensible, to pouring their black thoughts over white paper or canvas—and Juvenal has called it "an endless itch."

Before he had finished his first term at Albany Martin Van Buren knew that the Urge was in him, but he could no more lay it by than he could command the heavens to fall. Only in rare moments of despondency did he stop to consider his predicament, but when he did, it was to learn that what he had begun as a game had become an obsession, one that bound him mind and soul. He would not, because he *could* not, quit politics, yet there were times when he despised it as much as he loved. Once when he was a very old man, looking back over a lifetime of bondage, he recited an anecdote that is both revealing and downright pathetic.

Judge Bushrod Washington, nephew of the General, told the story during one of the Senator's visits to Mount Vernon. It seems that the First President, not quite so satisfied in retirement as is popularly supposed, sent for his nephew and John Marshall, ordering them to give up the Bench and run for Congress under his directorship. Bushrod refused; Marshall complied, and in less than two months after his only known attempt to enter party politics, George Washington was dead.

"I listened," said Martin Van Buren, "to the Judge's narrative with interest but with a painful sense of the danger to which it showed that General Washington had been exposed . . . a danger from which, in the inscrutable wisdom of God, he had been withdrawn by an early and otherwise premature death. . . .

"Who can regret that Washington's fair fame was snatched from further exposure to that fiery ordeal or who can hesitate to acknowledge that the goodness of Providence which had . . . directed all his actions . . . was scarcely less signally displayed in his death?"

Strange sentiments, these, to be coming from a man who above all men made a spectacular success of party politics; they lift a mask that was seldom lifted from the Little Magician's face; they serve well enough as a prelude to his founding of the Regency.

2

(February 1815–April 1815)

It was a high day of revelry at the Eagle Tavern, Albany. There was feasting and shouting and drinking. For this was Washington's Birthday, 1815, the War was over, peace was restored, and the Sons of Tammany rejoiced with appropriate hilarity.

They had good reason to be glad. The War which had made the country poor had made them rich; which had put the quietus on many less thorough-going patriots had brought them swimming into power and prosperity they never before had known. Grand Sachem Davis had made as much as $80,000 on a single contract. Tribesman Nathan Sanford had demonstrated how a mere District Attorney with advanced ideas could earn $30,000 a year, which was

$5000 more than the President's salary. So it was right on down the line, and happy was the occasion that brought them together.

Back in '05 Tammany had changed her name but not her nature. A charter passed by the Legislature had turned Tammany Society into Tammany Hall—a charitable organization "for the purpose of affording relief to indigent and distressed widows and orphans. . . ." There is every reason to suppose that the widows and orphans were promptly relieved, for within the five following years ten Tammany leaders including five Sachems were caught in the act of embezzling public funds, which mode of charity caused a quarter-million dollar deficit in Mr. Clinton's city budget.

Still there must have been other tribesmen who were more careful, since in 1811 enough donations were made by grateful members to abandon Brom Martling's Pig Pen and to erect an elegant $11,000 Wigwam in its place. Other changes too had come about since the old days of Mr. Burr's leadership. Not much longer would Tammany be an all-American institution, for the Irish immigration offered the possibility of swelling the ranks with useful floaters, and it was becoming an adage about town that St. Tammany was a brother of St. Patrick and had migrated over the water to make a place for the faithful. Also since the Indian massacres during the War, it had been deemed advisable to do away with much of the old pageantry, though the official parade costume still included the hat with the buck's-tail tassel and "Bucktail" continued to be the quasi-official name the Braves went by at Albany.

Loud were the shouts of acclaim which accompanied each toast as it was proposed:

> A toast to George Washington!
> A toast to Mr. Jefferson!
> A toast to Governor Dan!
> A toast to General Jackson!
> Aye, and a toast to their own Matty Van!

A smiling little gentleman, not much taller than the back

of his chair, daintily clad and possessed of a wavy golden-crowned head, rose and bowed into the gale of applause that roared through the rafters and caused a rippling of the huge banner stretched across the room—TOMPKINS & CRAWFORD.

Not on occasions like this did Abe's boy wish himself out of politics. At 32 the Boy Lawyer had come a long way from sweeping the floors for Francis Silvester. He was Columbia County's State Senator and first citizen, the chosen champion of the Sons of Tammany, the presidential campaign manager of Governor Dan, and already he had begun to extend his influence afar. At a recent election he had made a flying trip to Catskill to bring brother-in-law Moses I. Cantine to the Senate as an assistant. His friend and admirer John W. Taylor he had helped into Congress, from which vantage-point Taylor was keeping him posted with many epistles on the state of presidential affairs. Another valuable outpost he would soon plant in Congressman Henry Meigs, cousin to Return J. Meigs, the Post Master General—though who except Matty Van saw anything significant in that? Still another auxiliary was Jesse Buel, editor of the powerful Albany *Argus*—though who except Matty Van knew the real reason why the *Argus* was his most ardent supporter? A newspaper, Martin had learned, was not the only thing Buel published; he had a counterfeiting press hidden away in his cellar. On the day Senator Van Buren had gone before the Council to procure Buel the money-making appointment of State Printer, there was a letter in the Senator's possession proving this fact "without question," but if he had put his first thief in office he had begun to establish the most important of all political adjuncts: an obedient press.

And, added to all this, was the happiness that, with the War over and the threat of invasion removed, Hannah and the children could safely be moved to Albany and their home reopened after two years of separation. Bowing into the plaudits of the jubilant Bucktails, Martin knew that his cup of joy overflowed.

This post-War session, he had determined, was to be a

time of many adjustments. Several matters vitally important had been postponed in favor of the national crisis, and one of them pertained to Mr. Clinton. Too long, protested the Bucktails, had he been Mayor of the Wigwam's own city. He must be removed. That in itself was simple enough, for Martin need only nod to Governor Dan and the deed was done. There was, however, a complication. Tammany, being only one of the several subdivisions that composed the nascent Regency, could not expect to have all the advantage. If there were to be a vacancy in the mayoralty, an up-state clique, known by its newspaper name as the Coodies, demanded recognition. Just why any out-of-towner should feel himself entitled to be Mayor of New York seems not to have been discussed, but State Senator Peter W. Radcliff was in line for the job, and so was Grand Sachem John Furgerson. Who was to have the plum, Matty Van?

Why, that was easily decided. Furgerson should take the post for a month or so until Matty Van, through certain sources in Washington, procured him a suitably lucrative appointment. After that Radcliff should step in. So it was agreed and accomplished. Furgerson was Mayor for two months, then became Surveyor of the Port, while Radcliff replaced him at the City Hall. The matter of a new Sheriff for New York County also came up, and was settled with equal dispatch. This office was bestowed upon another State Senator, Ruggles Hubbard of Troy, who, though he lived a day's journey from the scene of his duties, managed to get there often enough to steal several thousands of dollars and two years later vanish to parts unknown.

Thus far the readjustments had been accomplished with amicable accord and straightforwardness. By naming the Mayor, the Sheriff and a federal job-dispenser for New York City, Matty Van had pretty well brought that province under his domination. There was a sound reason why his task, so far as it pertained to the City, was relatively easy. Only two of the Senators on the Council of Appointment acknowledged his leadership, but all were united in animosity to Mr. Clinton, whom experience, since the arrival in office of

Senator Van Buren, had endowed with an undying hatred of all things political. Since his demise as a presidential prospect Mr. Clinton had been conducting two newspaper columns devoted entirely to exercising this obsession. One was the *Ambrosiad*, purporting to be the life and opinions of Judge Ambrose Spencer but generously including all the Judge's political friends. And the other was a series of essays signed "the Traveller" which visited the Clintonian wrath upon the State at large. There was hardly a political personality in the region who escaped penal introduction into these pages and only the imminent threat of invasion had kept the able but inflammatory Mayor in office so long.

The rest of Senator Van Buren's program, not having to do directly with Mr. Clinton or the City, offered more difficulty, and called upon him for talented treatment. First of all there was the matter of the attorney-generalship. The brilliant Abraham Van Vechten held the post at present, but he was a relic of an erstwhile Federalist majority, and hence scheduled to depart. For the vacancy were two aspirants, Mr. John Woodworth and Senator Van Buren.

Other things being equal Mr. Woodworth, despite his abilities, would have had small chance against Matty Van's hold on the Governor, but Mr. Woodworth was fortunate in having a brother-in-law on the Council and in having the recommendation of the highly-regarded Judge Ambrose Spencer to boot. Two of the Council stood ready to vote for him, and Governor Dan, in this presidential season when friendships were especially sacred, dreaded to give the deciding vote. Affairs having come to this juncture, the assumption was that Matty Van with the Governor's interest at heart would do the graceful thing and withdraw.

Graceful as such an action might be it was not within the Senator's calculations. To him it was not so much that the attorney-generalship carried a salary of $5.50 a day plus travelling expenses and no negligible bonus in fees, but that the position would give him at 32 a remarkable eminence at the Bar. Therefore Mr. Woodworth, hinting at the Senator's withdrawal, was given to understand that Mr. Van Buren considered it "the desire of the Party that I be appointed" and invited to do some withdrawing himself. While the situation was thus deadlocked and Happy Dan in a frenzy of apprehension lest he should be forced to decide either against Tammany or the influential Judge Spencer, Mr. Woodworth sent his rival a messenger bearing compromise.

If Mr. Van Buren, said the messenger, would, in his persuasive way, convince the Legislature that two more judgeships should be added to the State's Supreme Bench and that Mr. Woodworth was the man to fill one of them, then there would be no more said about the attorney-generalship. As a pledge of good faith the messenger, who was a member of the Council, placed in the Senator's hands a signed letter promising support.

A less gifted schemer than the Little Magician would have snapped up the offer on its face value, but Martin Van Buren was too apt in such matters to do the obvious thing and too frugal an opportunist to miss collecting all possible dividends. As in the case of the Sudam challenge he seized upon the chance for effective histrionics. There being a third person present as a witness, and this being a pre-election year, the Senator whipped himself into a tantrum of outraged dignity, shouting shame upon "so profligate a proposition." Using the letter as an emblem of rejected temptation, "I threw it into the fire."

When report of this noble renunciation went abroad there was nothing for Governor Dan to do but break the tie in the Senator's favor, which he did "because," said Matty Van, "he knew that the People desired that I should have it." However that may have been, the Little Magician's coup is of twofold importance to the student of his methods. To see how he managed to become titular head of the New York Bar at so untested an age, illustrates again his ability for getting places with a minimum of legitimate labor. He was not Attorney General because he was a good lawyer, but because he was politically wily. And, secondly, to see how he utilized the renunciation act both to mask and to forward his designs is to discover a method he developed well nigh to perfection in the years ahead—the use of a moral alibi to shield his reputation for political wizardry. No matter of what he was accused, the Little Magician never lacked a plausible explanation with which to confound his detractors and to convince at least half of his public that he was only an innocent little man, more sinned against than sinning.

Having done the People's will concerning the attorney-generalship, Governor Tompkins generously remembered the neglected Judge Spencer. He sent word to the Judge that the post of Secretary of State was still open in case His Honor had any suggestions. Once more honest Dan had employed a half-truth, for it was well understood that Mr. Van Buren's good friend, Colonel Young, was to have the portfolio. However when Judge Spencer expressed a feeling that his own friend, Elisha Jenkins, would make a more suitable Secretary, the Governor again exercised his casting vote, and Mr. Jenkins was chosen.

Elisha Jenkins, otherwise fameless, may be added to political lore as the man whose tenure of office is among the briefest on record. When he sat down to supper one February evening, he was New York's Secretary of State, but by bedtime he was not. Mr. Van Buren himself was at dinner when news of the appointment reached him and it so visibly depressed him as to "attract the attention of the company" and cast a pall over the gayety of the banquet he was attending.

His gloom, though, was not for long. Staring moodily out of the window he saw his friend, Ruggles Hubbard, the absentee Sheriff of New York County, going under a street-lamp on his way to the re-convening of the Council which had recessed for meal-time. Suddenly aglow with inspiration, Mr. Van Buren turned to a fellow-guest, a Regency Senator, and leading him into the hall, whispered hurried instructions. The regencyman was to pursue Hubbard and tell him to move the Council for the immediate dismissal of Jenkins in favor of that valiant defender of the Erie shore, General Peter B. Porter.

That this plan, so abruptly devised, would work, Matty Van had little doubt. For one thing the Governor would hardly thwart him twice; for another, the Council would be very hesitant about rejecting Porter's name. With the War so close at hand, they might turn down a Colonel, but they would hardly treat a General so, especially, mused Martin, since Jenkins "had held a lucrative appointment in the Commissary Department," whereas "the General had fought gallantly in the War and, on his arrival at Albany, became the lion of the day."

Besides being lion, General Porter also became Secretary of State, though he did not even know himself to be a candidate until Senator Van Buren informed him. Hearing, while still at dinner of the Council's unanimous approval, Matty Van sent Porter word "to accept and . . . to hold the office until we could recover our ground and obtain the appointment of Young." The General humbly obeyed.

All the re-adjustments, here listed, the unhurrying Mr. Van Buren accomplished in the incredibly short span of ten weeks. By April of the post-War year he had erected a skeleton form of the Regency, modeled along the lines it would hold for the next quarter-century. The name itself was not yet in usage, but as clear recognition of the directorship, the term "Bucktail" had been expanded by common consent to include not only the legislative Sons of Tammany but all political followers of Matty Van. Controlling the chief organ of the Republican press as well as the City and State administrations, he was now ready to look further afield.

Dan Tompkins was panting for the presidency, but the despatches that reached Matty Van from Washington were not encouraging. Georgia's Mr. William H. Crawford seemed the logical successor to Madison, and Mr. Crawford's friends had been extremely put out to hear that the Regency dared yoke their man's name in second place to Happy Dan. Martin solaced the Governor with a promise to visit Washington when the session was over, and see what could be done. In the meantime there was the more immediate question of refilling the seat of United States Senator Obediah German, whose term would soon come to an end.

German was a stalwart Clintonian, hence fated much against his will to retire, and as the opening loomed up all eyes turned on him who by this time was considered the recognized manager of such affairs.

Among other eyes thus cast were the wrathful and injured ones of Judge Ambrose Spencer. Except for a conspicuous lack of handsomeness—for from his pictures he closely resembled the typical long-nosed, sharp-chinned caricature of the New England witch-burner—Judge Spencer was not unlike his brother-in-law, the Magnus Apollo. He was vain, vindictive, ambitious and extremely capable, inclined to be violent when crossed, and given to furious outbreaks of rage at dramatic moments of defeat. Migrating from New England, he had begun political life as a Federalist, but marrying one and then another Clinton sister, he had been converted to the Republican Party, and during the Clinton-Livingston jubilee he had been elevated to the Bench.

Until Brother De Witt had aspired to be Peace President, their relations had been admirably fraternal, but when the Judge's conscience had tugged him toward the Madison candidacy the *Ambrosiad* had been the result. For three years thereafter the two had made every social and public encounter an opportunity to fold their arms and refuse to speak. Theoretically the Judge's ermine precluded him from any political activity, but unfortunately for his happiness and peace of mind, he was victimized by the same Urge that was working its will in the beruffled bosom of Martin Van Buren. One day while the senatorial question was still in the air, the hero of the *Ambrosiad* asked the Senator from Columbia into his lodgings for a chat.

Now subtlety was a quality with which heaven had never blessed Judge Spencer, and the elephantine circumlocutions with which he broached his secret ambition moved Martin to considerable inward amusement.

What, inquired the Judge fumblingly, did Mr. Van Buren think of that worthy man, General John Armstrong, for the next Senator?

Of General Armstrong, Martin replied gently, he thought

136 ]

very little. After all it would hardly be politic to send back to Washington a man who had recently departed that city in haste and disgrace. Judge Spencer must recall that Armstrong had been one of the three Secretaries of War during the late hostilities, had fled the scene of battle neck-and-neck with Mr. Madison, and had been informed by the latter that there was no need to return.

Then if Armstrong would not do, pursued the jurist, what of his other friend, Elisha Jenkins, the short-termed Secretary of State?

Of Mr. Jenkins he thought, said Martin, even less. But if Judge Spencer himself would consent to be Senator, Mr. Van Buren would feel honored to support him.

When making the offer Martin knew he had no intention to fulfill it, for he had already committed himself to the candidacy of the Wigwam's thrifty District Attorney, Nathan Sanford. He knew furthermore that he was running small risk in making the offer once, since Judge Spencer was that ilk of candidate who demands being flattered and cajoled into acceptance. The Judge wanted to hear what politicians universally term "the Call," but he should have known better than to attempt any such coyness on the man who would develop that polite conventionality into a fine art. No sooner had Spencer replied with seductive modesty that "his pursuits had not been of a character to qualify him for the place," than Martin took him at his word, and said in that case he would support Mr. Sanford.

Frustrated in his first attempt to conjure up the Call, Judge Spencer refused to relinquish his hope. He need not even exercise his vanity to know himself by age and attainments much more entitled to the senatorship than was Sanford. Despite Mr. Van Buren's apparent stupidity in failing to take the hint, Judge Spencer felt that to win the Republican nomination and hence the election, he had only to let it be understood that he would consent to accept them. Therefore during the fortnight that remained to him, he sought to concentrate the somewhat doubtful charm of his personality on the legislators who would compose the Caucus. He entertained handsomely, spoke invitingly of his "unfitness" to be Senator, and finally succeeded in being understood. Meanwhile Martin had busied himself in behalf of his candidate, and when the Caucus convened in the Senate Chamber he was calm in the knowledge that, unless the law-givers stampeded at the sound of Spencer's name, all would go well. A Bucktail put Sanford in nomination, and when another rose to do likewise for Spencer, Martin leaped to his feet in feigned amazement.

Had the gentleman been serious in nominating Judge Spencer?

Yes, the gentleman had been quite serious.

Well, the Senator from Columbia could hardly believe it, because Judge Spencer had told him in so many words that he was not a candidate.

Nevertheless the gentleman and several others had dined with Judge Spencer not two hours ago, and knew whereof they spoke. Would the Senator like to have the Caucus recessed while a committee crossed the street to the Judge's home and corroborated the statement?

His hand called, Martin attempted to back down. No, if the gentlemen were so positive there was no need of a recess.

But the Spencerians were too well pleased at seeing the redoubtable Matty Van discomfited, and they pressed their motion only to see it voted down when Matty Van nodded authoritatively to his admiring Bucktails. Having proved by the test-vote that he held command of the Caucus, Martin proceeded to demonstrate again his unvarying faculty for getting the most out of every opportunity that confronted him. An ordinary strategist would have been perfectly content to nominate his man with no more ado, but not Martin. He knew for one thing that on a secret ballot the weight of Spencer's name might sink his plans; he knew for another that it would be far better to retain at least a semblance of the Judge's friendship than to humiliate him by an open defeat. Therefore he rose again and astonishingly repeated the same motion that a moment before he had had beaten, adding the kindly advice that the calling committee "would practice a cruel deception upon their friend" if they neglected to inform him that a majority was waiting to vote in Sanford at the next crack of the gavel. The committee departed, and soon returned with just the results Martin had foreseen. Spencer's vanity revolted at the thought of defeat; he sent back the sardonic message that he did not choose to run "because he would not put himself in competition with so young a man as Sanford."

Owning now more offices than it is necessary to recount, Martin Van Buren ended his Marvellous Session as a law unto himself in legislative Albany. He had banished a Mayor, beaten a Judge, taught a Governor to come at his beck and call. In the Caucus he controlled the Party nominating agency; in the Council he had his will of the State's administrative department; in the Senate he led a bloc of Bucktails that made him czar of the law-giving facilities. Yet monarch as he truly was of all he surveyed, uneasy lay the head that wore the crown. As the session prepared to disband in mid-April, Martin could see two black clouds converging to darken the brightness of his horizon. One was the voters; the other Mr. Clinton.

Had the Regency been a duplicate of the modern Machine, Matty Van need not have worried about either of these emergencies. Time would come when a candidate backed by a well-oiled organization could win office year after year without so much as bothering to campaign his constituency, and there is more than one example of instances when a Machine has manufactured votes for a dead man. But the Regency's power was largely circumscribed by what could be accomplished within the State House walls. It was at the mercy of the voting public. The adjournment of the 1815 session gave Martin one more year of his quadrennial term and little hope of re-election. Nor need he look so far ahead to see disaster. Even as the law-givers were departing from Albany, the spring elections for the House of Delegates were showing a violent reaction against the Regency-run Republican party. Seat after seat passed over to the Federalists. To lose the House was to lose the Council; to lose the Council was to lose dozens of vital appointments, including his own treasured attorney-generalship.

And closely related to this threat was the reappearance of Mr. Clinton as a hostile force. Martin had suspected, and said so at the time, that removing the Magnus Apollo from the mayoralty might be short-sighted strategy. He had hearkened to the demands of his Bucktails, but not without grave misgivings about making a martyr of Mr. Clinton. Just that had happened. However strongly the politicians reciprocated Mr. Clinton's low opinion of them, there was no doubt that the State at large solidly admired him, and that his treatment at the hands of the Regency only intensified the admiration. The People were all for him and, what was worse the better class of thinking citizens, most of the reputable moneyed interests, and in fact everyone who had reason to prefer good government to bad.

So long as Mr. Clinton remained only an injured personality he was merely a negative liability to the Regency, but he had hardly ceased to be Mayor before he began agitating again for his pet project, the Erie Canal, which had been forgotten during the stress of the War. A large committee of business men had approved the plan, public interest was being aroused, and at the next session Mr. Clinton was due to carry his plea to the State House. Backed by money, by influence, by popular acclaim, he would demand that the Legislature pass his Canal Bill. And win or lose, Mr. Clinton was certain to make things unpleasant for anyone who opposed him.

Throughout the summer Martin watched his apprehensions round out into actualities. The final count showed that the Federalists had captured the House of Delegates by the annoyingly close count of 61-62. Mr. Clinton was successfully publicizing his scheme, pointing out that the coming of peace had caused a period of expansion; that there were now more than two million Americans living west of the Alleghenies with no eastern outlet for their produce; that the Canal would bring a flood-tide of prosperity to the Atlantic seaboard and the inland pioneers alike. A man of Mar-

tin Van Buren's good sense could not fail to see the soundness of these arguments, but his patriotism would not for
many a year interfere with his personal objectives. Clinton
was a friend to the Republic, but a menace to the Regency;
for that he must be crushed. Martin endorsed the Tammany
resolution that the Canal was "so visionary and absurd that
no rational man for one moment could seriously consider
it;" he smiled approvingly over the Bucktail doggerel:

> "Oh, a ditch he would dig from the lakes to the sea,
> The Eighth of the world's matchless wonders to be.
> Good land! How absurd! But why do you grin?
> It will serve to bury its mad author in."

Deep in his heart Martin knew, and later he admitted, the
far-reaching majesty of the plan. But now it filled him only
with abhorrence. Packing his bags in December for his first
trip to the Capital City, he realized that on his return the
Bucktails would be expecting magical feats of him. Somehow or other he must save the Council and scotch the Canal.

They seemed a pair of impossible assignments, but the
Bucktails knew better than to despair. Matty Van was their
shepherd; they should not want.

3

(December 1815)

The firm and athletic strides that daily bore Mr. William
H. Crawford to and from his work at the War Office had
during the past summer and autumn taken on the gait of a
man who meditates as he walks. And in meditation the mien
of Mr. Crawford was a thing which caused admiring behold-
ers to pause and stare after, for his appearance was the in-
carnation of all that resident laymen of a Capital City
could rejoice to look upon. His manly body rose erect to
the height of six feet three inches from the ground he trod;
his thrust-out chin and clear blue eyes were pictures of inspired, aggressive statesmanship, and if the slovenly abandon
with which he wore his shabby and ill-sorted clothes did not

add smartness to his looks, at least it furthered the supposition that he was one who scorned all things trivial and artificial.

Moreover, anyone who happened to know the outline of Mr. Crawford's history could be aware that here was a figure representing what was fast becoming the flower of the American tradition. To future historians Mr. Crawford offered a ready-made subject for the presidential biography. He was a self-made man, a chip of the old pioneer stock, and one whose early privations and toil were writ large on his brow. Even his childhood, these historians could have found, was significantly entwined with famous names of the day. His father had pined in the same prison at Camden Town with the boy, Andrew Jackson; as a boy himself, Crawford had been the school-mate of John C. Calhoun; as a youth he had killed in an honorable duel the first cousin of Martin Van Buren. Poverty and the laudable aim to better himself had caused the elder Crawford to migrate from Virginia to the frontier lands of Georgia, where at his death the son had undertaken the livelihood of school-teaching. He was at it four years, studying law on the side, and he arrived at the bar in time to have a hand in prosecuting the most notorious scandal of post-Colonial days, the Yazoo land swindle, for which good work the people of Georgia had promptly sent him to the Legislature. There his steady cooperation had won the faith of his superiors, and when death produced a vacancy in the U. S. Senate he was shipped off to Washington to fill it. So commendably did he do so that he was soon re-elected to a term of his own; with the final illness of George Clinton he became President *pro tem* of the Senate; with the declaration of War Mr. Madison sent him as Ambassador to the Court of Saint Cloud, from which hectic scene he had but recently returned to take charge of the mangled War Department.

He had returned, too, for another purpose. It was commonly supposed in the inner circles that the passing of Mr. Madison's second term meant also the passing of the Virginia Dynasty, and with the presidential field wide open Mr. Crawford stood out as the logical Republican candidate. War Hawks Clay and Calhoun were too headstrong; Mr. Randolph of Roanoke, besides being of dubious sanity, was a Virginian, which latter disqualification also stamped Mr. Monroe. Had the North been able to bring forth a first-class Republican it might have been different, but the Party leaders, seeking a man fit to sit where a Washington and a Jefferson had sat, simply could not take Dan Tompkins seriously. Everything pointed to Mr. Crawford, yet despite this happy situation the furrows of anxiety that creased his lofty forehead deepened as the weeks and months slipped by.

"I am convinced," wrote Jabez Hammond, New York's political historian, who was a member of the sitting Congress, "that for six months the Caucus was ready to nominate Crawford."

Yet something always postponed it. Mr. Crawford was worried.

He could be reasonably certain what caused the delay, and he rightly guessed it to be an influence that emanated from Monticello. The aged Mr. Jefferson was not quite the closet philosopher he preferred people to think him. Having been President eight years himself, he had named his successor and was now busy naming his successor's successor. The country might think the Virginia Dynasty done for, but Mr. Jefferson thought otherwise. Not for nothing, deemed Mr. Crawford, had Long Tom descended from his mountain refuge to attend a celebration at Lynchburg, Virginia, in honor of that wild westerner, General Jackson; and not without prompting had the man of the hour offered a toast of allegiance to Mr. Monroe. That, together with the continuous putting off of the Caucus, was too much to be a coincidence, and Mr. Crawford needed no one to tell him that the longer the delay, the less were his chances.

Yet he did nothing about it. Mr. Crawford's aggressive appearance belied the patient and apathetic soul within. His progress thus far had been one to teach him faith in the adage that everything comes to him who waits. His very entrance into politics had resulted less from ambition than accident. He might have lived a whole life-time without stumbling on an opportunity like the Yazoo case. His two major advancements, the senatorship and the presidency of that honorable body, had occurred when men higher up had conveniently died. His own worth, of course, put him in line for these and other posts, but Mr. Crawford had never taken life by the horns. No man fraught with ambition and living on the restless frontier would have chosen to give four years of young manhood to the indolent, prosaic profession of school-teaching. And no man fired with a self-willed passion would have tolerated in those free days a seven-year engagement to a girl he fondly loved and finally married when he was thirty-two and wealthy. Mr. Crawford was disposed to wait for opportunity to seek him out, but this time he waited too long. By December Mr. Jefferson's insistence had taken effect: Monroe and not the tall Georgian was the favorite of the Caucus. Patiently Mr. Crawford sighed and remarked that he was "young enough" to wait another eight years.

That was true, for Mr. Crawford was not yet forty, but he was soon informed by his friends that being an appropriate age was not sufficient to keep him in line for future preferment. He must, they said, enter the competition, and if not beat Monroe at least register enough votes to make a respectable showing. Even this not over intricate problem confounded the lethargic Secretary. He did what he considered the honorable thing by naïvely telling Mr. Monroe that he had no hope of beating him in the Caucus but was merely running so as to file his application for the White House when the Virginian had finished his occupancy. And a short while later, when excited friends informed him that new events showed he still had a chance for the nomination, Mr. Crawford requested them not to press it lest he should be guilty of bearing false witness to his rival. Such quixotic high-mindedness might be all very well, complained the friends, but it would never get a man anywhere. What Crawford needed, they must have felt, was a manager.

If they had prayed for one the wish could not have been

more graciously or unexpectedly granted. One day in December, while the Caucus was scheduled to meet any moment, there appeared at the Capitol a smiling little dandy to whom the New York Congressmen were unaccountably deferential. That national legislators should show such marked respect for a State Senator was surprising enough, but when it was learned that Little Van (for so the Capital City soon learned to call him) had come to settle the presidential question, there was wonder indeed.

Little Van's first efforts were on behalf of Governor Tompkins, in whose name he had ostensibly made the trip. This Tompkins, it began to be whispered about Washington, was an outstanding and heroic statesman.

And what had he done, the curious law-givers wanted to know, to qualify him for running the Republic?

Why, practically single-handed, was the argument, Governor Tompkins had re-captured Fort Erie and hurled the British back into Canada.

Very likely this generous account of Happy Dan's deeds caused some mirth among its hearers, for Washington Irving had recently been Dolly Madison's guest and had doubtless recounted a story of which he was exceedingly fond. As aide-de-camp, Mr. Irving was wont to relate, one of his chief duties had been chasing Dan's horse, which had a habit of bucking its rider off at the first sound of gun-fire. And even supposing Happy Dan *had* beaten the British, pursued his chaffers, did that make him presidential timber. Consider General Jackson.

The very thought of Old Hickory becoming President was another great joke among the wiseacres of 1815, and the Tompkins canvassers perforce shifted their ground. At least no one could deny that their man had made a good Governor of the most important State in the Union. And if he had, came the rebuttal, did that mean he could govern the whole Union?

"We also have a good Governor in North Carolina," Hammond recorded a Congressman as saying, "but we do not on that account expect you to support him."

It was vain, Martin found, to argue his friend's qualifications. Monroe and Crawford had both done cabinet service, knew the details of national government and had the confidence of all. Clearly Dan was out of his class against these two, yet he had explicitly stated that he would not consider the vice-presidency. An informal calculation showed how the votes would fall. Tompkins could count on support from New York, New Jersey and from a few scattered in Ohio, Maryland and Kentucky. The situation gave him the semblance of a balance of power, not enough to nominate either candidate, but sufficient to swing the respectable quota which Crawford's friends sought for him. It offered the Little Magician a perfect setting to perform one of his sorceries, and as always, he looked past present benefits into the deeper possibilities of the future.

That being the situation, asked Hammond, how did the Regency want the New York. delegation to vote?

Matty Van looked him archly in the eye, and laid a tap of emphasis on two words of his answer.

"We say Tompkins, *of course.*"

Dan Tompkins never quite forgave the New Yorkers who deserted his cause for the presidency and wished the empty second office upon him. He insisted to his dying day that had they held out to the end and scorned all bargaining, Monroe must have weakened and his votes gone to New York. Somehow he seems to have borne no grudge against the real perpetrator of the plot, for Martin's glib gift of denial served successfully to exonerate him. Precisely what happened is not supported by documentary proof, but future events and the current understanding about Washington coincide to lay the blame where it doubtless belongs; and the too-late and too-loud protestations of Hammond, who was a party to the plot, rather substantiate than explode the theory. As nearly as can be deduced, what took place was this:

Having gone over the ground, Little Van went into serious conference with the Crawford men. No, Mr. Crawford was not interested in the vice-presidency, preferring to go into Mr. Monroe's cabinet if the Federalists were beaten, as they assuredly would be. If Little Van cared to withdraw his candidate from the first office, he could have the second—provided, of course, that most of the Tompkins votes went to Crawford. After all, the Empire State seemed to have as much claim on the vice-presidency as the Old Dominion did on the presidency. Tompkins would make the third New Yorker in that office as Monroe would make the fourth Virginian in his. Did Little Van agree?

Yes, Little Van was inclined to agree, but since looking toward the future was in order why should he not do the same. Since New York had such a monopoly on the vice-presidency, why not a New Yorker teamed with a Georgian eight years hence? In other words why not a Crawford-Van Buren ticket in 1824?

These several days in December of 1815 constitute one of the few periods when the Red Fox's trail is cold enough to baffle even the earnest hound-work of a curious biographer. Where the trail ends is on his pointed reply to Hammond, where it picks up is not far distant, but what happened in the interim can only be computed from the two points. That Martin and the Crawford men made the agreement which involved a waiting of eight years is as certain a conjecture as circumstantial evidence can make it, and the biographer can apologize for his flimsy sources without belittling his conclusions. If the bargain was not made, then some very remarkable coincidences occurred. The New York delegation promptly dropped Tompkins and gave Crawford enough votes to bring his total up to within 11 counts of top; the Crawford men fell in behind Tompkins and ordained that unwilling victim to be running-mate with Monroe. Thus Crawford was made heir apparent to King Caucus, and the Caucus of 1824 duly gave him the nomination, while the Georgia delegation as duly supported Little Van for the vice-presidency against Calhoun.

Enough was to happen in the next eight years to throw the nicest calculations out of order, but going home to spend Christmas with Hannah and the boys, Martin Van Buren could look before and after with no need to pine for what was not. Three years ago he had barely nosed out a victory in his first election; today he had lined up his third presidential prospect in three years, and this time one that looked like a certain winner.

Mr. Crawford, too, spending Christmas with his wife and eight children in their suburban mansion on Massachusetts Avenue, had a right to be complaisant. Since Little Van's appearance in Washington life had taken on a glow of anticipation for the Georgian. In his whole life, Mr. Crawford once confided, he had known only two dandies who were men of talent. One was Alexander Hamilton, and Mr. Crawford did not have to name the other. Nothing short of an Act of God, he must have known, could keep him out of the White House in a few more years.

And an Act of God, in fact, was exactly what accomplished it.

4

(November 1816–November 1817)

In Mrs. Keese's bon ton boarding house at Wall Street and Broadway, Judge Ambrose Spencer was dressing for dinner. The Court was sitting in New York for the autumn term of 1816 and, like most of the élite of the Bar, Judge Spencer stopped at Mrs. Keese's while in the city. He was dining this evening with Mr. Jacob Barber, banker and dabbler at politics, who was about to do the Judge a great favor. Ordinarily, being invited to sit at table with the author of the *Ambrosiad* was not what Judge Spencer might have deemed a boon, but politics is a great leveler of proud spirits, and he did not have to be any wiser than he was to know that there was plenty of precedent for what he was about to do. Judge Spencer was preparing, if necessary, to lick a better man's boots in hope of mending his political fortune.

It was, to be sure, a long series of tribulations that had brought the ill-fated jurist to this frame of mind. He could take no little pride in the knowledge that he had borne

148 ]

with fortitude the consecutive defeats visited on him by that unconscionable scoundrel, Mr. Van Buren. Without audible cry Judge Spencer had seen the Council reject one after another of his nominees, seen the Caucus turn down his own candidacy for the Senate, seen the Regency dominant at every turn. That was bad enough, but at the 1816 session just finished at Albany he had undergone the most rankling experience of all. Not a personal affront this time, but one that offended both Judge Spencer's schooled sense of justice and his native lust for revenge—two qualities closely coupled in his worthy New England soul. Worse, this last setback had come just at the moment when Judge Spencer was figuratively rubbing his long hands over an expected triumph.

He had watched the approach of the past session with gusto and yearning, for he foresaw it as the Waterloo of the Regency's dapper little ruler. The Federalist majority of one vote in the House was sufficient to wrest the Council from the Van Buren control, and Mr. Clinton's Canal Bill, if the Bucktails dared oppose it, was a vital enough issue to defeat and confound them for years to come. Yet faced with what seemed two unsurmountable difficulties, the nimble-witted Dutchman had overcome them both—had not only retained the Council but once again ravished Mr. Clinton.

The first of these feats had been accomplished by methods that enraged Judge Spencer beyond all expression, for he justly considered them nothing less than out-and-out fraud. On the convening of the House it appeared that while the Federalists truly had a majority by all fairness and right, the deciding seat hung momentarily in question. A Regency clerk of the court in Ontario county had thrown out 49 votes for the Federalist candidate on the grounds that that many ballots were signed "Hen" instead of "Henry" Fellows—enough to give the election to Peter Allen, Republican.

The Federalists naturally protested this seat on the opening day and there seemed little doubt that there were enough conscientious Republicans on hand to set the matter right. This, in fact, they eventually did, but Mr. Van Buren, abandoning his seat in the Senate chamber, had spent eight days on the floor of the House with no other purpose than to postpone the adjustment until after the Council was chosen. That having been accomplished, he unstemmed the tide of justice and the Federalist was duly sworn in with but one vote in the whole House against his claim. Then, to Judge Spencer's added indignation, Matty Van had used the Council to secure himself another high-sounding title—Regent of the State University—and the Bucktails topped off the fiasco by according a farewell banquet to the unseated Allen, who departed for home amid loud acclamation.

And the fate of the Canal Bill had been equally galling to Judge Spencer. Not that he hated Clinton less, but Van Buren more, had he hoped for its passage. He noted with pleasure that Governor Dan's annual message, which everyone knew was of Van Buren authorship, made only a vague reference to the question, saying it was a matter which "remained for the Legislature to decide." That meant, gloated the Judge, that the Bucktail captain feared to test his strength against the bill, and when it sailed unopposed through the House and came to the Senate there was every indication that a majority would bolt the Columbian's leadership, if he had the hardihood to stand against it.

Evidently the knowing little master was of the same opinion, for when he took the floor for debate on the Bill he treated his hearers to such unctuous phrases in its praise that even Mr. Clinton, standing by the wall, was convinced that his enemy was about to hoist the white flag. He was soon undeceived, however, for Martin ended his talk by offering an innocent-looking amendment, not at all altering the Bill but, by a devious net-work of phraseology, striking out the date set for the actual digging. The amendment with its nullifying joker was passed, and Martin then enthusiastically moved the passage of the corrected measure.

Nor was that all. Finding it necessary in April to stand for reëlection, Martin had once more made use of his tow-line method. The popularity of Dan Tompkins was all that kept the Regency afloat, and Dan, being candidate and certain winner of the vice-presidency, did not contemplate seeking

reëlection to the governorship, an office which he could hold
for only a few months of the three-year term. But Matty
Van had other plans. Desperately in need of Dan's aid, the
little manager persuaded him to make the run, thus insur-
ing the Middle District to the Republicans and to Senator
Van Buren's reëlection.

The sum total of the Little Magician's coups fanned
Judge Spencer's glowing rage into a blazing activity. His
Urge was, after all, a subjective passion, and one which hardly
became a man who wore the wig of impartiality and altruism. But now he could justify his feelings as belonging to a
higher stratum. With the "Hen" Fellows outrage, fumed
the Judge, this Van Buren person became a culprit at large,
a plotter against the public weal, and it behooved every moral
man to turn a hand against him. By this time it was only
too evident to Judge Spencer that his adversary was invulnerable to ordinary rivalry, that the one way to beat
him was at his own game. Since the popular Dan Tompkins
would soon be headed for Washington, the strongest man
in appeal to the voters would be Mr. Clinton, and the
Judge considered it a stroke of genius when it occurred to
him to patch up his quarrel with the Magnus Apollo and to
use him as a spear-head to break the Regency phalanx.
Hence the gleeful anticipation with which he put the finishing touches to his toilette and set off to the Barber house
in Beekman Street.

The Judge would have been less pleasurably inclined had
he known that at approximately the same moment no other
than the atrocious Mr. Van Buren was strolling down
Broadway in the same direction. Turning to the two companions who walked with him, Martin assumed one of his
mysterious airs, and asked whom they expected to meet at
the dinner this evening.

They offered a few casual conjectures, to which Martin
knowingly replied,

"De Witt Clinton."

"But Spencer will be there!"

Martin nodded wisely. "That is the very reason."

[ 151

Whether he had really divined the Spencerian plot, as he implies, whether someone had told him, or whether (and it is not unlikely) he merely wrote the anecdote into the *Autobiography* to enhance his own cleverness cannot, of course, be said. It is certain however that, arriving at Barber's, they found Clinton already there, and Spencer shortly followed them into the hall. In the presence of their common annoyance, the principals of the proposed reconciliation made scant progress in that direction, for whenever they raised eyes toward one another, there was always the mocking smile of the little schemer between them. During dinner the two haughty kinsmen exchanged not a single word with each other, and their cumbersome attempts to discourse through the medium of other guests only confirmed whatever suspicions Martin had brought with him.

His frustration again in true Matty Van style goaded the Judge to supreme efforts. "A more active and indomitable spirit," Martin says of him, "never existed." After dinner, when Mr. Clinton excused himself to be off to another party which he had promised to attend, Judge Spencer did likewise and dogged his brother-in-law's footsteps to the next function, where at last their hands met and they uttered each other's christian names for the first time in more than four years.

Elated, the Judge resolved to follow up this informal declaration of a truce by a definite treaty, so, learning that Mr. Clinton meant to sail for Albany on the Friday before the court adjourned for the week-end, he grasped this opportunity for a long confidential talk, free from interruption. It was necessary for the Judge to inform only one person, the Chief Justice, of his intended absence from the Bench, and this he did at the last moment to assure a secret departure. Conceive, then, his feelings to arrive on the deck with Mr. Clinton and to find himself effusively greeted by the one man he wished above all to avoid. Martin had been forewarned of Spencer's departure by the Chief Justice, Smith Thompson, who for this and other favors was two-fold rewarded. Little Van used his influence with the incoming Vice President to have Thompson created Secretary of the Navy, and his influence with Hannah to have their fourth son named after this benefactor.

The up-river trip, instead of being the confidential chat that Spencer had planned, turned into a banal, ineffectual trialogue which so disgusted Mr. Clinton that he disembarked at Newburgh to go the rest of the way to Albany by coach, leaving the infuriated Judge and the amiable Senator to talk things out between themselves. Secluded in an after-cabin, Spencer met Martin's inquisitive glance with what he intended to be a placable explanation of his strange behavior. He was hastening to Albany, he said, to be on hand for the choosing of presidential electors on Monday, when he would propose Mr. Clinton's name for one of them. After all, such an office was only an honorary one, and Mr. Clinton was an outstanding Republican deserving recognition for past services to the Party. Did Mr. Van Buren have any objections?

"If there were no ulterior motives," said Martin, "I would not object." But the Judge might as well confess that "it was his intention to bring Mr. Clinton forward as the candidate for Governor, to supply the vacancy that was expected to arise from the election of Governor Tompkins to the vice-presidency."

At this reading of his innermost thoughts Judge Spencer "became very excited," but recalling the futility of indignation toward Matty Van, he offered to bargain. If Mr. Van Buren would not interfere with Clinton's promotion, then Judge Spencer swore "he would be responsible for Mr. Clinton's good conduct toward me and my friends." Loftily Martin spurned the proposal, and the gage was down.

For the two days prior to the Caucus the Judge and the Senator canvassed among the legislators. Often they entered the same room with identical purposes, whereupon they would bow, and handsomely bid each other have the first chance. For all his unruffled good humor, Martin knew himself once more facing a crisis. Many of the up-state Bucktails, anxious to stay with their leader, weakened at the

[ 153

# The American Talleyrand

proposition of opposing Clinton for an office that had no
power and possessed but the vaguest of prestige. It was becoming progressively unwise to line up against the Magnus
Apollo's soaring popularity. A few hours before the Caucus
would sit, Judge Spencer accosted his rival with the jeering
boast that he had "a majority of twenty", at which Martin
hoped politely that the Judge would be present in the Senate chamber to witness the victory he had so masterfully
engineered.

It is unfortunate for Judge Spencer that something prevented his attendance, for he would have learned much to
his edification about the art of parliamentary manoeuvring.
Confronting this time the mathematical certainty of defeat,
Matty Van accomplished all but the impossible. There were
thirty electors to be chosen: one from each congressional
district and two delegates-at-large. Clinton's home constituency being the so-called Southern District where Tammany
held sway, he was to be offered as a delegate-at-large on the
theory that his state-wide popularity would swallow up the
Wigwam's opposition. There was a hush of curiosity as
Martin rose to address the Chair. Give Matty Van the floor,
everyone knew, and some sort of a surprise was in store. No
one was disappointed. His first motion was that the two
delegates-at-large be residents respectively of the Western
and Southern Districts. That, as well as the Clintonians
could understand it, was playing directly into their hands,
and they hungrily accepted the advantage. Then came
Matty Van's real effort. He moved, Mr. Chairman, that these
delegates-at-large be chosen by representatives of their own
Districts rather than by the vote of the whole Caucus.

The proposal was so manifestly absurd that it caused the
Clintonians nearly as much laughter as it did indignation.
How could the Senator from Columbia seriously suggest
that delegates-at-large be chosen by individual districts, when
the very terms themselves were contradictory? Nevertheless
the Senator did suggest just that, and he added the codicil
that the vote on the measure be taken *viva voce* instead of

154 ]

by ballot, so that no man present could make a secret of his feelings on this vital point.

A fight in the open was the last thing the Clintonians expected Matty Van to propose, but they failed to see through his subterfuge. He knew that his up-state Bucktails would be discomforted by a straight pro-or-con vote on Clinton, but this side-line motion could do them no harm. As for the *viva voce* clause, that was to prevent any of them attempting to bolt, which he knew they would not do under his watchful eye. The motion carried; Clinton was doomed to stand for the Southern District, and under the tender mercies of the Tammany delegation his candidacy went the way of all flesh.

Once again Matty Van had turned back the enemy at the very citadel gates, but he was on the defensive now. Not for long could he hope to hold out against the overwhelming forces that were massed against him. This was November; on March Fourth Dan Tompkins would resign as Governor, and the way would open for Clinton to take his place. Valiantly Martin gave himself to the defense of this breach in his walls. He did his best to inveigle Dan into holding both offices at once, there being no clause in the Constitution to prevent it. But Dan for once was obstinate. He would not hazard whatever chance he had of being Monroe's successor. Next Martin attempted a quibbling over the wording of the State Constitution to prove that the Lieutenant Governor was entitled to fill out the full three years of Dan's elective term. It was in vain. Following that, he pinned his faith on the State Caucus, which he had never failed to control, proposing to thwart Clinton by nominating that useful hero, Peter B. Porter. But Spencer completely offset this advantage by issuing loud and successful calls for an open Convention, the delegates of which were to be elected at the polls for the purpose of choosing the Party nominees.

This last seemed the knell of the Regency's fading hope. The Caucus Matty Van could handle, but not a Convention that sprang straight from the voters. The best the Regency could do was to set up General Porter as a graven image of the incomparable Dan, but Clinton won nomination on the first ballot. Too careful a Dutchman was Matty Van to linger any longer on the wrong band-wagon. The Braves insisted on a Caucus to send Porter into the general elections, but their champion refused to join them. Clinton, as Martin expected, was swept into office by the largest vote ever given a Governor, bringing with him a large majority in both houses. The Canal Bill, minus all jokers, rolled through to final passage with Martin not only voting for it but taking the floor to pronounce it "the most important vote I ever gave in my life."

It was, at least, one of the most expedient. There was no stopping Clinton or his project at this point, and when the axes, picks and shovels began swinging to the march of civilization, it was as if they were beating a death-roll to the smitten Regency. Undaunted still remained the Bucktails. They never understood Matty Van, but they never doubted him. Not Christian martyrs, trooping to a Caesar's arena, sang with more blind faith,

> "What schemes for Master Clinton's ruin
> The wily brain of Matt is brewin'!"

## 5

### (February 1819–July 1819)

High ran excitement at the $11,000 Wigwam; high soared the spirits of the Braves as the annual Washington's Birthday celebration approached. Many and gorgeous had been these occasions in the past, but the one of 1819 seemed in a fair way to eclipse them all. For no less a personage than the celebrated General Jackson was to be the guest of honor, and the General was the most-sought-after diner-out in the realm.

Only recently had he added to his laurels of New Orleans by leading a raid into the Spanish Floridas, and confiscating that property as American territory. Moreover he had accomplished this conquest without the loss of an

American life, and had added relish to the feat by lynching a pair of British citizens whom he happened upon in the process. The fact that both England and Spain were neutral powers did not at all detract from the public appreciation of Old Hickory's deeds, though it somewhat nonplussed Mr. Monroe and his associates. Mr. Adams, Secretary of State, had had to receive two rather irate Ambassadors; Mr. Crawford, Secretary of the Treasury, had had to dig into the shallow coffers for five million dollars with which to salve the Administration's conscience by "buying" the land from Spain; Mr. Calhoun, Secretary of War, had informed the Cabinet that the dignity of his Department demanded a court-martialing of this undisciplined marauder; Mr. Clay, Speaker of the House, was instigating a reprimand; and Mr. Monroe himself was on the point of banishing the troublesome hero to the ends of the earth by making him minister to Russia, when Mr. Jefferson interposed with:

"My God, you'll have a war on your hands within a week."

The execution of the two unfortunates brought the General's total of lethal victims up to a baker's dozen; which is not to count the eighty-some others whom (even his conservative biographers admit) he threatened with the assorted weapons of guns, knives, fists and a "red hot and-iron." Clearly this wildman was not one to be crossed, and when word came to Washington that he was on his way there vowing to "cut off the ears of anyone who opposes me," the official indignation vanished like a summer's cloud, and the entire Cabinet family came forth to meet him, hat in hand. There was doubtless more than one tremulous heart among these life-loving gentry, but the most tremulous of all belonged to the Hamlet-browed Mr. Calhoun, who had said in so many words that the General ought to be punished. None of his colleagues save the naïve Mr. Crawford seemed the kind to let out such a dread secret, but the Cabinet was sworn into a conspiracy of silence which Mr. Calhoun hoped his colleague of the Treasury would regard as a promise. As a promise Mr. Crawford was ready to con-

[ 157

sider it, but it is well for these pages that he broke it twelve years later, else *The American Talleyrand* might never have had a presidential biography.

About the diplomatic delicacies of the situation the Sons of Tammany cared not at all, and they failed to perceive any particular significance in the General's tour of the country which followed close upon his exoneration at the Capital City. They remembered, of course, how, immediately after the saving of New Orleans, Mr. Burr had predicted that Andrew Jackson, properly managed, could be President, but most of them put it down as one of the poor fellow's pipe dreams. If they knew that the General already had two presidential managers and was making the trip under their artful direction, the Braves, like the rest of the political nation, did not take it very seriously. Old Hickory was being tendered the banquet not as any sort of candidate, but as a conquering hero whose presence at the Wigwam might very handily be construed as a snub to the Magnus Apollo. All along the way General Jackson had been the official guest of Governors and Mayors, but in New York he had apparently ignored Governor Clinton in favor of the Bucktail invitation. That the General did or did not understand the importance of his action was immaterial, for the Regency newspapers would make the public think so anyhow.

That is, they would make the public think so should the banquet come off according to plan. All that concerned the hospitable Sachems was that the jubilee go on record as an unusually spirited demonstration of patriotism and good cheer. There was to be as much wine as the feasters could drink, and toasts and laudations to all good Americans, both the quick and the dead. Everything went smoothly until the climatic moment when the General rose in the teeth of a howling ovation and raised his goblet to offer a toast of his own. Any of a score of names he might have picked would have been greeted with equal enthusiasm, but the words that fell from the hero's lips left his hosts standing with unemptied glasses trembling in their hands.

## He Builds the Regency

"To De Witt Clinton! Governor of the great and patriotic state of New York!"

It was a bolt from the blue. Historians have never yet decided whether Jackson committed this breach of political and social etiquette purposely or by accident, whether he had the insolence to do so on his own initiative or whether someone mischievously put him up to it. At any rate, it did not matter that night. Only for a moment did the Bucktails remain in the petrifaction of their initial surprise. With a whoop of derision, one of the members flung his glass to the floor and an instant later all but one other had crashed there beside it.

That other remained in the hand of Andrew Jackson, and the "hawk-like eye" which had quelled mutinies and sentenced men to death for lesser insults than this, sweep balefully round the room. Back went his grizzled head, up came his arm, and tossing off the toast, he swung on his heel and stamped out the door. Consternation reigned behind him as the sobered tribesmen gazed on his vanishing coat-tails. What to do? Run after? Explain? Apologize? Such a dilemma called for the snap judgment of a masterful mind, but as luck would have it there was no such mind among them tonight. Matty Van was not there.

Indeed Martin was a long way from the Wigwam this February evening both in body and soul. Eighteen days ago Hannah had coughed up blood, closed her eyes on the babe at her breast and died. A pinched, pale, bitter little man drove her coffin through the snows to the Kinderhook churchyard. Ever since the birth of her last child he had known the end was not far, and the agony of the hopeless waiting had dealt harshly with him. For months the smile was gone from his lips and the honeyed guile from his tongue. For weeks the Bucktails had invoked him in vain. Already there were two graves in the burial lot which he had bought at Kinderhook, for Abe would damn no more tyrants and Mother Mary had said her last prayer. What thoughts can be read into the little man who stood at the new-turned mound beside which he himself would one day be laid? Nothing save what a biographer might invent. There is evidence aplenty that Martin and Hannah loved and were loved deeply, contentedly, exclusively, but he is never known to have said so. That he was numbed, embittered, bowed by her death is piteously clear, but not because he ever admitted it. Not once in all the seven-hundred-odd-pages of the *Autobiography* does he speak of Hannah either by that name or by the pet-name—Jannettje—which he is supposed to have called her. Only once in the 61 volumes of his letters and papers is she mentioned, and then by another man's pen. Never in the hundreds of anecdotes and conversations recorded by his contemporaries has it been possible for this biographer to discover the wife's name on her husband's lips.

There are two conflicting conjectures that may be drawn from this: either Martin cared too deeply for words or he cared not at all. Probably neither is true. With all its sentimental possibilities Hannah's death only proves again the utter futility of attempting to infuse into Martin Van Buren anything more than very average attributes. Entirely too normal a man to play the life-long suffering stoic, Martin grieved for a time and then, very humanly, forgot.

But humanly, too, his was a heart bowed down as he stood over her last resting place. Very possibly Hannah was the one person for whom he never bothered to pose; very possibly when she unseasonably died, there died with her America's only chance to know her Eighth President in his off-stage moments. With Hannah he had walked these same dusty roads to school, with her he had performed the daring adventure of elopement, marriage and parenthood. She must have been, if nothing else, such a companion of his inner thoughts as he never had before or after. Now she was gone.

In words less than these did Martin take farewell of his love. A line more mutely eloquent than any he ever wrote or spoke did he order engraved for her tomb-stone:

"Precious shall be the memory of her virtue."

## He Builds the Regency

For a week or so he stayed on at his brother's house in Kinderhook, but now or never was he far removed from the drama in which he played. A letter came from Cantine with political gossip, among it the report that Martin was about to be shorn of his attorney-generalship. The office would have been taken from him long ago had not Mr. Clinton been making a sincere effort to raze the spoils system from statecraft. As Governor he had removed only a handful of Bucktails who were ludicrously unfit for their jobs, and he had retained Martin because he was a good enough lawyer, despite their enmity.

Three times of late had Mr. Clinton extended the olive branch, proposing they put aside all differences and unite in giving the State their best efforts, but Martin found it impossible to accept peace on such terms. He must play politics or nothing at all, and his answer to the emissaries whom Clinton sent him was an impudent proposal that the Magnus Apollo resign as Governor and accept a foreign post, which Martin would procure through Vice President Dan. Even this saucy reply failed to upset the Clintonian serenity, and it seems Martin might have kept his post as long as he was willing to fill it dutifully. But this was the period of Hannah's parting and all was blackness and gall. His usual suavity shaded off into peevishness; his perpetual good humor into spite. One day when Clinton sent him word to go into Delaware county, there to take charge of a murder trial, Martin returned answer that travelling did not suit him "in such weather" and sourly advised the Governor to hire another counsel at the State's expense.

Such insubordination could not be brooked for long, but Mr. Clinton tried again. He sent ex-Senator German to the Attorney General to know if there were "some way to arrest the divisions that were spreading in the Party."

Martin met the advance churlishly with: "The Governor must either put us down, or be put out himself."

"Well," said German, "it requires no prophet to tell us which of those results will happen."

Contemptuously Martin received the order of his removal

that followed immediately. To a friend who had lately moved to Cincinnati he wrote what is, except for its wealth of misspelling and grammatical errors, the one uncharacteristic letter in his whole collection. Sneering at the "toadeaters" who "stunned the public ear and nauseated the public taste with their never-ending hallelujahs" of the Magnus Apollo and "his stupendous greatness," Martin gives notice that henceforth his one mission in politics is to overthrow Clinton and Spencer, the two enemies who had temporarily downed him. Though he addressed the man as "a friend who [sic] I dearly love" and though Hannah was but recently in her grave, Martin mentions her neither by name nor implication. But the bitterness that made him loathe the world is there in every line.

Back in Albany that spring he plunged into his work with an energy which for the only time in his life was motivated by hate. The Jackson toast had brought down a deluge of ridicule upon the Regency; another gubernatorial election was coming next year. Imploringly the Braves sought out their champion and begged him to lend a hand. The Regency waited to be reëstablished; the Bucktails, far and wide, longed to be led into new fields of plunder. Under the crust of his bitterness the old Urge was stirring in Matty Van. Whether he knew it or not he was glad to be back at this game in which he had no master. He scattered his four children among relatives and friends, looked over the field and prepared for the fray.

America never bred a political strategist who could stand against Martin Van Buren at the top of his bent. De Witt Clinton was so deeply entrenched in his office that it seemed nothing but death could dislodge him. Ambrose Spencer had been placed on the Bench for a life term, and was theoretically beyond reach of assault. Yet when Martin came to leave Albany two years later, both these men would have had their offices shot out from under them; Matty Van would have been elevated to a higher one than ever, and the Regency would be back in power with ten-fold strength.

It was during the period of his immediate bereavement

that Martin most seriously considered quitting politics, and is known to have told at least three men of his intention. He attempted through Barber to obtain a judgeship, and failing he returned to Albany half-expecting to make this session his last. But the Urge was not to be hushed. From Albany he wrote again to Cincinnati:

"I had intended to have left here . . . but, as it is, my desire to serve your dear friend *the Great Clinton,* will keep me here a few years longer."

6

(April 1819–November 1821)

Approaching the allotted span of three-score-and-ten, Mr. Rufus King also discovered himself approaching what to all appearances was the end of his long and praiseworthy career. His term as United States Senator was soon to expire and, being at the mercy of a Republican Legislature, he had no hope for reappointment. Not that the prospect of honorable retirement held any horror for Mr. King. To him public service was more of an obligation than an opportunity, and he could feel that he had done his share. He had helped to plan and then to fight the Revolutionary War; had sat in the Confederation Congress and the Constitutional Convention; had been New York State's first national Senator and sandwiched an ambassadorship between that first session and the one that was now waning toward its close.

Not a great man, perhaps, was Mr. King in comparison with some of those beside whom he had worked these past forty years, but he was an earnest, able, picturesque relic of a day that was fast fading. His was a creed of *noblesse oblige* which demands of the aristocracy that they rule with benevolence and rigor to protect the lower orders against false prophets. Sponsoring an imitation of the British system, he had violently opposed declaring the War of 1812; advocating freedom but not equality, he was far in advance of his time as a sane but active foe to Slavery. To him government was

[ 163

a guardianship, not a comradeship with the governed. Hand in glove with his close friend, Alexander Hamilton, he had fought the Constitution through to adoption, and labored thereafter for Federalist principles. When Hamilton fell, Rufus King had gone on as the acknowledged leader of the scattered forces, but as the Era of Good Feeling closed in, the Federalists practically ceased to be a national party. Mr. King had been their last presidential candidate in 1816 against James Monroe; this coming election of 1820 the Federalists would offer no national ticket. So far as service to the cause was concerned, Mr. King knew his usefulness to be at an end. Serenely he contemplated his retirement.

There were, however, four young men who lamented his passing almost to the extremity of grief. These were his two sons and the two sons of the slain Hamilton, all of whom had followed their fathers into what was left of the Federalist party, and all of whom regarded the old Senator as a sentimental bay tree in a wasteland of Republicanism. There was nothing, they agreed, they would not do to keep this grand old man in Washington. They found, during the spring months of 1819, a chance to prove it.

Returned to Albany from Hannah's grave, Martin Van Buren saw in the situation his opportunity to start re-founding the Regency. To entice the young Kings and Hamiltons into a bargain over the Senator's reëlection was not difficult, but there was a large moral barrier to hurdle. In the political decalogue there is but one cardinal sin. A man may knife his friends, rob the public and betray his conscience, but let him be even suspected of giving aid and comfort to the enemy, and there is no hell too low to hold him. Martin Van Buren was well aware of this dogma, and fully subscribed to it. Had he not consigned Mr. Clinton to this particular inferno for aiding King's election in 1812? But now the boot fitted another foot. The Clintonians held ample majorities in both houses, but a coalition of Bucktails and Federalists would overcome it. All unknowingly Rufus King, old-fashioned statesman and foe to everything that the Regency represented, was about to become the chief means for its restoration. Martin did not linger for long over the temptation. "Stimulated by the desire to obtain . . . . the votes and support . . . . of the Federalists . . . . I resolved to support his re-election."

The bargain was quietly made. It was understood and agreed that Matty Van should take command of both Federalists and Bucktails, working toward the double objective of Mr. King's return to the Senate and Mr. Clinton's return to exile. Once more in the lead of a deployable force, Matty Van spared no time at putting his program of reconstruction into action. His first move was to lay hands on some patronage, for the Bucktails were laborers worthy of their hire. The Council for the time being was not available but Martin, with his unvarying knack for opportunity, soon discovered a hitherto unexploited field, the winning of which would be a moral as well as a tactical victory.

For nearly two years Mr. Clinton's Erie Canal had been under construction, involving thousands of dollars in payroll and contracts. Needless to say, so long as the Governor had charge of his own beloved venture, there was no piracy aboard. Comfortably bulwarked behind a great personal popularity and legislative majorities, Mr. Clinton feared no evil either for himself or his project, but one day he knew that the Magician's hand had smote him again. Without warning or explanation, the Legislature suddenly upset the Governor's control of the Canal Board by removing one of his commissioners and substituting a notorious Bucktail.

Mingled with the Governor's scream of rage came gleeful shouts from the loot-hungry Regencymen. An inspection of the roll-call showed him that Matty Van had accomplished the deed by borrowing a bloc of votes from the minority Federalist party. Apparently there was some sort of a deal, but Mr. Clinton could not as yet guess the terms. Meanwhile he saw that the Regency was almost delirious with joy over its first taste of plunder in two years. The *Argus* insolently spread the glad tidings, announcing that it would no longer "be necessary for any person who wished employment on the Canal as agent, contractor or otherwise to avow himself a

Clintonian." Matty Van's abhorrence of the Canal turned to
gratitude, for, he says, "we derived more advantage from the
privilege and patronage attached to it than the Governor derived from the Council of Appointment."

From here on the work of reconstruction went speedily
forward. To clear the way for Mr. King's reëlection, Martin
dropped his own senatorial candidate, Colonel Young. To
clear the way for Mr. Clinton's departure, the Federalists
dropped their own candidate for the governorship. On behalf of Mr. King, Martin wrote a pamphlet which he felt
was better left unsigned, extolling the old Senator's patriotism and virtues. In damnation of Mr. Clinton, forty-eight
Federalist leaders issued an appeal to their constituents saying that "truly high-minded and honorable men" should
support the Bucktail candidate against the present Governor.
At this, Mr. Clinton perceived the extent of the plot to oust
him, and in his anger he became the Magnus Apollo of
yore. Reaching for the pen that had scorched Tammany and
flayed Spencer, he fell upon these defamers. Damning them
out of their own mouths, he added the expression High-
Minded to his already abundant store of invective, making
it live for a decade as a colloquialism for guilty hypocrisy.

But abuse from an adversary was never known to quell a
political plot. When the Legislature met to elect a Senator
in January, 1820, Martin noted with relish that the Clintonian candidate was no other than John C. Spencer, son
of the judicial Ambrose, who was now Chief Justice and
indulging his Urge vicariously as a party manager. Judge
Spencer's rivalry of the Little Magician enabled him to
witness many strange spectacles in his time, not the least of
which was to behold this day when a Republican Legislature
chose a Federalist candidate for the most coveted office in
its control. The Judge's candidate went down on the first
ballot before Rufus King, and the spirits that doubtless in-
fest Weehawken to this hour must have known astonishment
to see Mr. Burr's Sons of Tammany and Mr. Hamilton's Sons
of Federalism rejoicing over a common victory. Possibly the

most surprised person alive was Mr. King himself when he heard the news.

"The part taken by Mr. Van Buren," he wrote ponderously to one of his boys at Albany, "has indeed been most liberal . . . ; do not therefore fail to inform him that . . . . no occasion can arrive that I shall not be ready to prove him the personal respect and esteem with which he has inspired me."

"Respect and esteem" were not exactly what Martin was in need of at the moment, but he knew that having another United States Senator under obligations to him might some day come in very handy. Not to offend the old gentleman Martin voted in approbation of an anti-Slavery measure for which Mr. King was battling at Washington, and on top of this wrote him a note suggesting that Mr. Monroe might be probed into showing some interest for the Bucktail cause. Mr. Monroe responded by allowing Secretary Thompson to donate the Marine Band of the Brooklyn Navy Yard for parade purposes, but Matty Van's main concern with official aid from Washington was expressed in another epistle. Here marks the beginning of the Little Magician's scheme for a nation-wide Patronage System. Writing to Congressman Meigs, cousin to the Postmaster General, Martin demanded the instantaneous removal of three New York postmasters in favor of Bucktails. He could not hope as yet for the wholesale control of federal job-holders that he later accomplished, but he planned, as he wrote Meigs, "to alarm them with two or three prompt removals" for the sake of discipline. "If anything is to be done let it be done quickly." Quickly enough two of the postmasters were thrown out, and the net closed tighter about Mr. Clinton.

Martin had waited until the last moment for naming a candidate to carry the Bucktail colors against the Magnus Apollo. There is reason to think that he briefly regarded himself for the honor, but a few discreet inquiries soon convinced him that to give the voters a chance at his scalp would be a suicidal mistake. Even hope of winning reëlection as State Senator in his own Middle District was out of the question considering the widespread resentment against his methods. A little wistfully Martin agreed to keep his name off the ballot lest it weaken the Regency ticket. The Bucktails would need every advantage they could muster if they hoped to down the Great Clinton, and in the emergency Matty Van played his trump-card—he ordered Dan Tompkins to come home from Washington and stand again for the governorship. Grudgingly the Vice President obeyed.

Alas for Happy Dan! He allowed himself to play cat's-paw for the Little Magician once too often. His unwilling obedience cost him not only defeat but his honor, his health, his happiness and eventually his life. His would not be the first bright, trustful soul to be blighted when cleverer men have need of a tool to pick their political locks. Politics was never for the likes of Dan, but, as he, they usually find out too late. Back in the war-time, when Dan had first broken with Mr. Clinton and become affiliated with the embryonic Regency, large sums of money for military purposes had passed through his hands and through the hands of coöperating Bucktails, where some of it stuck. That Dan had appropriated any of it for his own use was never believed, but just the same his garbled accounts at the end of his term showed a shortage of some $110,000 for which he was undeniably responsible. The deficit had been known for three years, but had been put down under the inevitable waste of War. However, Dan's candidacy against Mr. Clinton was no sooner announced than the skeleton was dragged out of the closet and the press of the country blazed with the discovery that a Vice President's name was coupled with corruption.

That was the end of Happy Dan, though the shell of him lived on for the six years in which it required him to drink himself into a drunkard's grave. No more the bright lights of merriment knew him. Visitors who came to his Staten Island home remembered him sitting by the fireside or in the garden, a bottle always close by, his handsome face flabby and dull, his hand that had gripped a conqueror's sword trembling as it lifted a glass. Politics had done much for

Dan, had raised him from obscurity to honor, from farmer's son to Second Citizen of the Land, yet the last state of the man was worse than the first. Luckier he, if fame had left him alone.

But Dan's poison was meat to Matty Van. Advisers came telling him to scratch the name off the ticket, but the Little Magician knew better than that. Too well had he learned the value of martyrdom. From then on he directed the propaganda toward picturing Dan as a much-abused patriot. He wrote a pamphlet denouncing the denouncers, and he crowned the opportunity with the aforementioned speech, which was his masterpiece of sophistry. Rising in the Senate one day when the Vice President's reputation was in question, he made an address that Hammond heard and recorded as "most ingenious."

It must have been all of that. Instead of Dan's owing the State money, argued Matty Van, the State owed it to him, over whose official signature all the war-time loans were floated. Rather than ask the patriotic Tompkins to pay back $110,000, the State should regard him as its banker and give him 12½% accrued interest on all money obtained in his administration—which according to Mr. Van Buren's calculations came to exactly $11,870.50 over and above the disputed deficit. So inspired was the logic of Matty Van's deductions and so heart-rendingly did he depict the plight of this dear, noble patriot, unjustly besmirched, that a Brooklyn Bucktail burst into an uncontrollable spasm of weeping and had to be led from the room. The remaining Senators dried their eyes in time to give the resolution a 2-to-1 majority. The Attorney General, of course, declared the resolution unconstitutional but, though quashed, it furthered the theory of Dan's martyrdom.

Martin chose Washington's Birthday for his candidate's arrival in Albany to open the campaign. A crowd of the faithful met Happy Dan at the wharf, trailed his sleigh to the State House steps, and greeted his speech "with loud and repeated cheering." Once more the Farmer's Son and the Boy Lawyer swung round the circuit—a team that had never known defeat.

They lost—and yet they won. Dan did not beat Mr. Clinton, but he came within a scant 1457 votes of doing so, and Matty Van's Canal and Post Office patronage did the rest. "Clinton, though Governor," admitted one of his adherents, "was much in the condition of a pastor without a congregation." The Bucktails won a heavy majority in both chambers; they took over the Caucus; they recaptured the Council, and that was enough.

Out of office after eight years of service, Martin set up headquarters at 132 State Street, within two blocks of the State House. Spending most of his time in and out of the Senate Chamber and House he found it very convenient to be within walking distance. He was now in full command of both Republican and Federalist parties. One of his first cares was for the resolution to pay Dan's "interest." Unconstitutional or not, Matty Van had the measure passed, and coupled the gift to Dan with a renomination for the vice-presidency. One of his next was concerning Mr. Clinton's proposed investigation of a banking swindle which involved many Bucktails, including Matty Van's law-partner, Ben Butler. The investigation was blocked. Yet another was apropos of the Governor's attempt to prove an election fraud. Somehow Mr. Clinton had laid hands on Martin's incriminating letter to Meigs, and offered it with a mass of other data in the famous Green Bag Message. It was laughed off the floor.

When not busy at law-making Martin was in conference with the Council, for a house-cleaning was now in process the like of which had never been dreamed. The usual offices, of course, changed hands, but so did a multitude of others which no one had ever considered political prey. The State Comptroller had been at his post for fifteen years. He was ousted. The Adjutant General had been in for eighteen years. He was thrown out. The Superintendent of Public Schools had been in for nine years, ever since the beginning of organized education. He was replaced by "a mere collecting attorney." Never before had military commissions been tampered with. Over 8000 of them were thrown into the pot with something like 7000 civil offices, and were doled out with even-handed justice. There was only one qualification —friendship to Matty Van, who about this time was utterly overcome to learn that an appreciative coalition of Federalists and Bucktails had dragged Nathan Sanford out of his seat in the United States Senate and thrust that high honor upon their chieftain.

"I had," vows Martin in the *Autobiography*, "neither solicited the place nor taken a single step to promote the election."

In much the same spirit of *laissez-faire*, he continued fitting together his Regency. "Thousands and thousands of office-seekers," wrote the bedevilled Governor, trekked into Albany, howling for sinecures. Martin was building for the future. He bought a controlling share in the *Argus*, and made his brother-in-law editor. He added the New York *Advocate* to his string by creating its editor a Sheriff. William L. Marcy, another editor, was appointed Adjutant General. His father-in-law, a hat-maker, became State Treasurer. Martin's law-partner became District Attorney; Martin's half-brother became Surrogate; Martin's full-brother became Clerk of the Court; Martin's brother-in-law became State Printer. It were long to tell of the rest. Mayors and sheriffs; justices of the peace and notaries public—these and all offices in between were made and unmade under the supervision of the little Director.

And he had only begun. He had sworn never to rest until he had turned out Clinton and Spencer; this was not yet accomplished. Unfortunately there was no clause in the Constitution which commissioned a Senator-elect to oust a Governor and a Supreme Court Justice, but not even a Constitution was to stand in Matty Van's way. If it could not be discarded, it must be changed. And it was.

Among the recommendations which Mr. Clinton had put before his unruly Legislature was one to amend the Constitution so as to abolish the hated Council of Appointment and the equally hated restrictions on suffrage. None of his other suggestions had met with any success, so the Governor must have been mightily surprised when this one did. He had recommended simply putting these questions on the ballot, but Matty Van had the slightly different plan of letting the Legislature authorize a Convention to do the amending. The law-givers agreed; the Convention was called; the delegates were elected and met at the State House in August '21 for the alleged purpose of dooming the spoils system and giving the People their vote.

The Convention, however, did neither, and it was largely owing to a fair-haired little delegate from Otsego County who spoke several times on patronage and several more on universal suffrage with such ambiguous fluency that all agreed he was marvellously posted on his subjects, for he wafted his hearers into every State of the Union and into two countries of Europe. Martin, realizing that he stood no chance of being elected a delegate either from his home county of Columbia or his adopted one of Albany, had journeyed up the river and stood for a safe district in Otsego. His handling of the Convention was on a par with anything he had ever done in Senate, Caucus or Council. He did heatedly contend that such an autocratic institution as the Council of Appointment must go, but as chairman of the committee on that subject, he achieved the democratic triumph of shifting the appointive power out of the hands of five men into the hands of one: the Governor. He, furthermore, fell a-frothing over the thought that the People should be kept voteless, but somehow or other he deflected the Convention's attention to the plight of the American Negro in New York State, pointing out that the handful of blacks who had managed to attain both freedom and a little property were suffering the crime of taxation without representation. That atrocity was quickly adjusted, and in the furore everyone apparently forgot about the People. The voting qualifications were lowered; they were not abolished.

These defensive victories were but half of Matty Van's battle. When the smoke of combat cleared away the Convention saw that it had passed two very puzzling amendments which had nothing to do with the purpose for which the delegates had convened. One shortened the term of the Governor from three to two years; the other provided that Justices of the Supreme Court be shorn of their life-terms and that the personnel of the entire judiciary be revised.

It was July of 1820 when Martin ceased to be Senator at Albany, and December of the following year when he quitted the Convention to fare forth as Senator at Washington. As he set foot on the boat that would start him on the southward journey, his soul must have been sweet with the unction one feels for leaving a task well done behind him. In the last two years he had resurrected his fallen Regency and set it so firmly upon solid ground that it would stand unshaken for years to come. His enemies he had wholly vanquished. De Witt Clinton and Ambrose Spencer were already sentenced to private citizenship with carefully selected Bucktails waiting to step into their places. Truly, as Martin leant on the rail and looked up the hill to where he could see the roof of the State House, he beheld only a conquered province. There was nothing in Albany left for him to do.

The big side-wheels churned; the deck stirred beneath him. Once more a tide of his own choosing was bearing him on.

*BOOK III*

# CHAPTER I

# The Toga

SOMETHING else besides a conquered province did Martin Van Buren leave behind him as steam-boat and stage-coach bore him southward to the Capital City. Gone was the bitterness, the grief and the canker that had tinged his progress with vindictiveness since the parting with Hannah. Time, the great healer, had performed its cure quickly and completely with him. Removed from the scenes of his sorrow, he became once more his characteristic self. Blitheness and his sunny good humor returned; dispelled were the vapors that shut him off from his own personality.

Martin Van Buren was never a callous man, but essentially a shallow one. The loss of his love had stunned and hurt; it had not maimed or marked. The mind that found its favorite expression in petty intrigue and dandyism was as incapable of great, sustained emotion as it was of great ideas. Early in the term he was about to commence he is known to have proposed marriage to Ellen Randolph, a grand-daughter of Mr. Jefferson, and there are letters twitting him about having made similar advances to others. Had these been women of Hannah's own kind, it were possible to interpolate some sentimental motivation to his persistence, but all of them with whom he now associated were typical butterflies of society—as different from Hannah as he could possibly have picked. Yet a knowledge of these facts can reveal the man without degrading him. To be at 39 a United States Senator, well-to-do, well-known, widowed, handsome and simmering with social ambitions might have diverted one of a far sterner soul than his.

For both socially and politically, Washington of the early Twenties was a stage all set for the Little Magician's entrance. That is to say the social world was vividly alive; the political in a drowsy state of contentment. As the year 1821 came to its close, official affairs of the nation seemed truly to justify Mr. Monroe's pronouncement that America was living through an Era of Good Feeling. The passage of the Missouri Compromise Bill at the last session had stilled the echo of irate voices that were wont to rumble through the great dome of the rebuilt Capitol. The departure from Washington of Old Hickory had left the dignity of Cabinet meetings unrent by a major disturbance. In the White House Mr. Monroe looked forward blissfully to filling out his term without undergoing any of the harsh days each of his predecessors had known. In the State, Treasury, War and Navy departments, at the four corners of the presidential estate, Secretaries Adams, Crawford, Calhoun and Thompson pursued their labors with an industry uninterrupted by outside distraction.

Remarkable alone is the fact that the name which Mr. Monroe fastened on his administration has been accepted as an historical designation. War, corruption, strife and disaster are the usual milestones with which progress is blocked off, and the Era of Good Feeling stands as the sole example of a time that is remembered simply because national life ran smoothly. Most of the firebrand personalities who were soon to be setting things ablaze were not in action when Mr. Van Buren arrived. Clay and Webster were practicing law in voluntary retirement. Calhoun was enbalmed in a cabinet job. Randolph in the House was simmering quietly. Jackson, having resigned as Governor of Florida, was peaceably rusticating at the Hermitage.

It was the same with abstract matters. The two most threatening issues—Secession and Slavery—had momentarily been laid to rest with the failure of the Hartford Convention and the 36-30 agreement on Missouri's admission to the

Union. The two warring factions—the Republican and Federalist parties—had merged into one with Monroe's unopposed election in '20. Patriotism, fired by what General Jackson had turned into a victorious War, reached new heights of devotion. Westward expansion, aided by the ever-increasing network of roads and canals, by the sale of cheap land from the Government, by the encouragement of easy credit from the rechartered Bank of United States, was a triumphal procession. Post-war recovery of business, owing largely to Mr. Crawford's admirable work in the Treasury Department, gave promise of continued prosperity, and if there were skeptics who claimed to see lowering clouds behind the rainbow, they were an ignored and scoffed-at minority.

Looking back on the Era from the omniscient distance of another century, it is not difficult to identify it as a period of transition—a lull between two storms. It was the twilight hour for feudalistic government. So far, just as Mr. Hamilton had visualized, the country had been ruled by the ruling classes. Says a historian: "The Federalist party was destroyed by the success of its own principles at the hands of its opponents." The national Bank, the King Caucus, the Virginia Dynasty, were all Hamiltonian in spirit, though Jeffersonian in fact. Yet slowly and surely Republicanism was giving way to Democracy. The original Union of fourteen States had been safeguarded by voting restrictions, but since then ten new commonwealths had been added, all with universal suffrage, and the People stood on the threshold of power. The old order was passing, but knew it not, for neither Mr. Monroe, his four Secretaries or his patron saint at Monticello seemed at all aware that they were basking on the crater of a living volcano. And even Martin Van Buren, ever in readiness to board a new band wagon, almost misjudged the nearness of the People's day.

Not less socially than politically did the Capital City represent the innocent complacency of a passing régime. Dolly Madison had moved over the River to Jemmy's Montpellier, but her spirit marched liltingly on as ladies vied among each other for the queenship she had vacated. There was the enchanting Marcia Burnes, million-dollared wife of John Van Ness, who had hired Henry Latrobe, architect of the Capitol, to build her a $60,000 mansion at the foot of Sixteenth Street, facing the Potomac. Few could rival her in the flamboyancy of the parties she gave, but ladies like Louisa Adams, Sally Coles Stevenson and Cora Livingston—high-born Southerners all—could make things interesting. To own a front pew at one of the fashionable churches, to buy a houseful of slaves from the Market in Alexandria, to hold a box in the Washington Theatre, to run a winning horse on the National Race Course—all these were matters of stern competition among the peerage of the day.

Washington, in fact, had become the Versailles of the western hemisphere. No career—social, literary or diplomatic—was quite complete without presentation at the court. An out-of-town débutante was not really launched until at Washington she had sipped ice cream, a confection just coming into genteel usage; or at Washington had daringly essayed the waltz, a new-fangled step, the "decorum" of which, says Josiah Quincy, "was distinctly raised upon its first appearance." Mr. Jefferson's grand-daughters from Richmond, Dolly Madison's cousins from Philadelphia and the far-South —they and many others came to make their bow at the Capital city.

Of the American literati, not counting a host of journalists and pamphleteers, there was Washington Irving who arrived to match epigrams with Ambassadors and to call Jemmy Madison "a withered little apple-john." There was James Fenimore Cooper, who dashed off little dissertations to codify the official etiquette. There was Francis Scott Key who wrote satirical verses for the newspapers and hymns that were sung in the churches to please his proud mother. The parade of European lions that would culminate later on with Marryat, Dickens and Thackeray, had already begun. From Ireland came Thomas Moore who poked fun at Mr. Jefferson and jeered at the little City; from England came Harriet Martineau, reigning female essayist, and received six hundred callers on a single day. And among the diplomatists was the

Marquis de La Fayette, greatest of the years, who arrived aged and limping to be hailed by the President as "the guest of the nation."

It speaks well for the ingenuity of these gay villagers that they accomplished all this, for it was a strange pageant to be putting on against the background of savagery and wilderness. Here were Old World modes and morals transplanted from the Seine and Thames to the banks of a river which still flowed out of frontier country. Proud and loud were the praises of the new American culture, but real native customs, once a person crossed the District line, were looked upon with horror. Ladies and gentlemen dressed not in homespun and indigenous wool or cotton, but in the best silks and satins that ships could bring and money could buy. When Rachael Jackson was discovered to smoke a corn-cob pipe, she and this truly American way of enjoying good tobacco were denounced and derided; but when Dolly Madison performed the continental gesture of accepting a pinch of Henry Clay's imported Maccoboy snuff, she was distinctly a la mode and thus demonstrated the accepted procedure:

Holding in one hand a bandana handkerchief and in the other a flimsy thing of lace she said,

"Mr. Clay, *this* is for rough work and *this* is my polisher."

Thrift, simplicity, frugality were lauded as Jeffersonian, hence American, virtues, yet young gentlemen gambled away hard-earned fortunes, swilled unbelievable amounts of strong liquor, kept real and imaginary mistresses, fought comically Frenchified duels with the debonair abandon of King Charles cavaliers. Young ladies doted on secret trysts, swooned over love notes, planned unnecessary elopements as if they had just stepped out of a Sheridan comedy. It was all in the spirit of the day and place. When Henry Clay was said to have lost $8000 on a single evening of play and was delicately rumored to have kept anywhere from one to fifty mistresses, both black and white, it was blandly explained to a scandalized country that Mr. Clay was no different from the majority of his colleagues. When Andrew Jackson threatened to lop off the ears of his enemies, the threat was regarded in Washington as no less uncouth than it was terrifying; yet when Henry Clay shot a fellow lawgiver in the pantaloons, one of the seconds who later became a first-rate historian recorded the meeting "as about the last high-toned duel that I have ever witnessed." When Daniel Webster declined an affair of honor and offered to meet his challenger in a fist fight, he was considered no gentleman, but though the challenger, Randolph of Roanoke, appeared swinishly intoxicated again and again on the Senate floor, he was pointed out as the very pink of propriety. And when Peggy Eaton could have married any of several men in a perfectly respectable wedding, she bitterly complained that "marriage without an elopement would be heaven without harps and crowns and light and song."

Into the midst of this bizarre little world Martin Van Buren stepped as if it were one especially created for his talents and traits. He made, sad to relate, a rather inauspicious beginning by accidentally committing a social *faux pas*. Having a letter of introduction to John Randolph, Little Van hastened to pay his respects, only to be soundly berated by the Virginian for neglecting the custom that a Senator must never make the first call on a Congressman. But the rebuke whetted rather than dulled Mr. Van Buren's delight in formalities. Shortly afterwards some viceroys in Albany inquired whether, Spencer and Clinton having been ousted, Matty Van would like to be Chief Justice or Governor. "I answer no," he replied. "The situation I occupy is precisely the one . . . most agreeable to me."

His transfer from the State to the Federal Government broadened and matured the Little Magician, but it did not change him. He became at Washington the same mysterious conjuror of men and events that he was at Albany, made the same proportionate number of friends and enemies, dealt with them by methods he already knew to be effective. If his success was not quite so meteoric as it had been at home, that was because he was faced with a much larger task and, before long, with much strong opposition. Yet it is instructive to see that his general strategems in Washington were almost perfect parallels to those he had worked in Albany.

There was, for instance, his aversion to facing controversial issues and his agile ability to circumvent them. In this art he became increasingly proficient as he neared the presidency, but even in his senatorial period he was close upon perfection. When Henry Clay offered a Tariff Bill that put a heavy tax on woolen goods, Little Van, knowing that a vote either way would cause trouble in New York State, chose this moment to go sight-seeing around the new Congressional Cemetery, and at the end of the session to pay a visit to the Governor of South Carolina. Returning, he found the bill had passed the Senate by one vote and that he was being harshly denounced by the losing side at home. Therefore he went to Albany and made a speech which he promised would state his attitude emphatically. After the address the following conversation ensued between two of his listeners:

"Mr. Knower, that was a very able speech."

"Yes, very able."

A pause and then—"Mr. Knower, on which side of the Tariff question was it?"

"That is the very point I was thinking about when you first spoke to me, Mr. Wood."

Again, there was his glibness in easing his way out of personal embarrassments. One day in debate, finding himself about to be recorded on the wrong side of a dangerous question, Little Van rose and solemnly changed his vote. As he sat down, Senator Andrew Jackson, who then held the seat just in front, whirled and roared out:

"You give way, Sir!"

Little Van began one of his inspired explanations but "before I had finished . . . he stopped me and earnestly begged my pardon."

Yet again, and of greater importance, was his knack for coping with forces much stronger than himself. At Albany he had utilized Dan Tompkins and ambushed De Witt Clinton. He did the same with similar men at Washington. For Happy Dan whose popularity had been used to pull Matty Van's chariot, he substituted first Crawford and then Jackson. For the Magnus Apollo, whose higher conception of statesmanship had been troublesome, he encountered a legion of visionaries in Clay, Webster, Calhoun, Randolph, Adams and others. Every one of them became victims of the Little Magician's sorceries; every one of them became stepping-stones over which Little Van minced into the White House.

Where the once-pot-boy of a wayside tavern acquired the delicacy of social graces with which he was soon charming all Washington is another of the mysteries that continue to enshroud his memory. Surely none of his three home-towns —Kinderhook, Hudson and Albany—offered much training. In New York he stopped only briefly when the Court was in session, and if he really made a practice of rising before dawn to prepare his briefs, he could have small time for evening frivolity. For this problem there is a somewhat far-fetched solution which may not be as absurd as it sounds. Years later when Mr. Van Buren moved out of Washington, his household goods were sold at auction. Among these was an oblong rug which was remembered to have lain before a full-length mirror in his bedroom. The rug was worn threadbare and this, says legend, was because he used to stand on it for hours rehearsing his bows and foot work for the drawing-room.

If he did actually engage in this pantomime, it certainly served him well, for there is no doubt that he took the drawing-rooms by storm. Two months after his arrival Martha Jefferson Randolph wrote to her fiancé mentioning Abe's boy as the "rich, high-born Mr. Van Buren" and classing him with Senator Poinsett, "the most elegant man in the United States." Another gossiper says of him that he "was perhaps as polished and captivating a person as the social circles of the Republic have ever known." And still another bears detailed witness of his sartorial grandeurs:

"Mr. Van Buren was rather an exquisite in appearance. His complexion was a bright blend and he dressed accordingly. On this occasion he wore an elegant snuff-colored broadcloth coat with a velvet collar; his cravat was orange with modest lace tips; his vest was of a pearl hue; his trousers were white duck; his shoes were morocco; his neat fitting gloves were of yellow kid; his long-furred beaver hat with broad brim was of a Quaker hue."

It is not probable, though, that the Senator-elect burst upon the scene of his triumphs-to-be in any such glorious raiment or in any equivalent frame of mind. There was a double meaning to the proverb of the day which said that the closer a northerner came to the Capital City, the more multiple became his woes. To date six gentlemen residing north of the Potomac had seriously aspired to the mansion where Mr. Monroe now dwelt, and only one of them had ever attained it. He, John Adams, having successfully braved an election in which he beat Thomas Jefferson, came very near losing a wife in winning the victory. For attempting the ill-famed ride from Baltimore to the newly-named Washington, Abigail Adams lost her way in the swampy forests and might have perished miserably there had not a negroe squirrel-shooter come along and guided her through the morass. Nor had the two following decades made the last leg of the northern route much easier, and when Martin Van Buren made his first official trip it cost him $4.00 to be submitted to a forty-mile coach ride that would, according to all descriptions, have tried the soul and spinal column of a pioneer. Now the coach slithered hub-deep through mud and slush; now it bounded dismally over stony and frozen ruts; now it plunged crazily into treacherous fords where branches of the Patuxent River in winter flood sped over the road.

And even on entering the Washington environs there was little evidence of cheery civilization to lighten a traveller's heart. The forests had been only partially cleared away, a few fields were under cultivation, a cow or two nibbled dead grass by the roadside or was being milked there by a rustic who might stare vacantly at the passing coach.

How did he like Washington? a fellow-passenger once asked a foreigner who was gazing out on just this desolate scene for the first time.

"I will tell you when I see it."

"Why, you have been in Washington the last quarter of an hour."

Indeed in the Twenties and early Thirties anyone who came there expecting to see the City Beautiful was doomed to a shattered illusion. Capitol Hill and the presidential manor with their carefully kept gardens and meandering gravel paths, were sights to cheer the heart of either tourist or patriot, but in between and everywhere else was a forbidding expanse of stumps and mire. It looked to one observer "as if it has rained naked buildings upon an open plain and every man has made a street in reference to his own door." "As for lights," complained another, "if a pedestrian did not carry and provide his own he was in danger of discovering every mud hole and sounding its depth." "Everyone," scoffed a third, "knows that Washington has a Capitol, but the misfortune is that the Capitol wants a city."

Homes of the wealthy and fashionable were miles apart, separated rather than connected by roads worse, if possible, than the Baltimore pike. Until the mid-Thirties there was not a paved street in the District and except along Pennsylvania Avenue, no semblance of a unified town. Only when he rounded Capitol Hill and jolted on to the comparative smoothness of the Avenue could the traveller be at all sure that he, like the Second President's wife, had not gone astray in the wilderness. Here at last he saw, if not a city, at least a decent enough town with shops, taverns and three swinging hotel signs—Gadsby's, the Indian Queen and, nearer the White House, Fuller's. In case the traveller still felt skeptical about his chances for comfort he might proceed a little further and try one of the many boarding houses in Georgetown—where, in fact, most of the legislators chose to abide, and where of a December day, 1821, they were joined by the junior Senator from New York, of whom the senior Senator had written to forewarn them:

"He will not be there two weeks until he will know every man's opinion, but none will know his."

# The Toga

## 2

### (1822–1823)

Those two weeks—the time which Rufus King had allotted his junior colleague to acclimatize himself—were over,
and the fifth day of the New Year found Mr. Monroe's tall,
broad-shouldered, gawky body pacing the White House carpets in perplexity. Around him, though he could not have
guessed it, floated the tattered woof of his beloved Era. The
spell was broken; havoc was in the air, and a tempest, beginning in a tea-pot, would soon be sweeping the country to
uproot and rebuild its history.

In his quandary Mr. Monroe had just issued a hurry call
for a cabinet meeting; presently the Secretaries would be
there—wondering perhaps from the urgency of the summons
if another War were brewing. Had the trouble been of a
military or diplomatic nature, the President could have dealt
with it admirably, but for this sort of thing he had neither
aptitude nor experience. The gist of the whole commotion
was a disagreement on the naming of a new postmaster at
Albany—certainly of itself a trivial matter and ordinarily
not one to require the deliberations of a council of state. Yet
these, Mr. Monroe felt, were no ordinary circumstances and
two days ago the Postmaster General had paid him a frantic
visit to explain just why.

Any visit from the Postmaster General was enough to
upset the presidential peace of mind, for the doddering Mr.
R. J. Meigs was by all odds the most harassed and harassing
official in Washington. In 1812, as Governor of Ohio, he had
done notable work in blocking one of the British invasions,
for this good deed Mr. Madison had awarded him the
Post Office. It had always been the policy of the government
to use this department, and all other purely clerical jobs, as
honorary pensions for men past their prime who deserved
well of the Republic. Unfortunately for Mr. Meigs, however,
he assumed the post just at the time when the Union was

in its state of expansion, with the result that instead of inheriting a sinecure he was confronted with the baffling problem of managing 5200 branch offices on the same scanty allowance which Congress had granted him to manage the original 3000. Twice, when he unavoidably overdrew his budget, the Postmaster General had been hauled up before an investigating committee and, though he had come through both inquests with credit, the old man lived in mortal terror lest a misstep of some obscure subordinate would bring him dishonor. Going over his books at the end of the past year, he discovered that the much-dreaded catastrophe had finally happened. Solomon Southwick, postmaster at Albany, was several thousand dollars short on his accounts.

If shocked and chagrined, Mr. Meigs cannot be said to have been greatly astonished, for he long had reason to suspect that if corruption ever did come, it would come in the Empire State. They had, he knew, queer ideas of public responsibility up there. Shortly before he applied for the job, Southwick had been under indictment for bribery, but that did not seem to influence his supporters a bit. The Postmaster General had been informed that the Bucktails—whoever they were—insisted on Southwick and would hear of none other.

Bitterly Mr. Meigs berated himself for having agreed to the appointment, but it was too late now for vain regrets. The one thing was to remove Southwick as quickly as possible, and to replace him with a man of undoubted integrity. Just such a person Mr. Meigs had found in General Solomon Van Rensselaer—a wounded hero of two wars, brother of the Patroon and a gentleman whose very name was a guarantee of good faith. Moreover to appoint Van Rensselaer, who craved the $2000 salary so that "with strict regard to my duty I may sit down in comfort, peace and quietness with an affectionate family for the rest of my precarious days," would be both an act of deserving charity, and a direct rebuke to the Bucktails—for the General was an old-guard Federalist and one of those who had been swept out of office at the last Regency house-cleaning. On New Year's Eve, 1821, the New

York delegation in the House had endorsed Van Rensselaer and Mr. Meigs was on the verge of making the official announcement, when he received another communication— this one signed by Senator Van Buren, suggesting with ominous politeness that the appointment be withheld until "all concerned" had been heard from.

Here, Mr. Monroe might have summed up as he waited for the Cabinet to gather, was the real beginning of the whole affair. He might have added, had he been endowed with prophetic foresight, that it was also the beginning of Martin Van Buren's great gift to his country—the American Spoils System. The junior Senator, just settling himself in his new environment, had learned of Southwick's discovery in fraud too late to prevent the House delegation from backing Van Rensselaer. But learning, he acted quickly to rectify the error. Having dispatched the note to stay Mr. Meigs' hand, he lined up the fourteen men for whose presence at the Capital City either he or his Regency was responsible, and commanded them to stand firmly behind the ultimatum. Thus on January 3rd, and again on the 4th, Mr. Meigs burst in upon his chief with the unprecedented report that an aggregate of eleven Representatives, two United States Senators, a Secretary of the Navy and a Vice President were all up in arms over one of the most insignificant positions in the government service. What, he asked the President, was to be done?

Having no idea of the proper move for such an extraordinary circumstance, Mr. Monroe advised that they do nothing—nothing, at least, until he should have a chance to discuss the matter with Smith Thompson, New York's member of the Cabinet. He sent for Thompson and, although the conversation brought the President no closer to a decision, it did give Senator Van Buren more time to muster his forces, which he did with customary thoroughness. To Little Van there was more at stake than a mere $2000 plum for his Bucktails. Party politics was his life's work and this was a crucial moment in his career. There were 5200 postmasters in the country, each with four personally-appointed assistants, not to include the hundreds of other employees who owed their hope of livelihood to the Department. Allowing each of these men four or five dependants, it meant that to capture the Post Office was to assure himself of a solidly-voting nucleus in every State. It meant a chance to build up a nation-wide Regency, and as he wrote to a friend that week "I am for taking the bull by the horns at once."

He did. On the evening of the President's first talk with Meigs, Little Van was busy advancing upon his objective from several different angles. First he wrote another note to Meigs asking for a further delay of two weeks so that the matter could be leisurely considered. To his own signature he had Rufus King and Dan Tompkins add theirs. Then he called a meeting of the New York Representatives and had them draft a second plea for postponement, this one addressed to Mr. Monroe. Meanwhile he had begun a series of letters to his viceroys back home, calling on them to send individual protests, suggesting also that they organise a round-robin communication among the Republican members of the Legislature. Lest Southwick himself, that faithful Bucktail, feel offended at all this preparation to replace him, the Senator ordered him to be shown the correspondence "that he may know that we had not sought his removal" but were only acting in defense of the Party. And lest the President object on moral grounds to substituting one questionable character for another, Little Van picked the virtuous Chancellor Lansing as the Bucktail nominee against Van Rensselaer, reasoning that "the President being personally acquainted with the Chancellor, and entertaining a personal regard for him, we thought it the most likely mode of defeating the appointment of Van Rensselaer . . ."

But quickly as the Senator acted it was not quick enough to allay Mr. Meigs aversion to having a thief in one of his offices. To allow Southwick to remain at his post, drawing government salary for another fortnight while his very sponsors were arranging a substitute, was more than the old man could brook, and for the next two days he fairly hounded the President for a decisive opinion. Officially, of course, Mr.

# The Toga

Monroe had nothing to say about who should be postmaster at Albany, but Mr. Meigs, having made one poor selection, did not care to try again without the Chief Magistrate's sanction. All he asked was that Mr. Monroe give his approval of naming Van Rensselaer, but this the President considered too much of a responsibility to take without consultation. In the end—two days after the storm had broken—he sent for his councilors.

They came. The watery-eyed Mr. Adams, fast becoming ungracefully fat despite his vigorous efforts to keep off weight by breast-stroking nakedly across the Potomac all summer and tramping stolidly through the slush and mire of winter afternoons. The gigantic Mr. Crawford, no doubt casting covetous eyes about the First Citizen's palace and wondering how Susanna would care to refurnish it when they moved in on March 4th, 1825. The divinely-browed Mr. Calhoun, of whom a close friend once said "I never heard him utter a jest." The Regency's Mr. Smith Thompson, who harbored presidential yearnings himself and heartily wished Matty Van would choose someone else to pull chestnuts out of such injurious fires. And the Attorney General, the pious Mr. William Wirt, head of the Maryland Bible Association, and the only Marylander on record who ever received a presidential nomination—though he would have to join up with the malodorous Anti-Mason party to get it.

Mr. Meigs made his bow before the august Council, explained his side of the question and was excused from the room while the ministers bent their intellects to solve this perplexing problem.

He didn't, said Mr. Adams, see why the deputy postmaster couldn't take charge at Albany until Southwick's successor was chosen.

That, someone informed him, was impossible since the deputy happened to be Southwick's own son.

It seemed, put in Mr. Wirt, unworthy to be having a party squabble during this lovely Era of which Mr. Jefferson had spoken so sweetly: "We have called by different names, brothers of the same principles. We are all Republicans; we are all Federalists."

Such sweetness, interposed Mr. Thompson, might be all very well, but the Bucktails wanted the appointment and deserved to have it.

Mr. Calhoun loftily refused to enter into such a fruitless debate; Mr. Crawford, mindful of the coming day when he could not afford to have left behind any grudges, followed his example, and the President declared the meeting adjourned with the weary assertion that "he thought it very questionable whether he ought to interfere in the case at all."

Forced at last to decide the matter on its merits, Mr. Meigs dallied a day or two longer and then announced the appointment of Van Rensselaer. Once more the Bucktails at Albany knew that their Matty Van had suffered a reverse, but they were too wise in their old confidence to agree that he had lost the whole battle. Nor had he. Changing his tactics to suit the emergency, he despatched them more instructions. The Bucktails were now to hold a series of indignation meetings, protesting against the injustice of the Mr. Meigs' tyranny. They were to turn on him the full broadside of their invective, remembering, however, to spare all other members of the administration. Meigs must go. "Yes," replied a stalwart Regencyman by mail, "no other atonement can be made . . . to the injured feelings of the Republicans of this state than by the President's removing of the Postmaster General from office."

Meetings were held, pamphlets were published, cartoons drawn and editorials written. Mr. Meigs was the target of a barrage that damned him as the lowest of mammals. "Van Buren," a friend wrote to Van Rensselaer, "is determined, if possible, to remove the Post Master General, but he has not the *power*, though he possesses the *will*."

The gentleman was wrong about that. There was power and to spare behind these assaults. Mr. Meigs withstood them as long as he could, but in little more than a year he resigned and crawled back to Ohio to die, a man slain though no weapon had touched him. Into his place went John McLean, who understood so well what the Albany Director expected of him that he became in time the first official under whom that department gushed forth as the fountain head of party patronage.

This happy situation, though, was still in the future during Senator Van Buren's sessions of 1822–23, the most blissful, uneventful period of his entire career. Back at Albany the Regency was functioning smoothly under the lieutenants he had left in charge; his law business maintained itself without much need of detailed attention. In Washington the Era was falling apart, but the disintegration was slow and almost invisible. Political and social life there continued to represent the blind frivolity of a doomed epoch. There were portents of a coming unheaval, but the villagers and lawgivers found them easy to ignore. From his seat in the Senate Mr. Van Buren voted docilely to the Party's call, weaving his way as daintily among conflicting issues as he did among the dancers of the many cotillions he attended. Even on the matter of Mr. Monroe's successor he chose to be pleasingly vanburenish. His two papers, the *Argus* and the *Advocate*, were puffing Mr. Crawford, but Little Van, being reminded that both these editors were on the Regency payroll, declined to admit that they therefore expressed his sentiments. No one, not in his confidence, had the least idea where he stood on the question. A New York member of the House wrote home that "Van Buren is a Calhoun man." The Senator himself wrote a friend mentioning Adams, Clay and Crawford, overlooking Calhoun. A man as close to the Senator as Smith Thompson guessed so badly at his leader's intentions that he suggested himself for the nomination.

When neither at Washington, Albany nor before the Bar, Mr. Van Buren was using the recesses to widen his social acquaintance and with it his reputation as a willing candidate for remarriage. Hardly did the gavel fall on an adjournment than he was in his carriage and off on the rounds. The trail of calling cards which he left at famous houses from Massachusetts to South Carolina supports the theory that if he neglected anyone during his senatorial years, it was only Hannah's four orphans, who from her death until their manhood were farmed out among friends, relatives and boarding-schools. The four children also proved to be the only known circumstance which prevented Martin Van Buren from joining his line with that of Thomas Jefferson, for, according to her sister, Ellen Randolph's distaste for becoming a stepmother was all that kept her from accepting the charming Senator's hand.

In Ellen's company he visited her father, the Governor of Virginia, and later her grandfather at Monticello. The several days spent with Mr. Jefferson seem to have been equally delightful to guest and host, for the visit began a friendship and an intimate correspondence between them that lasted till death did them part. Not to overlook the proper formalities, the Senator followed his call at Monticello with a visit the next summer to Quincy, where old John Adams "received me kindly." And lest the shades of the First President should feel any neglect, Mr. Van Buren arranged his crowded schedule so that he might spend a Christmas at Mount Vernon as guest of its heir, Bushrod Washington.

Closely related to his infatuation for high names and bright places was the Senator's passion for elegant and sonorous titles. In 1823 this craving came very near losing America her Little Magician of politics. Visiting Rufus King's country home at Jamaica during the Easter holidays of that year, Mr. Van Buren, remarking that death had left a vacancy on the United States Supreme Bench, let it be known that he would like to have it. It meant a life term with no more elections to worry about and ample chance to indulge at social adventuring. Somewhat taken aback that a man of 41 and the most casual sort of a lawyer should aspire to this high tribunal, Mr. King agreed to help only if Little Van, once appointed, would forswear politics forever. To this promise the junior Senator readily gave his word and Smith Thompson was enlisted to the cause. King and Thompson both engaged themselves to write letters of recommendation to Mr. Monroe and the Secretary of State, but late in the summer the plans fell through. Thompson, being denied the Regency's nomination for the presidency, decided to go after the justiceship himself and succeeded at the price of his Director's friendship.

Not quite certain whether to be relieved or disappointed, Senator Van Buren returned that winter to Washington and to more congenial activities. For the time was now come when, as he expressed it,

"I made my début in the art and business of President-making."

### 3

### (1824)

The Act of God had fallen and laid Mr. Crawford low. No longer did he stride the Capital City's streets like a proud Goliath, but lay in his bedchamber at Fourteenth and Massachusetts Avenue, a broken and twisted wreck. Without warning, without foreboding symptoms, a stroke of paralysis had seized upon him and ripped the strength from his body. He could not walk, nor talk, nor read, nor even sign his name to the departmental documents. Only his mind remained intact, and into it, as into a lucid mirror, he could look and see the ironic pathos of his plight. For years he had patiently awaited his chance at the presidency, had stepped aside in 1816 and again in 1820 to let the Virginia Dynasty name its man, and now, himself the Dynasty's candidate, fate had tied his hands with the ambition of a life-time almost within his grasp.

His bodily affliction was not the only change that had come over Mr. Crawford during the past several years, and without much trouble he could have traced the beginning of his transformation back to the time when he first came into contact with the dapper little manager from New York. Till then Mr. Crawford's sense of ambition had been a thing which he scrupulously repressed, something that always took second place to his conception of duty to the State. Circum-

stance, his friends' belief in his ability and never his own aggressiveness, had thrust him into every one of the high offices
he had held. To have connived and bartered for selfish promotion was wholly beyond and beneath him—until, ever so
gradually, he felt himself becoming infused with an understanding of the new politics. Henceforward he was a different
man—one of whom John Quincy Adams could say with
more flattery than injustice—"His talent is intrigue."

It was not so much a talent as a lesson he was trying without much success to learn. He discovered that in order to
maintain his position as leading candidate for the presidency,
he must evade all injurious controversies, and this was the
easiest of his tasks. He discovered that in order to keep his
name before the public, he must spend money on editors
and pamphleteers, and when it came to recouping the funds
thus spent, he found that he could very handily use the inside information of his Treasury Department for speculative
purposes. Lastly, he discovered that in order to ensure help-
ful support for himself, he must give the appointments of his
Department to the right, though not necessarily the righteous, persons named by his manager.

These last two efforts of Mr. Crawford to live up to the
new creed of politics were so unnatural to his disposition that
before very long he made a frightful mess of them. When
word got out that the Secretary of the Treasury was reaping
some very large and suspicious-looking profits by speculation,
people began to talk, and finally he was openly accused of
malfeasance of office. A congressional committee, including
Webster, Randolph and Livingston, investigated the accusation, and though they exonerated Mr. Crawford on technicalities, it did his reputation no good. Worse than that was
the unspeakable blunder he made over distributing his patronage. One day he went to the White House with a list of
men he intended to recommend for office, and when Mr.
Monroe reprovingly declined to accept a single one of them,
the Secretary flared up and brandished his cane, made at the
President, shouting,

"You damned infernal old scoundrel!"

## The Toga

Mr. Monroe's spryness in grasping a pair of tongs with which to ward off his infuriated minister saved the presidential head a cracking, and in that position of defense he seized the bell cord and ordered Mr. Crawford off the premises before he should call the servants and have him thrown off. Recovering himself, Mr. Crawford departed and soon returned with profuse apologies, which were rather huffily accepted, but from then on Mr. Monroe gave no active assistance in aiding the man whom the Dynasty had chosen for his successor.

Despite the Georgian's distressing lack of finesse as a candidate, Senator Van Buren quietly stuck by his man and hoped for the best. Without giving the impression of personal interest he allowed his papers to fly the candidate's name, and during the investigation he remained in Washington as legal counsel. The secret pact with the Georgia delegation for a Crawford-Van Buren ticket still held good, and till the very eve of the presidential year it offered every promise of success. As heir to King Caucus, as candidate of the Dynasty and of the Regency, Mr. Crawford was protected both from the rivalry of fellow statesmen and from the onrush of the People, who by 1824 had gained the right to vote in 18 of the 24 States. So far as mortal mind could predict, William H. Crawford would be nominated by the Caucus, set before the country as the regular Republican candidate, elected without serious competition, and the Little Magician, whether as Vice President or presidential manager, would profit accordingly.

But the divine visitation of the Secretary's paralytic stroke altered the whole case. The Republican statesmen might be willing to accept the Dynasty's guidance in any reasonable matter, but they balked at the thought of putting a sick and apparently dying man in the White House. The Georgian's disability, they felt, removed him from consideration and opened the field to all comers. They needed no bugle to call them to the lists. At one time there were as many as 16 claimants for Mr. Monroe's palace, and when the dust of the cavalcade began to settle, Little Van saw that his man had slipped from first place in the rating to a distant fifth behind Adams, Jackson, Calhoun and Clay.

Here was a disheartening setback. However others might feel on the subject, Mr. Van Buren was not at all averse to being Vice President for a man whose days were numbered. And supposing he missed the vice-presidency, he was bound to go into the cabinet if Mr. Crawford became Chief Magistrate. Carefully as he guarded his secret there seems to have been one person alive at the hour who read the Little Magician's mind. Wrote a son of Rufus King:

"The apparent question now before the public is 'Who shall be our next President?' but the real question is whether Martin Van Buren shall be President of the United States on and after March 4th, 1833."

Nursing such thoughts, Mr. Van Buren wasted no time in lamentations for his candidate's misfortune. Already State Legislatures and impromptu conventions were nominating favorite sons with bewildering rapidity. The Capital City buzzed with the goodly gossip of an open season on the presidency. An enterprising firm in France was shipping over silk waistcoats "stamped with pretty good likenesses of Washington and the presidential candidates." No longer could the Albany Director afford to maintain his equivocation. He let it be known that Mr. Crawford was his choice, and with no more ado he set to work.

If he did not know so beforehand, Little Van soon found out what inspired jockeyship would be required of him. Not only was he attempting to win with a crippled candidate unable to lend any assistance, but he was competing with the strongest and most numerous field that had ever tried for the Republic's first prize. Moreover, he was carrying the additional impost of having to oppose the two popular issues of the campaign: abolition of King Caucus and the grant of universal suffrage, for the People's cry the country over was that they be allowed to nominate and elect their own First Citizen—nominate him in a series of open conventions and elect him through electors of their own picking.

Neither of these demands, of course, could the Director

agree to accept. The Caucus had been his favorite arena since the first day at Albany and it was Mr. Crawford's one hope for a respectable nomination. As for universal suffrage, that would decide the election then and there in favor of Old Hickory. The hero of New Orleans, considered a joke eight years ago, had been artfully brought along by his two Tennessee managers—Major William B. Lewis and Major John H. Eaton—and even with a fourth of the States not voting, he was certain to make trouble for the other candidates.

Deftly Little Van moved to preserve his meagre advantages. The institution of Caucus nominations was not founded on legal statutes; it was merely a traditional form that could not be abolished by act of law. Responding to the People's cry, a two-third majority of Congress informally agreed to a toothless resolution that the practice was "inexpedient" and should be dropped. Undisturbed, Little Van took the situation in hand and called a meeting of the Republican Caucus "to recommend candidates to the People of the United States for the offices of President and Vice President."

It convened at the House chamber February 14th, the last national Caucus ever to be held and also the only one of its kind. There were 256 Republicans in Congress at the time, only 66 of whom, representing but 4 States, dared attend this gathering held in the face of popular and official disapproval. Two of the members, torn between fear of the People and loyalty to Little Van, coped with the dilemma by sending proxies, while a group of others, arriving to find themselves so few, moved for immediate adjournment.

This, however, was not the will of their Director. He dismissed the motion with reassuring words and quickly arranged the nominations. For several weeks in advance he had come to realize that the best chance of electing Crawford was to team him with a strong running-mate. Obviously a Crawford-Van Buren combination would be tempting providence too far, but Crawford-Clay or Crawford-Calhoun would have the two-fold virtue of removing a rival and enlisting an ally. Accordingly Little Van had approached both these gentlemen only to meet with rebuff. Mr. Clay refused on the ground that the offer would have to be made to him "by the public having the right to tender it," while Mr. Calhoun frankly declared he would not care to be identified with the Caucus clique.

Unable to find a suitable Second Citizen among those close at hand, Little Van searched back among the elder generation of statesmen. There he found the aged Albert Gallatin, a wealthy Swiss-born French nobleman who had done excellent work in the Treasury Department under Jefferson and Madison, an intimate of La Fayette and now an adopted son of the highly important State of Pennsylvania. The hope that Citizen Gallatin might wean Pennsylvania's 28 votes away from its idol, Old Hickory, had suggested the nobleman's name to the hard-pressed Director and caused him to bring it before the assembled Caucus. Lest the farce be entirely too evident, the voting was arranged so as to give some suggestion of spontaneity and struggle. Mr. Crawford won a stirring victory for the nomination over three other candidates by the count of: Crawford 64, Adams 2, Jackson 1, Nathaniel Macon 1. And Citizen Gallatin likewise distinguished himself with 57 votes against 9, which were scattered among eight rivals.

Having preserved and utilized the Caucus to start Mr. Crawford along the way, the busy Senator now turned to his other problem—the much more difficult one of staving off the People. It would not do for him to be known as a schemer against their rights so, in order to place himself on the record, he offered a Constitutional amendment to the Senate which, after a long and elaborate preamble setting forth stalwart American principles of fraternity and justice, provided that all voting restriction in presidential elections be removed—*after this present campaign was over*. The measure was duly recorded, proving to anyone who cared to investigate that Senator Van Buren was a true democrat, and then it was referred to a committee, where it lingered and died.

So far the Red Fox had done not badly in the budding

campaign, but as it waxed hotter, troubles fell upon him thick and fast. First of all, the Gallatin nomination turned out to be a wretched blunder, and one unbelievably stupid for a man who a few months before considered himself well enough posted on the Constitution to try for the Supreme Bench. Article II Clause 5 was explicitly intended to disqualify anyone of foreign birth from holding either the presidency or the vice-presidency, and even if this difficulty could have been coped with, an alien seemed scarcely the right one to pit against a man so vehemently American as Andrew Jackson. The Bench and the Press mingled their cries of protest, and Mr. Crawford's chances sunk lower.

Finally Gallatin authorized his sponsors to cancel the nomination if they saw fit, but still the Senator hesitated. Despite the miscarriage of the plan, it is possible to construe Little Van's whole action as much cleverer than it appears. He may have grasped it as the one chance of combating Old Hickory with his own weapons. Gallatin represented the Revolutionary period, in which he had been conspicuously active as a hater of tyrants; he represented the last vestige of the Jeffersonian days, had the Third President's sanction and, what was more, had a very useful campaign ally in La Fayette, who was being fêted all over the country during the campaign. There was at least a vague chance that the combination of all these circumstances might stampede Pennsylvania away from Old Hickory. The prospect vanished, however, when a Jackson ticket swept the State, and thereupon Little Van removed Gallatin's name and substituted his own—which he may have intended doing all along.

If he did so intend, he certainly miscalculated the forthcoming results. In the midst of the race Mr. Calhoun withdrew as a presidential entry and announced himself as a candidate-at-large for the second office. All factions were urged to unite behind him, enough in itself to ruin any other man's hope, although the Senator now had no choice but to remain in to the end. Then, too, there was a group in the Georgia Legislature which was heartily ashamed of having their Mr. Crawford become a satellite to the Albany Direc-

tor, and soon they were expressing their opinion of Senator
Van Buren by nominating him first for doorkeeper, then
dog-whipper, and then for any other such honors as their
imaginations could invent. The whole country joined in the
sport of baiting the Red Fox, and Martin Van Buren experienced the première of what was to become a very familiar
ensemble—the nation-wide chorus of hoots and jeers. He
found himself the subject of ribald ballads and songs; he saw
his face in cartoons attached to the unflattering bodies of
snakes, cats, monkeys, foxes and minks, all of them conveniently labeled "Little Van," "Blue Whiskey Van," "The
Red Fox," "the Little Magician" and a few more of the
pseudonyms by which his fellow citizens came to know him.

Truly it was one of those periods of low tide with which
the story of Martin Van Buren is so prolific, and things
would have to get much worse before they could get better.
He had successfully diverted the People's hope for universal
suffrage by his facetious Constitutional amendment, but the
ghost refused to be laid and it appeared again in the home
State. If the national Constitution could not be amended,
came the demand, then why not the State Constitution? A
new faction—the so-named People's Party—had risen in the
Empire State, had won some seats in the Legislature and was
vociferously advocating a bill which would remove all voting
restrictions. Much depended on the Governor's attitude, and
Joseph C. Yates, whom the Regency had installed in that
office, was showing definite signs of restiveness against the
way he was being ordered about by Matty Van's agents.
Twice he had run afoul of the Director's pleasure by attempting to put men of high standing into appointive offices,
only to have the Senate—for he needed its approval—turn
them down. At the January session of 1824 the Governor had
allowed himself to be bullied into recommending "that the
State law remain as it stands," and the Electors Bill, having
passed the House, was beaten by the Regency majority in the
Senate. However, such a clamor had been raised over the
bill's defeat that the Governor suffered a change of heart
and with regained courage called a special session for Au-

gust, demanding that the Legislature give the People "their undoubted right." There was wide alarm among certain statesmen at the prospect of seeing New York surrender its feudalistic rule, and among the alarmists was—of all persons to express fear at seeing men become free and equal— Mr. Jefferson. Little Van calmed the old philosopher's fear with a letter to him promising that "the legislature will do nothing that they ought not to do," and set off to Albany to make certain.

The Senator need not and probably did not disturb himself much over the fear that the Electors Bill could possibly pass. He had 17 trusty Bucktails in the State Senate, a majority that could block anything the House or the Governor proposed. The Regency, in fact, made short shift of the trouble. The first motion in the Senate laid the bill on the table and the second called for immediate adjournment. Both carried, and that settled the Electors Bill, though it passed the House amid a four-day display of oratory that boded ill for the insolent Regency. When Matty Van reached his domain he found it in such a turmoil as he had never seen. Both banks of the Hudson rang with the clamor of indignation meetings; in the City ten thousand citizens met, marched and bawled maledictions on the Bucktails. In the fields as he drove along, he saw scarecrows labeled "Regency"; he saw stuffed dummies hanging from trees, tagged with names of his viceroys; he saw prescription lists of the "Immortal Seventeen" posted on the walls of the taverns where he stopped to dine.

The resentment over the Electors Bill accounted for part of the popular uprising, but not for all of it. Drunk with power and defiant of opposition, Van Buren's viceroys had signalized their high spirits by aiming a punitive blow for good measure at their old enemy, the Magnus Apollo. Since his retirement from the governorship, Mr. Clinton had been living contentedly among his family, interested only in his books, his writings and above all his precious Canal, the opening of which was scheduled for next year. He was serving as unpaid chairman of the Canal Board when, without warning or reason, the Bucktail Senate suddenly removed him. Matty Van had shuddered when he first heard the news, and by the time he reached Albany his worst fears were realized. It was a case of history's repeating itself. Just as the Bucktails had martyrized Mr. Clinton by dismissing him from the mayoralty in 1815, so they had acted again, and with the same results. Gubernatorial elections were now held in the fall and the People's Party, looking for a candidate who could beat the Regency, rallied joyfully around the Magnus Apollo at the close of the special session.

Even the presence of their matchless Matty Van could not save the Bucktails at this short notice. Yates was discarded for his insubordination, and one of the old war-horses, Colonel Young, hastily groomed for the forlorn hope of heading off Mr. Clinton. But it was no use. Day by day the People's party was gathering strength and, long before the polls were open, the Magnus Apollo was a conceded winner. It would have been difficult to find in Albany a sadder man on a morning of November 1824, than Judge Roger Skinner, the viceroy whose brain had conceived the scheme which had wrought such havoc. Timorously, and with hanging head, he slunk into Matty Van's dining room where the Director was gloomily eating breakfast, and announced that the returns were fast confirming the Clinton election.

"I hope, Judge," purred Matty Van, "you are now satisfied that there is such a thing in politics as killing a man too dead."

But it was no time for petty grudges. The post-Election Day was the date when the legislators would meet to select the presidential electors. Theoretically the Regency was still intact, but it was sorely shaken and its enemies heartened by yesterday's rout. The Immortal Seventeen still held sway in the Senate; in the House 43 Bucktails waited to do their manager's bidding, but the opening manoeuvres of the joint session showed that Matty Van lacked a majority over all. The first test vote revealed the situation:

## The Toga

The Bucktails shook in their shoes. Let the Adams-Clay men form a coalition, as they were threatening to do, and that would be the finish of Mr. Crawford. What irony if Matty Van, who had taught the use of the majority lash, should have it laid across his own back! But Matty Van was not worrying. To be sure, there was an Adams-Clay combine, but for weeks a Tammany Sachem named Henry Eckford had been working among them with good effect. He had contrived to bribe enough Adams followers to cast Crawford votes on the secret ballot, thus giving the Regency its majority, which Matty Van would quickly turn into 36 electoral votes for William H. Crawford.

So at least it was planned and would have turned out had not this been the occasion chosen by fate for Martin Van Buren's first meeting with the Nemesis which would be his final ruination. While Eckford's go-between had been trailing his prey, he in turn was being shadowed by a tall, swarthy young man whose name at the time meant nothing. Thurlow Weed, at 28, had been farm hand, blacksmith, vagabond, pot-boy, soldier and printer's devil, and several years earlier he had lost his job on the *Argus* for refusing to vote a Bucktail ticket. Wandering on to Rochester, he had founded an anti-Regency paper of his own and, feeling the Urge, made it his ambition to become a political manager. During the special and regular sessions of 1824 he had haunted the State House for whatever good it might do him, and several weeks before the November meeting he had smelled out a plot. Suspecting Eckford, Weed followed the go-between from Albany to Syracuse, from Syracuse to Albany, from Albany to New York and back again to Albany. He had overheard the bribery scheme and, calling together the Adams-Clay leaders, he proposed a counter-plot. Instead of making the discovery public, suggested Weed, they should simply corner the traitors and threaten them with exposure unless they performed the double deceit of betraying their bribers.

The plan was perfectly conceived and carried out. Two nights before the joint session Weed had printed Adams-Clay ballots and passed them among his cohorts. But not until that morning when the Regency chairman, Erastus Root, began his task of reading off the votes was the secret out. Instead of announcing what he read on the first slip, the chairman recoiled with astonishment and shouted:

"A printed split ticket!"

"Treason, by God!" yelled a Bucktail from the floor, and a moment later his companions were rushing from the room in order to prevent a quorum and to force a recess in which they might confer with the all-wise Director. But even against this ruse Weed had prepared. A Clintonian was on his feet, screaming at the fleeing chairman, who was leading the stampede to cover.

"I demand under the authority of the Constitution of the United States, under the Constitution of the State of New York, in the name of the whole American people, that this joint meeting of the two houses of the Legislature shall not be interrupted in the discharge of a high duty and a sacred cause!"

There was no defying such a wholesale invocation of political holy writ. Back to their seats slunk the Bucktails, shuddering to find that of the 32 electors chosen on first ballot not one was for Crawford. Once the tide was stemmed, Matty Van made a quick bargain for the 4 remaining votes, but he had been ignominiously trounced and no one knew it better than the man who had trounced him.

"Had our secret transpired before the first ballot . . ." rejoiced Weed in his journal, "the whole Crawford ticket would have been chosen."

Still there was glory enough for them both. If Weed's surprise attack had gained him the lion's share of the stake, then Matty Van's belated rally had salvaged enough to rescue his candidate from a larger defeat. Back in the summer the Senator had come to realize, along with the rest of the politically-minded country, that the presidential election would not be decided in November. With four runners in the field, none could win the clear majority required by the Constitution. The lowest would be automatically dropped and the other three fight it out in the House of Representatives as Jefferson and Burr had done at the beginning of the century. Little Van's sole anxiety had been that Crawford might be eliminated, and this the Director had prevented by the exact margin of those four votes from New York. Down in Washington for the meeting of the Electoral College, he saw how narrowly he had managed to edge his candidate into the finals.

| | |
|---|---|
| Jackson | 99 |
| Adams | 84 |
| Crawford | 41 |
| Clay | 37 |

Pride, if not complete satisfaction, the Senator could feel for his maiden attempt at "the art and business" he had chosen. He had not won a clear-cut victory but, operating under every known handicap, he had brought his entry up to even terms with the leaders. True he had erred on Gallatin, and was caught napping against Weed, but all in all he had had more bad luck than bad judgment. It was discouraging enough that his man was a bed-ridden cripple, regarded by most of the country as *hors de combat*, but even in the bloom of health Mr. Crawford would have been no ideal candidate against strong competition. Had he not been stricken the chances are that he would have been Sixth President, for he was the Dynasty's choice and his paralytic stroke was the deciding factor that discredited the Caucus and brought Adams, Clay and Calhoun into the contest. These three must certainly have supported the Georgian strenuously against the wild man Jackson, and though such mathematical post-mortems are at best conjectural, it is hard to see how Old Hickory could have won under any circumstances in 1824. By another four years only one State instead of six would still have restricted suffrage, and then the People's time would have come, but not before.

When the field was thrown open Mr. Crawford's physical

disability was but one of his drawbacks. He had been accused and tried for corruption; he had been caught in the act of playing politics with his patronage; he was severely judged by the company he kept with the unloved Albany Director, and he was in no sense a match for any of the three men running against him. On sheer merit for statesmanship he was not in the class with John Quincy Adams; for popularity he might as well have been running against George Washington as Andrew Jackson, and in Henry Clay he met a man who had never been equalled in American politics for the faculty of making real and affectionate friendships. "I don't like Clay," said Calhoun once. "He is a bad man, an impostor, a creature of wicked schemes. I won't speak to him but, by God, I love him." So did everyone else—and no one ever spoke that way about Mr. Crawford.

All things considered, the wonder is that the little Director kept his man in the running as long as he did. To have brought the Georgian through the preliminaries was of itself a remarkable feat, and the Little Magician was not yet finished, for at the House election he came within the proverbial hair's-breadth of pulling off a seeming miracle. He did not win with Mr. Crawford, but he came so close to doing so that it took the combination of Henry Clay and another Act of God to forestall him.

4

(December 1824–February 1825)

"I have, I think," wrote a young man in his diary, "found the way to be popular in Kentucky. Drink whiskey and talk loud . . . and you will hardly fail of being called a clever fellow."

The young man being, at the moment he penned these lines, a tutor in the Kentucky home of Mr. Henry Clay, it would not be strange if he were thinking of his employer in evolving this maxim of success. For Henry Clay was far and away the most popular man in all the Blue Grass State; there

208 ]

could scarcely have been a citizen to deny his being a clever fellow, and if whiskey and talk were not the most essential ingredients of his success, they were decidedly the most spectacular. For thirty years it was the abiding wonder of congressional and social Washington how this Harry of the West was able to consume the amount of intoxicants he did and yet retain the poise and perpendicular that he also managed. One gray dawn after a purple night he sauntered back to his lodgings with a friend for a few hours' rest before the House should convene at noon.

"How can you, under the circumstances," murmured the friend, "preside over the House today?"

"Come and see," the Speaker told him. The man says that he came and that he saw, but he never attempted to explain.

As to Mr. Clay's ability for talking there are such a legion of witnesses that to list them and their testimony would run *The American Talleyrand* into a second volume. There was, for instance, the Congressman who was sent to the House, so he said, for the sole purpose of "opposing Clay."

"Gentlemen," he confessed shortly after arrival, "I have been warned by the Legislature and threatened by the White House, but I'm damned if I can listen to Mr. Clay speak and believe he is wrong."

In 1797 the Mill Boy of the Slashes first set foot in the State that would elect him time and again to high public office, and never once over a period of five decades fail to give him a sweeping majority of confidence and votes. He had wandered out from Hanover county, Virginia, he said, "to grow up with the country." In his pocket he carried a license to practice law, and in his eye was an engaging sparkle that might have been either the light of unobtrusive good humor or the quickening flame of ambition. It turned out, as the inhabitants of Lexington soon discovered, to be a generous combination of both. He was not much to look upon, this immigrant just emerging into his twenty-second year, for in Kentucky of those days a man could be two inches over six feet, lean, high-headed and lantern-jawed without exciting much comment. But there was definitely a man-to-man attractiveness in the mobile expressions of his homely, oblong face, and give young Henry Clay a group of buck-skinned, long-riflemen about a tavern table, not even the tall tales of Daniel Boone could compete with the flow of his utterance on whatever subject that came up.

Seated, Henry Clay could spellbind an audience, but on his feet he could fairly hypnotize it. He was more than a speechmaker; he was an actor. His voice, men said, was the finest musical instrument they had ever heard. It could soar; it could roar; it could rhapsodize. It could, by the subtlest of inflections, set them slapping their knees in laughter; holding their breaths with suspense; blinking back tears, or turning derisive sneers on his adversaries as an insinuating vein of contempt flowed into his tone. And those gestures—! His hand laid over his heart to avow sincerity; his fist crashing to the desk to drive home a point; his arms stretched toward them in appeal; his long, freckled forefinger wagging at the sky. . . .

There must have been men in Kentucky, and later throughout the country, who believed Henry Clay to be a native, heaven-gifted genius of the oratorical art; that, perhaps, he had inherited his talents from his dead father, a Baptist minister known in Hanover County "for his fine voice and delivery." But the fact seems to be that this man, all in all the grandest speechmaker that America ever reared, came into the world gifted with nothing but the ambition to make himself just that. A pathetic stammerer in childhood, fellow residents in Hanover county were to remember, after he became famous, that many a time they had seen and heard him learning to master his tangled tongue while herding his family's hogs and cattle or riding to and from the mill at the Slashes. Later in young manhood he tells of himself that he made it an everyday rule to skim through a book on history or science and then recite it as an off-hand speech, "sometimes in corn fields, at others in the forest and, not infrequently in a distant barn with only the horse and the ox for auditors."

At Lexington he found the juries no more than his willing victims. Most of his cases at first were crimes of violence and it is said that he never lost a murder trial. Once a killer for whom he had gained an acquittal came tearfully to offer him thanks.

"Ah, Willis, poor fellow," said the attorney, "I fear I have served too many like you who ought to be hanged."

The conscientious qualm against misusing his talents moved Henry Clay to give up the exciting pursuit of cheating the gallows and to accept his first public office as Prosecutor. But he was never a man to pass judgment on his fellow-creatures, and after the rending ordeal of seeing his first case go to the hangsman he resigned and deserted criminal law for the less thrilling, but more lucrative, business of civil practice. Yet even when he became one of the highest-priced corporation lawyers in the country, he could never resist accepting gratis cases in the criminal courts when he felt that justice deserved a leavening of mercy. Till the end of his days, a widow in the toils of a mortgage shark, a negro in peril of losing life or freedom, had only to speak to Mr. Clay about it, and their troubles were half over.

Within eighteen months after his vagabond entrance into Kentucky he was able to marry Lucretia Hart, and soon afterwards he managed to buy himself a six-hundred-acre estate, which he named Ashland, and to settle down breeding livestock and children. From this existence he fondly hoped, but was never destined, to take much joy; his family life was one long, cruel tragedy. There was always Lucretia, of course, plain, loving, understanding and patient, who more than once "took him in her arms . . . as they wept together," but one after another the children, whom he loved with rapture, surfeited his soul with grief. Of his five sons, one was rendered insane by a carriage accident; another, his favorite, was killed in the Mexican War. Of his six daughters, all of them lived only long enough to win his heart and then died. Rumors were rampant of how Mr. Clay mingled infidelity with his other relaxations while away from home at Washington but, if true, the fact never affected his clinging devotion to Lucretia nor her sheltering care for him.

"Isn't it a pity," a lady once tried to taunt her, "that your husband gambles so much."

"Oh, I don't know," mocked Lucretia. "He usually wins."

When he was twenty-five the county sent him to the State Legislature; when he was twenty-nine the State sent him to fill out an unexpired term in the United States Senate, though at that age he was technically ineligible. After two short terms there he was elected to the lower House of Congress, where he accomplished the self-evident feat of becoming Speaker in his maiden term. That was in 1811 and for forty years thereafter he was in and out of House, Senate, and Cabinet, rushing home at will to replenish his fortune, hastening back to Washington to renew his reputation of being the most inconsistent, imprudent, magnetic personality of his day. At one session he flew into a tantrum against the national Bank; at another he became its fieriest advocate. At one session he was for "tariff for revenue only"; at another he became leader of the protectionist school. He signed one of the first anti-slavery resolutions ever circulated in Kentucky, but refused to free his own slaves and declined to vote for a single abolitionist bill in Congress. He was nicknamed a War Hawk at one stage of his career, the Great Pacificator at another, the Great Compromiser at a third—all of them given sincerely as terms of praise.

Yet far from being in any sense an equivocator, his headlong habit of self-expression was one of the very things that kept him out of the White House. He swore, he drank, he gambled, he was a professed unbeliever, he must have given some reason to imply that all his nights were not spent in holy wedlock. And he did it all with the open exuberance of a sailor on shore leave. He was, said one of his cult of worshippers, "the most imprudent man in the world." On the eve of one election, finding his funds low, he had the superb audacity to offer a bill raising Congressmen's pay; on the eve of another he had the amazing hardihood to oppose a bill giving a pension to the gray-haired mother of Admiral Perry, hero of Lake Erie, on the technical grounds that Perry had not died in line of duty.

# The Toga

What his detractors, living and dead, failed to see in Henry Clay was that his talent was less for practical state-craft than for a poetic, earth-spurning patriotism. If ever license were granted a poet to be impractical, inconsistent, imprudent, that allowance should be made for the Mill Boy. He suffered, it may be confessed, some sad relapses, but as his true and better self, if Beauty and Truth conflicted with practicability, consistency and caution, so much the worse for the latter virtues. He was too bedazzled at the vision of America becoming a continental empire to see the grotesque-ness of War. When Mr. Jefferson explained the Bank as a creature of monied aristocrats, Henry Clay helped to cry and vote it down; but when Mr. Calhoun, a few years later, asked for a recharter in order to open up and civilize the West, Henry Clay saw another vision of grandeur and resolved to stand or fall on the issue. His vision grew from a mere continental empire to a hemispherical one, including the South and Central Americas. He evolved a program of tariff, banking and foreign diplomacy which was collectively called the American System and for which he ranted and rhapsodized the rest of his life. Only the minion of Beauty could have felt such ecstasy as he expressed for the shrivelled boredom of law-making; only an enchanted apostle of Truth could have been credited with his famous epigram:

"Sir, I would rather be right than President!"

Whether or not he ever said it, Henry Clay was quite capable of having done so and (since he invariably believed himself right) of having meant it. What the sentiment amounted to was that he would like to be right *and* President, which was precisely how he felt in the middle of December, 1824. Even bad news had to travel slowly in those days but, when the election results were finally verified, Mr. Clay knew a bad moment. He had suspected that the contest would be close enough to prevent any candidate from receiving a clear majority, and in the suspicion was Mr. Clay's fondest hope. As Speaker of the House he felt without vanity that no man could beat him there. He had no delusions about gathering more votes than either Adams or Jackson in the

[ 213

general elections, but neither did he have any doubts about carrying more states than Crawford. Picture then his titanic rage and disgust to learn that, by some freak of arithmetic, the Georgian had nosed him out for third place in the Electoral College.

It was a bitter pill, but the Mill Boy tried manfully to swallow it with the proper show of philosophy and sportsmanship. "I shall yield," he said, "a cheerful acquiescence to the public decision." But the pose was all too transparent to the man who had manipulated his downfall. Meeting the Mill Boy in Washington on New Year's Eve, Martin Van Buren wrote home to a viceroy:

"He appears to me not to sustain his defeat with as much composure and fortitude as I should have expected. . . ."

The date for the House election being set for February 9th, Mr. Clay found himself in the intervening weeks in a position which he regarded as both grave and diverting. He could not be President this time, but as leader of the House he could say who would be. The humor of the situation was that Mr. Clay had only a modicum of admiration for any of the three candidates. Crawford, of late, had been a distinct disappointment and was fearfully incapacitated. Jackson had shown ability only as a military chieftain and "I cannot believe that killing 2500 Englishmen at New Orleans qualifies for . . . the chief magistracy." Adams he personally disliked, for they had been thrown together several months on the Commission to Ghent and had quarreled incessantly. Still, between the three there was only one choice to Henry Clay. Little as he cared for the querulous, unimaginative Puritan, Mr. Clay knew John Quincy Adams to be a sound forward-looking statesman, which was not true of the others. In fact the Mill Boy had already committed himself unofficially before leaving Kentucky for Washington, but until he made some formal announcement, he became the object of the most solicitous attentions from all three factions. He wrote to a friend:

"I am sometimes touched gently on the shoulder by a

friend, for example, of General Jackson, who will thus address me:

"'My dear sir, all my dependence is upon you; don't disappoint us; you know our partiality was for you next to our hero, and how much we want a Western President.'

"Immediately after a friend of Mr. Crawford will accost me:

"'The hopes of the Republican party are concentrated on you; for God's sake preserve it. If you had been returned instead of Mr. Crawford, every man of us would have supported you to the last hour. We consider you and him as the only genuine Republican candidates.'

"Next a friend of Mr. Adams comes with tears in his eyes:

"'Sir, Mr. Adams has always had the greatest respect for you and admiration of your talents. There is no station to which you are not equal. Most undoubtedly you are the second choice of New England, and I pray you to consider seriously whether the public good and your own future interests do not point distinctly to the choice which you ought to make?'

"How can one withstand all this disinterested homage and kindness?"

Mr. Clay withstood it fairly well and enjoyed himself hugely. Daniel Webster approached him with ponderous arguments on behalf the New Englander; Martin Van Buren, smiling impishly, came with sly insinuations of great reward in case Mr. Crawford acquired the purple, but most diverting of all were the clumsy advances of General Jackson's two Tennessee Majors—Lewis and Eaton.

Ever since the time, already six years ago, when Mr. Clay had tried Old Hickory's Florida War conduct before the House, there had been what Washington wits had called a non-intercourse act between them. Once they accidentally met at a Kentucky tavern where the General had pointedly snubbed Mr. Clay's polite salutations. But it was different now. The two Majors explained with lugubrious mirth that that night at the tavern Old Hickory had been "laboring under some indisposition." In return Mr. Clay's friends replied that the Speaker in the trial had only "expressed opinions in respect to public acts," and had the greatest admiration for the old hero. The result was that a dinner was arranged where the two men of the West met and cordially exchanged greetings. When it was over Mr. Clay started for the door where his carriage was waiting and found himself followed by the General and Major Eaton. Nothing would do, insisted the Tennesseeans, but that Mr. Clay dismiss his carriage and let them drop him at his door. It was done, and there followed a personal invitation to the General's own board, after which the ice was broken and they "frequently met . . . , always respectively addressing each other."

But the day was coming when Mr. Clay would have to announce himself officially for Adams, and as it approached friends warned him to be careful. Old Hickory and his two Majors were not men to be trifled with and the Red Fox had already wrecked the careers of several who had opposed him. All this Mr. Clay admitted but he declined to shirk the responsibility which, for all his amusement at the seducers, he felt keenly.

"I shall risk without emotion" he wrote to such an adviser "these effusions of malice. What is a public man worth if he will not expose himself on fit occasions for the good of his country?"

Mr. Clay was not surprised at the sudden cessation of attentions which marked his endorsement of Adams. He had expected that. But there are no words to tell his rage when on the last day of January he picked up a Philadelphia paper and read an open letter which accused him of having traded his support to the Puritan for a promise of the State Department portfolio.

"And," went on the letter, "the friends of Mr. Clay gave the information that if the friends of Jackson would offer the same price, they would close with them. But none of the friends of Jackson would descend to such mean barter and sale."

The letter was unsigned, but it purported to come from a member of Congress and Mr. Clay immediately put it down for a forgery. No Congressman could possibly have been in possession of such information, for the very idea of the conscience-bound Puritan countenancing a bargain was too absurd for anyone who knew either him or his reputation to believe. For a fact Mr. Clay, as history would reveal, had had at least one chance to sell his support, but it had not come from John Quincy Adams or any of his following. One day James Buchanan, Congressman from Pennsylvania and henchman of the two Majors, had cornered the Speaker and whispered to him certain inducements, which had been properly spurned. Either the letter was a forgery, deduced Mr. Clay, or else Buchanan, Eaton or Lewis, inspired by their own iniquity, had written it. Such an insult called but for one answer, and the next day Mr. Clay gave it. He published a card in the *National Intelligencer*, opining that the letter was a fraud:

"But if it be genuine, I pronounce the member, whoever he may be, a base and infamous calumniator, a dastard and a liar; and if he dare unveil himself and avow his name, I will hold him responsible as I here admit myself to be, to all the laws which govern and regulate men of honor."

Nothing would have pleased Mr. Clay more in this moment of his wrath than to have out and shoot down any Jacksonian in sight, but two days later his rage was turned to contemptuous mirth. In answer to his challenge came one George Kremer—a ludicrous, insignificant, inoffensive Pennsylvania Dutchman—who admitted himself to be author of the offending publication. The idea of going through all the pageantry of the *code duello* with George Kremer or of butchering such an innocent was too absurd a thought to be entertained. Obviously he was no more than a decoy for schemers higher up, but since they refused to show themselves Mr. Clay could only do the next best thing and ask the House for an investigation of the charges against him.

It was short notice—only five days before the election—but a committee was named and Kremer summoned to appear with his evidence. Here the whole farce evaporated, for Kremer, who seems to have been somewhat fascinated by the glory of facing the great Mr. Clay in mortal combat, slavishly refused to meet the committee. Mr. Clay was pronounced exonerated, and so he was in the eyes of his peers, but there was never a charge of corruption in politics that died for want of nutrition. All good reason to suspect Henry Clay vanished two days after the accusation was made, but the cry of "Bargain and Corruption" was a campaign slogan against him for thirty years to come, and it dogged him to the grave.

But having set it temporarily behind him, Mr. Clay now bent every effort to putting Adams in the White House. His enemies had showed their mettle, had confirmed his original opinion that they were unfit to lay hands on the government. With Daniel Webster as an active ally he plunged into the work of saving the Republic from the impending calamity. The Kentucky Legislature sent him instructions to vote for Jackson. Hearing from one of Mr. Clay's friends that they were supporting Adams, Little Van attempted to frighten them off:

"Mr. Johnson . . . if you do so you sign Mr. Clay's political death warrant."

Ignoring threats and petitions alike, the Speaker set about his task of garnering the votes. The poll of the House would be by states, of which there were now 24, with each delegation bound by the unit rule to adhere to its majority. Their preliminary canvass showed Mr. Clay and his assistant just where they stood:

Adams . . . . . 12 states.  Six in New England, Illinois, Kentucky, Louisiana, Maryland, Missouri, Ohio.

Jackson . . . . 7 states.  Alabama, Indiana, New Jersey, South Carolina, Mississippi, Pennsylvania, Tennessee.

Crawford . . 4 states.  Delaware, Georgia, North Carolina, Virginia.

To their chagrin the canvassers found themselves lacking the one necessary vote and what was still more disconcerting, the only State at all uncertain was Little Van's own New York. This could not have surprised them greatly, for the fact that Senator Van Buren had been discreetly in the background ever since New Year was proof enough that he had found work to keep him busy. The Senator, indeed, was immensely satisfied with the pivotal position he now held, and Mr. Adams was correct in writing five days before the date of election that "they have not yet abandoned all hope of the success of Mr. Crawford."

Occupying the most strategic of all positions—the balance of power—Little Van was far from beaten. More than a year ago the wiseacres had counted his candidate out of the contest, but here at the home-stretch he was still in a contending place. A doctor was found to pronounce the paralytic a well man; the poor sufferer was lugged from his bed to the Capitol and propped up against a pillar while friends formed a cordon about him lest onlookers should see what a pitiful wreck he really was. Fortunate for him, Mr. Crawford could have been thinking, that he had heeded the little Director's advice and eschewed all arguments. The Adams and Jackson men might hate and distrust each other, but they held no bitterness for him. Let the election deadlock again, then trust Little Van to pull off another of his miracles. He, Mr. Crawford, and his Susanna would move into the White House yet.

The same thoughts at the same moment were no doubt teeming in the brains of Congressmen Webster and Clay. They saw that even if Senator Van Buren did not actually elect his man he would certainly be in a position to name his own price for whatever he wanted, and the Tennessee Majors had proved themselves capable of meeting a bargain halfway. Somehow New York's vote would have to be wooed away from the Albany Manager before the noon hour of February 9th. Desperately the two orators turned from a canvass of the House to a canvass of the New York delegation, and what they discovered gave them a vestige of hope. Of the 34 members, 17 intended voting for Adams; 15 for Crawford and the other 2 for Jackson. To persuade one of the Jacksonian pair to change his affiliation was the only hope, and happily not too vague a one. For one of the pair was the Patroon, General Stephen Van Rensselaer—close upon his dotage, piously patriotic and suitably unsettled in his brain.

On the old Patroon Clay and Webster concentrated the fire and persuasion of all their talents. He weakened. They had at him again and again. He floundered. Two weeks ago the Patroon had written his brother that "I feel inclined for Old Hickory," but Little Van in the meantime had weakened the resolve and now Clay and Webster were tugging in a third direction. On the morning of the election the Patroon felt himself so enfeebled by indecision that he stopped at the Senator's lodgings to sharpen up his spirit with some gentle exercise. Bravely he told Little Van that he might relieve his mind by voting Jackson on the first ballot and Crawford on the second. So long as he voted against Adams, the Senator did not care, but he allowed his visitor to tussle with a mild argument for Crawford which so invigorated the old man that he set off for the Capitol bountifully restored in self-confidence. But Clay and Webster, lying in wait for the last word, waylaid him there and for half an hour they submitted him to a thorough going-over in the privacy of the Speaker's retiring room.

A shaken and uncertain man, the Patroon emerged and tottered to his seat. A page passed down the aisle putting three ballots on each desk. Soon came a teller with a box into which each member would drop the ballot bearing the name of his choice. The Patroon cringed; a rudderless conscience stirred within him. He had promised Little Van he would vote either for Jackson or Crawford, but the arguments of the two mighty debaters would not be still in his brain. They had told him that the fate of a nation lay in his hand. Feeling himself slipping again, the Patroon flagged Louis McLane, of Delaware, and besought him to run across the hall and fetch Mr. Van Buren from the Senate Chamber. But the House in executive session is no place for a trespassing Senator, and Little Van only sent back an encouraging cheer. As the fateful teller drew closer, the Patroon dispatched another emissary. Even professional etiquette could not deny that second call; the Patroon was evidently *in extremis*. Little Van left his Senate seat and hastened across the hall. But he came too late.

As the ballot box neared him with the Senator not yet in sight, the Patroon abandoned all hope of human comfort and sought guidance from on high. Bowing his gray head to the desk he prayed: Which, Oh Lord, of these three men shall it be? He opened his eyes. On the floor at his feet lay a ballot that had slipped off the desk. It read for Adams; the Lord had spoken. The Patroon picked it up, dropped it in the box, and thus it happened that Henry Clay below and God above, were forced to unite in thwarting the Little Magician.

But it never happened again. . . .

5

(1825–1828)

Nude, deluded and disgusted, the Sixth President of the United States lay prone upon the river bank and hoped that his Maker would spare him the indignity of being discovered in this moment of his shame. About him Fairfax County, Virginia, had risen, yawned, breakfasted and fared forth to do a day's labor under an April sun. Beyond him over the river, the magnificent dome of the Capitol arched upward toward a sky that would be looking down on many a governmental head not yet off its pillow. And across the Long Bridge, the President's servant, in the President's dripping shirt and pantaloons, was scurrying to find a closed cab in which his master might be decently smuggled back to the White House.

This morning, following his usual custom, Mr. Adams had risen at dawn, tramped to the river and there embarked with Antoine in a canoe, intending to paddle to the opposite shore and swim back. But part way over the concurrence of a leaky boat and a gust of wind had capsized them, bearing away all of Antoine's clothes and most of the President's and leaving them to make the best of their way to safety.

This April 13th marked only the fortieth day of Mr. Adams' official residence on Pennsylvania Avenue, but even in that short period it was not the first which had found him in a similar state of distress and with similar grievances. Another craft besides his canoe had been capsized in a sudden squall, leaving America's First Citizen to struggle through hostile elements to an indifferent and humiliating refuge where the best he could hope for was to be left alone.

"I am a man of reserved, cold, austere and forbidding manners," wrote Mr. Adams of himself.

His life's career and his chosen attitude toward it had contrived to make him so. Self-inflicted loneliness from his fellowmen was his only escape in times of trouble, which times rarely had much distance between them. On March 4th, Mr. Adams had been inaugurated; on March 5th, he had sent his cabinet recommendations to the Senate. Then the storm had broken, for when Mr. Clay's name appeared as choice for the State Department, seven Senators had pointedly removed themselves from the chamber, fifteen more had voted against the nomination, and only a scant majority of twelve sanctioned the new Executive's first measure. Throughout the nation the press of the defeated candidates howled with delight. Henry Clay's appointment, came the cry, proved beyond further question that the presidency had been bought and paid for. Bargain and Corruption in high places!

Lying there on the Potomac's shore, John Quincy Adams could have remembered how years ago in the pride of his youth he had written to a friend: "I am cultivating the stoic philosophy, so if the world frowns upon me I shall be prepared. And if the world smiles, I can always turn myself into an epicure." The world, by not smiling, denied itself what might have been a most diverting spectacle—to see a born-Puritan attempt the transformation into a hedonist— but Mr. Adams had opportunity enough to practice his stoicism. And this, too, despite the fact that he offered his country a brand of conscientious and informed leadership with which she could ill afford to dispense. The idea that statesmanship is some inherent, mystical quality, something that needs and will tolerate no training, has become so precious a creed in America that to point a child deliberately for public office would be considered nothing short of heresy. An ideal American statesman is no product of the Aristotelian theory of rearing scholars from childhood to be of service to the Republic. Rather it is the Roman conception of a Cincinnatus who can turn from his furrows at an instant's notice and do a patriot's duty, whether in council or battle. But the Greek, and not the Roman, doctrine was in the minds of John and Abigail Adams when they undertook the education of their second-born. From the first conscious moments of his life, John Quincy Adams had been schooled for statecraft—and Duty. By the time he emerged from his nonage he had studied foreign languages and diplomacy at three different capitals of Europe, had taken a Phi Beta Kappa key at Harvard and was perfecting his knowledge of American law. By thirty he had been an Ambassador whom George Washington called "the most valuable public character we have abroad"; by forty-five he had been state legislator, congressman, senator, ambassador again, envoy and cabinet minister and, when at fifty-six he came into the presidency, it was with the Miltonic, God-fearing knowledge that his were advantages and talents which were death to hide —something, as his "Honored Mamma" had written him in Paris years ago, "of which an account will be required of you hereafter."

But even a Puritan's hopes and fears of a "hereafter" were not enough to goad or comfort Mr. Adams this April morning. Gazing over the water toward the realm of his Duty, he could behold a chasm wider than the expanse of the river. The Powers of Darkness, aligned against him, composed more than a handful of scheming, ambitious men. There was also to be faced a great tide of evil elements which no man, even were he mailed ten times in the armor of righteousness, could be expected to stem. The new era

[ 223

of politics had dawned, backed by the lure of plunder, by the power of the People. Mr. Adams, trained in the old school, stood helpless before it.

If he had any lingering doubts about it in April, they were shattered in December when Congress met for its regular session. During the interim the President labored in collaboration with his Secretary of State to draw up a Message that would sound the keynote of his administration. Between them, the Mill Boy and the Puritan pieced together their personalities, bringing forth a program that was the marriage of Beauty and Duty. Where Henry Clay saw gorgeous poetic possibilities of an American Empire, John Quincy Adams beheld a realistic field of ripening opportunities that it would be criminal negligence to leave unreaped. The rolling plains, the towering mountains, the sweeping rivers of the West offered a store of boundless resources which if properly harvested might be used to banish such scourges as poverty and ignorance from the People's home.

"The great object of the institution of civil government," Congress heard, "is the improvement of those who are partners to the social contract . . . ; moral, political and intellectual improvement are duties assigned by the Author of our Existence."

It was the awful voice of a Puritan's God speaking through His earthly disciple. Mr. Adams' Message advocated a peaceful expansion by means of Government-built roads and canals; the careful trusteeship of all public lands; a national university; a geographical and astronomical observatory; the exploration, mapping and development of rivers, coast-lines, mountains and plains.

Prepared as he always was to expect and accept the worst, grimly content to be cursed and reviled in the name of Duty, Mr. Adams could hardly have pre-supposed the pestilence of ridicule and wrath that fell upon him now. The Message was as godly, practical and foresighted a document as a Chief Executive had ever presented, and that men calling themselves patriots should dare oppose it seemed next to incredible. Yet they did, and with such vehemence and vindictiveness that the several sessions of Congress during Mr. Adams' term were occupied with little else than a dismembering of the Message, clause by clause. Further and further within the shell of his turtle-like stoicism, the President withdrew himself, and America would have to wait many years before it knew what horrid sorrow he was hiding there. He lived to see this splendid Utopia of natural wealth debauched to make political plunder and the People's heritage squandered with sickening waste by persons who posed as their benefactors. Wistfully, as an old man, he wrote:

"Ages and ages of continual progressive improvement, physical, moral, political in the condition of the whole People of this Union, were stored up in the possession and disposal of those lands."

But it was too late then—a vision had passed.

And his enemies, Mr. Adams discovered before his term was half over, were not content to center their assault wholly on his legislative program and the personalities of his Cabinet. They carried the feud even into the social realm. It has ever been the tradition among law-giving bodies to separate personal and professional affiliations. Thus one man may attack another by a speech on the floor and yet with linked arms the two can march off to lunch together after adjournment.

That, at least, is the theory, and if it sometimes suffers the fate of most ideal arrangements, nevertheless the pose is usually maintained, though at the cost of awkward moments. But even this balm to his injured spirits was denied Mr. Adams. As President, he and his wife were supposedly on the receiving end of many social contacts and calls, but during this administration the White House stood as if a plague were on it. Nor could this be explained by Mr. Adams' "cold, austere and forbidding manners," for he had married Louisa Johnson, gay daughter of Maryland, whose Tuesday Evenings, when they lived on F Street, had been a feature of the social week. Sourly Mr. Adams confided to his diary that those "skunks of party slander who have been squirting round . . . and perfume the atmosphere of the Union" had not the decency to treat him with respect. Only one of the tribe he exempted from the charge, and that was an "obsequious," "fawning," "sycophantic" little gentleman whom the Diary further designates as "the great electioneering manager for General Jackson, as he was before the last election for Mr. Crawford."

Had the Sixth President been a man less spiritually muscle-bound, and less concerned with bearing his suffering like a proper Puritan, he might have derived a very apt object-lesson from these contacts with the Manager from New York. For Martin Van Buren, also, had recently known the capsizing of a cargo of hopes. The same chain of events which sent Mr. Adams to the presidency had nearly sent the little Senator to political oblivion. The election which made De Witt Clinton Governor in 1824 had all but prostrated the Regency. The ranks were so gutted that hardly a Bucktail up for reëlection that year had been returned. A swarm had been swept out of the House of Delegates; the Immortal Seventeen in the State Senate had been reduced beneath majority strength, and though Mr. Clinton did no general housecleaning of office-holders, many Regencymen felt themselves compelled to resign, three of these being the viceroys who had been respectively Treasurer, Comptroller, and Attorney General. The defeat of Mr. Crawford and his departure for Georgia had been another staggering blow to the Director's strength and prestige. Moreover, the three other high-ranking officials who had served him at Washington were all departed from the sphere of his influence. Dan Tompkins was dead; Rufus King had been sent to the court of St. James's, Smith Thompson was on the Supreme Bench. John McLean, whom Mr. Adams mistakenly continued in the Post Office, was Little Van's one henchman in the new administration. And, to crown the whole calamity, his own senatorial term was drawing to a close and the Clintonian majority at Albany was preparing to name his successor a year ahead of time.

Certainly it was all very distressing, and Mr. Adams would have done well to note with what cheerful fortitude the

Senator bore his tribulations, with what measured precision he went to work restoring his broken power. The little Director's first task was to reëstablish his kingdom at home; the second to see what could be done at Washington, so putting first things first, he had set his face resolutely toward Albany in the autumn of 1825.

His intention was, if possible, to use the annual election for the House of Delegates as an opportunity to put a working nucleus of Bucktails back in the Legislature. Tammany Hall could usually be counted upon to send a snug delegation from the City, but these must be supplanted by enough up-State brethren to make the combination formidable. As his chief assistant in this particular election, Matty Van had the wise and subservient Edwin Croswell now editing the *Argus*. Together they set forth upon what the historian of this campaign calls a "political still-hunt." Quietly they moved, without fanfare or trumpeting; issues were gently laid to rest in the *Argus* columns; controversies were hushed and jealousies healed with bargains, promises and soft speeches. So noiselessly it all happened that not until it was over did the Clintonians realize that once more their man was ambushed. There were enough Regencymen in office to block, if not carry, whatever measures might come before the Assembly, and the talk went round that Mr. Clinton would never see reëlection in '26.

Matty Van, however, had other ideas. He, too, would be a candidate that year. Now that he was personally removed from State politics, he felt there was room enough for the Magnus Apollo, provided, of course, that that gentleman could be brought to terms. Accordingly the Senator despatched to Mr. Clinton his friend Benjamin Knower, with the proposition that each should do nothing to prevent the other from maintaining his present office. That is, that if Mr. Clinton would support Mr. Van Buren for the Senate, Mr. Van Buren in turn would see to it that Mr. Clinton did not fail to succeed himself as Governor.

It was a type of manoeuvre just beginning to be known as "log-rolling." Ten years ago the Magnus Apollo would have spurned any such offer, but time and politics more often soften than cement a man's intolerance for shady dealings. Mr. Clinton could remember how he might have compromised with his convictions in 1812 and himself, instead of James Monroe, been Mr. Madison's successor. Like most men infected with the presidential rabies, Mr. Clinton had never recovered. In '24 he had been one of the sixteen original candidates, only to withdraw when his hopes faded. But the gala celebration at the opening of the Canal in 1825 had brought him again into a prominence which he did not care to risk by opposing the Little Magician. Gratefully he accepted Matty Van's proposition.

It was a secret pact. Matty Van knew well that for the rank and file of Bucktails to find him in connivance with their natural enemy would be hard to explain. A month preceding the gubernatorial election the Regency Republicans were to meet in convention to name a candidate, William Paulding being conceded to be their best choice. This was one time, however, when Matty Van did not want the best choice brought forward. Either Mr. Clinton had to win or else New York would have a new Senator. Therefore, a few days before the convention was to meet, certain Regencymen (among them Silas Wright, who later became a Regency Governor in his own name) were summoned before the Director and informed that Paulding must not be nominated, but a gentleman named William B. Rochester.

This somewhat surprised Matty Van's viceroys, for Mr. Rochester's sole identification with politics was that he happened to be a friend of Henry Clay and one of Mr. Adams' envoys to Central America. To oppose Mr. Clinton by a candidate thus connected with an unpopular administration, with both principles of the Bargain and Corruption slander, seemed a strange procedure, and the little Manager's explanations, sleek as they were, hardly justified it. In the *Autobiography* he claims that he persuaded his followers with the argument that to be identified with the Adams administration would help the Regency, but this is too palpably absurd to believe. Probably what he did was to confess

228 ]

his agreement with Mr. Clinton and admit that Rochester was as good a man as any for the sacrificial rites.

What happened corroborates the guesswork. Not only was Rochester overcome by Mr. Clinton, but several Regency strongholds, hitherto impregnable, accomplished astonishing landslides to the Magnus Apollo. And though Rochester lost, his Bucktail running-mate for the lieutenant-governorship beat Clinton's team-mate almost as badly as the latter beat Rochester. Such happenings were too unusual in politics to be deemed accidental, and Rochester went down to his grave crying that Matty Van had sold him out. Before that, however, he sought vengeance and vindication by opposing his seducer for the senatorship and gained, though not victory, the satisfaction of finding that his accusations were well founded. Senator Van Buren was reëlected in the Legislature by votes which Mr. Clinton was generous enough to lend him. Safe for another six years, Little Van was now able to give his undivided attention to affairs at the Capital City, where the Adams Diary had meanwhile discovered him "making a great effort to combine the discordant elements of the Crawford, Jackson, Calhoun men into a united opposition against the Administration."

For Mr. Adams to have called the Senator "the great electioneering manager of General Jackson," indicates that Mr. Van Buren's sentiments must have undergone considerable change since the political demise of William H. Crawford. During that campaign Little Van had given ample proof that he was of a mind with most experienced men in looking upon Old Hickory's candidacy with trepidation. The late Mr. Jefferson had called Jackson "one of the most unfit men I know of for the place," and Matty Van's own *Argus* had stated editorially that the old hero was culturally and mentally "an immeasurable distance from the Executive Chair."

Here it may be reiterated that if a single positive belief can be ascribed to the man who made his name synonymous with evasiveness, it is that he dreaded and distrusted, above all, the will of the People. For years he had taken every opportunity to keep the People down; his whole aspect, atti-

tude, association and appearance were aristocratic. But by
1826, when New York had finally achieved universal suffrage under Mr. Clinton, Little Van succumbed to the inevitable. The expediency of cajoling the People had occurred
to him long ago. Ever since the day he had offered the resolution praising Andrew Jackson for his defense of New
Orleans, the Senator had been holding himself in readiness
to make use of this tow-line. His support of Crawford from
1816 to 1824 shows that he, like many others, underestimated
the rapidity with which the People were charging forward.
Crawford represented the oligarchic theory of government,
Jackson the democratic, yet it must be stressed that in the
Little Magician's shift from one type of candidate to the
other there was really no inconsistency at all. Till 1824
Crawford seemed the man most likely to be next President;
after 1825 that man was Andrew Jackson. Both times Martin
Van Buren was on the side of political expediency; both
times he was backing a favorite.

Nor is it out of character that, proclaiming himself a
friend of the People, Little Van should have served them in
so dastardly a fashion as to oppose the program of the Adams-
Clay Message. It was not because he failed to see its deeply-
lying importance, but that he saw it too well. In Albany
he had done all he could to thwart Mr. Clinton's splendid
Canal scheme, for the simple political reason that it never
pays to let an adversary succeed. In Washington, acting on
the same principle, he dedicated himself to frustrating the
Message. Jackson's two managing Majors were doing their
man yeoman service in popularizing him both as hero of
New Orleans and martyr of the Corrupt Bargain, but what
they needed was a parliamentary tactician to discredit Mr.
Adams as an executive. That, and also (so it was said) because Mr. Van Buren's social acceptance would help to offset
Old Hickory's supposed uncouthness, was the reason the
Tennessee Majors approached the Albany Director and in-
vited him into their camp.

For a man to undertake the parliamentary bear-baiting of
the unfortunate President, they could scarcely have made a

better choice. Senator Van Buren had two qualities that admirably fitted him for just this work. First was the disarming politeness, both in public and personal address, that enabled him to injure an adversary without insulting him. These were days when an insult usually had to be answered for on a field of honor, but it was maddeningly impossible to find that kind of effrontery in the tinselled barbs with which the gracious little Senator impaled his opponents. It always seemed to be with infinite regret that he rose ever so delicately to goad the suffering Puritan and the raging Mill Boy. And once the gavel had fallen on recess, what could be said to rebuff the cherubic smiles with which he would greet the men whom he had just crucified. Always he contrived to be, as Mr. Adams fumingly dashed off in his diary, "like Sosie of Molière's *Amphitryon*—'l'ami de tout le monde'."

And the other advantageous quality was his gift for sophistry. The tortured arguments with which he had proved Dan Tompkins to be the State's creditor instead of its debtor were as mere gibberish compared to those he concocted while engaged in the process of stoning Mr. Adams out of the White House. So persuasive are they, even to read, that both of Mr. Van Buren's serious biographers to date were almost, if not wholly, convinced that they had laid hold upon an unsung statesman. And how the speeches must have sounded, dropping in honeyed syllables from his tongue, no man can ever know. This was in the period of his career when the little man built up what small reputation he gained as an orator. Pridefully he relates how, when the Congress-going ladies' arrived in the galleries, he would rise and salute them before beginning. His orations have not the grandeur, the depth, the sparkle, the passion of his immortal contemporaries—Clay, Webster, Randolph, Calhoun—but they served their temporal purpose and evidently the ladies enjoyed them.

"Sophistry—specious but fallacious reasoning," Professor Noah Webster's new dictionary defined it, but no mere definition ever did justice to a stylist of an art. When Senator

Van Buren undertook to fashion an apparently sound argument out of mere nothingness, it was so finished a product that supposedly intelligent men failed to see the cracks. There was an Adams-Clay majority in the Senate when Little Van first took charge, but under the subtle alchemy of his reasoning it vanished away.

Usually his points were made by drawing reference with bated breath to some sacred document of the mystic past— the Declaration, the Constitution, the Farewell Address, the Jeffersonian Creed. He was as the village atheist who, by citations from the infallible Good Book, can conclusively prove up to be down. When the Administration brought out its vast plan for building a network of roads and canals under the title of Internal Improvements, the Senator pounced on it as a degradation of the Jeffersonian State Rights that would set Long Tom writhing in his grave. When the President proposed, as an adjunct to the Monroe Doctrine, to appoint a good will commission to attend the meeting of South American delegates at Panama, the Senator declared himself scandalized at this heresy to the Farewell Address, which had warned against foreign entanglements. When Mr. Adams proposed to strengthen the Supreme Court in its present status as a Court of Appeal, the Senator, professing to believe that this constitutional safeguard would threaten the People's rights, fell a-trembling for the Declaration. By the slyest of innuendo he implied that Mr. Adams, being a President's son, was like a prince ascending his father's throne; by a most incredible exhibition of imaginative agility, he tied up the Sixth President's appointment of commissioners to Panama with the Second President's hated Alien and Sedition Laws; by a preamble attached to a bill he was sponsoring, he turned prophet of woe with the strained analogy that because Caesar and Napoleon had become Emperors of their respective Republics, the scheming Puritan in the White House might somehow become the same thing.

This was not all. Not caring—or daring—to deal in personal slander, the Senator uncovered, in Randolph of Roanoke, just the man to do his dung-hurling. To call the Virginian three-fourths insane is perhaps as charitable a version as a conscientious biographer can do for him. Gifted with supersensitive powers of intelligence and a corrosive vocabulary, Randolph employed these talents solely as weapons with which to perform the sadistic rites of public torture. Presidents were his especial delight. From the day in Richmond, 1795, when he had startled a political banquet with the toast: "George Washington—may he be damned!" this demented genius had been the holy terror of each successive régime. With the ascendency of John Quincy Adams, however, it appeared that finally John Randolph had found a First Citizen with whom he could pick no fault. But that was before someone reminded him that Mr. Adams was a Yankee, a Puritan, and the son of the man whose coachman had once been rude to Randolph's brother.

After that it was only a question of how much bile and brimstone the Virginian could heap upon the President and his Secretary. Mr. Calhoun, in mortal terror of the madman, whimpered that a Vice President had no right to call a Senator to order, so Randolph would occupy the floor for hours on end, flinging off one salacious epigram after another, until finally Little Van, to stop him, had to arrange a signal whereupon the Senators would walk out, leaving less than a quorum in the chamber and the session would be automatically adjourned. Before things came to that pass, though, Randolph had done his work. Using the Corrupt Bargain invention as a springboard, he soared daily into a series of scurrilities that ranged from unsavory literary allusions to the vernacular of likening Mr. Clay's Kentucky to a harlot who had sold her charms to Mr. Adams' Massachusetts, and from there to the famous climax where he termed these gentlemen's alliance: "a coalition between a Puritan and a blackleg."

Mr. Clay, of course, called him out for it, and Randolph, with his usual eccentricity, appeared on the field with a white linen duster under his coat. Missing his first shot, Mr. Clay savagely called for another, and missed that too, while his opponent grandiosely fired into the air. The burlesque affair served the Van Buren cause admirably in dramatizing the Corrupt Bargain story, and the Senator, meanwhile, was not idle on his own behalf. He now came forward with an extravaganza that outdid for audacious absurdity even the best of his sophistry. In conjunction with Thomas H. Benton, Mr. Clay's Missouri in-law whom the specious arguments had weaned away from him, Little Van brought out two sheaves of bills—one to curtail Post Office and other governmental patronage; the second to prevent presidential elections being decided in the House, suggesting to a now-aroused country that Mr. Adams had been guilty of both the implied abuses.

Probably in all political histories of all nations there was never a more brazen attempt at re-incrimination. The Senator happened to be one of the few persons in the country who knew how completely unfounded was the Corrupt Bargain story. He knew what Mr. Adams was too proud to announce, that the State Department had been first offered not to Henry Clay but to De Witt Clinton. And for Martin Van Buren, of all persons, to have accused John Quincy Adams, of all people, of misusing political patronage is a comic atrocity that beggars comparison. So scrupulous had been the beleaguered Puritan that during his entire four years he had replaced exactly twelve government employees, all presumably for cause. At the very moment he was drafting and presenting these bills Little Van, in connivance with John McLean, was laying plans to use the Post Office as means for a nation-wide Spoils System, and Mr. Adams was helplessly writing in his Diary: "Some think I have suffered for not turning my enemies out of office, particularly the Postmaster General."

It was, naturally, never intended that these bills should be taken seriously by anyone except the public, much less that the important phases of them should become law. They were held in committee until a few days before the close of the session and then brought out when it was too late to do much but debate them. Senator Van Buren valiantly led a sham battle in which the dangerous privilege of appointing cadets and midshipmen was snatched from the power-hungry Puritan, but the Post Office and Custom Houses remained unassaulted. Better to capture such arsenals than destroy them; Old Hickory could use them later.

With Congress in recess and the pre-presidential year at hand, Little Van headed northward in the autumn of '27. There was trouble at Tammany Hall. Three sachems—Judge Henry Barker, Henry Eckford and old Mathew Davis —along with a host of lesser tribesmen had been indicted and convicted of a swindle that ran into the millions, the largest on record at the time. Unfortunately this fiasco coincided with the coming of the vital local election in which the City would vote for the first time with unrestricted suffrage and in which it had been hoped to poll a huge majority for the Jackson candidates. But these exposures in fraud had a way of doing the Wigwam no good, and to make matters worse a clique of braves known as "The Élite" had declared themselves disgusted with such barbarities and about to run an Adams ticket.

A schism in the ranks at this eleventh hour threatened disaster, but on Matty Van's appearance at the Wigwam things were soon set in order. That Tammany eventually carried the City for Jackson is ascribed by her best historian to two factors: first, the personal popularity of Old Hickory; second, "the organizing genius of Martin Van Buren." Immediately upon arrival the Senator went into conference with the Sachems and promptly suggested that, as a way out of their difficulties, they issue official orders for all Braves to vote only for Jackson candidates. This was done, but the dictatorial policy resulted in a revolt in which the Adams men counter-attacked by forcibly seizing the Wigwam assembly hall and going into parliamentary session to nominate their own ticket. Not to be outdone, Matty Van ordered the loyalists into the cellar and in the renowned Coal Hole meeting the Jackson slate was chosen.

The election of November '27 was an experience Manhattan had never known before. In previous years there had been all manner of tumult, breakage and shouting, but this first popular election eclipsed the past as it forecast the future. In addition to the native-born People, flocks of Irish immigrants had just been enfranchised by the reduction of the eligibility period from twelve years to three. Old Hickory was presented to them as a son of Irish parents, and in some wards it was worth an Adams man's life to come within sight of the polls. Challengers, stationed there by law to watch out for foul play, were chased away and men symbolically armed with hickory sticks patrolled the voting places. Cartloads of repeaters were hauled from one poll to the next; immigrants underneath the three year limit were known to have voted six times apiece, and anyone who protested was, if he escaped a clubbing, arrested by the Tammany police force for disturbing the peace.

But, such is the unrestful tempo of a political manager's life, Matty Van had hardly had time to rejoice over the Jacksonian victory in the City than he was threatened in another quarter. By now he had completed his parliamentary tasks and was managing the campaign proper, doing more, said Webster, "to obtain General Jackson's election than any other man—yes than any other ten men—in the country." He had made a speaking tour of the South,. conferred with leaders there and, back at his desk in Albany, had become by common consent the directing genius of the Hickory forces, which now included in its first rank the two managing Majors and five regional editors of great subsequent importance: Duff Green in Washington, Frank Blair and Amos Kendall in the West, Ike Hill in New England and Thomas Ritchie in the South.

At Albany Mr. Van Buren set up a general headquarters, composing, as he described it, a one-man "board of censors." He secured the assistance of a very able coadjutor in James A. Hamilton, son of the great Federalist, and by Hamilton's aid he kept in touch with the situation in every state. He made a check list of all papers and pamphlets, mailed out instructions to the Majors, the Editors, the General himself, concerning how to deal with this situation, how to circum-

## The Toga

vent that one, when to speak and when to be silent. The greatest mud-slinging epoch of American history was now at its height. The Jacksonian press was calling Mr. Adams a pimp, a thief, a gambler. In Russia, they said, he had sold a beautiful American girl into the lascivious clutches of a Moscovite Blue Beard; as Ambassador he had inflated his expense account and pocketed the profit; as President he had installed a billiard table in the White House, turning that sacred mansion into a gaming hell. Lustily the Adams papers reciprocated by calling General Jackson an adulterer, a murderer, a bastard. Hadn't he lived two years with another man's wife? Hadn't he killed thirteen men? Wasn't it true according to the Cincinnati *Gazette* that:

"General Jackson's mother was a common prostitute brought to this country by British soldiers. She afterwards married a MULATTO MAN with whom she had many children, of which General Jackson is one."

Industriously Little Van labored to dilute this deluge of libel, scurrilities and half-truths with which his candidate was being showered. There was, he knew, no use replying to the worst of them, but fearing that Old Hickory would play into the enemy's hands by showing some violent reaction, he wrote the old hero begging him to be patient and silent "under the torrents of malignant vituperation to which you have been exposed." Nothing, he assured the General, could hurt him except "some indiscretion of our own." In order to offset the fame of Old Hickory's well-known ferocity, the little manager wrote Hamilton: "Does the old gentleman have prayers in his own house? If so mention it modestly." In order to make full use of the General's one claim to election, he helped organize an anniversary celebration of the great victory, and sent Hamilton down to New Orleans to represent Tammany Hall and the Regency. In order to reach the hearts of another faction at home he ordered an agent to hasten a large shipment of wine "before Thursday . . . on that day I give a dinner to all the young Jackson Blood in the city."

Careful as always not to soil his own fingers, the Senator kept clear of the skirmishing, acting only in an advisory capacity. Whether from disapproval or caution he had no part in the mud-slinging but, as a contemporary put it: "His hand was full of cards and all his cards were trumps." The Majors had given him to understand that if New York State did its expected share in the election he should have his pick of the cabinet posts. Regencymen were urging him to speak for the Treasury Department, since it had the most spoils within its gift, but Little Van saw more attractive advantages in another portfolio. Every President since John Adams had matriculated in the State Department; it was considered the doorstep to the White House, for which reason Mr. Van Buren picked upon it as his next abiding place. By New Year of 1828 it seemed that nothing could happen to deny it to him. But suddenly something did—murder!

Actually the killing had taken place many months before, but only of late had it become nationally significant. In September, 1826, William Morgan, a bricklayer, had mysteriously vanished from his home at Batavia, in western New York. Since Morgan was known locally only as the town drunkard, his disappearance could scarcely be mourned as a loss either to his townsfolk, family or humanity at large, but there were attached motives that made for a widening importance. It seems that Morgan, a member of the Masonic Lodge, had contracted with a publisher to write a book exposing the Society's secrets, a volume on the same subject having lately achieved a large sale in England. Visualizing wealth and a cessation of his bricklaying labors, Morgan in a moment of intoxication had boasted of his prospects. Warned by his Lodge members to abandon the idea, he persisted. Then suddenly he was gone.

A long-drawn-out investigation revealed that he had been kidnapped and imprisoned for five days in a powder magazine at Fort Niagara, and there the trail was lost. It would be fifty-six years before that enterprising sleuth, Thurlow Weed, solved the case by producing an affidavit of one of the kidnappers, who definitely declared that Morgan had been murdered, but mystery and suspense were enough at the time to stir the national pulse. The Adams leaders, hard-pressed, seized upon this as a straw that might save them. Andrew Jackson was a Mason! So was one of his heartiest supporters, Governor De Witt Clinton! True-minded Americans were called upon to express disapproval of such terrorism at the presidential polls.

New York State, of course, was the hotbed of it all. Ever since the abduction Masons had been proscribed from the local tickets in the Western counties, and those who ran independently were overwhelmingly beaten. The formation of an anti-Mason party was the next step, and the alliance of this new faction with the National Republicans, as the Adams camp now called themselves, was only a stride beyond. Once more Matty Van found himself at grips with his Nemesis, for Thurlow Weed immediately assumed command of the allies and was in exactly the same position as four years earlier, when he had so unexpectedly shattered the Regency's hopes for Crawford.

To lose New York after so much preparation and promise became the nightmare of Matty Van's pillow. Dropping the State's 36 electoral votes would very possibly lose Old Hickory the whole election and most certainly lose Little Van his cherished portfolio. Something must be done. Fortunately for the Director's plans Mr. Clinton chose February of the presidential year to suffer a heart attack and die. That, at least, removed one major difficulty, for Mr. Clinton, flourishing as the Masons' Grand High Priest of the Grand Chapter of the Royal Arch, and also as Old Hickory's leading candidate for the vice-presidency, had been a broad target for assault. Little Van, acting as chief oratorical mourner for the memorial services at the Capitol, deposited a goodly quota of tears at the bier before hastening northward again to rearrange his plans. Thus he ended his panegyric:

"I, who, whilst living, never—no never—envied him anything, now that he is fallen, am greatly tempted to envy him his grave with its honors."

Whatever his thoughts concerning Mr. Clinton's grave

there is no doubt that Matty Van had designs on Mr. Clinton's gubernatorial honors. Prowling about the western counties to discover the extent of the Anti-Mason feeling, he wrote back to Hamilton that "The excitement has been vastly greater than I supposed." He was not long in devising a plan by which to drive a wedge between the two enemy factions. In July the National Republicans rushed Justice Smith Thompson up from Washington to accept nomination for the governorship on a ticket with Francis Granger, one of the milder Anti-Masons. It did not please the ultra-avengers that their man should be relegated to second place, but they were somewhat placated when Matty Van quietly shifted some of the Jackson campaign funds to Solomon Southwick and encouraged that enterprising Bucktail to announce himself as the genuine Anti-Mason candidate for Governor. There being now three tickets in the field, it was possible for whomever bore the Regency colors to win on a minority vote. Not unmindful of the possibility, Mr. Van Buren paid a call on his friend Judge Enos T. Throop, whose chance it had been to preside over the original kidnapping trial and to win universal applause by sentencing the abductors to the fullest extent of the law.

How, inquired Matty Van, would the Judge like to be Governor?

The Judge gave an unhesitating assent, whereupon the Senator unfolded his plan. The Regency convention would nominate a Van Buren-Throop slate for the State election, which coincided with the national one. By the combination of Old Hickory's popularity and a divided opposition, they would assuredly win, after which Mr. Van Buren would serve briefly, resign the governorship to Judge Throop, and himself become Secretary of State.

The plan worked out with mathematical precision. Although informing posterity that he accepted the gubernatorial nomination "against my wishes," Matty Van bore the imposition bravely in private and did not hesitate to compensate himself for the additional burden of another title. "Bet for me on joint account," he instructed Hamilton, "five hundred dollars that Thompson will be defeated and a hundred dollars on every thousand up to five thousand." He had not miscalculated. In November General Jackson became President-elect, and Senator Van Buren, three thousand dollars richer for his wagers, became Governor-elect by a minority victory over his two rivals. Inaugurated on January 1st, he was enormously surprised forty-six days later to be tendered the portfolio of the State Department—"a wholly unsolicited step." He remained Governor a total of ten weeks, time enough to execute another complete housecleaning, and then set off once more to the Capital City to do the will of the People.

## The Portfolio

### (1829–1830)

REVOLUTION in the Capital City!
A Coup d'État soon to be followed by a Reign of Terror!

"John the Second" had been routed from his Palace and "Andrew the First" was come to town for the coronation! "The noisy and disorderly rabble," wrote an uneasy aristocrat ". . . brought to my mind descriptions I have read of the mobs at the Tuileries and in Versailles." Truly, groaned another, "the reign of King Mob seemed triumphant." The "warm and springlike" morn which the deposed Mr. Adams viewed from his refuge at Meridian Hill near the Maryland border was hailed with "cannon-firing, drum-beating and hurrahing." "By ten o'clock," remembered an eye-witness, "the Avenue was crowded with carriages of every description, from the splendid Baronet and coach down to wagons and carts. . . ." By eleven there was such a mob as Mr. Webster "never saw before. Persons have come five hundred miles . . . and they really seem to think the country is rescued from dreadful danger." By noon the steps, porticoes, and terraces of Capitol Hill were black with a mass of sweating, shouting, happy humanity that caused ecstasy in the poetic soul of Mr. Francis Scott Key.

"It is beautiful," he murmured. "It is sublime."

From the west wing of the Capitol there came a scream

of delight. Those there, looking down the Avenue, beheld
a group of men issue from Gadsby's Hotel. All wore tall
beaver hats save one—a lean, grizzled, gray-haired soldier
who strode in their midst. It was the Conqueror walking
bareheaded and unguarded among his People. Came shout
upon shout that must have churned havoc in the heart of
Mr. Henry Clay, brooding all day behind locked doors.

Then, as the tumult subsided at the westward, it broke
out again to the east. Here was the place of vantage—a
fenced-in garden facing a flight of marble steps at the top
of which was a table, draped like a pagan altar in red, and
behind the table a door leading to the rotunda. From
it now came the coronation procession. The marshals first,
their tall hats doffed; next a venerable gentleman, garbed
like a high priest in flowing robes, and last, the Hero bowing to the cheers, bearing himself "with a grace and composed dignity" which a haughty Governor of South Carolina
had to admit "I never saw surpassed."

A hush fell upon the multitude and it strained forward.
The Hero was reading his Address, but in so low a tone that
few could hear. It did not matter, though, for the words were
not his own. A speech turned by his own "rist" he had
brought with him from the Hermitage, but it was revised
first by the Majors, then by the Editors, so that this third
version was less his than theirs. He finished, and Chief Justice John Marshall, whose life's labor found only a mockery
in this moment, stepped forward to administer the oath.

"I, Andrew Jackson, do solemnly swear . . ."

Now was an unexpected climax. Taking the Bible from
an attendant, the grizzled Hero bowed once more to the
crowd, reverently bent his gray head and laid his lips to the
Holy Book in his hands. For a moment there was a thrilled
and heavenly silence; an instant later a roaring stampede.
Bursting through the guard line, the multitude stormed up
the steps to wring the Hero's hand, to touch his garments,
to come as close as possible to the Presence. Even then the
dignity and poise did not leave him. Gravely he pressed
among them, down the steps to the gate where his horse was

waiting. Not in a coach with liveried outriders would he go to his Palace. Some of his predecessors had done so, but like Citizen Jefferson, Old Hickory would go as a plain man to a plain man's home. With difficulty he stretched for his stirrup and swung to the saddle. Slowly, through the mud, trailed by his People—"countrymen, farmers, gentlemen, . . . boys, women and children, black and white"—he rode to the White House.

The solemnity of the occasion was over now. Ceremony turned to carnival. Into the First Citizen's new home rushed the People, bringing with them a goodly portion of the Capital City's mire. They leaped upon chairs and sofas for a better view of Old Hickory, and he, attempting to shake hands with his guests, came so close to being crushed that some thoughtful gentlemen had to form a bodyguard about him to preserve the Seventh President for a higher destiny. Even this devoted band seemed in a fair way to fall before the onslaught until reënforcements came in the shape of a corps of black mercenaries, bearing not arms, but plates and bowls of refreshments. With renewed clamor the People fell upon these reserves. China was broken; glassware smashed. Eyes were seen to be blackened, noses to bleed, while women fainted and strong men turned pale from suffocation. In the confusion Old Hickory executed a strategic retreat, slipping out a back door and staggering off to Gadsby's for recuperation.

If the People noticed his departure, it did not slacken their appetites nor depress their spirits. Ever the front door was a horn of plenty, rolling them in, and when that entrance proved insufficient the windows were flung open —and still they came. "A mob . . . scrambling, fighting, romping." "Black, yellow and gray, poured in in one uninterrupted stream of mud and filth . . . many subjects for the penitentiary . . . tyros for Liberia . . . a stout black wench eating . . . jelly with a gold spoon . . . We had a regular Saturnalia," wrote James A. Hamilton to the absent Director.

"We" might have had worse than that, except that some

level head conceived a method of raising the siege. Huge tubs of heavily-spiked punch were carried from the kitchen to the lawn and, at sight of this, the flood turned back upon itself. Out of the windows and doors tumbled the President's guests, leaving behind them breakage and ruin that would be estimated in the thousands of dollars. But what did it matter? It was the People's day and no more than their due, though the very thought of what it all meant so affected Mr. Clay that he "drew out his handkerchief, turned away his head and wiped his eyes." His Vision was passing; theirs was just rising before them. Mr. Jefferson's Republicanism lay in the grave beside Mr. Hamilton's Federalism and the young giant of Democracy had reared itself from their dust.

It remains one of those cheerful inconsistencies of History that July Fourth and not March Fourth stands on the calendar as Independence Day; that 1776 instead of 1829 is widely celebrated as the American holy year. For it was the Second Revolution, not the First, which freed the People. Until the Jackson election, the People as an entity had never spoken, had never elected their own First Citizen, had never doffed the historical chains of taxation without representation. The affair of '76 merely transferred their subjection from George the Third to George Washington and, during the first four decades of the Republic, they may have been ruled by wise, benevolent gentlemen but, very decidedly, they were not ruled by themselves.

Nor is it sound treatment to pass over the Revolution of 1829 in any patronizing or belittling fashion. Reasonably bloodless, it is nevertheless a perfect example of its type. In causes and results, in sequence of events, in reaction and aftermath, it resembled every red revolution, as distinguished from white, that the world ever knew. As always in the case of popular uprisings, there was a social as well as political grievance. In Andrew Jackson's files at the Hermitage were hundreds of letters urging him on to right governmental wrongs, but there was also one of another kind entirely, purporting to come from "near two hundred thousand freemen" and begging him to reform the "court etiquette and pompous perade (sic)" of the pampered aristocrats. As always, too, there lurked behind these legitimate causes the charlatanism and scheming ambition that invariably characterizes revolts of this sort. There was never a Military Chieftain called in from the fields to put on the purple who did not bring with him a disreputable swarm of camp-followers and scavengers, loudly bawling the Hero's anthems but simultaneously rolling envious eyes toward the public coffers. The Coup, the Coronation, the Carnival. No perfect Revolution could stop there. Followed then the Reign of Terror.

Long before Inauguration Day it had been widely assumed that heads would roll when Old Hickory came into his power. Under the ingratiating titles of "reform" and "rotation in office," the Director, the Majors, the Editors had circulated the campaign pledge that "the General will cleanse the Augean stables," that "the barnacles will be scraped clean off the ship of State"—which was correctly interpreted to mean an ousting of all office-holders so villainous as to have displayed any loyalty for the luckless Puritan. During the three weeks just prior to March Fourth, the President-elect had sat at Gadsby's, flanked by the two Majors, receiving applications for all posts from Cabinet memberships down, and the fur-flying scramble which marked the selection of these six councilmen was of itself a portent of what was to come. Half of these positions were fixtures before the selecting ever began. The invaluable Director, Martin Van Buren; the senior managing Major, John Henry Eaton; the useful Postmaster General, John McLean—these were certain choices, but over the remaining three there developed a battle royal with all rules suspended. Applicants from a dozen cliques and communities moiled about Gadsby's, breast-beating in praise of their own claims, befouling their rivals, until finally two survivors stood facing each other over the prostrate forms of the rest. They were James Alexander Hamilton of New York, representing Governor Van Buren, who was at home rehabilitating the Regency; and James Hamilton of South Carolina, spokesman for Vice President

Calhoun who, though not absent, was somewhat reluctant to demean his dignity in such an unworthy combat, especially since he had already tried and failed to get his friend Senator Tazewell the State Department.

Daily the two Hamiltons encountered each other at the General's headquarters, each striving in his master's behalf to gain any or all of the remaining portfolios. From the first all advantage was with the Carolinian, and in the end he prevailed. Mr. Calhoun was allowed to name Samuel D. Ingham for the Treasury and John Branch for the Navy Department over Louis McLane and Levi Woodbury, the Van Buren claimants. That left the Attorney Generalship at the Director's disposal, but when McLane declined it, fearing, he said, to meet such spartans as Webster, Clay and Wirt in the Supreme Court, the appointment went to still another Calhoun candidate—John M. Berrien.

All was apparently decided, but later on John McLean, hearing that the Administration was contemplating a wholesale massacre of job-holders in the Post Office, suffered a rather belated attack of conscience. Mr. McLean was in his spare time a lay clergyman and his flock had already expressed dubious admiration at the way in which he had played Judas to the pious Mr. Adams. Demurring at further removals, he allowed himself to be kicked upstairs to a seat on the Supreme Bench, and Judge William T. Barry, who had been promised the elevation, willingly traded his ermine for the privilege of plundering the Post Office. It was a decision which the Judge never had reason to regret, for it made him Mr. Van Buren's sole representative in the Cabinet, and as such the only member whom the Little Magician suffered to remain there for a full term.

Of themselves these ministerial appointments were revolutionary enough. The precedent had been that a Cabinet should be composed of the best minds at the Executive's disposal, with little regard for favoritism or friendship. That Old Hickory's councilmen made up the "most unintellectual cabinet we ever had" was one of the mildest pronouncements which contemporaries made upon it. With the debatable exception of Governor Van Buren, not one of the ministers had ever distinguished himself in governmental work, though four had been drawn from Congress and the other from the Bench. In their former positions they had been only so many time-servers, and in the Cabinet their one claim to mention is for the comic relief which they would soon be inserting into the solemn drama of History.

But the apportioning of a mere half-dozen jobs was in no way sufficient to satisfy the hungry mass of scavengers who descended upon the Capital City in the wake of the conquering Chieftain. First came the Editors, who were variously rewarded with posts ranging from auditor to foreign minister. After them stormed a nondescript crowd with no other claims than their willingness to share in the spoils. All sorts and conditions of men thronged to the City, lined up outside Gadsby's, dogged the gift-givers about town, demanding to be remembered. None found it necessary to feel any bashfulness in regard to ability or character for, as Matty Van's Hamilton remembered it, "no thought appeared to be given as to the worth of the person for the places. I am sure I never heard one word in relation thereto." So long as a man had dutifully voted and supported the Hickory ticket, he was qualified for any job that happened to be open. The one danger was that, with such a multitude to feed, there might be a shortage of loaves and fishes, but to take care of this emergency, the in-coming Administration soon set up the guillotines, and heads began to roll in earnest.

After the Carnival then—the Carnage. The five preceding Presidents had removed 74 office-holders over a period of thirty-two years. Within a few months the Jacksonian spoilsmen dismissed, by conservative estimate, "as high as two thousand" on the avowed principle that "no damned scoundrel . . . for . . . Adams . . . is entitled to the least lenity or mercy save that of hanging." In order to ferret out a maximum number of victims an espionage system was established, after which, as a lady complained: "Why a man dare not . . . . shake hands with a personal friend if he happens to differ from the powers that be." Those holding office, observed Mr. Clay, came to feel "something like the inhabitants of Cairo when the plague breaks out: no one knows who will be next." The suspense was maddening. In the State Department a clerk went crazy; in the Treasury another committed suicide. Still the Terror swept on.

Seeking to justify the pre-election charge that the government was honeycombed with corruption, elaborate investigations were held; at first with an embarrassing poverty of results. A search of the court and jail records proved that some of the clerks were in debt, for which disgraceful offense they were condemned to annihilation. The public, however, failed to respond with any enthusiasm to this display of Old Hickory's honest severity, and efforts were redoubled to uncover a real scandal. Finally it was discovered that Tobias Watkins, an auditor already dismissed without cause, had taken with him from the Treasury about $7000. With wild yelps of exultation the People's avengers dragged him from retirement, tried, convicted and imprisoned him. Here, they pointed out, was a personal accomplice of Mr. Adams, a typical example of the rogues whom the ex-President had employed. In order to make the exhibition a complete success, General Jackson was persuaded to order a sign placed over the wretch's cell-door: "Criminal Apartment"; but it was doubtless removed later on when one of Old Hickory's personal appointees, Sam Swartwout, made off to Europe with $1,222,705.69 of stealings from the government.

The gruesomeness of the carnage was greatly enhanced by the longstanding policy of using minor clerkships as pensions for old and disabled soldiers. Richard Rush, Secretary of the Treasury under Adams, had called his office force the "Octogenarian Department," and to drop the axe on such venerable necks touched even the iron hearts of the executioners. "I turned out six clerks on Saturday . . . The most painful thing I ever did . . . Among them was an old man with a young wife and six children." "My feelings have been severely crowded with various applications for relief . . . A lady applied to me with tears in her eyes . . . her children were starving and to buy them a morsel of bread she had

# The American Talleyrand

had to sell her thimble." But thoughts of mercy were seldom allowed to interrupt the work. When old Solomon Van Rensselaer, notified to evacuate the Albany post office, journeyed to the White House and tore off his coat to exhibit his honorable scars of battle, Old Hickory relented; but when a friend attempted by the same graphic argument, to save William Henry Harrison, hero of Tippicanoe and the Thames, the President was adamant.

"If you'd seen him as I did on the Thames, you would, I think, let him alone," said the Postmaster General.

"You may be right, Barry," sighed Old Hickory. "But thank God I didn't see him there."

So went the Revolution, rounding out its cycle, destroying —as what revolution does not?—its one sensible excuse for existence. The aristocrats were out and the democrats in, but as reaction and aftermath began to crystallize and permanent results became visible, it grew apparent to anyone who cared to observe that the goal of improved government and social equality were further off than ever. The camp followers had inveigled the Conqueror. Left to their mercies he became little more than a gullible old man who, despite his utter sincerity and rugged patriotism, eventually did his country as much harm as good. So long as he remained in the White House plunder and pillage had to be cloaked under the thin guise of "rotation in office" and "reform" but, when he was gone, an Horatius had left the bridge. Henceforth the Spoils System became an integral and accepted factor of American politics, and charlatanism a candidate's most conspicuous quality. The ensuing century would prove that no man need look to the most powerful office on earth unless he were willing to buy it with the People's own money and win it by out-capering his opponent in a jig-dance of demagoguery and hypocrisy. Henceforth babies must be kissed and backs must be slapped ere a man could aspire to leadership. Henceforth a candidate must learn to fawn and to flatter, lie and to libel before he could hope to rule.

Such was the ultimate outcome of the Revolution, and

250 ]

behind the scenes moved a figure of destiny. Too dainty and immaculate to be picturesquely sinister, Martin Van Buren nevertheless was, as a friend wrote him, "the prime mover" of the whole transition. At forty-seven he had transcended his mere mortal existence and belonged to posterity. He was, in truth, a Founding Father. For the Little Magician's whole life up to this point had been but a prologue to the epoch that was now inaugurated. No man but he had nurtured the fledgling Spoils System, brought it to full flower on the Hudson's shore, and transplanted it to the Potomac, whence it would shower its seeds the country over. No man but he had developed political chicanery from an outlawed, spurious practice to a national profession. He had not instigated the People's rebellion, but at the propitious moment he had mounted upon the thunder clouds and directed the storm. He had not made Andrew Jackson a Hero, but he had done more than any man to make him a President and had done so with a knowing eye cocked toward the future. More than that, Martin Van Buren had accomplished the cosmic feat of re-architecting a universe which he found hostile to him. Born into a nation that knew how to select its Washingtons, its Jeffersons and its Adamses, and to reject its Burrs, its Tompkinses and its Crawfords, he recodified the system of values so that mediocrity, instead of true greatness, might thrive and prosper.

Delayed in Albany by the demands of his Bucktails (and very likely by his innate dislike for risking dangerous responsibilities), Mr. Van Buren arrived in Washington eighteen days after Inauguration and when the Carnage had already begun. Besides his portfolio, Little Van came bearing the commission of chief patronage dispenser. Knowing from experience what a rush to expect, he had suggested a more orderly method than simply throwing open the doors to all applicants. His plan had been, as explained in a letter to Hamilton, "to get the streets of Washington clear of office-seekers" by stating that no removals would be made until after due consideration. But in his absence the situation had gone far beyond control; there was nothing to do now but go ahead with the guillotine work. Though no formal announcement had been made of the Prime Minister's secondary commission, such was his reputation for authority in such matters that apparently none was necessary. On the evening of March 22, when his coach pulled up at the hotel door, a host of job-hunters was awaiting him on the curb and "followed me into and filled my room."

Lecturing them severely on the uncouthness of such undisguised eagerness for loot, Mr. Van Buren allowed them an hour to talk and then hastened off to the White House for the purpose of salvaging some ambassadorships for his friends who had been left out of the Cabinet. He soon arranged with the President that Levi Woodbury should be offered Spain, but to his annoyance Little Van heard that the two choice missions had already been disposed of. A pair of very able and scholarly gentlemen, Senator Tazewell and ex-Mayor Edward Livingston, at that time of Louisiana, had been named respectively for Great Britain and France. That, of course, would never do, but it required only a small dose of the Little Magician's persuasiveness to induce Old Hickory to revoke these men's appointments and to send in their steads Louis McLean and William C. Rives.

Another problem later arose over the disposal of Randolph of Roanoke, who at an early hour of the Carnage became violently envenomed of the Democracy which he had inadvertently hastened. Lest this congenital President-hater vent his passions against Old Hickory, Little Van advised that he be shipped off to Russia, adding the hopeful suggestion that "it would expose him to an unfavorable climate . . . and little harm would be done if it should turn out we had made a mistake."

With all of his accustomed efficiency Little Van took charge of "clearing the streets." He did not immediately assume his waiting duties of the State Department, but devoted the first fortnight after his arrival to finishing up the Carnage. Under his practiced direction the guillotines worked double time and, to facilitate matters, the inconvenient cant about rotation and reform was temporarily dropped. As rec-

252 ]

ognized head axeman, he was waited upon by a committee of protest who demanded to know why twelve good officials in far-off Florida had been replaced by as many worthless hirelings.

"We give no reasons for our removals," he told them smilingly, and from then on explanations were neither expected nor given. By April 4th the unsavory work had been done, and Mr. Van Buren was formally sworn in as Secretary of State, which post, along with the senatorship and governorship, made three high offices, embracing a total term of ten years, which the Little Magician had held in less than half that many months.

The rôle of Prime Minister in a presidential Cabinet was easily the most congenial one he ever played. A few months ago he had tried his last case and he was now definitely retired from law practice with enough money to forget all financial worries. The simultaneous withdrawal from lawgiving life gave him opportunity to devote his whole time and talents to a pursuit for which he was most admirably suited. With no more briefs and speeches to write, no more elections to distract him, he now became a full-time, fullfledged courtier—flattering his monarch, out-scheming his adversaries and charming his social circle.

The truth is that, up to this point in his life, Martin Van Buren had succeeded more in spite of his natural bents than because of them. Never a first-class orator and always an unpopular candidate, he had convinced his audiences and won his elections, but his heart was never in the rostrum or on the hustings. By temperament a pacific character and by cultivation a dandy, he had never cared for the rough and tumble of parliamentary debate or for feigned friendship with the voting bourgeoisie. The drawing-room and the privy council were his happy hunting grounds and, becoming Prime Minister, he discovered himself in proverbial clover. Called upon to display his ability for polite intrigue among both sexes, for polished cabal among schooled diplomats, the Little Magician shone as never before. As with each of his former offices, he had won this one less by intrinsic worth than by masked manoeuvring, and he would make it serve him less for his country's good than his own. In Albany and on Capitol Hill, his most outstanding successes had been in extra-curriculum activities—matters that had nothing to do with the work for which his salaries were paid. The same would be true with his incumbency of the State Department, yet in this post, because it fitted him so perfectly, he did manage to do a certain amount of legitimate labor.

Entering the Cabinet he found that his official duty as presidential adviser fell fairly under two heads—domestic and foreign relationships. The first had mainly to do with guiding the President's legislation through Congress; and since that body, though none too friendly, had great respect for what Senator Webster called Old Hickory's "out-door popularity," this portion of the Prime Minister's task was not overwhelming. At the regular session which convened in December '29, the Senate registered its formal protest against the Spoils System by rejecting appointments for the two most objectionable editors, Ike Hill and Henry Lee. But the first parliamentary rift appeared over the question of Internal Improvements, which the thwarting of the Adams-Clay Vision had left hanging fire.

Several such bills were introduced early in the session, but no issue was drawn since there remained reasonable doubt as to where the President and his Secretary stood on the measure. During the Monroe administration Little Van had voted for Internal Improvements, only to change his mind when Mr. Adams made it part of his program. Old Hickory, as a Senator, had also voted pro and con on several occasions. Being a Westerner, the President was assumed to be for expansion at government expense, being a State Rights advocate he was judged to be against it, so that, until he made some definite statement, his attitude remained a mystery. All depended on what interpretation he found in the Constitution which he had sworn to uphold, and his reputed illiteracy added largely to the speculation.

How the General, left to his own devices, might finally have decided this vital point will never be known. Evidently it occurred to him that Mr. Van Buren, who was about to be ordained a Phi Beta Kappa member by Union College, must be a very erudite gentleman—and what were scholars for, if not to give bookish advice? The matter came to a head with the passage through both Houses of the Maysville Road Bill, proposing to build a highway across Kentucky with governmental funds. In his quandary the President was on the point of calling his Prime Minister into conference when the Minister himself broached the subject. Mr. Van Buren had been watching the Bill ever since its introduction in the House, had marked it for destruction mainly, he admits, because it involved Henry Clay's own State. He now laid before his chief a fully-written veto message, intended to submerge not only this particular measure but the whole question of Internal Improvement.

Old Hickory's pre-conception of his Secretary's scholarship was amply justified by his reading of the message. "As far as I have been able to decipher it," he wrote Little Van, "I think it is one of the most lucid expositions of the Constitution. . . . I have ever met with." Henceforward Mr. Van Buren became the Administration's acknowledged criterion on constitutional matters, and the President's indispensable aide. It is pleasant to relate that in this capacity he served wisely and well, proving himself fully competent of level-headed, informed statesmanship so long as it did not interfere with his personal plans. There is no need to weigh either the sincerity or soundness of his interpretations except to observe that they were strictly Jeffersonian, being very largely the opinions of ex-Presidents Madison and Monroe, with whom he frequently consulted by letters. Yet it is always impossible to divorce the man from his underlying motives. General Jackson applied the veto message, and from the West came a storm of protest that threatened to shake the "outdoor popularity" on which the Administration was heavily counting. The President stood firmly by his action and gloried in the strife. Not so his Secretary. Questioned on his opinions concerning the matter, Little Van gave out such contradictory and evasive statements that, coming under the

Senate's fire several months later, one of the charges against him was that he had secretly opposed this same veto which he himself had written.

Still there should be no underestimating the Prime Minister's usefulness to the President during the early duels with Congress, of which the Internal Improvements question was the outstanding example. He was in the Cabinet to support his superior, and since this support served the Secretary's own purposes, he accomplished it admirably. Of equal ability was his handling of the highly combustible question of foreign relationship. The elevation to power of a Military Chieftain, and one who had already caused them woe, naturally had a disquieting effect upon European nations. Especially was this true of Great Britain and France—the first, America's traditional foe; the second, just becoming her traditional debtor through large indemnities incurred during the Napoleonic days. To calm the fears of nervous Ambassadors became one of the Prime Minister's main duties, and one to which he attended with habitual delicacy and tact.

Soon after arriving in Washington, he had called on his fast friend and "brother Dutchman," the Chevalier de Huygens, Minister from Holland. Through the Chevalier he made it a point to establish personal acquaintanceship with each member of the diplomatic corps and to treat all to a goodly amount of flattery and charm. Then, having carefully coached Old Hickory on what to say and what to leave unsaid, the Prime Minister brought, first, Sir Charles Vaughan of England, then each of the others, to informal little dinners at the White House, exhibiting the dread Chieftain as a harmless, home-loving host. By the aid of these amiable contacts he was able to accomplish the two diplomatic feats for which his incumbency in the State Department is chiefly known—the West India Trade Treaty with Great Britain; the Debt Compromise with France.

But it would be an unpardonable violation of truth to imply that Mr. Van Buren gave all or any large portion of his energy to running the State Department. He made a moderately good Secretary, but is not to be seriously compared

to the best of those who came before and after him. He was
as good as he was because of his natural fitness for the post;
he was no better because his mind was elsewhere. "To be
President," he wrote, "has ever been my most earnest desire."
What he called "the great goal . . . the Ultima Thule of
political life" was now within sight. The four preceding
Prime Ministers who ascended to the Chief Magistracy had
done so by devout attention to statesmanship, but it could
hardly be expected that the Little Magician, having prospered so well by his wits, should change his tactics. By
adroitly tacking across the winds of circumstance, by
shrewdly contriving that the moving tide of men and events
continually bore him forward—so had Martin Van Buren
progressed thus far and so would he go further.

The neat uniformity of his career shows that at each step
of his progress the Red Fox met and mangled one or more
men whom History has justly rated his superiors, despite the
fact that he invariably overcame them. With Mr. Adams laid
low and Mr. Clay in full flight toward Kentucky crying that
he'd "make a better farmer than statesman!" the distinction
of being Little Van's next major opponent fell to the luckless
lot of Mr. John C. Calhoun.

It was inevitable that this should be, for the gaunt and
gloomy Carolinian, besides being irreconcilable to anyone
of such political dexterity, stood as the logical heir to the
presidency. Of exactly Little Van's age, Mr. Calhoun had
come into national office when the Boy Lawyer was just
breaking into the State Senate, had given honorable service
in Congress and Cabinet and twice had been elected Vice
President. Furthermore, Andrew Jackson had specified that
he would hold office only one term, and in 1829 his choice
for successor was unquestionably Mr. Calhoun, whom Old
Hickory had toasted up and down the Atlantic sea-board as
"An honest man—the noblest work of God!"

To ambush one man and woo himself into the favor of
another, these, then, and not foreign or domestic affairs,
were the problems to which the Prime Minister gave his fore-
most attention. To him there was nothing new about such

[ 257

objectives, having been about them all of his public life. Yet, if he paused to calculate his chances, Martin Van Buren could only see that every advantage was with his rival. Bearing the public's confidence, the President's blessing and the Cabinet's support, Mr. Calhoun appeared well-nigh invulnerable.

One by one these advantages must be cut away from him. And one by one would the Little Magician bring these wonders to pass.

2

(1829–1830)

Over the fallen figure of a beautiful woman two men stood face to face, aghast. An instant before Major Eaton's fist had been moving through space in the exact direction of the Reverend J. M. Campbell's jaw, only to be intercepted as the lady plunged in front of the blow and went down beneath it, gashing her head against a piece of furniture.

It was not, as Peggy Eaton might have wished, a properly ladylike swoon, and it may only be called deplorable that this prostrate position between friend and foe was so symbolic of her plight. Yet she at whose feet so many men had flung themselves, now lay in that posture herself; and the same Capital City which she had seen to burn under the British torch had finally brought her to the stake and was preparing to apply torch to her. She was no witch they were burning, though two men were reputed to have taken their lives for her charms. She was no queen, though Queen Dolly had danced at her wedding and King Andrew had wept in her arms. She was no saint, though the Church it was which had ordered her execution.

"Would to God," cried the Reverend Campbell, as he saw her crash to the floor, "that I never had anything to do with this!"

Unquestionably his utterance was wholly sincere, for this was the second time in as many days that his victim's anguish

258 ]

had brought the churchman into physical peril and embarrassment. Only yesterday he had been summoned to face the lethal rage of Old Hickory and had been forced to stand as her prosecutor before the assembled Cabinet. Yet much as he may have regretted these public ordeals and wished himself through with them, the Reverend Campbell might have been consoled to know that he had accomplished what few of his cloth ever did. He had won himself a deathless, if distasteful, rôle in the American drama.

It all came about because young Mr. Campbell in his earnestness had done what he considered his duty as custodian of the Capital City's morals. Pastor of Washington's fashionable church, which included among its congregation the President and all but one of the Cabinet families, he very naturally came into indirect contact with the gay social world that buzzed about him. Shortly after the beginning of the revolutionary year he had heard a collection of horrific tales and, seeking advice, had relayed them to his friend and spiritual confidant, the aged Mr. Ezra Stiles Ely of Philadelphia, who happened to be in town for the inauguration. It seems, began young Campbell, that on New Year in celebration of Peg's marriage to Major Eaton, the British Ambassador had given a ball, at which a guest was heard to remark of the bride that "she had forgotten the time when she used to sleep with him."

Such evidence of lewdness in court circles only vindicated Mr. Ely's life-long opinion of the upper classes, whose doings it was his livelihood to denounce. Avidly he pressed his young colleague for more data, which Mr. Campbell had no difficulty supplying. At this same party, he reported, word went round that Major Eaton had requested the mission to France instead of the War Department, and ladies and gentlemen were freely offering wagers that there was a sound biological reason for his preference.

"Oh, you can't go to France," her friend Minnie Bankhead had warned Peg. "You are not in a condition to leave the country, you know. You must have that child first."

Blushingly, the bride had accepted the challenge. "I will not leave the soil of America until nine months . . ."

At this Mr. Ely must hear more. With so much smoke there must be fire. There was, Mr. Campbell assured him, at least plenty more smoke. The present Mrs. Eaton was the 30-year-old daughter of William O'Neil, for many years proprietor of Franklin House, a popular tavern in Washington. There as a child Peggy had grown up and served as barmaid, while her ever-growing reputation for saucy beauty and flippant familiarity with the male guests became the talk of the town. Three times she had tried to elope; a rejected lover had killed himself over her, and then she had married a seafaring man, John B. Timberlake, whose own suicide, the Capital City's best people agreed, had been caused by her flirtations—or worse—with this same Major Eaton. In support of this popular theory there was a shocking story ascribed to the late Dr. Craven—if Mr. Ely felt he could hear it. Mr. Ely was certain that with grim fortitude he could. It was thus:

One day in 1821, with the husband at sea, Dr. Craven had been called in to attend Mrs. Timberlake for slight injuries incurred in a carriage accident. Entering the bed room, the physician was greatly surprised to find the patient and her mother in gales of hysterical laughter.

"You should have been here a little sooner," Peg was reported to have giggled. "You would have seen a little John Henry Eaton."

"Yes, Dr. Craven," supplemented the mother, "you lost a good fee, for Major Eaton would have paid you well."

Hungrily Mr. Ely made note of all this and, being personally acquainted with the incoming President, he appointed himself the tale-bearer. Unable to find opportunity for a conference during the turmoil of Inauguration Day, he returned to Philadelphia and from there sent the President a long letter detailing the charges and begging him "for your own sake, for your dead wife's sake, for your Administration, for the credit of the government and country," to dismiss this sinful Secretary of War and his infamous bride.

## The Portfolio

The letter reminded Andrew Jackson of a rain-swept grave in Tennessee where he believed just such scandalmongers had laid his Rachel, whose sudden death just after the election Old Hickory always claimed to be not heart failure but heart break at the loathsome attacks upon her good name. Mr. Ely's letter also reminded the old soldier of how one night he had lain across that grave mingling his tears with the descending storm, and how Peggy Eaton had found him there and, lifting him up, guided him into the house. Desert such a friend in time of her travail? Not Andrew Jackson! He ragingly answered Mr. Ely that the letter "gives me pain" and dedicated the rest of the spring and summer to compiling documentary proof that Peg was, as he called her "chaste as a virgin."

Detectives were hired, affidavits taken, records searched, and in September the two churchmen were called to the White House and confronted with 90-odd pages of rebuttal to their accusations. No hotel register revealed, as they had insisted, that Mrs. Timberlake and Major Eaton had travelled together before marriage. Dr. Craven was unfortunately dead, but his mother, his wife, his pastor all testified that he had never been on anything but friendly and unprofessional relations with the defendant. His books showed that the only time he had been called to Peg's house for medical services was to treat one of the servants. And the crushing destruction of the prosecution came when Timberlake was proved not to have been at sea in 1821 nor for five years thereafter.

Somewhat flustered but staunch in their cause of righteousness, the churchmen admitted that perhaps they were wrong about the date, the doctor, the accomplice to Peg's iniquity. Perhaps it was another year, another physician, another lover—nevertheless she was a scarlet woman. They would stick to that. Gruffly Mr. Ely agreed that he had no evidence against Major Eaton.

"Nor Mrs. Eaton either!" roared Old Hickory.

Mr. Ely set his lips. "On that I would rather not give an opinion."

Wrathfully the President drove them from his presence
and dismissed the Cabinet meeting which had been convened to review the case. He heard next day of how the
Eatons had cornered Campbell at the rectory in a vain attempt to wring from him a confession of error. That night he
called to find Peg a-bed with a bandaged head.

"Major, how could you keep your hands off the scoundrel?"

"My wife held me back or I would have throttled him,"
fumed the husband.

Home in his own room at the White House, the President
found comfort in a picture that hung on his wall—one that
represented a now-familiar countenance adorned with soft,
furry sideburns and a beaming, confidential glance. "It appears to look upon me and smile," the tired old warrior once
commented. "I say to you frankly," he told the Senator from
his own state, "that Van Buren is one of the most frank
men I ever knew . . . *a true man* with no guile. It is said
that he is a great magician—I believe it, but his only wand is
common good sense which he uses for the benefit of his
country."

Indeed the picture had every right to be smiling down
upon Old Hickory, for it portrayed a Prime Minister who
in his maiden year had performed a courtier's first mission
of becoming the monarchial favorite. Mr. Van Buren was
barely resettled in Washington before he made his first move
to that end. Calling on Mrs. Eaton, he confided to her that
he "had been reading much and thinking deeply on the
character of great men and had come to the conclusion that
General Jackson was the greatest man that had ever lived—
the only man among them all who was without a fault."

"But don't tell General Jackson what I have said," he
cautioned her. "I would not have him know it for the
world."

Needless to say Old Hickory heard it before the next sunrise. He looked at Peg "with tears in his eyes":

"Ah, Madam, that man loves me; he tries to conceal it,

but there is always some fixed way by which I can tell my friends from my enemies."

After that the Prime Minister was no longer "Mr. Van Buren" to Old Hickory in familiar discourse but plain "Van," and anyone who attempted to malign the little favorite was a certain recipient of the General's roaring displeasure. Who but Van could make such touching and tender references to his departed Rachael or such solicitous inquiries concerning an old man's failing health? It was in Van's company that he took his daily exercise, riding out into the open country beyond the George Town Bridge; on Van's arm that he frequently climbed the steps to his bedchamber at night; on Van's advice that he signed or vetoed a bill; on Van's opinion that he relied for solution of puzzling questions. Jealous politicians might sneer at the Prime Minister's supposed insincerity and fopperies, but Old Hickory knew better than they. Didn't Van once tell him: "I wished I had a window in my breast through which you might read my innermost thoughts"? Was that insincerity? Hadn't Van sat about the White House many an evening in shirt sleeves, puffing a pipe when he might as easily have been mincing over a snuffbox in some drawing room? Was that foppery? By the Eternal, Andrew Jackson knew a friend when he met one.

So it happened that the "man with no guile" was soon able to apply his "common good sense . . . for the benefit of his country" whenever he found it necessary. For instance, in December the President became so enfeebled with a flare-up of his multitudinous afflictions that it seemed advisable to procure from him some sort of political will. Therefore, with the connivance of Major Lewis, who lived at the White House, the General was propped up on his pillows and aided in writing a statement which named Little Van for the succession. The General's unexpected recovery made it unnecessary to publish the document, but Lewis confessed years later that it had been procured for the above purpose.

Again during the next month, it now being supposed that Old Hickory might survive one term but possibly not two, the "common good sense" was evidenced once more when the *Courier and Enquirer* (whose editor was a Tammany Sachem) nominated Mr. Van Buren for an election which was still three years distant. And still again in February, with the General completely recovered, "the most frank man I ever knew" wrote to Albany that the Bucktails should re-nominate Andrew Jackson for 1832 with a suggestive omission of Mr. Calhoun's name for the second office.

All these, however, were only emergency measures and not at all of a kind with the larger plan which the industrious little courtier was mapping out for himself. It is instructive to note that, during his courtiership, nearly every-one of the Little Magician's coups were staged at a social function—mostly at balls and banquets. After these many years he had succeeded in building up a national Regency and manning it with assistants capable of doing all visible labor themselves. Ben Butler and Silas Wright were managing the Bucktails back home, collaborating with C. C. Cambreleng in the House of Representatives and Charles E. Dudley, Little Van's successor in the Senate. William M. Barry was running the Post Office according to instructions; J. A. Hamilton and Major Lewis were aides-de-camp in and about Washington; Edwin Croswell still edited the *Argus* and there were others, such as Jesse Hoyt, handling less conspicuous details. Behind the scenes machinery might now and then be heard to creak, and stage hands seen to strain and sweat, but the dapper little figure that moved before the footlights seemed alone in his glory.

Peg's trial being over, life in the Capital City assumed an ominous state of calm. The frustration of her accusers and the discrediting of their evidence, would have been sufficient to gain her an acquittal in any court of law, where a person not proved guilty is assumed to be innocent. But no such charitable code prevailed among the select jury that sat on her case. Theoretically cleared of adultery, Peg was none the less convicted of the higher crime of social-climbing. A barmaid and a tavern-keeper's daughter simply had no business marrying a Cabinet Minister. Her sentence was pronounced with finality. Burn she must.

Only the date of the execution remained indefinite. The torch-holders gathered and prepared for the rites. Floride Calhoun, returning from a visit to Fort Hill, her husband's Carolina estate, found that the Eatons had called on her and left their cards, but she flatly refused to return the courtesy. In this she was upheld by her mate, the Vice President, who declared with his Presbyterian severity that her decision was "a great victory in favor of the morals of the country." The other ministerial ladies—wives of Secretaries Ingham and Branch and the daughter of Berrien—joined forces with her, making no secret about town of their intentions. All that was needed was for the President to give the Cabinet dinner which was considered, since the reign of Dolly Madison, the official opening of the social season.

But to end Peg's days of grace was something Old Hickory was in no hurry to do. He knew, as did everyone, what mutiny was brewing and, untrained in handling female insurrections, he resorted for once in his life to Fabian tactics. From March '29 till November '30, still no presidential fête, and so it might have continued had not the Prime Minister taken a hand. A suave suggestion on one of their afternoon rides stirred Old Hickory out of his delay. He remonstrated a little, but not for long. If Van said so, then, by the Eternal, the thing should be done.

When the cards went out the debate waxed hot around tea tables as to whether the Four Executioners would consent to break bread with their victim. But an invitation to the White House was a royal command, and on the appointed evening the ministers arrived with their ladies to go through the pantomime of peace and good will. It was, the Prime Minister noted, "a formal and hollow ceremony," a fitting last meal for the condemned. The flames about Peg's pyre were now lighted and diligently did the Red Fox fan them, knowing whose hide they would eventually scorch.

His first move was to issue invitations for a Cabinet dinner of his own. "Just as I had supposed" the Four Executioners grasped the chance to give Peg her first singeing. They all pointedly declined to attend for reasons, as their husbands

[265

explained, "unnecessary to detail." Little Van's next effort had yet more satisfying results. His first invitations had been for an exclusive affair, but to bring officialdom *en masse* to the orgy he now gave one large dinner-dance himself, and is credited with having incited a pair of his fellow-courtiers and bachelors, Sir Charles Vaughan and Baron Krudener, the Russian Minister, to give two others.

The three balls, individually and collectively, did the Prime Minister more good than three elections could have done. They completely separated the Calhoun element of the Cabinet from Old Hickory's confidence and strengthened his faith in the altruistic fidelity of Little Van who, Mr. Adams observed, "is notoriously engaged in canvassing for the presidency by paying his court to Mrs. Eaton." Sir Charles' party resulted in a flood of newspaper articles which baldly stated that Mrs. Eaton was an undesirable element in polite society and that Mr. Van Buren was trying to force her upon her betters. Little Van's own dinner witnessed a shoulder-shoving contest and an exchange of insults between the victim and one of her torch-bearers. The third saw the Dutch Ambassador's wife dramatically leave the table at sight of Peg, and it served also for the trysting place where the evergrowing band of Executioners took oath to organize spite parties which would leave the War Department unrepresented.

As New Year of 1830 approached the Eaton Malaria was beginning to find its way into the hearts of the several Muses. Ballads and songs hymned the Princess Immaculate and told of her sorrow; cartoons pictured La Bellona in various settings and poses; at one of the less reputable theatres a five-act comedy made merry allegory of the commotion, and in the local newspapers Francis Scott Key offered jingling verses to commemorate its progress. Old Hickory played deaf and blind as long as he could, but when he heard and saw that Peg was being excluded from the parties she loved so much, he rallied to her defense. Emily Donelson, his niece and the White House hostess, refused to coöperate; he chased her home to the Hermitage. He sent his Prime Minister in person to the Dutch embassy with the warning that any more boycott would call for immediate dismissal. He whipped off letters with Little Van's aid to each of his erring Secretaries, stating that snubbing the lady in question would be considered *lèse majesté* and answerable directly to him.

The ultimatum, given in January, made the Prime Minister supreme. After that the other Cabinet members ceased to be councilors and degenerated into mere department heads, no longer even called into executive meetings. The real Privy Council became known as the Kitchen Cabinet and was composed of the same personnel as the preëlection board of strategy; that is, the Majors, the Editors and the Director. Over this coterie presided the Little Magician, the affairs of the nation at the tips of his nimble fingers.

Prime Minister, constitutional authority, court favorite, power behind the throne—the courtier from Kinderhook was moving ever closer to his Great Goal. Yet before him there still stood, though shaken, the dark menacing figure of the Pretender—Mr. John Caldwell Calhoun.

### 3

### (1830–1831)

Under his upright spiky hair and gloom-ridden brow the "glorious yellow-brown eyes" of the Seventh Vice President looked down on a crowd that filled the little Senate Chamber to capacity and over-flowed through the open doors at the rear. Everyone who could get there this 27th of January, 1830, had come to the Capitol to hear the finale of the Great Debate, and "to accommodate the ladies who thronged the vestibules, not only the lobbies and passages were filled with chairs, but even Senators had the gallantry to yield their seats." Spread before Mr. Calhoun was a bright panorama of flashing colors and wrapt faces, all turned on the burly, barrel-chested orator in shiny, gilt buttons and buff waistcoat who stood just below the rostrum, "sway[ing] his right arm like a huge tilt hammer up and down . . . like Vulcan in his armory, forging thoughts for the gods."

For six days the Webster-Hayne encounter had dragged on, mainly because Mr. Webster found it necessary to ask for frequent postponements while he rushed out to see after a lucrative case of his before the Supreme Court. Beginning with the ever-active question of Internal Improvements, the subject-matter had ranged through every live issue of the day—Slavery, States Rights, Tariff, the Constitution—and had finally come down to a head-on collision between North and South with Mr. Calhoun's own Nullification theory the *causus belli*. Two days ago the two champions had definitely squared off when South Carolina's Senator Hayne, cheered on by grimaces of encouragement and frequent notes of advice from the chair, had risen and set upon New England in general and Mr. Webster in particular with a sparkling assault that seemed unanswerable. And yesterday Mr. Webster boasting, "I will grind him as fine as a pinch of snuff!" had commenced a speech he was finishing today—one that would make him famous on two continents and, being published, would bring him in royalties that rivaled Washington Irving's.

Viewing the spectacle from his lofty dais, Mr. Calhoun was becoming progressively aware that it was mistaken tactics to have roused this lion from his customary indolence. Left to himself, Black Dan Webster was inclined at this period of his career to take his legislative duties extremely lightly. He had wandered into the Twenty-First Congress three days late with a new bride in tow and John Jacob Astor as a client. Only by accident had he been passing the Senate door during the early stages of the Internal Improvements debate and heard New England's name taken in vain. It greatly harassed Mr. Webster to hear Mr. Hayne allude to the embarrassing subject of the Hartford Convention and to accuse his beloved Northland of having bought western support for the Tariff by backing government subsidies for improvements out beyond the Alleghenies. The policy of protecting the infant industries of the North might be the

268 ]

Tariff of Abominations to the southern planters, but to most of Mr. Webster's constituents and nearly all of his clients it represented good yellow gold. To hear Mr. Hayne voice the sentiment that any State Legislature had a right to nullify an Act of Congress pinched Mr. Webster's thrifty sense of business as well as his patriotism.

"It's high time," another nervous New Englander enjoined him that morning on their way to the chamber, "that the people of this country should know what the Constitution *is*."

"Then by the blessing of Heaven," Black Dan had rumbled, "they shall learn this day before the sun goes down what *I* understand it to be."

They were learning, as Mr. Calhoun was in a position to observe, a great deal, much of which had very little to do with the Constitution. Out of that massive chest rolled syllable upon syllable of eloquence that needed only the majestic presence of the orator and the organ-like tones of his voice to make them impressive. Breath-taking flights that thrilled the crowd when, ever so endearingly, he mentioned this land of liberty for which our forefathers had nobly died that it might live. Searing darts of irony that caused Mr. Hayne to slink within his chair as the doctrine of Nullification was exposed in its shameful nakedness. Fluid streams of pathos at which a visiting delegation from Massachusetts was reported to have "shed tears like girls" when he recalled how the heroic old Bay State had so often stood as the watchdog of the endangered Constitution. Then, ignoring the twelve pages of notes which lay on his desk to guide him through what his admirers insisted was an unprepared speech, Black Dan plunged into a peroration that rose and seethed like a foaming tide. It reached a climax that caused even the phlegmatic Mr. Adams to go home in a daze and put it down in his Diary ". . . remarkable . . . It demolished the whole fabric of Hayne's speech, so that it leaves scarcely a wreck to be seen."

"Liberty *and* Union, now and forever, one and inseparable!"

Bobbing his leonine head toward the galleries, Mr. Webster made to resume his seat only to find that a lady had usurped it when he had risen. Mr. Calhoun leaped up and pounded the desk with his gavel lest some forbidden applause should spontaneously break forth to insult the dignity of the Senate. It was an unnecessary apprehension, for the audience was so completely mesmerized that it sat silent several moments before it rose and numbly departed, ignoring Mr. Hayne who was on the floor again to attempt a feeble rebuttal. Mr. Webster heard him through, replied in a few hasty sentences and then scurried away to continue his money-making before the Court. That evening he met his rival at a White House levee.

"How are you, Colonel Hayne?"

The Carolinian smiled wanly. "None the better for you, Sir."

But Mr. Calhoun was not so certain that his cause had received a mortal wound. With mixed emotions had he watched Black Dan dismember the Nullification argument and, though it was a discomforting scene to have witnessed, the Vice-President had secret reason to rejoice. Here at last was an opportunity for which he had been yearning these many months—a chance to embrace a common cause with Andrew Jackson. When Mr. Calhoun had deserted the Adams camp, against every one of his avowed principles, it had been with the mutual understanding, and possibly with the promise, that he should be Old Hickory's successor. But shortly after Inauguration, and remarkably coincident with the tardy arrival of the Secretary of State, events began to shape themselves in a way which Mr. Calhoun could not fail to see were sundering instead of cementing his ties to the President. The Eaton Malaria was now in its most contagious stage; the Ultimatum to the Cabinet had severed that body of allies from presidential influence.

To assuage all these mortifications Mr. Calhoun was ready to make concessions. The humiliation of the Cabinet he could refuse to admit was a personal affront, and though he could not force his wife to call on the Princess Immaculate, he

270 ]

could at least temper the wind of Old Hickory's displeasure by sending Floride home to Fort Hill, which he soon did. To span the ever-widening chasm of presidential disfavor, the Nullification problem came, thought Mr. Calhoun, as a godsend. Here was an issue that made a cleancut division between North and South; between nationalistic Federalism and Jeffersonian States Rights; between industrialism and agrarianism. Andrew Jackson, as a born-Carolinian and one who had advocated hanging the New England-bred Hartford Convention, seemed bound to side with the Calhoun interests and had, in fact, given indications that he would. The Nullification moves had begun in 1828 before the election, when Congress had passed and Mr. Adams had signed the Tariff of Abominations. During the campaign and since then, Old Hickory had been sounded out on the doctrine and had gone so far as to say that, so long as Nullification was a State Rights program and not Secession, he saw no harm in it. Its advocates had hastened to assure him that their policy was purely a legislative one with no implication of treason to the Republic, and the President had responded so warmly as to send Hayne a note of congratulations following the masterful arraign of his opening speech.

Hence it was not without a certain amount of elation that Mr. Calhoun gathered his colleagues after the Great Debate and laid plans for the future. At one of their meetings someone came forth with a truly inspirational thought. April 13th was Thomas Jefferson's birthday, just the occasion for a State Rights demonstration. Why not rent Brown's Hotel, proclaim a large public banquet at which the President would be guest of honor and, under the sanction of the great sage's name, launch their program anew.

The plan was quickly adopted; the arrangements made. There would be twenty-four formal toasts, "all save six or seven" of which would pertain to Jefferson, the Old Dominion and the South. Then Old Hickory, called upon for the first volunteer toast, would undoubtedly give one pertaining to the occasion, after which the Vice President would offer a health that swore fidelity to his chief, and with the room full of Congressmen, citizens and newspaper editors, Nullification and Mr. Calhoun would soon be riding the crest of the General's "outdoor popularity."

Well it was for John Caldwell Calhoun that posterity has not looked too deeply into his character during this mid-portion of his life. Coming into Congress during the prewar enthusiasm of 1811, he had, though calling himself a Republican, taken up exactly where the Federalism of Alexander Hamilton had left off. Favoring a strongly centralized government, he had sponsored bills that might have been taken directly from Mr. Hamilton's files: a re-charter of the National Bank, a protective tariff, internal improvements at government expense and control. Finding by 1828 that these measures, especially the high tariff, worked great injustice to the South, Mr. Calhoun was too much of a statesman to fear the empty charge of inconsistency. He completely reversed his position, embracing the ultra-State Rights doctrine of Nullification.

For this perfectly sincere exercise of his better judgment Mr. Calhoun undeniably deserves the wreaths of glory with which sympathetic biographers have garnished him. But if he had all the moral courage that a leader of a doomed cause might need, the Carolinian was sadly lacking in its bodily cognate. There was a musty little corner in Mr. Calhoun's life which most of his commentators have done well to leave unexplored. He came very close to being an abject physical coward. Several of his contemporaries have remarked with what poltroonery he allowed the mad Randolph to cavort about the Senate and to hold up proceedings day after day with meaningless noises that degenerated at times into insane babbling, while the Vice-President cringed behind the transparent excuse that he had no parliamentary right to call a Senator to order. But the terror in which Mr. Calhoun held this swashbuckling maniac was valor incarnate compared to his quakings at the thought of Old Hickory.

Poor Mr. Calhoun had died many times since that day Andrew Jackson was reported to be heading for Washington with the intent of lopping off a few ears. Deep within the

Vice President lurked the fearsome memory that in the
Monroe Cabinet he had suggested court-martialing the General, and though rumor had credited Mr. Crawford with the
suggestion, there was no peace in Mr. Calhoun's soul lest
the truth be some day known. From that day forward his
manners toward the old warrior had been fraught with an
unwholesome amount of fawning servility—so much so that
John Quincy Adams always attributed the Carolinian's desertion of him to "terror of Andrew Jackson."

Consequently the chance to flatter Old Hickory into a
salutary state of friendship was another of the hopes which
Mr. Calhoun had for the Jefferson Day Dinner. As the day
approached and the plans progressed, he grew ever more
ardent. He considered, as well he might, that all was cleverly
arranged and would be perfectly executed, but he missed
seeing the one ruinous flaw in the whole strategem. Had Mr.
Calhoun been less the statesman and more the politician, he
would certainly have hesitated to meet his rival for the
presidency on the latter's home ground. Giving Little Van
another social function at which to spin one of his plots was
an error which the Carolinian lived many years to rue.

Not even on the fateful evening, when he saw Old Hickory
arrive in the Prime Minister's company, did the Vice President suffer any foreboding symptoms. Sitting on one side of
the toastmaster, with General Jackson on the other, Mr. Calhoun was prepared only to enjoy a great moment. He did not
know—for how could he?—that for an hour or so beforehand, Mr. Van Buren had been closeted with the President
in the White House study, had writen his toast, and worked
the old man into such a passion over the hidden dangers of
Nullification that "we repaired to the dinner with feelings
on the part of the Chief akin to those which would have been
animated in his breast if the scene . . . had been a field of
battle instead of a festive board."

All went well throughout the meal. The twenty-four
healths and the accompanying remarks came off according
to plan and with reassuring applause. Secretary Ingham and
his Pennsylvania delegation, perceiving the true nature of

the affair, stalked from the room, and the fact that Old Hickory made no such move argued that he would certainly do what was expected of him. Came the moment for the first volunteer toast. With a flourish the chairman presented the President of the United States, and those who noticed must have been surprised to see the proper Little Van abandon all pretense of social decorum and suddenly stand upright on the seat of his chair. Table manners might be very well in their place, but the Prime Minister was not to let his stunted stature deprive him of the pleasure of watching the Vice President's face—something, he knew, which would soon be a sight to behold. The old Hero stood for a moment without a word. Now, thought the Nullifiers, a good strong allusion to the sanctified doctrine of States Rights.

Old Hickory barked: "Our Union—it must be preserved!"

The silence that proceeded was engulfed and forgotten in the one that followed. No one stirred. Glaring about him, the President lifted his goblet to the level of his eyes—a sign that the toast was to be drunk standing. Haggard and aghast Mr. Calhoun stumbled to his feet. "His glass trembled in his hand and a little of the amber fluid trickled down the side," as he raised it to his lips. All but he and the President resumed their seats. General Jackson, with a conqueror's glance about him, strode from his table to a corner of the room, leaving Mr. Calhoun in the center of attention. The gage was down. Let him take it up who dared.

Blurted Mr. Calhoun with the courage of despair: "The Union—next to our Liberty, the most dear."

But the deed was done; the Nullifiers had been dealt a public thrashing, and men were fleeing the scene of humiliation so fast that soon less than a third of the original remained. Even the Prime Minister's characteristically soothing health to: "Mutual forbearance and reciprocal concessions!" failed to bring either ease or levity to snap the strain. Mr. Calhoun trudged home that night beaten and bowed.

Yet it was merciful that the tortured Vice President did not know what fiends his enemies were sending to dog his retreating footsteps. Content Little Van might have been

274 ]

with this maiming of his rival, but he was now making ready the *coup de grâce*. As he left the banquet hall with his man Hamilton, the Little Magician learned something he had never known before. He learned the truth about Mr. Calhoun's dread secret. Hamilton told him.

Two years ago, related Hamilton, when Matty Van had sent him to New Orleans for the anniversary celebration, he had been joined at Nashville by Mayor Lewis. Lewis, apprehensive over the possibility of losing Georgia in the nearing election, had asked Hamilton to stop off at Mr. Crawford's home on the way north, and procure the latter's unqualified endorsement of Old Hickory. This he promised to do but, finding that Woodlawn, the Crawford estate, was many miles off the main highway, he had turned his mission over to Governor Forsyth, who expected to call on Mr. Crawford shortly. A few weeks later Forsyth had written to relay Mr. Crawford's endorsement and also to echo the surprising statement that not Crawford, but Calhoun, had suggested punishing General Jackson for the raid into Florida.

On receipt of this communication, continued Hamilton, he had merely showed it to Lewis and then locked it up in a drawer where it had remained ever since—and the secret with it. On one occasion the General had heard Lewis mention his knowledge of it and had demanded to see the proof, but no real effort had been made to get it for him, presumably because neither Lewis nor Hamilton cared to sow seeds of dissension in the Administration. The Prime Minister, however, had no such compunctions and though he spends several pages of the Autobiography attempting to prove that "I had no more to do with the proceedings than the man in the moon," it would be passing strange if he had not. For over two years the letter to Hamilton had remained hidden, yet immediately Little Van heard of its existence it was brought into play.

Forsyth—now Senator—was called on for aid, and he readily consented that the President be shown his quotation of Mr. Crawford. But that there be no possible doubt, he was asked, and agreed, to write to Woodlawn and procure the evidence over Mr. Crawford's own signature. Forsyth's letter left Washington immediately after the Nullification Dinner, the answer came promptly and was as promptly laid before Old Hickory. Beholding how basely his supposed friend had lied and pandered to him, the General no doubt yearned to complete his threat of having the traitor's ears, but as was his habit by this time he first sought the Prime Minister's advice. Lewis was sent to place the Crawford letter in the Secretary's hands, but after a brief glance over the contents, Mr. Van Buren returned it to the President, saying nobly that he would have no part in the quarrel.

"I reckon Van is right," mumbled Old Hickory. "I daresay they would attempt to throw the whole blame on him."

And they did—probably with no more justice than the case deserved. When Mr. Calhoun received Crawford's letter accompanied by a curt note from the White House, he knew that his last hour of hope had come. He did attempt to reply with some belabored explanations, but they were cut short by Old Hickory's second note saying that "No further communication with you is necessary." No longer was Mr. Calhoun a suppliant, but an avenger. "Under the firm persuasion that the author of the combustion is Martin Van Buren who has used the agency of James A. Hamilton . . . as . . . a go-between," his dearest object in life became to destroy the Red Fox.

In Duff Green, editor of the *United States Telegraph*, he had a willing helpmate. The Calhoun and Green children had intermarried, but that was only a bond that tightened an already firm friendship. Ten years ago Mr. Calhoun had brought Green to Washington to run an administration paper and Green now proved his gratitude by pulling out of the Kitchen Cabinet at the first signs of animosity toward his benefactor. To fill his place there Frank Blair was imported from Kentucky, set up in business with a large slice of government printing and ordered to run the *Washington Globe* as a Kitchen Cabinet mouthpiece. All through the summer, autumn and winter of 1830 these two journals clashed in furious encounter—one to prove the Prime Minister guilty of low intrigue; the other to deny it. Mr. Calhoun sat down and wrote a voluminous pamphlet charging that he had been knifed from behind. Mr. Van Buren responded with a brief notice disclaiming all responsibility. Green thundered in the *Telegraph*; Blair thundered back in the *Globe*.

So raged the storm to the ineffable delight of the gossip-mawed Capital City, and it need not be wondered if Little Van made the gusty blasts fit into the sails that propelled his destiny. One day that autumn, as they rode through the Virginia countryside, Old Hickory turned to his little companion with a proposition the like of which no American except George Washington has ever been known to receive. It was to make the Little Magician Ruler of the United States without either the grace of God or of the People. He would stand for re-election, said Andrew Jackson, with Van as his Vice President. Then, after a year or so, he would resign and his little favorite would be First Citizen.

"I thanked him for the kindness . . . but I could see nothing but danger to myself in the proposition."

A Caesar had rejected the crown and there was no Cassius present to say with what gentle reluctance he thrust it aside. But Little Van, having become designated heir to the throne, had more orthodox plans for ascending it. He knew the time was not ripe as yet. He had seen what had happened to a lady with a past, and he could feel that his own record was not one to stand close scrutiny. The changing seasons offered no abatement either in the Eaton Malaria or the Calhoun disclosure. In the spring of '31 it became known that Duff Green was preparing a mammoth attack and was arranging with editors all over the country to join with him in hunting down the Red Fox. Early in June Green published an advertisement and an appetiser for his pending diatribe against the Prime Minister.

"He came like a mercenary and having divided the spoils among his followers, he seems resolved to expel the native troops from the camp.

"I will expose him!"

One afternoon as they rode to their exercise, the President spoke hopefully, saying that "we should soon have peace in Israel."

"No, General, there is but one thing to give you peace."

"What is that, Sir?"

"My resignation."

For several months the Minister had been screwing up his courage to broach his latest scheme and Duff Green's advertisement gave him the necessary push. As he expected the President was alarmed and chagrined at the thought of losing his favorite, and especially sympathetic at the prospect of Van having to go back to dull work at the law. A subtle trend in the conversation let him understand that "I should consent to run for the office of Vice President . . . against my will" and that meanwhile the mission to Great Britain would overcome the frightful prospect, which all politicians dread, of returning to civilian labor.

The conversation, begun on horseback, was completed at the White House, and Little Van had his own way. Before Mr. Calhoun and his editorial associate could steady their aims for a sure shot, the Red Fox had vanished, leaving behind only the evidence of his delicate handiwork. The Cabinet, except for the useful Postmaster General, was wholly refurbished. Eaton took his cue and resigned with the Prime Minister; the others were unceremoniously dismissed, and into their places went men over whose names Little Van had carefully thumbed.

That was not all. The secretaries were only presidential appointees, removable at the First Citizen's pleasure, but the Vice President had been elected by the People. Nevertheless it did not please Little Van that Mr. Calhoun should finish out the term. Nor did he. Old Hickory's ever-mounting fury against the Nullifiers caused him to remark several times that he was tempted to "Hang them, Sir, as high as Haman!" and such threats made Mr. Calhoun exceedingly miserable. His friend Hayne sounded out the President's friend Benton on the subject.

"I tell you, Hayne, when Jackson begins to talk about hanging, they can begin to look for the ropes."

That was enough for John Caldwell Calhoun. Being Vice President no longer had any charms and eventually he did what no other American has ever done. He resigned the second highest office within the People's gift.

But before affairs had reached this crisis the Red Fox had put an ocean between him and his pursuers, though not until he had made certain arrangements for a timely return. Heading for the Court of St. James's with an Ambassador's portfolio in his pocket, Martin Van Buren had left behind a nation-wide audience which he had taught to gasp and wonder at his magic, but never to understand.

"Well indeed may Mr. Van Buren be called the great magician," breathed one admirer in print, "for he raises his wand and the whole Cabinet vanishes."

4

(1832)

Forty-nine, fleshy and famous, Mr. Washington Irving sat at his breakfast table in Stratford Place and read the overseas dispatches in the London *Times* with the irritation of a man moved at once by annoyance, regret and commiseration. It must have been mildly surprising to this gentleman, whose literary fame had recently been crowned with fellowships to the Spanish Royal Academy of History and the British Royal Society of Literature and an LL.D. at Oxford, that the misfortune of a mere politician should stir his sympathy. For Mr. Irving had spent most of his life poking fun at political antics and abhorring any contact with men who practiced them. A quarter-century ago his brief experience in journalism during Aaron Burr's day in New York had caused the creator of Ichabod Crane to pronounce "such haranguing and puffing and strutting among little great men to be a nauseous business," and the seventeen years he had now spent away from America had been sweeter for the

[ 279

absence of it all. Penniless and jobless in London at 36, Mr. Irving had refused a $2400 a year post as naval attaché solely because he loathed politics, and he would live to turn down a Tammany nomination for Mayor of New York, for Congressman, and for a place in a presidential Cabinet on the same grounds.

Only the pinch of circumstance had induced him in the early months of 1831 to accept the position of Chargé d'Affaires and later the post of Secretary at the London Embassy, though "I fear the beef and pudding of England will complete the ruin of my figure." He had been in Spain for several years writing the *Life of Columbus* and gathering notes for his *Tales of the Alhambra*, when the failure of one of his numerous business investments had left him embarrassed for cash. The offer of a diplomatic post gave him a chance to await royalties from *Columbus* and to finish the *Tales* in comparative leisure under the tolerant and inoffensive Louis McLane, then Ambassador. But in the summer when news came that Martin Van Buren was on his way to replace McLane, Mr. Irving immediately sent in his resignation, to take effect the moment of the new minister's arrival. The Red Fox's fame had travelled before him, and to Mr. Irving such a man could only be the most obnoxious specimen of his type. However, the day following the Ambassador's landing at Cowes found Mr. Irving, not resigning, but writing to friends in New York:

"I have just seen Mr. Van Buren and do not wonder that you should all be so fond of him. His manners are most agreeable and ingratiating. I have no doubt that he will become a favorite of this court."

That had been in September, and in February, reading that the Ambassador's appointment had been rejected by the Senate, Mr. Irving was ready to consider his friend no schemer but a victim of schemes. That "one of the gentlest and most amiable men I ever met with" could be the abandoned scamp of the Little Magician's reputation was more than Mr. Irving could swallow. His first favorable impression had been much enhanced when, shortly after arrival, the

Ambassador rented a fine house in Stratford Place for the princely sum of $2500, manned it with a staff of liveried servants for $2600, and invited Mr. Irving to make it his home. And when, on top of this, Mr. Van Buren purchased a $1550 coach and insisted that his Secretary accompany him in a pilgrimage to literary and historical shrines, Mr. Irving began to hail him as a Mycaenus.

Their tour had seen the beginning of a friendship that would last the two men the rest of their mortal days. To Oxford and Blenheim; to Hardwick and Warwick Castles; to Shakespeare's Stratford and Dr. Johnson's Lichfield; to Sir Walter's Kenilworth and Lord Byron's Newstead Abbey, and finally to Barlborough—Mr. Irving's own "Bracebridge Hall." Here they spent an old-fashioned Christmas Eve with "mummers, morris dancers, the glee singers from neighboring villages, great feasting with the boar's head crowned with holly, the wassail bowl, yule log, snap dragon dancing and all kinds of merriment."

Mr. Irving soon came to see something not a little pathetic in the hungry eagerness of his companion, who for the first time in twenty years was now removed from the rancor and intensity of all he had left behind him. He saw the diminutive Ambassador as a success-wearied man, rushing to pleasures and play with a childlike delight. Returned to London for New Year, Mr. Van Buren had conferred with the British Foreign Secretary and, finding "no point of special importance in our national relations," plunged wholeheartedly into the season's festivities. His gaiety and charm soon captivated the Town. No other American minister—certainly not Rufus King, James Monroe or John Quincy Adams— had ever shown such aptitude for the superficial graces of courtiership. Mr. Van Buren was a social success from the start and diplomatic London clutched him to her bosom.

So much more the pity, Mr. Irving must have been ruminating over his *Times*, that those dolts in the United States Senate could not appreciate such qualities. Doubly unbearable was the news of rejection at this particular moment, for Mr. Van Buren, out late last night at one of Prince

Talleyrand's soirées, lay upstairs in a delicate state of health and had sent down word that he could not face breakfast, much less attend the Queen's first drawing room this evening. A servant had just ascended bearing the stricken Ambassador a large packet of mail which, Mr. Irving knew, would surely contain mention of the catastrophe and probably reduce his friend's state of mind to new depths of unhappiness. But to the Secretary's unbounded surprise he looked up to see the sick man come bouncing gleefully downstairs and into the dining room, where he shoved an open letter under Mr. Irving's most intellectual nose.

Washington, 27 Jan'y. 1832.

My dear friend,

I most sincerely congratulate you on your rejection by the Senate—23 to 23 and by the casting vote of the Vice President. . . .

I consider this as a providential interposition in your favor. A more reckless act was never committed by men in their senses —indeed, altho' I earnestly desired it, I could not persuade myself to believe that their passions would drive them into a measure the inevitable result of which might have been seen by a schoolboy. . . . The votes were exactly as they should have been—we could not have had them better.—Poor Hayne has laid himself in the grave of Calhoun—and Webster and Clay die in each others arms. . . . The thing is admirable—you will be our Vice President . . . and you will ride over your adversaries or rather you will drag them after you *à l'Achille* . . . In the midnight of the Senate they have done the deed—but "Birnam wood will come" . . .

Come back as quick as you can—we have no triumphal arches as in ancient Rome, but we'll give you as royal a reception as ever Conqueror had.

Sincerely your friend<br>C. C. Cambreleng.

The perusal of this strange epistle failed to enlighten Mr. Irving. How the Ambassador and his viceroy could read victory into such a patent defeat was beyond the man of letters. All he understood was that Mr. Van Buren had been sternly rebuked by the highest law-making tribunal in America, and even Little Van's excited explanations about the value of martyrdom in politics fell upon barren ground.

A glance through other of the Ambassador's letters—they came from nearly all his henchmen: Lewis, Wright, Butler, Blair, Hill, Hamilton and others—told in more detail how bovinely his enemies had walked into what Little Van considered a masterful ambush. His appointment by the President had been during a congressional recess, but immediately upon the reconvening Mr. Calhoun and Duff Green had sought once more to level an aim at their elusive quarry. The *Telegraph's* columns blazed away at the Red Fox's reputation, while in the Senate Mr. Calhoun arranged for the last rites. The incriminating data, which Green had collected, was passed among the conspirators and written into twelve set speeches, including blistering arraigns by Hayne, Webster and Clay. A four-point indictment of the culprit was drawn up for all the world to see; several Senators were asked to absent themselves at the proper time so the Vice President might have the exquisite pleasure of the casting vote, and when all was ready the Senate retired into secret session to vote on the question:

"Whether the said Martin Van Buren, then Secretary of State, participated in any practices disreputable to the national character . . ." concerning:

1) The instructions . . . to reopen negotiations for the West India Trade.
2) Making a breach of friendship between the first and second officers of the Government . . . for the purpose of thwarting the latter and helping himself to the Presidency.
3) Breaking up the Cabinet for the same purpose.
4) Introducing the system of "proscription" (removal from office for opinion's sake) for the same purpose.

In his panting lust for revenge Mr. Calhoun and his help-mates could not see the waiting noose into which they were thrusting their assembled heads. But the Regency had seen it. "Now for the secret desire of some of your best friends,"

Cambreleng had written his Director at an earlier date. "They wish most sincerely, and I among the number, that the Senate would reject you." And so had two of Little Van's more astute enemies realized how perilously the Carolinian was risking his political neck. The Red Fox removed, warned Thurlow Weed, "would return here as a prosecuted man, throw himself on the sympathy of the Party, be nominated for Vice President and be huzzahed into office on the heels of General Jackson." "To reject the nomination," pleaded Mr. Adams, now a member of the House, "would bring him back to do more mischief here."

But Mr. Calhoun had scented blood and was not to be whipped off the trail. Nothing, he felt, could go wrong this time. Charge No. 1 had been trumped up to give some semblance of dignity to the assault; it was the only one in which there was no case against the accused. Charge No. 4 had been added to gain public sympathy; it was the only one of which he could be proved guilty, and Senator Marcy's "Spoils to the Victor" speech was the lone defense. Sandwiched in between these two allegations were the Vice President's personal grievances. Men were to tell years later with what barbaric leers he descended from the rostrum to give the deciding vote on all four counts.

Mystified as he still remained after this lengthy explanation, Mr. Irving was nevertheless delighted to hear the Ambassador say that in his rejuvenated spirits he now felt well enough to attend the royal reception. Together that evening, and in full court regalia, they drove to the Palace, where they found Mr. Van Buren's rebuff the main subject of conversation. The King drew him out of the receiving line to express royal and personal regrets. Lord Palmerston, the Foreign Minister, and Sir Robert Peel, the Prime Minister, were only two of a dozen who offered their condolence.

The two months which Martin Van Buren spent in England after the inglorious loss of his portfolio show how deeply he had imbedded himself in the good graces and affection of his acquaintances there. No longer was there any ulterior reason for his popularity. Indeed his removal might more reasonably have had the opposite effect, yet he was feasted and fêted as never before. Week-end invitations to Windsor Castle were honors reserved for members of the Home Government and the Diplomatic Corps, and Mr. Van Buren's two-day visit there was said by experienced authority to be "the first case of departure from that rule." King William IV, one of the fifteen children of George III, turned out to be an affable old gentleman with bluff, hearty manners and "an easy and natural way of wiping his nose with the back of his forefinger." The man who had tamed Old Hickory had no difficulty in fascinating his good-natured host, and with the more regal-mannered Queen he seems to have scored even a greater hit. On his departure she presented him with four colored engravings of the Castle, each signed in her own hand, and on one of them she coyly placed a cross-mark beside the window of her visitor's bedchamber. So affectionately did Her Majesty come to regard him that several years later, when the King died, she remembered the American courtier well enough to send him a copy of Lady Wellesley's *Life of William IV.*

The final weeks of his stay were a prolonged fiesta in the little man's honor. He was the guest of knights and earls and dukes and princes. It reveals his inner personality to see what unconscious emphasis he puts on the glamour of court life and the lure of the titled nobility. He was in England during the strife that accompanied the passage through Parliament of the Reform Bill, which gave the English People a voice in their government. Yet both in his letters home and in his *Autobiography,* this professed bulwark of democracy mentions the Reform only in passing and dwells at length on the names and events of the social world. Covering this brief period of his life, the mention of 31 members of the peerage studs the *Autobiography* as against that of 11 commoners. Among the latter Gladstone and Disraeli are allowed to share one sentence between them; the epoch-making feats of Cobden, Bright, Denniston and Labouchère are consigned to one short paragraph, while the appearance and accomplishments of the noblemen require 40 long ones, totalling more than

that number of pages. Faintly comical is a letter which Little
Van wrote from London to Andrew Jackson. Having described in affectionate detail the week-end at Windsor, he
suddenly becomes apprehensive lest "I might be regarded
as placing undue estimate upon attentions of their character
—so far from that being the case, I assure you, that I have
derived no small share of self-compliment since I have been
here from seeing how well grounded my Republican principles are."

But the person in London who fascinated him most was
no Englishman. Prince Talleyrand at seventy-eight had become the world-wide symbol for unmoral and strategic courtiership. This gentleman whom the urbane Madame de Staël
called "the most impenetrable and undecipherable of men"
had begun public life as a Bishop of the Holy Church only
to fling off his cassock at the beginning of the French Revolution and enter upon a career of diplomacy that has linked
him in History to Metternich and Machiavelli.

"His patriotism," said Mr. Irving, "is a mere local attach-
ment, like that of a cat who sticks by the house, let who will
inhabit it."

The Prince's incredible record to date was to have served
under five different and hostile French governments—the
Directory, the Consulate, the Empire, the Bourbon Restoration and, finally, the House of Orleans which had just
crowned Louis Philippe. A hideous cripple from birth, M.
de Talleyrand in old age had become a tragic and grotesque
caricature of his own reputation. Shifty gray eyes under a
scowling brow imbedded in a deeply-stained, hair-tufted face;
a ponderous upper lip that protruded and overhung its mate;
an unearthly, demonic expression that writhed over his
twisted features; a voice that broke silence only with oc-
casional and terrifying gutturals—this was the Minister Pleni-
potentiary from the Kingdom of France when Martin Van
Buren first looked upon him, hardly one, it would seem, to
invite the admiration or confidence of an American pro-
vincial. Yet the Little Magician was so intrigued with this
past master of the political art that, striking up an intimacy

with the Prince, "I visited his house as often as the habits of society in relation to persons of his position would justify."

On his last day in England Little Van's patient curiosity was rewarded with an example of subterranean diplomacy that no other man in the world could have shown him. For six months the American Ambassador had been inconvenienced by the fact that neither he nor the object of his admiration used each other's language. All of Prince Talleyrand's conversations with, for instance, Lord Palmerston, were carried on in French, which encouraged British statesmen in the Frenchman's presence to talk freely in their native tongue without fear of giving away any secrets. Hence when Mr. Van Buren on this last day sent the Prince a gift of a leg of American venison, and later encountered him alone in an antechamber of the Palace, they were both much encumbered for lack of an interpreter. Peering carefully about in search of some third person and finding none, Prince Talleyrand "smiled and, without the slightest embarrassment and in very tolerable English, entered into conversation on various subjects, concluding by thanking me for the venison and inviting me to dine with him . . . and partake of it."

Ruefully, and with a reluctance he found it hard to bear, Martin Van Buren departed next morning from this hospitable shore and set out via France and Germany for his ancestral Holland. Here he was entertained by another court, and given the chance to disclaim with no very great emphasis that his peasant forebears might have been some relation to the Dutch royal family. Asked by the Queen how far back he could trace his family, he replied democratically:

"As far back as Kinderhook, may it please Your Majesty."

His progeny rather than his ancestry caused Mr. Van Buren his only worry during this time abroad. He had brought with him his son John, a wild young sprig whose brilliance and energy in these untamed years were causing the father as much pain as they were later to cause him pride.

"You say," wrote parent to son, "you have spent $150 in six weeks and instead of giving me an account of it . . . you

tell me of the expenditure of other boys. . . . The money is
the least by far of my concern. . . . It has given me great
pain to receive a letter from the President of the College informing me . . . that your conduct in refusing to attend
chapel in the morning was a cause of dissatisfaction . . .
that you had been twice carried drunk from the race course.
. . . My reflections on the conduct of the course of life
which you appear to have marked out for yourself, and in
which eating and drinking and dressing appear to be the
most important, not to say the least exceptional of your per-
suits (sic) have given me a feverish and sleepless night."

But Prince John, as he came to be called, would have to
run his course. The parental neglect of the early years was
not conducive to discipline; his father's remonstrances came
both too late and too early. Arriving in England Prince John
had at once cut out for Paris and surrounding areas of gaiety
where it required the combined efforts of the American em-
bassies in France, Italy and England to locate him in time
to accompany his father home.

That very question—when to go home—was the main tactical problem which had concerned Little Van and his advisers ever since the rejection. All were agreed that he was in
direct line for the presidency, but they differed as to the
next move. Every post brought him enthusiastic advice. Some
would have him hasten back in time for Governor Throop
to appoint him to his old seat in the Senate, which his successor, Mr. Dudley would be ordered to resign. Others would
have Throop himself resign and Matty Van stage a vindication campaign for another short term as Governor. Still
others insisted that he go directly to the vice-presidency,
urging him to arrive before the first Democratic National
Convention which would meet at Baltimore in May. The
President only asked him to return as soon as possible.

"I am anxious to have you with me . . ." pleaded Old
Hickory. "There still remains a vacancy by your absence
. . . which is not filled."

Twice in letters to London the sick old General had repeated his offer to retire soon after reëlection and thus smug-

gle his favorite into the White House, but Little Van knew such a plan would never do. The safest and surest way of attaining his aim was just the method he had chosen. Had he been able to plot out his rejection, he would not have had it otherwise. He wrote back that the most auspicious moment for his reappearance would be *after* the Convention, when he could more plausibly maintain the pose of a surprised and unwilling candidate.

His will prevailed. Under the well-trained viceroys the situation was in perfect control. Editors were busy building up his martyrhood and, though public indignation was a trifle sluggish, the political press by this time was well versed in the ventriloquism of speaking the People's mind. The Regencymen at Albany and the Braves at Tammany Hall both passed resolutions deploring the Senate's action and damning Calhoun, who very soon executed his retreat from the vice-presidency. The Spoils System made it easy to pack the Convention with federal job-holders, and the few delegates who, like Major Eaton, balked at nominating the Red Fox, were promptly whipped into line with Lewis's calm assertion that they had better take orders "unless you are prepared to quarrel with the General." The Convention chose Little Van as its candidate for Vice President, but the Wigwam went it one better by looking four years ahead. At their Forty-Second Anniversary banquet the Braves secured the honor of being the first to nominate the Little Magician for his ultimate goal. They toasted:

"Martin Van Buren, the Grand Sachem of the Eagle Tribe ——

"The Great Spirit is pleased with his faithful support of the Great Grand Sachem of the Nation and smiles upon the sages and warriors of the tribe who aim to elevate their chief in 1836 to the highest station in the country."

Boarding the homeward ship at Havre in June, 1832, Martin Van Buren must have felt satisfaction to see how neatly his pattern of advancement had worked out. Whether or not Old Hickory lived through his second term (and Marcy had written to doubt it) the once-Boy Lawyer appeared destined to become First Citizen. But his three years as courtier, at home and abroad, had left him with a nostalgia he would never quite lose. The anticipation of meeting the People in a raucous, cut-throat election gave him the harsh thrill of combat, no pleasure. In the polite intrigues of drawing-room and privy council he could shine and sport his talents as nowhere else; more than ever he dreaded the American necessity of feigning brotherhood to Demos. Martin Van Buren knew himself a man born too late and on the wrong side of the Atlantic.

Still the Urge owned him. While it possessed him there was no turning back. In New York the Sons of Tammany, under Cambreleng's guidance, were preparing a festival of welcome to acquaint him with the "surprise" of his nomination. On shipboard the "surprised" candidate devoted his time to preparing an acceptance address, but he was glad on arriving at the Narrows to find an excuse for not delivering it. A ravaging siege of cholera was upon the City; he sent word to call off the celebration and not risk spreading the contagion. A messenger bearing a note from the President was there to meet him.

"I want your aid . . ." wrote Old Hickory, "Let me see you as early as you can."

Evading all others at the dock, Little Van set out posthaste for Washington. He was the courtier no longer, but the Director again. An election waited to be won, rivals to be hoodwinked, power to be grasped. General Jackson, pale and drawn with sickness, lay on his bed at the White House, but his face lighted up fondly as he caught sight of his returned favorite. Not a man who often uttered a cry for help, the President's letter to the boat had been nothing else. Congress had just passed a re-charter of the National Bank and, emboldened by support in Cabinet and Kitchen Cabinet, was daring Old Hickory to use his veto. "Holding my hand in one of his own and passing the other thro' his long white locks," Andrew Jackson viewed his friend with loving confidence.

"The bank . . ." he snorted from his pillow, "is trying to kill me, *but I will kill it.*"

There was, the Director knew, more to the Bank Bill than met the eye. The charter, granted in 1816 for a twenty-year span, still had four years to run. This premature raising of the question could have naught but a political explanation, and one not far to seek. Henry Clay, in nominal retirement when Ambassador Van Buren sailed away, had since received the presidential nomination from the National Republican or Whig Party. Writing his own platform, he brought forth his American System again on a three-point program: Internal Improvements, Protective Tariff, the National Bank. To press his candidacy, Mr. Clay had returned to the Senate in time to take part in the Ambassador's recall and at the present session of 1831-2 had introduced measures covering all three of his points. That being the genesis of the Bank Bill, it must, explained Little Van, be smashed, and he himself would be at the Capitol to see that the veto was not overridden.

As good as his word, Mr. Van Buren, clad in the best handiwork of a Pall Mall tailor, ascended Capitol Hill on the morning of July 10th and was to be seen tripping about the corridors, bestowing enigmatic smiles on friend and foe alike. There he was greeted warmly by a gentleman whose oblong, homely face wore a broad smile of satisfaction, and when Senator Clay took the floor later in the day to assail the veto, he was gracious enough to remark:

"By the bye I have just had the pleasure of shaking hands in the other House with our late Minister to England, Mr. Van Buren, and was gratified to find him in excellent health and appearing to great advantage in his English dress."

The whimsical admiration in which Mr. Clay held his friend from New York was not the only cause for his good humor. As well as the Mill Boy could understand, everything was breaking happily in his favor. Little Van mustered enough votes to prevent an overruling of the veto, but Mr. Clay, like many another Whig, was thoroughly satisfied to have it so, since the question was now squarely before the

[ 291

People as a campaign issue. The Democratic nomination of Martin Van Buren had pleased the Mill Boy enormously. A few months ago he had written to Kentucky:

"The attempt to excite public sympathy in behalf of the Little Magician has totally failed and I sincerely wish that he may be nominated as Vice President."

Tying the Red Fox to Old Hickory's coat tails, deduced Mr. Clay, would both weaken the appeal of the Democratic ticket and increase its vulnerability. As their author saw them, each of the three planks in the Whig platform was a tower of strength against which even the General's "outdoor popularity" could scarcely prevail. Internal Improvements would certainly fetch the West; Protective Tariff, the North; the Bank, the business and commercial interests of the East. As for the South, Virginia was offended by the Jacksonian scrapping of State Rights, as was South Carolina by his coldness to Nullification. And the Anti-Mason Party, with William Wirt as its candidate, was confident of offsetting Little Van's organization in the State of New York. He was, deemed Mr. Clay, as good as elected.

But the campaign of 1832 was to show Henry Clay and the several generations of politicians who followed him that issues were never again to win an election, that an appeal to the People must be made not to its head but to its heart. The Mill Boy was a wiser man than Old Hickory, a more skillful, higher-gifted, better-educated statesman, but Andrew Jackson had conquered the British Army, and Henry Clay had not. Historically the '32 election is important on two counts. First, it marks the original attempt to deify the Big Businessman as a god of American idolatry. As the Jupiter of this forthcoming hierarchy was the Byronically-handsome Mr. Nicholas Biddle of Philadelphia, who not too oddly combined an effeminate, fastidious personality with the muscular philosophy that the People be damned for the sake of what his bright lexicon called Prosperity. Being President of the National Bank which controlled government as well as commercial credit, Mr. Biddle came naturally by his Joveship over business. He saw in Henry Clay's American

System the gilded promise of his own Parnassus, and was therefore willing to donate the Bank's name and capital for the promotion of mutual interests. Until and during Mr. Biddle's connection with the Mill Boy's Vision, the American System was very largely a liberal rejuvenation of Federalism, but from here on the saving grace of Alexander Hamilton's humanity was missing. Mr. Biddle planned no guardianship of the People; instead, a financial autocracy which was not to see its best days until a Civil War had cleared the way for its rule.

Second of the innovations of 1832 was the fact that for the first time two national parties met in combat with full arsenals of political ammunition. Ere now each party had used whatever weapons came to hand, but never before had both been organized battle-camps with regimented troops of workers and heavy artillery of prepared propaganda, slander and intimidation. By precept and example the Albany Director had demonstrated a method of political warfare which would not be improved upon for more than a century. Rationed by the Spoils System, generaled by the Kitchen Cabinet, gunned by a trained and obedient Press, the Democrats lined up to win again for Old Hickory. And against them, armed with a lesser store of the same equipment, stood the embattled Whigs, led by the energetic Mill Boy.

The opening salvo was a wholesale charge of corruption from both sides. A Whig investigation of the Spoils System was begun which would eventually show an $800,000 deficit in the Post Office and a similar condition in the Treasury; a check-up on government patronage revealed a total of 100,000 persons as beneficiaries of the State. In answer to this the Democrats uncovered some very mysterious "loans" made by the Bank at the beginning of the campaign. Mr. Webster, stumping the country for the Mill Boy, had received not less than $32,000, of which a third had been given him after a particularly inspired attack upon the Jackson veto. Two newspapers, one neutral and the other Democratic, the Washington *National Intelligencer* and the New

York *Courier and Enquirer,* suddenly became enthusiastically Whig, and were exposed in the possession of $59,000 which their editors found hard to explain. Duff Green's *Telegraph* was richer by $20,000; two other sheets in Philadelphia received loans of $35,000, and a lump sum of $80,000 was down on the Bank's books under the inclusive heading of "stationery and printing."

In conjunction with the corruption data went the usual slander of personalities. The graves of Old Hickory's mother, wife and victims were ransacked once more; the Eaton affair was tastily served up; Little Van's career as a master-spoilsman; Henry Clay's foibles as gambler, adulterer, drunkard and Corrupt Bargainer were bared for public edification.

Slight but significant was the difference in generalship between the two hosts. Whereas the Whigs ran their campaign mainly from a central headquarters, the Democrats made a headquarters wherever there was a poll. Here was the beginning of the national political Machine with its myriad of petty bosses serving as cog-wheels. The postmaster or Federal revenue agent in any small town belonged to the Kitchen Cabinet's far-flung battle-line, it being his recognized duty to awaken public enthusiasm and get his majority to the ballot boxes under peril of losing his own job if he failed.

Again: the Whigs depended on their urban newspapers to carry the propaganda, thus confining the work to cities and large towns, while under the Kitchen Cabinet editors—Kendall and Blair—the glad tidings of Old Hickory's Second Coming reached into hamlet and farm. Many an editorial from the hurrying pen of Amos Kendall appeared in journals a thousand miles away but over the local editor's name. Pamphleteering as a political weapon was barely holding its own, but cartooning was on the increase to replace it. Blow for blow the opponents exchanged their compliments. Old Hickory was St. George slaying the Monster Bank; Old Hickory was a burglar climbing through the window to rifle the People's safe. If Andrew Jackson was pictured as King Andrew, then Nicholas Biddle was pictured in one degree worse as Czar Nicholas. If the country's President was shown as receiving a sceptre from the Devil, then the Bank's President was shown as Old Nick himself about to gobble up the country.

In the matter of slogans the difference was mostly a question of anatomy. The Democrats aimed straight at the People's heart with "Hurrah for Old Hickory" and "Stick by the Old Hero!", while the Whigs attempted an appeal to the belly with the "Full Dinner Pail" promise that was to prove so successful in later years. To break the Bank, they argued, was to break the country. They offered several telling examples of what to expect unless Big Business were endorsed at the polls. In Cincinnati wholesale buyers of pork advertised offers of $2.50 a hundred if Clay won; $1.50 if he lost. In Brownsville, Pennsylvania, a large manufacturer discharged all his employees until he should see how the election would go. A Whig paper in Pittsburgh announced that "not a single steamboat will be built this season"; one in Baltimore noted that "a great many mechanics are thrown out of employment by the stoppage of building". It was all attributed to the threat of another four years of Old Hickory.

The day had not come when personages as dignified as candidates for national office should swing round the circuit. They were supposed to remain aloof from all display of personal interest, only answering public questions addressed to them in writing. To Mr. Van Buren came a letter from some curious Democrats at Shocco Springs, North Carolina, asking his views upon tariff. He returned an answer that discouraged all further attempts to probe him out of his silence. He was, he wrote, against "oppressive inequality" and in favor of "a conciliatory measure." So, of course, was everyone else, but each of the other candidates had defined the terms. The enemy papers opened on Little Van again for his vanburenism, whereupon he addressed another letter to the Young Men's Democratic-Republican Club of New York, not mentioning tariff but bemoaning the fact that he was a misunderstood patriot to whom there was no respite from partisan hatred and slander. Loyally the Democratic press flew to the defense of his martyrdom, and the tariff question plagued him no more.

Except for these two, and supplementary utterances, the Red Fox remained in covert during the entire campaign. Secretly he worked, but the heavy correspondence that passed between him and his lieutenants showed that he was far from idle. As in '28 he was directing the campaign from a distance and confining his visible activities to garnering New York's electoral votes without which it was judged that no party could win. Up and down the Hudson he roamed, interviewing Regencymen, spurring them on, and in the City he kept a watchful eye on Tammany. The huge influx of immigrants from famine-stricken Ireland and middle Europe was a windfall for the Wigwam, besieged by the combined forces of Anti-Masonry and the Bank. Davy Crockett, the frontiersman, remembered when he came to write his *Autobiography* how he visited "the glorious Sixth Ward—the regular Van Buren groundfloor."

"I thought," wrote Davy, "I would rather risk myself in an Indian fight than venture among those creatures after night."

But "those creatures," as Falstaff once remarked about his ragged soldiers, were mortal men and good enough for cannon fodder, which was all Mr. Van Buren asked of them. They could be herded to the polls like so many cattle, and the man who was recently exchanging immaculate pleasantries with courtiers and kings must be there to make the arrangements.

As the campaign drew toward its close Senators Webster and Clay began trading congratulatory letters. The brains and wealth of the nation were on their side; the masses had been frightened away from Old Hickory by the fear of starvation. Everyone was telling the Senators so; they heard it said wherever they went. But what they did not hear was the still small voice of the People which could not rise in volume save through the amplifying medium of the ballot boxes. Had the two Senators been aboard a certain Ohio River steamboat on a particular day that autumn they might have felt some suspicion of uneasiness. General Jackson, on his way to the Hermitage for a rest, was saying good-bye to Ike Hill at Wheeling.

"Isaac, it'll be a walk. If our fellows didn't raise a finger from now on, the thing would be just as well as done. In fact, Isaac, it's done now."

And it was. Outdoor popularity plus superior organization had set everything else to naught. Old Hickory whipped the Mill Boy worse than he did the Puritan, and the Red Fox could now come out of hiding, for though trailing the ticket by 30 electoral votes, he had moved still a step closer to his Ultima Thule.

# CHAPTER III

# The Ante-chamber

## (1832–1833)

LESS like a fox than the proverbial ground-hog did Martin Van Buren emerge from his covert, for he stayed out only long enough to look round for his shadow and then vanish again from the public view. It was a cloud-ridden horizon which greeted his sight at the Second Coming of Andrew Jackson. Anarchy and Sedition followed in wake of the Revolution. Violence, vandalism and the menace of civil strife. Exultant in the renewal of their freedom and inspired by the wild man at the head of their government, the People gave vent to their feeling in an unconfined orgy of lawlessness. In his outdoor popularity, Old Hickory became to America of the early 30's what Victoria would later be to England—the dictator and fountain-head of the Zeitgeist. His example of reckless endeavor, his headlong individualism became incarnate throughout the land he ruled.

"The People of the United States are out of joint," reviewed Niles' *Weekly Register,* a leading periodical. "A spirit of riot and a disposition to take the law into their own hands prevails in every quarter."

Following this comment came several columns of solid print, listing the organized disorders which marked the first half of the old Hero's second term. In New York a mob attacked an abolitionist's home and heaved the furniture into the street for a bonfire and was barely prevented from demolishing two churches by the arrival of troops. Near Boston seven hundred masked men raided the Ursuline Convent, chased sixty nuns out of bed, fired the building and fought off the firemen. In Philadelphia thirty houses, including two churches, were destroyed, men were seized in their sleep and flung out of windows, negroes were hunted through town to the whoop of the death-halloo. A post office in Charleston, a newspaper office in Cincinnati, school-houses in New Hampshire and Connecticut—these and much else were pillaged in the names of Justice, Democracy and Humanity.

Came no remonstrance from the White House. In Washington the enthusiasm for self-expression was bespoken among upper circles by a revival of the *code duello*: among the townsfolk by riots, tarrings and terrorism. Even officialdom was not beyond reach. The President actually had his nose pulled by an irate naval officer; the Vice President had to sit over the Senate with two cocked pistols under his coat-tails; Congressmen going to and from the Capitol were fired at and "cruelly assaulted". But Old Hickory refused to rebuke this spirit of his which had marched abroad. When a committee of citizens called to ask police protection for non-combatants in Washington streets, he sent it off with a contemptuous refusal. When others suggested that something might be done to preserve the lawgivers from snipers, he snorted aloud that:

"After a few more examples of the same sort, members of Congress would learn to keep civil tongues in their heads."

Anarchy, with its attending wear and tear on life and property, Old Hickory could tolerate and even encourage. It was, after all, only the spontaneous overflow of the People's feelings. But Sedition—planned and plotted mutiny—that was something else. The same season which brought in the second Hickory ticket also brought to the Legislature of South Carolina a majority pledged to Nullification. Under the rebellious triumvirate of Calhoun, Hayne and James Hamilton, the Nullification Convention met on November 3rd, adopted its own Declaration of Independence and set February 1st for the date of enactment. Medallions were struck off enscribed "John C. Calhoun, First President of the Southern Confederacy"; arms were stacked, militia was marshalled, and the bewildered nation looked fearfully toward its First Citizen.

But Old Hickory was on familiar ground now. Once, single-handed and with an unloaded rifle, he had quelled a regiment of Tennessee mutineers; he was not likely to be disturbed with the entire Army and Navy at his disposal. Nor had he any misgivings about his duty. Others might quibble and cant about the sovereignty of State Rights, but Andrew Jackson had learned his Constitution from Little Van. That Jefferson Day toast was ever on his lips and on his pen. While the Nullifiers were gathering in convention he wrote to Hamilton: "We are wide awake here. THE UNION WILL BE PRESERVED; rest assured of that." He longed, he told several persons, to put himself at the head of a posse, march into Carolina and "hang every leader . . . sir, by martial law, irrespective of his name, or political or social position." Realizing reluctantly that his place as commander-in-chief was in Washington, he placed Winfield Scott in charge, prepared to move 50,000 men within striking distance of the rebel border and ordered a fleet of warships into Charleston harbor. Then, when the Congress met in December, he hurled South Carolina his thunderbolt, the famous Nullification Proclamation, which, written by Edward Livingston, his Secretary of State, stands as the Seventh President's one documentary claim to statesmanship.

Setting forth its theme in a single clause—"The United States is a government and not a league"—the Proclamation drew the last tooth of Jeffersonian state sovereignty, and thus horrified old-school Republicans as much as it delighted the few die-hard Federalists who were left. It was, said Henry Clay, "entirely too ultra for me"; it set John Randolph to screaming that Old Hickory "had disavowed the principles to which he owed his elevation," but it thrilled to the core such a staunch old Tory as John Marshall, and it caused the cult of Daniel Webster worshippers to call it a plagiarism on his Reply to Hayne—the highest unintentional compli-

ment they could imagine. Credit for the Proclamation, however, belonged neither to Senator Webster nor Secretary
Livingston. It was no more than an echo and an elaboration
on that toast which King Andrew's obliging little favorite
had written for him more than two years ago. And yet when
Old Hickory looked to Little Van for approbation and advice, he looked in vain.

For oddly enough this national crisis found Mr. Van
Buren not at his chieftain's elbow, but up in Albany super-
vising a reshuffling of the Regency. There were two sen-
atorships to be awarded this year. William L. Marcy's unfortunate frankness in pronouncing the creed of the Spoils
System made it advisable to replace him, so he was shifted to
the governorship. Into his Senate seat went Silas Wright,
erstwhile Comptroller; into the other one went the Bucktail choice, Nathaniel P. Tallmadge whose election Matty
Van would later repent. Busy as he was with these and other
local matters, the Director was not too absorbed to be severely chagrined over the Proclamation. The Jefferson Day
toast had been devised for the particular purpose of confus-
ing Mr. Calhoun's presidential hopes and now, nursing those
same hopes himself, Little Van perceived that a boomerang
had swooped back to smite him.

His winning of the second citizenship had graduated
Martin Van Buren into an attitude of mind he had never
known before. Hitherto he had been aggressively fighting his
way upward. There had always been an intrigue to be con-
summated, a rival to be cozened. But being now Crown
Prince to a popular régime, he became as intent on avoiding
trouble as he had formerly been in making it. He hoped
his vice-presidency to be an unobtrusive, almost imper-
ceptible, evolution into the higher office. Peace and the
preservation of the *status quo* was all he craved; to be delivered from controversy and perilous decisions was the whole
of his litany. In the Nullification question he saw the potential ruin of all his work. If he wholeheartedly approved
the Proclamation, he would offend the host of State Rights
voters below the Potomac. If he came out against it, he

would alienate Old Hickory. Both alternates were unthinkable. So he did nothing.

He did nothing, that is, for the time being, but with ever-increasing difficulty. Mr. Calhoun, resigning his lame-duck vice-presidency, had returned to South Carolina where the Legislature immediately appointed him to Hayne's place in the Senate. When Congress met in December, his seat was empty and gossip had it that his courage had failed him at thought of facing Old Hickory again. But shortly after New Year he appeared like, someone described him, Luther coming to the Diet of Worms. Crowds flocked to the Capitol to scrutinize the torture on his face as he took an oath of allegiance to the Constitution. At his arrival the Nullification drama reached its climax. The President brought forward the Force Bill, authorizing him to collect revenue in South Carolina at the point of the bayonet; Henry Clay, temporarily deserting his American System for a larger cause, was pressing a reduction of the tariff by way of compromise, and meanwhile the country continued to totter on the verge of war.

Even in this hour of direst need there came no word from Albany, but still the old Hero refused to suspect the sincerity of "the most frank man I ever knew". He requested Hamilton to stir up the Director with a letter. And when Matty Van returned the letter, opened but unanswered, Hamilton told the President in disgust that "this unfriendly, nay offensive course resulted from Van Buren's fear of offending the dominant party in Virginia." Still Old Hickory would not doubt. In the midst of his other labors he found time to dash off a note to his favorite.

"Whispers and innuendoes . . . are circulated to injure you, carrying the idea that you . . . through fear are silent . . . And the silence . . . gives a coloring to these false suggestions."

At this there could be no more delay. With his heart in his teeth, Little Van set his practiced mind to creating what must stand among his works as the masterpiece of evasion. By mid-January nearly every Legislature in the country had expressed itself on this matter so vital to the Union. A Whig minority at Albany had offered a resolution praising the Jacksonian staunchness, only to have the measure tabled at Matty Van's personal command. The Regency could not speak without orders; it patiently awaited the document which the Director, closeted in the Congress Hotel, was known to be writing. It would, the Bucktails guessed, be a hymn of praise to Old Hickory and at the same time an olive branch to the disgruntled Jeffersonians.

It was all of that. Advocating "mutual concession and compromise", it exalted State Rights "in their highest sovereign capacity" in one paragraph, and "the illustrious man so providentially at the head of the Government" in another. Without justifying Nullification, it upheld Jeffersonism; without endorsing the Proclamation, it declared that "the official course of our present Chief Magistrate . . . has established for himself imperishable claims to . . . gratitude, respect and confidence." In a word it succeeded in saying that everybody was right, nobody was wrong, and everything was sweetness and light in a country that had already taken up arms for a civil war.

Proudly Matty Van's Legislature put its stamp of approval upon this strange treatise and dutifully Matty Van's *Argus* proclaimed it: "The sound Republican doctrine of 'Ninety Eight—the creed of the Democracy in the old times and at all times." Off to the White House, the Director sent it, accompanied by a letter to salve over the rough edges with his accustomed sleekness of explanation. But Old Hickory for the first time seems to have had suspicions concerning his favorite's wonderful frankness. A. J. Donelson, his private secretary, tells how the General "read all the papers very deliberately, placed the letter on his files without saying a word."

By the time Little Van found it necessary to come to Washington for the Inauguration, the trouble had blown over. Late one night Congressman Letcher of Kentucky had routed Mr. Calhoun out of bed with the news that the Presi-

dent had decided to arrest him for treason and hang him
without further ado.

"There sat Calhoun", recounts a contemporary, "drinking
in eagerly every word, and as Letcher proceeded, he turned
pale as death . . . and trembled like an aspen leaf."

That was the last of Nullification. The next morning, Mr.
Calhoun sought out Henry Clay, agreed to the compromise,
and then hurried southward to disband the conspirators. To
his friend Van the President was painfully silent about the
whole affair. He never acknowledged either the Regency's
resolution or the Director's letter; "nothing further ever
passed between us in relation to them."

At this harrowing escape from seeing his hopes anni-
hilated, Mr. Van Buren seemed resolved to keep a safe
distance between himself and any more such adventures.
On March Fourth, 1833, he was sworn into the vice-presidency by the venerable John Marshall and soon afterwards
departed the Capital City, though the Kitchen Cabinet was
in executive session and Old Hickory had urged him to
remain as a White House guest. There were matters a-foot
which the Vice President hoped would not involve him. He
stopped briefly at Albany to put a few finishing touches on
the Regency; dawdled for a while in New York where, according to Philip Hone, diarist, he was "all the fashion,"
and then moved on to Saratoga Springs, most modish resort
of the day.

But much as he hoped to be spared any more embarrassment, it was not to be. In June came a letter from the
White House threatening no less a calamity than had Nullification. Old Hickory wrote:

"The Bank and the change of deposits have engrossed my
mind much, is a perplexing problem and I wish your
opinion."

The question was no new one. Mr. Van Buren understood, of course, that his chief had long been considering
a complete destruction of the Bank. It was not enough for
Andrew Jackson that "the Monster," as he called it, would die
a natural death in March, 1836, when its present charter

would expire. He must slay it at once, and the surest way
to do so was to remove the several millions of dollars which
the Bank held as government deposits. To this end the
President had had Senator Benton introduce a bill for removals at the last session, contending that the Bank was
insolvent, but an inquest by a House committee proved it
to be perfectly sound. Here the matter could reasonably have
ended and the Bank allowed to close its books in an orderly
fashion, but Old Hickory on the trail of a foe was unrelenting. If Congress would not act, he decided, then he would
wait till the recess and act himself.

That he legally had any such authority is, at best, questionable. The charter provided that the Secretary of the
Treasury should keep a certain percentage of government
funds in the Bank unless he found "adequate reason" to do
otherwise, and even then he was required to submit these
reasons to Congress. The phraseology was slightly ambiguous about the right of Congress to reject the Treasury's
reasons, but it was certainly never intended that deposits
could be removed at the President's whim and fancy. That,
nevertheless, was the way Old Hickory chose to interpret
the charter. Louis McLane, Secretary of the Treasury, refused to act, so the President moved him into the State
Department, substituted William Duane, whom he thought
more malleable, and was then ready to strike. His plan, as
devised by Amos Kendall, was to spend the deposited funds
for current running expenses of the government, but to issue a decree that no more moneys would be placed there to
maintain a balance.

While still in Washington for the Inauguration, Little
Van had sought to dissuade Kendall from pushing Old
Hickory into such rashness. Quite willing that the Monster
should go, the Vice-President saw plainly enough that
the Removal Decree was certain to wreck more than the
Bank. When Kendall, flying into a temper, had threatened
to break off friendly relations, Little Van soothingly told
him, "You were right and I was wrong," but he had left

Washington hoping that the President would be restrained by the more level heads among the Cabinet.

The letter he received in June undeceived him. The General was passing through New York on his way to New England, where Harvard would grant him a LL.D., and he wanted Little Van to join him for a conference on the final details of removal. Here was a frightful predicament. Clearly Old Hickory's mind was already made up. To cross him again so shortly after the Nullification episode would be courting a terrific disaster. Yet to permit or encourage him to break the Bank would be risking national welfare, the livelihood and daily bread of thousands of citizens. There can be no doubt of how fully Martin Van Buren realized his responsibility and the spineless manner in which he shrunk from assuming it makes him guilty of the one major crime he ever committed against his generation—always excepting the Spoils System which transcends mere temporal importance. It is difficult and distasteful to picture this dapper little adventurer in the deliberate rôle of a Judas, but it can scarcely be denied that by criminal negligence and selfishness aforethought he consigned his country to the Gethsemane of a devastating economic depression, and did so at his own price—the presidency.

Beginning in Andrew Jackson's first term and continuing nearly to the end of his second, America enjoyed a period of soaring prosperity, hauntingly similar in its general cause and eventual débâcle to the one she was to know nine decades later under the leadership of two patriots yet unborn, Presidents Harding and Coolidge. In the Nineteenth Century, as in the Twentieth, this happy delusion was based on the over-expansion of fiscal credit, nourished by blissful confidence from the White House, and it ended when both credit and confidence wilted at the sight of naked actualities. In both cases there was a contributing factor of dishonesty among the money-changers and profiteering among the law-givers; in both cases the nation was found upon autopsy to have one organ which was its financial heart, and this, ceasing to beat, prostrated a whole country. In the 1920's this heart was Wall Street, New York; in the 1830's it was Chestnut Street, Philadelphia, where, girt by tall Grecian pillars, stood Mr. Biddle's Bank of United States.

The day Martin Van Buren received the President's letter he was in full possession of knowledge and experience to tell him how calamitous would be any sudden overturning of the financial system. For one thing he had come into the State Senate at the time Hamilton's Bank of America had expired, and he had had a close view of the brief confusion that resulted when wildcat, or what was then called "kiting" banks sprang up to replace the national one. One of his boasts in Albany had been that only once (and then as a war measure) had he ever voted to charter one of these, yet Andrew Jackson's plan would bring about an exact replica of what had happened twenty years ago. The President proposed to transfer the Government moneys to local banks, any of which would be permitted to issue their own notes as the recognized paper currency of the country. A man with even the rudiments of economic education must have been scandalized by such a system, and Martin Van Buren, besides his experience with banking matters in New York, had been for seven years a member of the Finance Committee of the United States Senate. It would be strange if he did not foresee what was bound to happen. Almost immediately the number of local banks increased from 330 to 634, each turning out their own notes and many of them located in mythical towns which the eye of man had never seen.

Furthermore, the Vice President had received from Louis McLane an exhaustive study showing how deeply the national finances were rooted in Mr. Biddle's institution and how essential it was to effect a gradual divorce between State and Purse. "God knows," McLane wrote him, "I have no love for the present Bank and my opinions are the result of honest convictions." They were also the result of cold, undeniable facts. In the East and near-West the building of canals and the dredging of rivers had put an average of 25 new steamboats afloat each year and in four years had

doubled the tonnage of cargo. In the far-West the population, counting by thousands, had stretched from 60 to 400
in Illinois; from 170 to 600 in Indiana; from 450 to 800 in
Tennessee; from 80 to 240 in Mississippi; from 70 to 350 in
Missouri; from 10 to 200 in Michigan. In the South, where
the money crop was cotton, prices had jumped from 6
cents a pound to 20 cents. In the cities, where real estate
value was the criterion of the times, prices had sky-
rocketed. In Mobile the assessed city property went from one
million to 27 millions in six years; in New York it went
from 139 million to 390 in five years.

Upon the Bank of United States rested almost the whole
weight of this expansion and the credit of the government as
well. Business and the Treasury Department had their interests inseparably entwined about Mr. Biddle's Grecian pillars.
At the defeat of the Adams-Clay program for conserving the
West, the price of public lands had been left at $1.25 an
acre and sold to all comers. As a result great tracts were
passed out, not to homesteaders, who would cultivate and
improve them, but to speculators whose sole interest was to
hold on until they could sell at a profit. In order to buy up
as much land as possible and to organize boat-making and
river-dredging companies, these empire builders borrowed
freely from the Bank, paid the Government with the money
thus received, and the Government in turn put it back into
the Bank where it was promptly lent out again to the same
and other speculators. Business boomed; the Bank expanded
its credit and out of this giddy inebriation was born prosperity.

By the same process the Government had also profited.
The steady income from land sales enabled the Jackson
Administration to accomplish what was thought to be an
economic miracle: the paying off of the national debt. In
other words, the Administration had conceived and con-
summated the extraordinary bargain of trading the country's woods and templed hills, its vast plains and fertile val-
leys, its potential wealth in mountains and rivers—all this—
for the wonderful scraps of paper that rolled off of Mr.

308 ]

Biddle's printing press. Coming at last to see the seamier side of the bargain, Old Hickory had effectively cancelled it with his veto of the re-charter bill, but his plans for crushing the Bank by force was merely cutting off a nose to spite the face.

Absurd and ominous as the proposition was, Martin Van Buren had no notion of risking his future by opposing it. Now, if ever, was the time for all good men to come to the help of the Party, but the Vice President simply did not possess that kind of goodness. The particulars of the Removal Decree were "considered and discussed between the President and myself on our journey" through New England, but the trip was abruptly cut short when Old Hickory's health collapsed and he had to be hurried to a seaside resort in Virginia in order to recuperate. While the President was there, Little Van met Kendall and McLane in New York and made a feeble attempt to avert the disaster. He proposed they suggest to Old Hickory that the matter be postponed till Congress should meet and then fought out in full view of the public. The plan was relayed to the General, who responded by returning to Washington and summoning the Cabinet to inform them of his intention to act at once.

Faced with a showdown, three of the ministers, including his Treasurer, balked. It meant another reorganization of the Cabinet and, as usual, the old Hero sought his favorite's advice.

"Whom shall I select for the State, War and Attorney General?" he asked in September. . . . "I had to struggle with my private friendship opposed to my public duty— but I could not struggle long. My God told me that the measure was right."

Old Hickory's God in this case was far more communicative than his friend Van. Seeing to what a pass the affair had come, Mr. Van Buren ordered out fast horses in an effort to escape. With Washington Irving, who had followed him back from London, the Vice President laid plans for a protracted tour of upper New York, leaving no address

behind. Not knowing where to find him, the President en-
trusted an insistent letter to Viceroy Cambreleng, who made
the wretched mistake of locating his Director "just as I was
stepping into my carriage."

Again, as with the Nullification question, the Red Fox had
been tracked to his den not by his enemies, but by his best
friend. And again he resorted to tactics of laying low and
saying nothing. He utilized the Cabinet reorganization to
put in two more of his friends—his old law partner, Ben
Butler, and his henchman of the Calhoun plot, John Forsyth. But he steadfastly refused to identify himself with the
Removal Decree. Instead of returning to the White House,
as Old Hickory had requested, he sent tender messages of
affection and declared that he would remain away lest his
presence in Washington deprive the President of sole credit
for the momentous step he was about to take.

How Old Hickory's high opinion of his favorite's unselfish
devotion survived all this is a mystery which has never
been solved. The Removal Decree was announced in late
September and Little Van was far from the tumult and the
shouting that accompanied it. Taken together, this and his
shadow-dancing around the Nullification question heap new
laurels upon the Red Fox's already over-burdened brow.
He had proved himself as impervious to the inconveniences
of friendship as he had always been to those of hostility.
To be nominated and elected to the presidency he needed
the continued good grace of Andrew Jackson, and he needed
a record which was unencumbered by debatable opinions.
During his first few months in the Ante-chamber he had,
though sorely beset, hung on to these assets. Old Hickory
still thought him nonpareil; neither the Jeffersonians of
the South or the Philistines of the business world could
call him their enemy.

But the time was approaching when he must come out
of his hiding again and take up his duties as presiding officer
of the Senate. Awaiting him there would be three men
fondly anticipating their chance to confront him. Nor would
Little Van find in Senators Calhoun, Webster and Clay

the same upright ignorance which had enabled him to slaughter most of his victims to date. Statesmen all, these three had been tempered and toughened at the political forge. They were wiser than the many who had played fly-to-the-spider for the Little Magician in days gone by. And joined with them in the common cause against all things Jacksonian was Nicholas Biddle, a desperate and deadly foeman, armed with the most effective of all political weapons: money.

Between Little Van and his Ultima Thule stood this formidable array. He would not pass if they could help it, and they were ready and waiting when, in December, 1833, he set his unwilling feet in Washington.

2

(1834–1835)

A manly and monumental ornament to any assembly, Mr. Black Dan Webster sat in his Senate seat on March 7, 1834, and watched a scene that was warmly reminiscent. Three years ago he had stood before galleries that were packed even tighter than they were today, and tormented a Vice President in a speech that had made him famous. At this moment there was another Senator on the floor attempting the same torture upon another Vice President—and with Mr. Webster's complete approval. The intervening years had changed the rôles, but not the drama. It was Henry Clay this time who was wielding the thong, and Martin Van Buren, enthroned on the rostrum, who was receiving it.

There was, too, Mr. Webster might have been thinking, another shift in the cast that was rather important. In the former instance Henry Clay had been the one with presidential hopes and had therefore kept out of the dispute; on this occasion it was he, Dan Webster. Within a few months the Whigs of Massachusetts would formally announce his nomination which was already decided upon, and from now on till election day, the best he could hope for was to see Martin Van Buren undergo as much discomfort as possible. It was therefore with interest, and not without anxiety, that the man from Massachusetts watched his Kentucky colleague go into action.

Mr. Webster could approve his friend's motives without saying an amen to his methods. There was, Black Dan always believed, something about the Mill Boy's speechmaking that kept him perpetually teetering between the ridiculous and the sublime. For when Henry Clay undertook to hypnotize an audience he very frequently succeeded in hypnotizing himself as well. Give him a sentimental subject, and his feelings habitually eloped with his facts, bearing him full-sailed into those narrow straits so barely dividing pathos from bathos. Often enough Old Harry of the West had come through the treacherous channel, not only unscathed but trailing additional clouds of glory, yet Mr. Webster, with so much of his own cargo aboard, was apprehensive to see him attempt it again, and especially in the presence of so resourceful a pirate as Little Van.

Rising to voice the Opposition's protest against Andrew Jackson's Removal of Deposits, the Mill Boy was now painting a lachrymose picture of how horribly the President had betrayed the People. Black Dan had guilty reasons to know better than that. To be sure, there was no denying that the Removal Decree had been followed by a considerable amount of distress in certain elements of the country, but this was something which both Senators Webster and Clay should have found mightily embarrassing. The Panic of '34, now at its height, was only a mild forerunner of what was to come three years later, but such as it was, it was wholly the work of Mr. Nicholas Biddle, their employer and political patron. Acting upon advice from Senator Webster and Thurlow Weed, Czar Nicholas had embarked upon the plan of starving the nation into submission, having, he said, "no doubt that such a course will ultimately lead to a restoration of the currency and the recharter of the Bank."

312 ]

Mildly described by Black Dan as "discipline", and by the period's ablest historian as "the frankly avowed purpose of blackmailing the American people into granting another charter," the Bank's policy since the Removal Decree had been to produce an artificial depression. Mr. Biddle, taking Weed's word for it that "Nothing short of general ruin will cure the People of their delusion," had set to work applying the cure. Able to do so because of his monopoly on business control, Old Nick had ordered a sharp contraction of credit, a recalling of loans and a hoarding of cash and paper currency. Within a few months, nearly 18 million dollars in paper and 20 million in specie had been taken out of circulation, with the result that stocks and all speculative values immediately landslided; commercial houses in the eastern cities closed their doors, and hundreds of industrial employees were thrown out of work.

All through the autumn and winter the President and the Czar had been engaged in a tug-of-war, with their countrymen, as usually happens in such cases, serving as the rope. Committees begging relief came to the White House only to be advised in Old Hickory's best snort to "see Biddle", and at Chestnut Street they were similarly recommended to carry their pleas to the President. Even Mr. Webster's somewhat tardy remonstrance that "the Bank ought . . . occasionally to ease off—where it is prerequisite to prevent suffering", touched not the mercy of the Czar. "The Bank," he replied, "feels no vocation to redress the wrongs of these miserable people. Rely on that." It was to be a fight to the finish. Let the President surrender to the Czar, or let the People take the consequences.

The consequences, of course, were the theme song of Mr. Clay's philippic today, and he characteristically managed to forget at whose door the original causes belonged. Seeing only the opportunity to flagellate his friendly enemy, Little Van, the Mill Boy warmed to his work with moistening eyes and a breaking voice. Abandoning his stand beside his own desk, he advanced to the rostrum and addressed the presiding officer in person, pleading with him to go to the President with a message from the anguished People.

"To you, sir, in no unfriendly spirit, but with feelings softened and subdued by the deep distress which pervades every class of our countrymen, I make this appeal. . . .

"Depict to him, if you can find language to portray, the heart-rending wretchedness of thousands of the working class cast out of employment.

"Tell him of the tears of helpless widows, no longer able to earn their bread, of unclad and unfed orphans, who have been driven by this policy out of busy pursuits, in which but yesterday they were gaining an honest livelihood. . . .

"Tell him that he has been abused, deceived, betrayed by the wicked counsel of unprincipled men around him. . . .

"Tell him that in his bosom alone, under actual circumstances, does the power reside to relieve the country; and that unless he opens it to conviction, and corrects the errors of his Administration, no human imagination can conceive, no human tongue can express the awful consequences which may follow. . . .

"Entreat him to pause and reflect that there is a point beyond which human endurance cannot go; and let him not drive this brave, generous, and patriotic people to madness and despair."

Exhausted from his exertions and overcome with emotion, Mr. Clay dropped into his seat, and in the pregnant hush that followed all eyes turned eagerly on the Vice President, who throughout it all had sat there "looking respectfully and even innocently at the speaker as if treasuring up every word." Here, saw Mr. Webster, was a trap from which even the Red Fox could hardly escape. Plainly some reply was expected of him, and anything he said was bound to be an anti-climax to the Kentuckian's tearful tirade. Jubilantly Black Dan saw the Little Magician lay down his gavel, beckon another Senator to the chair, and descend the rostrum steps, preparatory to taking the floor. Mr. Webster was elated, but a moment later his joy was turned to gall.

For once again the uncanny little trickster rose grandly

to the occasion, and so skillfully did he counterattack that in another instant Mr. Clay's tragic masterpiece was turned into a cheap and tawdry farce. Instead of wheeling about to address the chair, the Vice President walked calmly down the aisle till he stood before the panting Mill Boy.

"Mr. Clay," he lisped, "may I borrow a pinch of your excellent snuff?"

Aghast, the Kentuckian handed over his snuff-box and, thanking him profusely, Mr. Van Buren delicately applied the powder to his nostrils, bowed deeply and continued serenely out of the room, leaving behind a superb and spectacular triumph.

Despondently Mr. Webster rose and followed the victor from the scene of frustration, and as he passed out the door, he beckoned wearily to his diary-writing friend, Philip Hone, New York Whig and financier. Together they collapsed in a nearby committee room where, for more than an hour, the Black Lion "unburdened his mind on the state of affairs and future prospects." Obviously, they agreed, the only chance of defeating this incredible Magician was to cut him down from behind. Formidable and unquenchable as he was in personal encounter, he would be helpless on Election Day without the reënforcements that always came to his aid from New York. Smash Tammany, break the Regency's back, and the Red Fox would be cornered at last. In April, the next month, New York City would be holding its mayoralty election, and in November Governor Marcy would be called upon to run on his record. If the Whigs could take these two elections, the battle was half won.

Thus they reasoned and the idea was no sooner conceived than put into motion. Hone, assuming the managerial duties, rounded up Henry Clay and "that sagacious man", Congressman John Quincy Adams; found that both agreed to the plan and then began enlisting volunteers for a raid into the enemy country. A meeting was arranged in Philadelphia where it was resolved that "Martin Van Buren deserves, and will receive, the execrations of all good men;"

three of the first Whig orators in Congress—Poindexter, McDuffie and Preston—were selected for their ability as rabble-rousers and sent to New York to bait him. Gulian C. Verplank, a Bank Democrat, was chosen to oppose the Wigwam candidate for Mayor; and, to meet Tammany on her own level, great mass-meetings were organized in public parks where sedate bankers and corpulent businessmen danced about "liberty poles . . . a hundred feet high" in emulation of the Braves.

But it was useless endeavor. To beat the gentlemanly Mr. Verplank the Wigwam whitewashed her ticket with the equally aristocratic Cornelius Van Wyck Lawrence. To off-set the Whig mass meetings the Braves held one in every ward of the City, where hogsheads of beer were rolled up and flowing health drunk to Old Hickory. In desperation the Whigs followed Tammany's example of hiring thugs to patrol the voting-places, but the best mercenaries obtainable were no match for the embattled Sons of the Saint. On Election Days streets were torn up and the paving stones hurled. With knives, clubs and fists the contest was waged. One man was killed; the outgoing Mayor, seeking to command peace, was grievously wounded, and eight policemen were carted to the hospital before a detachment of infantry and two squadrons of cavalry arrived to capture the ballot-boxes and hide them away in the City Hall. The Tammany candidate was winner by the lean margin of 179 votes, and the Braves escorted him triumphantly through the devastated streets in a "barouche drawn by four white horses."

Dismayed but undaunted, the Whigs concentrated their forces against the state-wide Regency in hopes of dislodging Governor Marcy in November. Back to his old stamping ground hastened Matty Van to direct the fight. In an effort to lift the depression, he ordered Marcy to lend $6,000,000 of State money to local banks and thus bolster up business. He prepared an Address to the People in behalf of the Democracy; he supervised the writing of pamphlets and speeches, and no doubt he found time while rolling about the countryside in the $1550 coach, which he had brought from England, to help compose the Regency's two campaign slogans—"Down with the Aristocracy!" and "The Rich against the Poor!"

In September the bookmakers in New York were offering even money on the Regency's defeat, and confident Bucktails covered all bets. John Van Buren, latest addition to his father's organization, made $9000; Jesse Hoyt, the family's Man Friday, won a list of wagers that ranged from cash profit to loads of firewood and cases of champagne, while the Vice President, who seldom missed such opportunities, must have added a sizable sum to the satisfaction of another victory.

Back in Washington for the December session he found no respite from the onslaught of his foes. An editorial in one of the papers he now controlled had referred to Senator Poindexter as "that bloated mass of corruption", and awaiting him in his mail was a note from the Senator hinting at an apology or else satisfaction in the customary manner. It was patently an attempt to provoke a challenge or, even better, to expose Little Van's well-known timidity and humiliate him in the eyes of Old Hickory and the Capital City at large. The gossip about town had it that, failing to entice the Vice President to the field of honor, Poindexter meant to give him a public beating.

Once more Little Van had his back to the wall. It would never do to show the white feather to Andrew Jackson and much less did the Vice President relish the thought of risking life or self-respect in any fracas with the bloodthirsty Senator from Mississippi. As always, he found a way out. In answer to Poindexter's note he wrote a quite dignified letter disclaiming any responsibility for what the papers had to say, but offering neither apology nor challenge. He showed the letter to the President before mailing it, and then, buckling a brace of pistols about his waist, went his usual way to the rostrum and about the streets.

What might have come of the matter remains in doubt, for Henry Clay, in his fondness for Little Van, came to the rescue by sternly ordering Poindexter to "drop it where it stood." Soon afterwards the Little Magician found more congenial means of protecting himself. Emerging from the Capitol one day, Andrew Jackson was twice fired upon by a workman in the crowd. An inquest quickly proved that the would-be assassin was a lunatic who had acted on his own initiative, but the proof did not prevent Little Van's editors from hinting in print that there was organization behind the attempt. Poindexter, it was implied, headed a plot to kill off both the First and Second Citizens. Old Hickory leaped to this wild conclusion, aired it widely among his friends and after that Little Van was too well guarded by public opinion to need his pistols. But a stout heart and a quick wit stood him in good stead as the Opposition redoubled their efforts to maim him.

Daily, and by every conceivable method, his position as presiding officer was made more untenable. Commotions were staged in the galleries to complicate his task of keeping order. Tie votes were arranged to force him into expressing an opinion with the casting vote. Once, attempting to dodge one of these, he stepped off the platform for a stroll, whereupon Mr. Calhoun leaped at the opportunity to humiliate him by calling "eagerly and loudly" for the Sergeant-at-Arms to go fetch the Vice President by force. Day after day that great triumvirate of Calhoun, Webster and Clay, along with their associates, followed each other to the floor to take potshots at the Red Fox. But through it all he remained suave, smiling and unruffled, meeting each new sally with a new defense, never losing his temper and never for a moment giving any indication but that he was at peace with the world. A reporter, covering one of these scenes described him thus:

"He received his fusillade of snubs and sneers as the ghost of Creusa received the embraces of Aeneas—he heeded them not. He leaned back his head, threw one leg over the other, and sat there as if he were a pleasant sculptured image, destined for that niche of life."

Thwarted in all attempts upon the man and his Regency, the Whigs sought another solution. They planned to trap

318 ]

the Little Magician by his own method of ambush. As well as may be deduced, the plot originated with Henry Clay, though he unquestionably had plenty of outside advice. Henry Barbour of Virginia wrote to the Mill Boy:

"We have no prospect of excluding Van Buren but by the plan you suggest of selecting two candidates who will be strongest in their respective sections."

In a word, the scheme was to recreate by artifice the situation which had existed in 1824 when the presidential election was thrown into the House. The idea was soon amplified to include four anti-Jacksonian candidates instead of two, each to be the favorite son of his own district. The plan, if successful, would whittle away the Democratic vote, gut the Kitchen Cabinet's organized ranks and make it next to impossible for any one man to gain the clear majority.

Hopes renewed, the Opposition bent to forwarding their scheme. Mr. Webster, already in nomination, was counted on to carry New England. Someone was needed for the Jeffersonian South, and he was found in the person of Senator Willie P. Mangum of North Carolina who received and accepted the endorsement of Mr. Calhoun's ex-Nullifiers. There remained the West which, like the East, was divided longitudinally into Southwest and Northwest. For the first of these sections, the Whigs received what looked like a boon from on high. It seems that the young wife of the elderly Senator Hugh Lawson White had long cherished the ambition to be mistress of a certain house on Pennsylvania Avenue, and though her husband, hailing from Old Hickory's own State, at first loyally scoffed at the idea, he was soon talked into accepting the third nomination.

But it was in the fourth of their candidates that the Whig leaders showed the profundity of their inspiration, and showed also how indelibly the Little Magician's influence had made its mark on the profession of statecraft. No longer were wisdom, experience and nobility the necessary qualifications for a First Citizen. A term, then new in politics, but destined to grow gray in service, covered the whole subject: Availability. Henceforth men were to be picked not

[ 319

to make good Presidents, but good candidates; not because there was something in their favor, but because there was nothing against them; not because they would serve well the country, but because they would serve the Party.

Each of the first three nominees was only a decoy to catch a few sectional votes. None of them except Webster had any national reputation, and Black Dan was too tarred with Federalism to carry much weight south of the Hudson River. Had the Opposition wanted to bring forth their best man for the fourth nomination, he would certainly have been Henry Clay, wisest in council and oldest in service. But the Mill Boy was entirely too opinionated a statesman for the present purposes, and though ever anxious for a chance at promotion, he recognized the emergency and abided by it.

For what the Whigs needed at the moment was an anchorman; a candidate who would both brace their Party against the vicarious tug of outdoor popularity which Old Hickory's endorsement would transmute to his favorite, and one who could match Martin Van Buren tit-for-tat in non-committalism. He must be, if possible, a Hero; if necessarily, a synthetic one, and the less he knew about current issues, the better. As Thomas Benton trimly put it, "Availability was the only ability sought by the Whigs."

To find the exact man was indeed a problem. But the Whigs found him.

3

(1835–1836)

In his fine and spacious manor house, set in the midst of teeming acres and on the banks of a picturesque river, a retired Major General was writing a letter.

Lean, shattered and sickly, his sixty-year-old body still retained the unmistakable tautness of military training, and the infirm hand holding the pen had once clutched a sword that had routed the Indians and defeated the British Army.

His home, filled with trophies and memoirs of these glorious days, was famed miles about for its openhanded hospitality, yet so simple and unpretentious was the host that one could forget how cities had received him as a public guest, how Congress had voted him a gold medal and the thanks of a grateful nation.

The General, however, was not Andrew Jackson at Nashville-on-the-Cumberland, but William Henry Harrison at North Bend-on-the-Ohio, and his marked similarity to Old Hickory was the reason Old Tippecanoe happened to be writing this particular letter on January 15, 1835.

"I am," he was informing Solomon Van Rensselaer, an old comrade-at-arms, "the Clerk of the Court of Common Pleas of Hamilton County at your service. But I have news still more strange to tell you, if you have not already heard. Some folks are so silly as to have formed a plan to make a President of the United States out of this Clerk and Clod-hopper."

There was in Old Tippecanoe's estimate of himself as a Clod-hopper, a great deal more truth than modesty, and even the "silly folks" planning to force this astonishing honor upon him did so in knowledge and not ignorance of the fact. For to have actually found a man who was both a graven image of Andrew Jackson and bumpkin enough to appear as noncommittal as Martin Van Buren, was to the Whig managers a dream come true. Here, they rejoiced to one another, was the perfect candidate, "the only one likely to overthrow the Champion of the Empire State."

It was fortunate for these merry gentlemen that they did not have to insist beyond superficial appearances upon the similarity between the two old Heroes. True, both at an early age had migrated into the badlands of the West and there manfully grown up with the country. Both had industriously built themselves prosperous-looking plantations, but had remained conveniently poor in regard to monied wealth. Both had killed Indians and Englishmen and borne the forthcoming honors with a certain amount of modesty and grace.

The American Talleyrand

But to push the comparison any further would have been perilous for the Whigs. For whereas Andrew Jackson had truly personified the American saga by working his way up from the bottom, William Henry Harrison had very nearly done the reverse. At sixteen Old Hickory, the orphan of an Irish immigrant, was turning his hand to whatever work he found in an effort to keep clothes on his back and food in his belly. At sixteen Old Tippecanoe, son of a wealthy Virginian, a Signer of Mr. Jefferson's Declaration, had dawdled his way through college; and been set up by his father in medical apprenticeship with the famous Dr. Benjamin Rush of Philadelphia, from whom he separated without having made perceptible progress. Smitten with the wanderlust, both boys headed westward, young Jackson alone and friendless, young Harrison with a commission, secured by family favoritism from Governor Richard Henry Lee. In Tennessee, Mr. Jackson became a leading citizen by dint of his hard fists and sharp shooting eye; in the Indiana Territory, Mr. Harrison became Governor at twenty-seven on $2000 a year through the influence of his late father's friend, Mr. Thomas Jefferson.

His ability, as prosecuting attorney, to preserve law and order first made Andrew Jackson locally famous. His ability to entice Indian chiefs (especially, according to official records, when they were "a little mellowed with Wine") to sell two-and-a-half million acres of their hunting grounds, earned William Henry Harrison his first commendations from Washington. When it came to fighting, both young men gained conspicuous notice, but with this difference. General Jackson beat the Creeks at Horse Shoe Bend by surrounding and killing every one of them. General Harrison beat the Swanee at Tippecanoe by accidently allowing himself to be surrounded and driving off the 400 assailants with a force of 1000 United States Regulars, and to the count of nearly 200 casualties as against not more than 30 dead redskins.

At New Orleans, General Jackson, though outnumbered, defeated the veterans of the Peninsular campaign cooperating with the British navy. At the river Thames, General

Harrison, vastly superior in forces and cooperating with Admiral Perry's navy, defeated a British detachment mostly composed of Canadians and Indians. Old Tippecanoe resigned his commission a year before the War ended; Old Hickory ended the War several years before he resigned his commission.

Moreover, there was no little dissimilarity between the manner in which each man received the worship of his countrymen. After Horse Shoe Bend, the War Department gave Jackson a regular commission; after Tippecanoe, the Legislature of Indiana omitted Harrison's name from a resolution of thanks on the charge that he had dastardly sacrificed a lieutenant's life to save his own. After New Orleans, cities rivaled one another in entertaining Andrew Jackson, and Congress coined him a gold medal. After Thames, New York welcomed Harrison but refused to grant him a sword and the freedom of the City as she did Perry, who accompanied him there. And though Congress did eventually give General Harrison a medal, it was not until 13 years after the War and when the honor had been several times voted down in the Senate.

Indeed, whereas Jackson entered post-War politics because of his war record, Harrison entered in pursuit of his. When Congress in 1816 refused his recommendation for the trophy, he secured an appointment to fill out an unexpired term in the House that he might be in Washington to see after his interests. And again: whereas politics made Andrew Jackson progressively more industrious and independent, it made William Henry Harrison inversely more shiftless and seeking. Apparently believing that the country owed him a living because of his military service, Old Tippecanoe's career from the Battle of the Thames to the Election of 1836 was a 23-year quest for sinecures. His farm went into decay, he into debt, and but for the speculative sale of the lands which he had thriftily staked out for himself while Territorial Governor, his wife and eight children must have known lean days. No less than ten times did he attempt to win an elective post, and seven times he failed. Seven times

more he vigorously sought appointive place, and four times
he was disappointed.

"This person's thirst for lucrative office," wrote President
Adams, "is positively rabid. . . . He has been in this session
as hot in pursuit as a hound on the scent of a hare. He is a
Bayard of lively and active but shallow mind, a political
adventurer not without talents but self-sufficient, vain and
indiscreet. He has withal a faculty of making friends and is
incessantly using them for their influence in his favor."

Finally in 1828, through friendship with Secretary Clay,
General Harrison secured an $18,000 ministership to Colum-
bia, but unluckily he arrived there shortly before Old Hickory's Reign of Terror and was summarily removed.
Returning to North Bend during 1830 he attempted in rapid
succession the Governorship, the Senate, the House in an effort to escape having to go to work, and at last received a
minor clerkship as a plain act of charity. Indebted to the
Bank of United States for $19,000, he put his sons and rela-
tives-in-law toiling on the farm and in the clerk's office, and
was just resigning himself to an old age of genteel poverty
when the Whig Convention of Ohio unaccountably nominated him for President of the United States.

A mere State nomination meant very little on the face of
it, but it was soon evident that there were powerful forces
behind his destiny. In Mr. Biddle's Pennsylvania, in Mr.
Clay's Kentucky, in his native Virginia, in Maryland, in
Delaware, he became the Party nominee. Henry Clay, bowed
low by the recent death of his daughter, came out of mourning to speak for him at Lexington. Thurlow Weed assembled
a thousand men in Albany, and nominated him in the name
of the Empire State. In New York City, Gulian C. Verplank
presided at an anniversary celebration of the Battle of Tippecanoe. In Louisville a testimonial dinner was given in the
General's honor, and from then on, Tippecanoe and the
Thames began to rival Yorktown and New Orleans as the
Republic's most hallowed victories. Unfortunately these an-
niversaries came but once a year, but the Whig managers
soon discovered that wherever men could be gathered to-

gether for barbecues and beer, for shouting and song, the memory of the great battles could be recalled, and the name of the victor exalted.

Dazzled and dazed by it all, the Old Clod-hopper scarcely knew what had happened. A short time ago he had wanted to be Clerk of the Court, and now thousands of persons apparently wanted him to be President.

"How little we can judge our future destinies. . ." he once wrote to Henry Clay. "Fate, as Bonaparte would say, has placed me where I am, and I wait the result which time will determine."

Not fate, though, but very realistic politicians took charge of his progress. Speeches were written for him; statements obligingly issued in his name; and questions put to him for which he had been carefully coached in the answers. Featured particularly was the questionnaire sent him by Congressman Sherrod Williams of Kentucky, containing five queries which his rival Mr. Van Buren had declined to answer, stating that a Vice President in session could not be asked to express opinions. These, having to do with State Rights, the Bank, Internal Improvements and presidential tyranny, were all aimed at the Administration's weak points, and were frankly disposed of with naive earnestness and generalities by the Perfect Candidate. Another issue just rearing its ugly head was Abolition, a fighting word to the South, but a man born in slave-holding Virginia and grown up in free-soil Ohio was a veritable flag of truce to both sides.

These were trying days for Little Van. By 1835 the government largess had been transferred to the so-called pet banks and the panic was temporarily abated. But returning prosperity brought no relief to the hunted Red Fox. When not under full fire on the rostrum, he sought peace and seclusion at Kinderhook or more often at Saratoga Springs, the fashionable watering-place. He would have had to take the wings of the morning and fly to the uttermost parts of the sea to escape the barrage of slander and abuse which the Whigs laid down around him. Well it was for the Little

Magician that he had no skeletons in his closet during this open season on his reputation. Whatever the foemen might say of his politics, they rooted in vain for some proof of his moral depravity. Some use was made over his rumored son-ship to Aaron Burr and of the fact that Major and Peggy Eaton had named him godfather to their child. But that was all. No one could deny with any conviction that he had clean hands in money matters and a pure heart toward woman-kind. His drinking was entirely a social habit; his gambling was mildly and quietly done, and his only association with corruption was in his relationship to Tammany Hall and the Spoils System. This last, together with his far-famed vanburenism, his subtle stratagems and fastidious tastes, had to be the whole subject of the Whig lampooning, but they succeeded in making their mite go a long way. Denied facts, they dealt in vague generalities.

Said the New York *Courier and Enquirer*: "Every paper almost that we open speaks contemptuously of Van Buren's prospects for the presidency; but they speak without knowl-edge of . . . the vast machine of intrigue and corruption that he has set in operation in every part of the Union—they do not see the fox prowling near the barn; the mole burrow-ing near the ground; the pilot fish who plunges deep in the ocean in one spot and comes up in another to breathe the air."

And the New York *American*: "Mr. Van Buren consorts most naturally with the degraded and vile—for among them he is a superior. . . . The good we desire we may not be able to attain; but the evil we dread, the great and menacing evil, the blighting disgrace of placing Martin Van Buren, illiterate, sycophant, and politically corrupt, at the head of this great republic . . . we *can* avert and such a consumma-tion is surely worth some trouble. . . ."

Where the Vice President came in for his worst flagella-tion was in one of the strangest publications that ever saw print. Davy Crockett, of late a Congressman from Tennessee, had written an *Autobiography* of his frontier days which, by virtue of his native wit and picturesque slang, had had a large popular sale. He was now hired, supposedly by Senator White, to turn off a *Life of Martin Van Buren*, and surprised everyone by producing what was, in spots, a remarkable work of slapstick satire. Where Davy, possibly through the agency of a ghost-writer, attempted to deal with issues, he failed miserably; but the imaginary chapters on Little Van's childhood, the burlesque of his character and appearance were so saltily said and so hilariously obscene as to justify, for amusement's sake, anything he violated in the way of decency and truth.

"Van Buren," said Davy, "is as opposite to General Jackson as dung is to a diamond. . . . It is said that at a year old he could laugh on one side of his face and cry on the other at one and the same time. . . . His mind beats round like a tame bear tied to a stake in a little circle no bigger than the head in which it is placed. . . . When entering the Senate Chamber he struts and swaggers like a crow in the gutter. He is laced up in corsets, such as women in town wear, and if possible, tighter than the best of them. It would be difficult to say from his personal appearance whether he was man or woman, but for his large red and gray whiskers."

Any clipping of his passages does the author no justice, but the book sold far and wide, and, satire being ever a sharper weapon than slander, Little Van's stock continued to fall. If the Vice President's dignity were injured or his humor prodded by the attack he gave no one the satisfaction of knowing it. Philip Hone, paying a friendly call about this time, found "his outward appearance like the unruffled surface of a majestic river, which covers rocks and whirlpools, but shows no mark of agitation beneath." Instead of protesting, the inscrutable little man merely arranged for three of his own hack writers to turn out more orthodox biographies, one of which, in German, assured that race of immigrants that Mr. Van Buren was "von deutschen abkunft, mit deutschem herzen, und deutschem sinn"—of German ancestry, heart and thought.

There was really no need for the Whigs to stress his knack for combining non-committalism and organization.

The Democratic Convention meeting at Baltimore on May 20th, 1835, should have been proof enough. The Convention held four years previous had only seconded Andrew Jackson's nominations from the various States; this was the first one ever to name a President, and as such it becomes an enduring monument to Martin Van Buren's claim for the Founding Fatherhood of American Politics. The first, it was also the model and ancestor of its type, not to be improved upon for at least a century to come. No National Convention of any period or party ever functioned more smoothly than this one operated from remote control by the Little Magician. He won, and he won so effortlessly that the fiction of his being the unseeking candidate read like gospel truth. Probably a dozen other Democrats more acceptable to the People might have been named, but the unloved Little Van was not only nominated, but nominated unanimously. Probably there have been few presidential years when more live issues loomed ahead, but Little Van wanted no platform to encumber him, and so none was adopted. Because Colonel Richard M. Johnson of Kentucky had shared the glory of Thames with General Harrison, the Director wanted him for a running-mate. Because the Two-Thirds Rule would enlarge the credit of his nomination, the Director demanded its adoption. His word was law among this parliament of Federal job-holders. Everything his spokesmen—Lewis, Blair, Wright and Hill—demanded for him was granted. Formally acquainted with his nomination, the candidate addressed the public in an open letter which was supposed to state his views on the various questions of the day:

"I am not aware," he wrote, "that there is a single point of interest in the general policy of the Federal Government in respect to which my opinions have not been made known by my official acts—my own public avowals and by the authorized explanations of my friends. . . . I shall, if honored with the choice of the American people, endeavor to tread generally in the footsteps of President Jackson—happy if I shall be able to perfect the work which he has so gloriously begun."

Just what this gloriously-begun work could be, no one was quite certain, unless it were the Spoils System, which was the only constructive accomplishment of the past eight years. Several things had been demolished—notably the last vestige of Alexander Hamilton's financial policy and most of Thomas Jefferson's state sovereignty principle—but Old Hickory's one legacy to statecraft was his own personality. To this Little Van hitched his ascending star, in full confidence that it would suffice him among the mass of the voters. But even his promise to walk humbly in the steps of his master was not wholly unqualified, and the Whigs raged to see how skillfully the Red Fox proceeded to nibble the sharp ꜰdges off the more dangerous issues.

After considerable delay he had finally consented to answer the Sherrod Williams questionnaire and had done so with (for him) surprising straightforwardness. He was, of course, for State Rights and against all government subsidies—except in "emergency." He opposed a recharter of Mr. Biddle's Monster, but he was understood by the "authorized explanations of my friend" Senator Benton, to be open-minded on "*a* bank but not *the* Bank;" and, in fact, was known to have suggested to Old Hickory that a bank with curtailed powers be established in the District of Columbia. He did not agree with Mr. Williams that any presidential tyranny had been practiced, but promised, if elected himself, to "exercise the powers . . . in a spirit of moderation and brotherly love."

But none of these matters had the emotional elements of the Slavery Question and, finding here a chink in his armor, the Whigs laid to with unstinted ferocity. Why, in 1819 Mr. Van Buren in the State Senate had voted for a resolution urging the Missouri Compromise, the first legislative attempt to curb Slavery! In 1820 he had supervised the election of Rufus King, forefather of Abolitionism. In 1821, he had voted to extend citizenship to freed negroes, a plain attempt to incite the blacks to rebellion.

This time Little Van could not afford to be evasive. To be in any way connected with the Abolition movement was branding oneself a fanatic, an anti-Unionist, a disturber of the *status quo*. Vehemently he disclaimed ever having held "views and opinions that are justly obnoxious to the slave-holding States," but the Whigs knew they had cornered him and they pressed their advantage. An inquiry was sent him asking if, in his opinion, Congress had the right to prohibit slavery in the District of Columbia. There was, the Whigs fancied, diabolical cunning in this epistle. The only possible answer was yes, for Congress could as legally regulate slavery in Washington as it could regulate the paving of streets. But let Little Van give this reply and he would be pilloried from the Potomac to the Gulf as a rabid Abolitionist, an enemy to the South and a menace to the Union at large.

The Vice President, however, was not so blind as to walk into this sort of a trap. Instead of answering the question, he used the opportunity to give a stirring dissertation on the sacred right of one man to enslave another without interference from the government. He pointed out that, since Maryland and Virginia had ceded the site of Washington, it would be rank injustice to make it free soil except by consent of these States. That had nothing to do with whether or not Congress *could* rule emancipation in Washington, but it enabled the Little Magician to tightwalk his way across another chasm. The Whigs in striking had had the weapon wrested from their grasp and turned against them, for Mr. Van Buren now flourished under the serio-silly title of "A Northern Man with Southern Principles." His friends used it to illustrate his broadmindedness; his opponents to depict his two-facedness, but the South had been mollified and the Red Fox went his way unscathed.

Meanwhile the campaign was running its course. Beginning in the summer of '35 it spanned a twelvemonth and drew to a close with the falling leaves of the next autumn. The four Opposition candidates continued their efforts up to the very closing of the polls, knowing that their plan of deadlocking the election could hardly go wrong. Webster was certain to carry Massachusetts, possibly two or three more of the New England states. Mangum could not fail in South Carolina and was running strong elsewhere in the South. White already had Georgia in his grasp and Tennessee would be his despite Old Hickory, who hastened there and made six informal speeches in hope of saving the home State for the Party and his favorite. As for the Old Clod-hopper, he was gaining at every stride. Ohio, Indiana and Kentucky were safely tucked away; he was crowing with exultation.

"Rely on me," he counseled a friend. "I may beat him 6 or 8000 [in Pennsylvania]. . . . Virginia is safe."

If Harrison or any other of the Opposition candidates took either Pennsylvania or New York the decision would automatically go to the House, where anyone but Little Van or Mangum, the Nullifier, would have a chance. In 1836 the Election Days varied in each state, stretching over the first fortnight of November, so that the reports dribbled slowly into Washington, creating a suspense which Mr. Van Buren could not have enjoyed. By the end of the month there were enough States heard from to show that the Whig plot had wrought a stalemate over the vice-presidency. Johnson and Francis Granger, one of the Opposition candidates, would have to fight it out in the Senate. That in itself was not disturbing, since the Democrats held a majority there; but it would be a sad day for Little Van if his election went to the House, where his erstwhile victim, old John Quincy Adams, was now the dominant force.

Not until the first week of December was there positive news about the presidency and, presiding over the Electoral College where the votes were counted, Martin Van Buren could see how barely he had nosed out a victory. The Regency had delivered New York with an increase over 1832, but elsewhere his lack of popular appeal took heavy toll against the machine-made majorities. As the reading clerk droned off the count, the Director heard that he had lost five States which the Party had carried in '32, that he had dropped over 130,000 in the popular total. In Louisiana and Mississippi he had scraped through by only 300 votes; a shift of a meagre 2500 in Pennsylvania would have meant his doom.

Still a miss was as good as a mile. The Red Fox had made another hairbreadth escape and could not know it was destined to be his last one. The closeness of the decision forecast stormy days ahead, but the Great Goal was his at last, and that was all that mattered today. Henry Clay, grinning wickedly out of his rectangular skull, sauntered up to the rostrum:

"It's a cloudy day, sir."

"The sun will shine," beamed Little Van, "on the Fourth of March."

CHAPTER IV

## *The Crown*

(1837)

*intro*

---

C ELEBRATION in the Capital City.
Another Coronation, but one that held no threat of
a Reign of Terror.

The change of monarchs this time was no change of
dynasty, and it did not matter if the twenty thousand souls
in Washington for this bright and balmy Fourth of March
had come less to cheer the incoming Director than the outgoing Hero.

At a few minutes of noon four dappled grays were spank-
ing out of the White House driveway, drawing a varnished
phaeton which had been made for the occasion out of the
wood of Old Ironsides and presented to Andrew Jackson
by the worshipping Sons of Tammany. Boisterous shouts of
acclaim as the carriage rolled down the newly Macadamized
Avenue toward the Capitol. A reverential hush as the Inaugural procession appeared on the famous east portico. Bareheaded and bowed with age, the grizzled Conqueror stood
for the last time in the assembled presence of his People,
while the little favorite gravely took oath and launched into
an Address that was simultaneously a panegyric to the departing Chieftain and a promise of peace and continued
welfare to the Land.

Indeed the Ides of March gave the Eighth President every
auspice of a quiet and happy reign. Spring was on the Poto-

[ 333

mac. The last remnant of the winter's snow lay on the hill-
tops, and this almost dissolved under the gleaming sun, just
as the lingering effects of Mr. Biddle's personally-conducted
panic were almost dissolved under the sunny optimism of
Old Hickory's last two years in power. A few chilly gusts
tossed the whitened locks of the General as he drove back to
the Palace where he was now a guest. A few indistinct rumblings of an approaching storm might have been heard, as
for instance from Manhattan, where "The prospects of Wall
Street," sighed Philip Hone, "are getting worse and worse";
where only a few weeks ago a hungry mob had charged out
of City Hall Park and raided a warehouse for flour.

The gusts and the rumblings, though, seemed insignificant
—not at all in character with the occasion at Washington.
The day was both temperate and invigorating enough for
Old Hickory to have crawled out of a sick bed, to which
he did not return until after attendance at the Inaugural
Ball that night at Carusi's. The country, too, seemed firmly
on its feet again. Government funds were out of Old Nick's
grasp, and the pet banks, urged by the Treasury Department
"to afford increased facilities to commerce . . . to individuals
. . . (and) merchants engaged in foreign trade," had responded with a flood of paper money that gave the well-
known aspect of prosperity. The national debt was zero; a
surplus resided in the coffers; the harvests had been plentiful, and the new President seemed amply justified in his
Inaugural pronouncement that:

"Overlooking partial and temporary evils as inseparable
from the practical operation of all human institutions, and
looking only to the general result, every patriot has reason
to be satisfied. . ."

Not until three days later, when he escorted Old Hickory
to the new railroad station and started him off to the Hermitage, did the Eighth President's administration really
begin. In his Address he had reiterated the promise to tread
faithfully in the master's footsteps and had dramatized this
policy by retaining the entire Cabinet which, however, included such of his own associates as John Forsyth, Levi

Woodbury, Ben Butler and Amos Kendall, who had taken over the Post Office after the latest exposé. The presidency was Andrew Jackson's parting gift to his favorite, but one could scarcely make any critical examination of the heir-looms while the corpse, as it were, was still in the house. And when he did find time for a close scrutiny, Mr. Van Buren was shocked to discover that all that glittered about his prize was not gold. The quest of it had been sport royal, but the final winning proved a mocking delusion.

"The truth of the matter can be stated in a word," he wrote. "Whilst to have been deemed worthy . . . to fill the office of Chief Magistrate of the Republic is an honor which ought to satisfy the aspirations of the most ambitious citizen, the period of his actual possession of its powers and the performance of its duties is . . . one of toilsome and anxious probation."

The Emperor of Morocco was soon to send Martin Van Buren the present of a caged lion, but this gift was in no wise so hazardous as the legacy he had inherited from Andrew Jackson. There had been Jeremiahs aplenty—Clay, Webster and Adams—to preach the inevitable woe in wait for the country, but they had been heeded not, and cried down for a pack of Cassandras. Yet in retrospect it is plain to see how the weird fiscal policies of the Jackson administration and the fantastic fathering of speculation, did much to make the Depression of 1837 a logical and inescapable result. Millions of dollars on credit had been sunk into unproductive, uncultivated lands of the West; millions more into imaginary steamboat and river-dredging companies; into unmarketable supplies of cotton and woolen goods; into urban real estate, and rural highways and wilderness canals. The absence of a national debt and the seeming presence of unbounded government credit were both as mythical as the paper values on which they were laid, yet these mirages attracted a rush of foreign investment which served to swell the tide that was soon to be a backwash. The whole country, from the White House down to the humblest shanty on the frontier, seemed to believe that producing wealth and prosperity demanded no more labor than merely rubbing an Aladdin's Lamp.

In his final year of office Andrew Jackson signed two measures that did not create, but certainly helped to hasten, the axe that was destined for his favorite's neck. The first of these was the Distribution Act, whereby all Treasury surplus above five million dollars should be divided and passed out to the individual States for public works and relief for the needy. It seems incongruous that an Administration which had crushed Internal Improvements would agree to such a proposition, or that such proud Jeffersonians as Senator Calhoun would accept it. But Andrew Jackson signed the bill with what he termed in his last message to Congress "a reluctant approval" and lest (as his floor leader, Senator Benton, admitted afterwards) a veto of so popular a measure would inconvenience Little Van, then in the heat of his campaign. And the Jeffersonians justified their acceptance of the gift on the facile argument that it was a "loan," though Mr. Clay "did not believe a single member of either house imagined that a dollar would be recalled."

The Distribution Act took effect on January 1st, 1837, when the 36 millions of government surplus would be paid out in four annual installments. Thus the first 9 million was wiped off the Treasury books two months before Mr. Van Buren went into office, and the second only a few weeks afterwards, with the third and fourth yet to come. The total result of this was to drain the capital of the pet banks and to start the State governments off on a splurge of spending and debt in which they took no thought of the morrow, dreaming, of course, that the next installment would soon be due. And to team up with this measure, Old Hickory trotted out another which pulled, however, in the other direction and thereby added uproariously to the confusion. Someone, apparently, had pointed out to the General the idiocy of selling land for $1.25 an acre and receiving for it nothing but promissory notes to pay. Therefore, as in the matter of the Removal Decree, he waited till Congress was in recess and then struck suddenly with his renounced Specie

Circular, the gist of which was that all public lands must be paid for in cash.

Immediately there was another violent dislocation of capital as the large Eastern banks began trundling gold and silver across the continent, where it could be paid into the land offices. It took very little foresight to see what this could do to the business sections along the Atlantic coast, and coming in July of '36, the Circular gave the Whigs hope that a return of the panic would aid their cause. The Clod-hopper, the Mill Boy and Black Dan had rent the air with dire predictions but, to the dubious good fortune of their opponent, the panic did not break at once, but lurked out of sight until he was safely elected and sworn in.

Andrew Jackson had not yet reached the Hermitage, and the new Administration was barely a week old, when America's first major Depression began sweeping its vicious circle. Everything, it seemed, depended on everything else, and nothing was stable. In mid-March, irate landlords began agitating under slogans: "No more rag money. Give us gold and silver." In April, brokerage houses, their credit gone, began to collapse. By the 8th of that month, 98 of them in New York City had declared bankruptcy; by the 11th their casualties were 128, and after that their brethren in other cities began to expire with such rapidity that the count of failures was completely lost.

In the North, factories, and especially textile mills supported by these brokerage companies, shut their doors. Employees were turned out on the streets where whole families vainly sought refuge in the overcrowded Almshouses, willingly committed felonies to get into jail or desperately risked their lives, and often lost them, by charging the soldiers who guarded warehouses where food was stored. In the South, cotton growers, relying on sales to the northern mills, saw their product, which had been selling for 20¢ a pound, go begging at 10 and 8. Nine-tenths of the clearing houses in Mobile closed shop. Eventually over two hundred plantations were deserted for want of money to pay the taxes, and the initials "G. T." became grim slang for "Gone to Texas,"

whence ruined planters migrated with their slaves in hope of
making a fresh start in the new Lone Star Republic.

Everywhere, as the value of speculations went down, the
cost of necessities went up: rents in the cities, clothing in the
country, foodstuffs all over the land. Grain and meat, which
had been hoarded for rich markets abroad, were now on sale
only at prohibitive prices. A country that reaped the greatest
harvests in the world was forced to reimport two million
dollars worth of wheat for home consumption. "Meat and all
kinds of poultry are dear . . ." moaned Philip Hone. "The
shad, the cheapness of which in ordinary seasons makes them,
as long as they last, a great resource for the poor, are not to
be bought under seventy-five cents and a dollar. . . . Are
the fish afraid to come out of the water lest they be caught in
the vortex of Wall Street?"

The panic gathered momentum in its second month, and
the Hone Diary, the barometer of the financial classes,
showed new lows of despondence. "No man can calculate
to escape ruin save he who owes no money. Happy is he who
has little and is free from debt." Fortunes dissolved over
night; suicides became commonplace. News came from
abroad that the Bank of England was tottering, and foreign
capital began to disappear. A group of Hone's friends woe-
fully reckoned their losses at 20 millions in the stock market
and 40 millions more in their real estate holdings. On May
10th every bank in New York City suspended payment. On
the next day banks in Philadelphia, Baltimore, Albany,
Hartford, New Haven and Providence followed suit. On the
next day it was Boston and Mobile; on the next New Orleans; on the 17th, Charleston and Cincinnati. With currency practically out of circulation merchants of ready wares
resorted to the use of barter and script. Cards like these were
the nearest thing to money.

| | |
|---|---|
| The Bearer will be entitled to fifty cents worth of refreshments in the Auction Hotel, 123 and 125 Water Street. | This ticket will hold good for a sheep's tongue, two crackers and a glass of red eye. |

For the first of many times to come, Capitalism in America was on trial for its life, and the People crowded about the scaffold crying for blood. The masses might be starving, but it was comfort to witness the agony of their enemy. A left wing of the Tammany Democrats broke off into the Equal Rights Party, or Loco Focos, as they were called. Through their editorial spokesman, William Cullen Bryant of the *Evening Post,* they demanded justice for the workingman, an end to class privilege, an end to wealth by speculation, no more banks, no more paper money. The Loco Focos put up a mayoralty ticket for New York, but only succeeded in splitting the Democratic vote and letting in the Whigs. The movement spread to other cities, to Baltimore and Philadelphia, where at tumultuous mass meetings the workingman's principles were lauded and resolutions adopted wherein: "We hereby pledge our lives, if necessary, for the support of the same."

Just what a President may or must do in such crises the America of 1837 did not know. Financial disturbances the country had experienced before, but nothing so terrifying and all-inclusive as this one. There must have been, of course, thousands of farmers living on their own produce whom the Depression did not measurably affect, but these are the silent many always ignored in historical generalizations. So far as voluble America was concerned, the situation could hardly have been more desperate. Here was starvation in a land of plenty; bloodshed inflicted by uniformed soldiers in times of peace; universal bankruptcy in a nation that owned the richest resources on the whole wide earth. Where could the country turn for leadership and advice save to its First Citizen and, turning, what confidence could it have in a man who was by all odds the most notorious politician in America, one whose twenty-five years in public life had been only a series of intrigues and evasions?

Gloomily at first, and then resentfully, the Republic demanded some recognition of its plight from the White House. To all appearances Little Van was utterly oblivious to what was happening. At the Executive Mansion, instead of weighty discussions and councils of state, a great renovation was taking place. Carpenters, interior decorators, and salesmen thronged the halls, hammering, measuring, presenting their bills. The private office was completely refurnished and the dining room redecorated. Bed chambers and sitting rooms were done over with new carpets, new curtains, new wallpaper, new fixtures—all at a total cost of $27,000, which Congress would be asked to pay.

Gossip had it that either the Patroon's daughter or Dolly Madison's niece would marry the President's eldest son, and become social mistress of Washington, but there was no report on who was going to stem the Depression. Rumor was corroborated that Mr. Van Buren had imported an English chef to feed the White House guests, but there was nothing definite on how he intended to feed the People. A delegation of fifty New York businessmen paid him a call and insisted that a special session be convened to pass relief measures, but Mr. Van Buren replied the emergency did not warrant such action. Nicholas Biddle, still considered the financial genius of the age, dropped in to offer assistance, but "found the President profoundly silent on the great and interesting topics of the day."

Headlong the affairs of the nation continued to go from bad to worse. With the closing of all but two of the eighty-four pet banks, the government itself was embarrassed for cash to meet its daily running expenses. The banks, counting on more government deposits, were informed by the Treasury Department that tax officers and revenue agents would henceforth keep what little they collected in their own strong boxes. The State governments, awaiting the third and fourth installments under the Distribution Act, were shocked to hear that the payment would probably be suspended.

More riots followed more mass meetings. Papers were saying that the President dared not show himself for fear of being assassinated. In New York a gathering of financiers asked: "What constitutional or legal justification can Martin Van Buren offer to the People of the United States for having brought upon them all their present difficulties?" In Boston the head of a large textile firm told his audience that soon "the time might come when the crew must seize the ship." In Washington, journalists dropped the formality of the First Citizen's title, addressing him as "Mr. Matty Van Buren" and mimicking his cheery Inaugural Address with insolent jibes: "As for the Presidency being 'the highest of all marks of the country's confidence' we are compelled to confess that your election utterly overturns that idea."

"Where will it all end?" wailed Philip Hone. "In ruin, revolution, perhaps civil war!"

March passed and April and two weeks of May, but still no action from the White House and when, finally, the President apparently came out of his trance, it was only to exhibit his well-schooled faculty for getting his own way. He had good cause for not wanting a hostile Congress on his hands so early in the term, yet he could no longer be deaf to the hysterical demands for a special session. Accordingly on May 15th he issued the call, but he set the date for convening at the first Monday in September—nearly four months away.

At this rose another indignant roar from People and Press, but the Chief Magistrate merely retired into closer seclusion. The announcement that he was busy mapping out a recovery program with which to greet Congress only added to the impatience, contempt and despair. Either the Little Magician would do nothing, went the common opinion, or he would do something outrageous. If there were any thinking men in the country who posed the slightest confidence in the little trickster, they must have been few and exceedingly far between. But up at Sunnyside, his estate on the Hudson, Mr. Washington Irving permitted himself to fear the worst and hope for the best. A fortnight before Congress would meet, and while the President was putting the final touches on his Message, Mr. Irving took it upon himself to send some anxious advice.

"Never heed," he wrote to the White House, "how any measure is to affect your political fortunes, *and dare to be unpopular rather than do wrong.*"

2

(1837–1838)

Strange and fortuitous advice, nearly any living American would have said, to be offering a man whose whole career had prospered under just the opposite philosophy. From the Tavern by the roadside to the Palace on the Avenue, Martin Van Buren's progress had been a single-minded and highly successful march in which taking heed for political fortunes was the central motivation. That he could, even if he wished, abandon such tactics now, seemed more than the sublimest faith could accept.

But though no one, save himself and Mr. Irving, seemed to have guessed it, the Martin Van Buren on whom the sun of March Fourth had shone six months ago, was no longer the Little Magician nor even the Red Fox. He was not the first or only man whom a sacred trust, no matter how undeservedly achieved, has suddenly sobered and ennobled, but the courage, wisdom and unselfishness he would show as Chief Magistrate was far and away the most astonishing miracle he ever performed. That "common good sense" which Andrew Jackson had been hypnotized into seeing years ago, unaccountably became a reality. Those talents, so long directed toward personal ends, were actually to be applied, as Old Hickory had imagined, "for the good of his country."

This is not to say that Martin Van Buren became overnight a seer and a statesman. His was never the profundity of mind to permit that. What he did was what any man with ordinary intelligence, a sense of balance and a practical education in government could have done—were he willing to take the consequences. If America's political history proves anything it is that common sense, character, and unselfish devotion are qualities to be rated far above genius and experimental intelligence. A mediocre man rarely has all these gifts unshakably in him, but assuredly no genius has either.

# The Crown

Between the two is a happy medium, be it homely or austere, which America has seen incarnated in several personalities of which George Washington and Abraham Lincoln are the most obvious examples. The remarkable thing about Martin Van Buren was not that he had brains enough to make a good President, but that he had fortitude enough to make an unpopular one.

Nor will it do to extend over-much sympathy to the Eighth President for having inherited so baleful a legacy from his predecessor. The whirlwind which Martin Van Buren reaped in 1837 was only the wind he had been sowing for the past eight years. No man had been closer than he was to Andrew Jackson, and no man—not even Old Hickory himself—was more responsible morally for the blunders of that administration. Andrew Jackson was headstrong and ignorant of state-craft, plunging into his errors with a good conscience, but Martin Van Buren, level-headed and in full knowledge of his subject, perpetrated his sins of commission and omission with open eyes. Unofficially as Party Director, and officially as Prime Minister and Vice President, he had been, in the truest sense, the power behind the throne. Where he could lead Old Hickory, he did so; where he could not lead, he followed—and into at least four policies which were contrary to his conscience and his better judgment. He was privately against the Nullification Proclamation, the Removal Degree, the Pet Banks and the Distribution Act. Yet on none of these did he have the courage to risk a break with his benefactor. Whether he could have succeeded in dissuading Andrew Jackson from any of his errors does not matter so much as that he did not try. Martin Van Buren allowed his country to be brought to the threshold of ruin so that he himself might be brought to the threshold of the White House. Both of them entered together upon their separate destinies.

And neither can it be argued that his reformation in any large degree redeemed his past record. Nothing he accomplished in the White House at all compared to the havoc he had wrought while making his way there. He would serve splendidly as a buffer against an onrushing tide of destruction, but none of his measures ever had the enduring importance of the Spoils System, and no example he set as President is to be rated with the precedents he set as a politician. History would do him scant injustice to forget the first and remember the second, to put him down as one of the most paradoxical characters who ever crossed the American stage —a Forgotten President and a Founding Father.

It was, nevertheless, a matter of extraordinary good fortune for the country over which he presided that Martin Van Buren laid aside his wizardries at the time he did. Ungrudgingly and unqualifiedly may it be said that no President, before or afterwards, ever faced a disheartening problem more stoutly, or carried one through to solution in more masterful fashion. His seeming indifference during the first several months had, in fact, been no indifference at all, but a daring and deliberate policy. If Martin Van Buren ever believed anything about statecraft, it was that government was meant to be supported by the country, not country by the government. As he saw the Depression of '37 it was a distemper which only time and retrenchment could cure. Other than ordering the Treasury to withhold money from the suspended banks and warning business and State governments to expect no more gifts, he purposely procrastinated until the first hysteria should dwindle. And when he did act it was to meet the furor with a combination of nonchalance and severity which were themselves reassuring. He called for a restoration of confidence by no demogogic appeal nor by any masking of the facts, but by a practical diagnosis of the ailment. And he prescribed a remedy that was no sugar-coated quackery, but painfully and distastefully sound.

What are a President's constitutional rights and duties in such a crisis raises a question which a later century has never solved. Given on one hand a scrap of paper called the Constitution and on the other a pressing emergency, the several Chief Magistrates who suffered panic administrations have showed several responses. But of them all there can be little doubt that the easiest and most popular thing a President can

344 ]

do is to reach into the public vaults and dole out government money and credit. In such a policy he will be supported by all enterprises which hope to be benefited, by all politicians who hope for reëlection, by all ignorant and shiftless masses who merely understand that once they were hungry and now they are fed. That a First Citizen should, if possible, afford relief for acute suffering is only humanely sensible, but whether his duties include rescuing prostrate gamblers (genteely known as brokers and businessmen) is something else.

And momentarily dismissing his moral and political rights in the matter, he may also consider the practical wisdom of such a course. It is not too broad a generalization to say that a financial panic in peace time is universally a case of deflation caused by previous inflation, whether of confidence or currency. To attempt a remedy by more inflation seems remarkably like attempting to revive a drowning man with a refreshing dash of cold water. If by any chance it shocks him back to consciousness, it will hardly do him much permanent good. There never was a process of alchemy which could turn the symbol of values into values themselves; there never was a government mint or printing press which could create a substitute for the sweat of its citizenry's brow.

Still it remains a persistent fantasy that any large government possesses the golden touch, and the illusion increases in proportion to the country's distress. It requires a mental steadfastness on the part of any ruler not to be duped into this superstition. It requires a moral heroism of him to tell the unsavory truth to an impatient and infuriated public. Much easier and much more expedient is it for him to accept the fable, or pretend that he does so; to be weak instead of strong, and shortsighted instead of farsighted. Temporary glory and gratitude will surely garland his name, if he patriotically mortgage the country and cry oblivion upon the inevitable day of reckoning.

Certainly mental steadfastness and moral heroism were not traits which had distinguished Martin Van Buren up to the winning of his Great Goal. No doubt the Opposition, having seen him yield to the plea for a special session, were

[ 345

quite confident that he would gracefully surrender to the rest of their demands; or, at most, attempt some dexterous manoeuvre to gain credit for plans which were already theirs. Three things the Whigs had been howling for ever since March: a repeal of the Specie Circular, a passage of Mr. Clay's Land Bill for another distribution of federal largess, a re-charter of Mr. Biddle's Monster for the subsidizing and reinflation of business.

Back to the Capital City trooped the lawgivers in the autumn of 1837. Southerners still came mostly by saddle or coach, but those from West and North were now spared the torturous trip over the Baltimore pike, for the B. & O. Railroad covered those forty miles in perfect comfort and in the amazing time of five and a half hours. Great preparations had been made to spread the President's Message to distant cities with all possible speed. A relay of steamboat, train and horsemen awaited the word, and Philip Hone would note with pride in the march of progress that a copy of the Message reached Boston "in the inconceivably short time of twenty-four hours."

At noon on September 5th the Houses met jointly under crowded galleries. Abraham Van Buren, his father's private secretary, was ceremoniously announced by the Sergeant-at-Arms, and walked up the aisle to the reading desk, bearing a bulky manuscript. Congress and country prepared to hear the Little Magician's theory on how to beat the Depression.

What they heard was one of the most admirable state documents ever penned in America, and coming from Martin Van Buren, one of the most incredible. Here was the vapid Little Magician speaking with the authority of a Jefferson and the fearless aggressiveness of a Hamilton. Here was the perpetrator of the sinister Spoils System calling idealistically and sincerely for faith in the homely honesty of first American principles. The Republic, he said in effect, had only herself to blame for the woe. She had deserted her creeds and consorted with the Philistines. Where was the agrarian state of self-sufficient freemen which Mr. Jefferson had visualized? Where was the proud simplicity that the forefathers had

346 ]

loved? A yearning after unearned wealth, a "spirit of reckless speculation" had inveigled the nation into a "diversion
to other pursuits of much of the labor that should have been
applied to agriculture." And "the rapid growth among all
classes, and especially in our great commercial towns, of
luxurious habits, founded too often upon merely fancied
wealth," had sapped the nation of its vigor and its traditional identity.

Concerning the Philistines, their "over-action in all departments of business, an over-action . . . stimulated to its
destructive consequences by excessive issues of bank paper,"
was the fundamental cause of the panic. Now they came
asking the Government to assist their nefarious schemes.
Should the Administration countenance a repeal of the
Specie Circular so that more of the People's Land might be
bought with paper money, when the Treasury already held
29½ million dollars of it? Should it advocate measures for
giving away more public funds when all but a million dollars
of the Treasury surplus was tied up in closed banks? Should
it allow the re-charter of the Monster, so that sums turned in
by honest taxpayers could be lent out again for private and
thriftless enterprise?

The Administration, said the Message, would do none of
these things. Rather than extend its activities, the Government would contract them. A bond issue must be floated to
meet current expenses; some concession would be made to
actual settlers of the West and to importers caught in the
maelstrom of foreign exchange. But beyond that the President would not go. He would insist on a policy of hard
money and, most important of all, he would present a plan
for the complete separation of Bank and State.

Then, as text and climax of the whole Message, came a
passage which might have fallen directly from the lips of the
Sage of Monticello.

"These who look to this government for specific aid . . .
lose sight of the ends for which it was created, and the powers
with which it is clothed. . . . It was not intended to confer

special favors on individuals or on any classes of them; to create systems of agriculture, manufactures or trade. . . .

"All communities are apt to look to Government for too much . . . especially at periods of sudden embarrassment or distress. But this ought not to be. The framers of our excellent Constitution, and the people who approved it with calm and sagacious deliberation, acted at the time on a sounder principle. They wisely judged that the less Government interferes with private pursuits the better for general prosperity. It is not its legitimate object to make men rich, or to repair by direct grants of money or legislation in favor of particular pursuits, losses not incurred in public service. . . . Its real duty—that duty the performance of which makes a good Government the most precious of human blessings—is to enact and enforce a system of general laws . . . and to leave every citizen and every interest to reap, under its benign protection, the reward of virtue, industry and prudence."

All in all, the Message was as sound and profound a pronouncement of creed as had ever come out of the White House. Considering each in its own capacity, it yielded not a whit to the Farewell Address, the Monroe Doctrine, the Adams-Clay Vision or the Nullification Proclamation. Had it remained only a pronouncement, it would possibly have been widely admired and spiritedly debated over many a teacup and after-dinner brandy, then gone the way of most good advice. But Little Van now assumed the rôle of Party leader, as distinguished from Party Director. His suggestion of separating Bank and State was no empty boast. Through his floor leaders he next presented the Divorce or Sub-Treasury Bill which, coupled with the Classification Act of 1814, make the only important and disinterested pieces of legislation that ever bore his name. The Divorce Bill did more than finish what Old Hickory's Removal Decree had begun. Whereas the Jackson measure only substituted one injurious system for another, the Van Buren plan was a thoroughgoing reformation of the whole fiscal structure. By its proposal, the Government would build its own vaults, keep its own bullion, and issue its own notes under careful control by the Treasury Department. It was, in general, the plan which, after several stops and starts, became an integral part of the permanent American policy.

At its introduction, the Divorce Bill split Congress into two factions where party lines were entirely obliterated. On the opening day of the Panic Session the Democrats were seen to hold slight majorities in both chambers, the first test vote being for Speaker of the House, where the President's friend, James K. Polk, was chosen 116 to 103. But the dividing issue was now hard money against soft; between a renaissance of Jeffersonism against Mr. Clay's American System. These new divisions made strange bedfellows. Nathaniel P. Tallmadge, the Regency's junior Senator, and William C. Rives, for whom Little Van had once procured an ambassadorship, bolted to the Opposition. Mr. Calhoun, who hated Little Van as he hated Lucifer, came over to the Administration. Hand outstretched, the Great Nullifier appeared one day at the White House office:

"Mr. President, you have removed the difference in our political relations; I have called to remove that of our personal difference."

The Carolinian's alliance strengthened the Administration hold on the Senate, but in the House, where members looked to nearby election, the mutiny shifted 27 votes and with them the majority control. The Divorce Bill was desperately fought through the upper chamber, only to be soundly beaten in the lower one.

While the President failed to establish the Sub-Treasury, he succeeded in blocking all attempts to reinflate business, though not without heavy casualties in popularity. The Ides of another presidential March were still far distant but Henry Clay and Daniel Webster, foreseeing bright futures, were beating the big drums of demagoguery for all they were worth.

"It was paper money," screamed the Mill Boy, "that carried us through the Revolution, established our liberties and made us a free and independent people. . . . I have thanked my God that he has prolonged my life until this present time to enable me to exert myself in the service of my country against a project far transcending in pernicious tendency any that I have ever had the occasion to consider."

"Over-trading, over-buying, over-selling, over-speculation, over-production," rumbled Black Dan, were things that he "could not very well understand." He was petrified, he said, by the President's "disregard for public distress," by his "exclusive concern for the interests of government and revenue, by his refusal to prescribe for the sickness and distress of society."

The Panic Session faded into the regular session with only a few weeks of recess between, and new problems rose to test the President's mettle. The Slavery Question was taking shape as a rampant goblin to North and South. Nick Biddle had circumvented the law by reissuing 10 million dollars worth of government notes under re-charter as a State Bank in Pennsylvania. On three of the nation's borders was bloodshed and the prelude of War. The Seminole Indians in Florida were up in arms against being transported from their Everglade hunting grounds and dumped down somewhere west of the Mississippi. Mexico was refusing to settle indemnities accrued in the Texas Rebellion, and the Lone Star Republic was begging entrance to the Union at peril of complications abroad. From Canada came a graver menace. Some rebels in the Dominion were reënacting the scene of '76, demanding of Great Britain an end to taxation without representation. Several American soldiers of fortune had led raids across the border; the loyalists had reciprocated by a counter-invasion, burned some United States property, sentenced some American LaFayettes and were next contemplating "freeing" Maine as Sam Houston had "freed" Texas.

All these situations called for extreme delicacy, accompanied by a proper amount of sabre-rattling, at which new business the reformed Magician proved himself remarkably adept. He asked and received of Congress the powers to carry on, if necessary, a war. He sent General Scott to the Canadian border and General Jessup to Florida, and emphatically told the Texan emissaries that he would not consider annexation under their present status. He paved the way for a settlement with England of the boundary dispute between New Brunswick and Maine; he began negotiations with Mexico which finally resulted in having the quarrel decided by an international umpire, the King of Prussia.

Meanwhile, going into the second year of his term, he saw that his cure for the panic was its own justification. The Depression did not vanish into nothingness with the year for which it was named, but the high tide of despair had subsided. Under the natural law of survival of the fittest, order came majestically out of chaos. By the spring of '38 the better banks were preparing to resume payment. The harvests this time were used for home consumption and, as he had predicted in the Message, "the proceeds of our great staples will furnish the means of liquidating debts." Cotton prices were finding a reasonable level; import revenues picked up, and business began moving once more.

Most gratifying of all was the pleasant surprise of finding that his coolheaded judgment had touched some chord of appeal among the voters. The Regency, sad to relate, had suffered a monstrous setback when Tammany lost the City again, and Thurlow Weed's "Little Bill" Seward beat "Big Bill" Marcy for the governorship. But the congressional elections were those that counted, and in November the President's party won itself a majority of one vote in the House. Still more reassuring was that this victory had been gained with little recourse to the Spoils System. Federal coöperation in New York had thrown the aged Solomon Van Rensselaer out of his long-contested post mastership, but elsewhere the President seemed to be testing the British use of patronage. Washington Irving, as America's leading man of letters, was offered the Navy Department, and when he declined Mr. Van Buren gave it to James K. Paulding, co-author with Mr. Irving of the *Salmagundi Papers*. George Bancroft, historian, and Nathaniel Hawthorne, promising young scribbler, got custom house jobs, an indication of the Government's new policy. The incoming Congress would not sit for thirteen months, but its election meant the eventual passage of the all-important Divorce Bill. Again, as in that brief period during the War of 1812, Martin Van Buren had become a true leader of men and causes.

Not victory, defeat, nor responsibility, though, prevented the little dandy from being the man he was. His now were the Palace and the Ultima Thule, and heavens might fall before he would fail to feed his fastidious vanities on the social ambition of a lifetime. Coming into the presidency with no thought of doing any more than enjoying it, Mr. Van Buren proceeded to do so. On his first New Year in office he opened the season with a gorgeous reception, his first step in restoring the presidential court to the glories of its pristine days. It is paradoxical in the light of existing conditions, but in perfect keeping with his character, that while the ragged Loco Focos were whooping his name through the slums of New York, the chosen and immaculate few were filing down his receiving line.

So long as Andrew Jackson had dwelt there, the White House had been the People's shrine. Now it became once more the Palace. "A few years ago," wrote Frederick Marryat, the reigning literary lion, "a fellow would drive his hackney coach up to the door, walk into the saloon in all his dirt and force his way to the President. . . ." But Mr. Van Buren, he went on, "has prevented the mobocracy from intruding itself upon his levees. The police are now stationed at the door to prevent the intrusion of any improper person."

Until November 1838, when Abraham settled rumors by marrying Angelica Singleton, Dolly Madison's niece and protégée, the White House had no mistress. But it never lacked a feminine touch in the dainty knowingness of Martin Van Buren. He himself had overseen the interior decorations and passed on the embellishments of glass doors, tinted chinaware and floral carpets. Under his inspiration the imported chef surpassed himself in cuisine, which possibly explains the notation in the Adams Diary: "Mr. Van Buren is growing inordinately fat."

Formal dinners of the time ran sharply to pattern, the only

variation being in elegance of cookery and service. At the White House a banquet would begin with delicately tinctured soup, followed by the choicest of fish, meat, fowl, several platters of highly seasoned vegetables, and ending on pudding, pie and the inevitable ice-cream. Sherry wine preceded dinner in true English style; Madeira (surnamed for its potency "The Supreme Court") was served throughout, with Port or Brandy to follow. If there were ladies present, they retired while the gentlemen lingered over their cigars, after which the carpets were rolled back and the floor chalked for figure-dancing, music for which seems to have been invariably supplied by two violins, a flute and a harp.

Hand in hand with the Eighth President's revival of court life, went the amnesty he declared on partisan enemies. For twelve years before him, the White House portals had received only brethren of political faith. Few except their followers ever called on the Puritan or Old Hickory, not caring to do so in the first instance, nor daring in the second. But to the Eighth President social acceptance took precedence over all else. His policemen might exclude "improper persons," but no person was improper because of his politics. To his regular Saturday night dinners came such of his stalkers as Henry Clay, Philip Hone, John Quincy Adams and Winfield Scott, the last being groomed by the Whigs as another "Old Hero" possibility. Even Mr. Biddle found an invitation and a welcome, and Mr. Calhoun reëntered a White House drawing-room for the first time since the Nullification Dinner.

The courtier once more, Mr. Van Buren was in his element. Whatever stiffness prevailed at first among these ill-assorted messmates was soon dissipated by the President's habitual good humor and impartial attentions. Men dined with him, then went home and paid tribute in their journals and correspondence to his prowess as a host. Justice Story had "a splendid dinner"; Nathan Sargent noted "the high art of blending dignity with ease and gravity"; Henry Clay did homage to "a generous and liberal hospitality." Especially notable seems to have been the little man's ability for making every visitor feel himself to be the favorite guest. On minds as far apart as the crabbed Mr. Adams and the urbane Mr. Hone, he made this identical impression.

"The President was, as usual, courteous to all and particularly to me."

Adams Diary

"There is no fuss about the business and every guest has his full share of the attentions of the host. I thought myself particularly favored, and so I presume others did."

Hone Diary

Yet for all the chivalric display of good feeling, these were queer banquets where a man's victims could come to sit at his board. Many a Banquo, the gashes still raw on his head, must have drunk gall with the Little Magician's wine, and downed it, as the next presidential year approached, with a silent toast for better days. On one such evening, while the party sat at table, a servant entered to report that the kitchen was on fire. A few buckets of water quenched the flames, but as the meal was resumed, the irrepressible Mill Boy rose with a hand laid over his heart:

"Mr. President, I am doing all I can to get you out of this house, but I assure you I do not want to burn you out."

Little Van bowed; others, he could know, had no such inhibitions.

3

(1839)

A tall, swarthy man stood in the doorway of the cloakroom and beckoned across the Senate Chamber to Mr. Webster. Few persons could so cavalierly command the Senator from Massachusetts, and correspondingly few politicians in the spring of 1839 could afford to ignore the gesticulations of him who now beckoned. It was, as it were, the hypothetical problem of the invincible force meeting the immovable object, and this time the object it was that yielded. Mr. Webster left his seat and made for the cloakroom.

Arriving there, he committed what turned out to be the saddest blunder of his political life. Would Mr. Webster, asked Thurlow Weed, like to be the next Vice President? Black Dan emphatically would not, having aspirations for the higher office. He said:

"I think I shall be the Whig candidate."

The tall man shrugged: "It looks to me like Harrison. . . . The question is who will poll the most votes."

Being reminded how easily the Clod-hopper had out-distanced him in '36 did not please Mr. Webster and he returned to his seat all unaware of the opportunity he had missed. A little more prescience on Black Dan's part would have suggested certain advantages to being Vice President for a man who, if inaugurated, would be sixty-eight years old and in feeble health. As for Thurlow Weed, he continued in Washington a few days in search of a team-mate for Old Tippecanoe, and then returned to Albany where minor problems awaited him.

History, in Albany, was repeating itself, but with significant variations. Twenty years ago a man had sat in a room close by the State House and ruled it in an unofficial capacity. Another sat there now. One man was short, the other tall; both had secured their positions by studious application to back-stage principles; each wore the iron fist of power under a silk glove of affability. Yet between Martin Van Buren and Thurlow Weed was a definite difference. The former had been always concerned with advancing to a higher public office; the latter wanted no office at all. Thurlow Weed was the first memorable example of a great American profession. He was a political boss.

Nature had endowed the man richly for his niche in life. No less than Matty Van, he possessed the talent of conversational persuasion; no less, he possessed the ability of picking subordinates, organizing his forces and assuming generalship in campaign and parliamentary manoeuvres. He could not, he admitted, deliver a speech, but his shrewdness as an editor made it unnecessary. In any other state but New York he would have come to the top long before he did, but the

Little Magician had a head start there and, other things being equal, was difficult to overtake. Opportunity came to Weed when Matty Van went off to Washington, leaving affairs of the Regency more and more to his viceroys. After that the Boss's ascendency was only a matter of time.

Patiently he had camped on the Regency's trail; minutely he put his Machine together, piece by piece. In the 1820's he enlisted the Anti-Masons to the Whig standard. In the 30's he enlisted the Abolitionists. He found a hard-fisted Irishman, Captain Maher, and put him in command of a gang of longshoremen to serve as shock troops on election days. He recognized promise in a young writer named Horace Greeley, and brought him to Albany as an editorial assistant. He saw possibilities of a great orator and vote-getter in another young man named William H. Seward, and took him away from the bar to be his star candidate. He perceived in the growth of Big Business and banking the chance to match the Regency's spending power of patronage, and he imported money from New York to be used where it would do the most good.

All this merit was bound to have its reward. At last it did. In 1838 Boss Weed's Mr. Seward was elected as the first anti-Regency Governor since De Witt Clinton and the first anti-Republican Governor since John Jay. At that election he swept the Bucktails out of the House of Delegates; at the next he swept them out of the State Senate and proceeded to a house-cleaning of job-holders which had not been approached since the last days of Happy Dan. No one, least of all Governor Seward, bothered to deny that Thurlow Weed was Boss.

"I never knew," the Governor used to say, "that dictators could be such amiable people."

"Thurlow Weed:" became one of the Whig toasts. "Who so long served in the office of Governor Seward."

The approach of the presidential year saw Weed's ambitions grow taller. His predecessor in Albany had gone on to be a national Director. Weed yearned likewise to be a national Boss. So it came about that there ensued one of the unsung battles of American history between a pair of champions, each supreme in his own field. A fight to the finish between the two types of political rulers—the old order against the new, the Boss against the courtier.

Martin Van Buren, despite his reformation, was not so quixotic as to make no effort for his own reëlection. No presidential season since the turn of the century had found him idle, nor would this one. The dignity of his office would keep him out of the campaign proper, but till then he could have his innings. Accordingly, in June he left the White House and set forth on what he disarmingly announced was a sentimental journey to the place of his birth. He longed, said the Administration press, to forget the cares of office among old friends and old scenes of his childhood. This great and simple soul, who had been unjustly pilloried as an aristocrat, would travel as a plain man, in an open barouche, accompanied only by two of his sons. As Andrew Jackson had returned each summer to the Hermitage, so Martin Van Buren would return to Kinderhook. Two great Democrats.

For one hastening to hallowed scenes of repose the President's was a remarkable pilgrimage. He made only two set speeches in Maryland and New Jersey, but Maryland had only 10 electoral votes and New Jersey only 8. In Pennsylvania which had 30, he made five speeches. In the Empire State which had 42, he made well over a dozen. And it was rather strange for a plain man en route to a haven to address a crowd in New York City as "my fellow-Democratic citizens," and to discuss such things as his iron hand in the Canadian troubles, instead of his anticipated joys of recreation. Suddenly it dawned upon the Boss that the courtier had stolen the first march; he was making a political canvass.

The reception accorded his adversary in Manhattan irked Thurlow Weed tremendously, especially since he could do nothing about it. At the last election Tammany had enticed the Loco Focos renegades back into camp and recaptured the City—Mayor, Council and all. Left to their own devices, the Braves put on a welcome for Matty Van which

was said to equal that of La Fayette fifteen years before. The
President put off from Jersey City in a navy cruiser and, not
content with crossing directly, navigated "gracefully for
some time among the vessels that thronged the bay." His
Navy Department had thoughtfully arranged that the frigate
*North Carolina* should be there to give him a double broadside salute. The Army Department, not to be outdone, had
ordered salvos from the forts on Governors, Staten and Bed-
loe's Islands, as well as from the several companies of field
artillery lined up along the Battery.

Landing, the President was greeted by a holiday crowd,
generously estimated at one hundred thousand, escorted to
Castle Gardens, lauded with affectionate panegyrics from
the Braves and then placed astride "a spirited black horse"
to review six thousand marching regulars. Following that he
paraded up and down Broadway and the Bowery between
cheering masses, and finally he was greeted at the City Hall
by Mayor and Council. The restful charms of Kinderhook
still beckoned, but the next day found him closeted in Washington Hotel talking politics; the next, sailing to Staten
Island on Captain Vanderbilt's private yacht for a Fourth
of July Sunday School picnic; the next, shaking hands with
nine thousand callers and attending the theatre with a box-
party of Loco Focos. After that he crossed over to Brooklyn
to inspect the Navy Yard amid another demonstration, and
at the end of a hectic week he continued northward, escorted
clear to Harlem village by the Wigwam Mayor and Council,
and ushered into town by the Young Men's Democratic Club
on horseback.

The duel between Boss and courtier was now properly begun. Until his prey ventured from the environs of the City,
Weed could do little to plague him, except by having Governor Seward refuse to join in the welcome because, he said,
showing hospitality to the President of the United States
would be "evidence of inconsistency and insincerity." Once
the First Citizen emerged into open country, Weed's bombardment roared into full blast. He owned the press and
most of the township governments. Matty Van's visit to Sing

Sing was pronounced "a disgrace to our place." At Hudson, his home town for many years, the aldermen passed an ordinance declining to receive him. At Albany, the scene of his many triumphs, he was greeted only by ex-Governor Marcy. At Troy the town council "Resolved: That the President's visit calls for no public action." At Schenectady he met a similar rebuff.

No shade of his former self would be the Little Magician if he failed to match these tactics in kind. By aid of his deposed Regencymen he saw to it that, even if officially snubbed, he was not therefore neglected. It was always possible to gather a crowd of villagers and rustics, anxious to boast that they had seen a President, and especially among the up-country Dutchmen, who were assured by Bucktails that it was a great honor to have one of their own race in the White House. Large travelling delegations were transported from town to town in order to swell the number. Touching spectacles were arranged to enhance the First Citizen's glamour. In one instance three old farmers were concurrently moved to rush up and kiss the President's hand. In another, a group of school children lined up before him and recited verses, for which occasion the great man was prepared with a pocketful of $5 gold pieces, one of which he thrust into each palm. In a third, as a Weed paper furiously noted, "a person was appointed to hold over his head an umbrella after the fashion set by the slaves of a Chinese emperor."

The native's return to Kinderhook recouped all of the setbacks elsewhere. Mounted on the second-story balcony of Stranahan's Hotel, he looked first to one hand where lay the tumbledown remains of Abe's Tavern; then to the other where, through the trees, lay Father Abraham and Mother Mary in their last resting place; then down to the crowd in the village square, and allowed tears to come rolling out of his eyes. Ignoring the four pages of notes in his hand, Mr. Van Buren spoke, in what the reporter from the Albany *Argus* dutifully recorded as "one of the most effective and beautiful addresses I have ever heard," of himself as Abe's Boy and the Boy Lawyer, of his childhood playmates and

[ 359

playtimes, but most emphatically of the extreme bodily labor he once performed here. At this (though the heaviest of his burdens seems to have been a basket of vegetables or Francis Sylvester's brief case) "all hearts were melted, and he himself was almost overcome by the bare repetition." But somehow he finished and, descending to the street, "took by the hand all that approached him and exchanged congratulations with old friends and neighbors."

It would be shameless cynicism for a biographer to read anything extraneous into so tender a scene, but there could have been persons present who believed the President's tears, if not premeditated, then a little implausible. It was not as if Martin Van Buren were looking upon these sights and old neighbors for the first time since childhood. Hundreds of times he had gazed, presumably dry-eyed, upon the same scenes which so moved him now in the presence of voters and newspaper men. Still this would be his best chance before Election Day to prove how closely his greatness resembled that of Andrew Jackson in their mutual love of dear memories, simple folk and home.

Unfortunately (though the Democratic press had refrained from stressing it) the only home Martin Van Buren ever had in Kinderhook was Abe's Tavern, now reduced to an uninhabitable hovel. Much as it might have helped the cause, he could scarcely lodge there during his stay at the village; and even if he could, there were certain disadvantages to reminding the country that its First Citizen had been born and reared in a drinking-house. Little Van's insistence on his remarkable likeness to the beloved Andrew Jackson and the revered Thomas Jefferson could be best foisted if he owned an estate somewhat remindful of the Hermitage or Monticello. Consequently he had quietly arranged for the purchase of Billy Van Ness's old home, Kleirood, of which he now took possession. It would never do, of course, to use that name, so reminiscent of another family, and all along the journey the presidential company had been wracking their brains for a pseudonym.

"The old man . . ." wrote the youngest son to his brother

# The Crown

at Washington, "spent a day and dined at the Van Ness Place—Kleirood no more. . . . We tried hard to get up a good name, but it is very tough work. The present favorite is THE LOCUSTS, of which there are a great many about. The only objection is that it is the same name used by Cooper in the *Spy.* . . ."

Having come over three hundred miles and waded through a whole month of speech-making for the professed purpose of inhaling Kinderhook's bucolic quietude, it might be supposed that the weary First Citizen would indulge himself in some of the indigenous pleasures. But the hope of prolonging his residence on Pennsylvania Avenue seemed to have a stronger appeal. He remained at Kinderhook only four days and these he spent not in rustic solitude or neighborly visitations, but at public banquets and private dinners "of fricassé and ham, washed down with champagne." From the village he pushed on to larger towns for addresses and public appearances, finally settling down for a rest at Saratoga Springs where, instead of sylvan bliss, he was dining and dancing; instead of his boyhood companions were more recent acquaintances among the gay and idle rich. Included among the hotel guests were Mr. and Mrs. Philip Hone, old Morgan Lewis, Winfield Scott and two ladies whom Mr. Van Buren seemed particularly anxious to charm. One was Mrs. De Witt Clinton whom he approached with bows and beamings, only to treat an interested audience to the rare privilege of seeing a President frigidly snubbed on a ballroom floor. And the other lady who merited his attentions was the beauteous Countess of Westmoreland, with whom the Chief Magistrate struck up a flirtation that would soon be ringing through the halls of Congress.

At Saratoga the contest between courtier and Boss took on a new aspect. Henry Clay was reported to be heading for the Springs, intending to make it the headquarters of his own pre-season campaign for New York. Having stepped aside for other candidates at the last election, the Mill Boy was in no mood to do so again. Anybody, he felt, could beat the Little Magician this time, and that anybody might as well be himself, founder and acclaimed leader of the great Whig Party. To become Whig nominee for 1840 was Mr. Clay's present ambition and, reasonably enough, no one concurred in his wishes more warmly than Martin Van Buren or less than Thurlow Weed. Courtier and Boss both looked upon the enthusiastic Mill Boy as a perpetual loser, the most logical and, at the same time, the most luckless of all Whig possibilities. Mr. Clay's destiny was therefore become the stake for which the two master manipulators now competed, each to his own purpose.

Cannily from Albany Thurlow Weed plotted to give Mr. Clay much the same unwelcome that Little Van had received in the Empire State. The task, as the Boss saw it, would be much simplified since the Mill Boy did not have the facilities of Tammany Hall in the City, and could not be received with much profusion at Saratoga, where Philip Hone and other Clay enthusiasts were waiting to greet him. Etiquette at the Springs would forbid any undue demonstration for a mere Senator while a President was on the premises.

Of both these impediments the Little Magician was quite aware, and aware also of his ability to remove them, which he lost no time in doing. Too late the Boss learned that the courtier's rapier had pinked him again. When Mr. Clay arrived at the Springs he found that the President had departed on a three-day coach trip, thereby facilitating a highly publicized reception in which the Mill Boy was welcomed into the Empire State with brass band, garlands of roses, speeches and a parade. And, planning to go to the City, Mr. Clay was overjoyed to hear that the patriotic Braves would do scarcely less for him than they had done for their Eagle Sachem. They would (and they did) fête him through town, give him the Governor's room at the City Hall, and even donate to the welcoming Whigs the same "spirited black horse," so that everyone might know with whose blessing he came to Manhattan.

"I hope I don't obstruct your progress," cried Little Van as he greeted his friend on returning to the Springs.

"Not at all," replied the innocent, "I have found the utmost facility in my progress since I entered your domains."

So far honors of the contest were all with the courtier, but the Boss, sensing his disadvantage at long-distance fencing, pressed into close quarters. Leaving Albany, Weed hastened to Saratoga for a conference with the joyous Mill Boy. He found Mr. Clay aglow with the memory of his recent successes in Little Van's home State, and confident that the nomination and the presidency were his for the taking. Vain were the Boss's arguments that the only candidate to beat the Little Magician was Old Tippecanoe. Mr. Clay regarded himself as the favorite Whig, but he promised a little condescendingly that, if the Convention thought otherwise, he would cheerfully back the Party choice.

That promise was enough for the Boss. Deftly he moved to complete one of the cleverest intrigues ever perpetrated by an American politician. In order, as he later confessed, "to keep New York away from Clay," he arranged the nomination of Winfield Scott, guardian of the Canadian border, and then proceeded to the strategem which has come down through history as the Triangular Correspondence. By his direction Whigs in different parts of the State commenced writing to one another:

"Do all that you can for Mr. Clay in your district, for I am sorry to say he has no strength in this."

Gradually the idea was implanted that votes for the Mill Boy would be support thrown away, and his boom dwindled. Setting off in December for the Whig Convention at Harrisburg, the Boss felt out New England delegations whom he met on trains and in the hotels. With Mr. Webster concededly out of the race they were open to suggestion. By the time Weed arrived in Harrisburg he had formulated a plot that could hardly fail.

Henry Clay's name, all admitted, would poll a plurality on the first ballot. After that Scott's votes would be quietly shifted by pre-arrangement to Harrison, swelling the Clodhopper's total till it approached and passed the Mill Boy's. If necessary the bait of the vice-presidency would swing other candidates into line and the deed would be done. The Boss would take charge of the organization for the campaign; Old Tippecanoe would supply the outdoor popularity, and the Little Magician, dissolved by his own magic, would be conjured away.

4

(1840–1841)

Drunk, profane and disorderly, Mr. Henry Clay paced the carpet of his lodgings at Brown's Hotel, "lifting his feet like a horse string-halted in both legs, stamping his steps upon the floor," and treating his three visitors to "such an ebullition of passion, such a storm of desperation and curses" as "we never witnessed before and pray never again to witness."

"I am," he wailed, "the most unfortunate man in the history of parties: always run by my friends when sure to be defeated, and now betrayed for a nomination when I, or anyone, would be sure of an election."

Pausing by the sideboard he poured out a stiff drink and tossed it down. It seemed to steady him. He bowed.

"Gentlemen, for aught I know from your cloth you may be parsons, and shocked at my words."

They were not parsons but messengers from Harrisburg bringing news that the Convention had nominated General William Henry Harrison. Their account of the proceedings showed how flawlessly Weed's plan had worked. On the first ballot Old Tippecanoe was a bad second to the Mill Boy with Winfield Scott a distant third, but Scott's votes were gradually transferred until they boosted Harrison to the top. In the turmoil that followed, the Clay supporters to a man refused to accept the secondary nomination, and it was finally given to Virginia's excellent Senator, John Tyler, because, as Weed said, "we could get no one else to accept." Once more Mr. Clay had allowed himself to be kissed by a Judas, once more the glittering prize had been dangled before his eyes

and then snatched away. He had given his word as a gentleman and a politician; there was nothing he could do but
repeat his promise to back the Clod-hopper.

"My friends," he howled, "are not worth the powder and
shot it would take to kill them."

Up the Avenue at the White House, Martin Van Buren
received the tidings with no less disgust, but with a nonchalance that hid his feelings. He could not fail to see the
irony of his position, the poetic justice of his lot. Twelve
years ago another President had sat in this same house in
the same predicament. Like Mr. Adams, Mr. Van Buren
had launched a program of national scope, and needed, was
entitled to, another term in which to complete it. Like the
Puritan, he was now set upon by unscrupulous schemers who
had no thought or motive save their own profit. He, as the
Albany Director, had thrust Old Hickory on Mr. Adams;
now Thurlow Weed, as the Albany Boss, was thrusting Old
Tippecanoe on him. A Military Chieftain to enchant the
People and heave a statesman-like President into the dust-
bin. The plan had worked to perfection in '28; what would
prevent it from working again in '40? Little Van had taught
the methods not wisely but too well.

He could take comfort, but small confidence, in the knowledge that he had done splendidly as Chief Magistrate. Without having played either the tyrant, the demagogue, or the
trickster he had become everything which the People ought
to ask of its First Citizen. By the application of nothing more
magical than common sense and conviction he had pulled
the country out of a quagmire and set it upon firm ground.
The advent of his fourth year in office showed the first ripe
fruits of his efforts. A Congress was now in session which
would pass the Divorce Bill. Quiet had been restored on the
national borders. The uprising against Slavery had been
calmed by his steadfast position on State Rights. An economy
in government had cut 11 million dollars from overhead expenses. True, the recent failure of Old Nick's Pennsylvania
Monster brought a short relapse into depression, but this
only justified the President's fight for hard money and sound

[ 365

credit. He had breathed health into economic leprosy, substituted confidence for despair, and was preaching a doctrine of safe-and-sane, frugal government that the country was just beginning to appreciate.

Still Martin Van Buren needed only his memory to tell him how much chance statesmanship had against politics in an open election. For the first time in his life Little Van was prepared to stand on his record. He had all the personal reasons for wanting a second term. It was the recognized token of the nation's esteem, and no President of his Party had ever been denied it. But being First Citizen had come to mean more to him than the empty vanity of the title. In assuming leadership he had assumed a mission. He was regarded, and so considered himself, less the heir of Andrew Jackson than of Thomas Jefferson. He was restoring the Party to its first principles. Had Henry Clay, successor in many ways to Hamiltonism, been named to oppose him, the election might have been waged along fairly rational lines. The two theories of government might have been threshed out again, and despite the inevitable amount of claptrap, issues would have been clearly drawn. But the nomination of the Clod-hopper was emphatic proof that the administration's case would not be tried on its merits. The Whig Convention offered no platform, gave no hint of its policies except what might be understood from the instructions to their candidate.

"Let him," commanded Nicholas Biddle, "say not a single word about his principles or his creed—let him say nothing, promise nothing. Let no committee, no convention, no town meeting extract from him a single word about what he thinks now or will do hereafter. Let the use of pen and ink be wholly forbidden."

Against such a totality of evasion no one but the Little Magician of yore could hope to compete. And against the machinery of demagoguery and organization which the Whigs soon set in motion no one but Little Van of the Kitchen Cabinet days was worthy to direct a fight. The glorification of Old Tippecanoe, his feats, his character, his victories, began just where it had left off in '36. Not Charlemagne was more tigerish in battle or more sagacious in council than this incredible old Hero. Marathon was not more gallantly fought, Waterloo not more efficiently generaled than Tippecanoe and Thames; and the fate of a nation never hung more breathlessly in balance than over the outcome of these two frays. Beloved by his friends, worshipped by his soldiers and called by his country, no saint was kinder, no sage was wiser, no savior of his People ever more deserving of honor and faith than this grand old Clod-hopper of North Bend.

The Opposition stayed not at mere sound and fury. Under Boss Weed's pragmatic direction all hands set to work building a Machine that would triumph over the federal Spoils System. Where States went Whig in local elections new job-holders replaced the old. Governor Seward blushed to admit that he replaced 1400 at Albany. Henry Clay dragooned his forces in Kentucky, urging in a letter home that "when parties are nearly balanced the one which is disciplined and in a state of complete organization is almost sure to prevail." A Whig manager in Pennsylvania gave details of the Boss's system:

"In this county we are polling the townships and thereby ascertaining the certain strength of our friends—dividing them into tens and giving each 10 into the charge of a committeeman, making him responsible for bringing his men to the polls by 4 P.M. of the day of election."

No busier man in the United States than Thurlow Weed. His was precisely the position Little Van had held while managing Old Hickory. His double duty was to carry New York for the old Hero and to direct the national campaign at the same time. He sent out a shining array of orators into the provinces: Clay, Clayton, Corwin, Choate, Webster, Wise, the ornate Edward Everett, the fire-eating Prentiss and the plausible Reverdy Johnson. He headed a column of poison-penned journalists: Horace Greely, William Lloyd Garrison,

James Gordon Bennett, Charles King, Mordecai Noah. He plucked the richest angels for campaign funds: Nicholas Biddle, Gerrit Smith and Philip Hone. In April he brought to New York an unusually large consignment of Philadelphia hoodlums for a valiant but vain attempt to whip Tammany again. In May he contrived for 30,000 Whigs to meet at Baltimore at the same time as the Democratic Convention. There resulted a free-for-all battle in the streets where brickbats and cudgels caused, among other casualties, the death of an innocent bystander, whose widow had to be solaced with $7000 out of the campaign chest.

The Convention gave Little Van his second unanimous nomination, but there was a wide difference between this and the one four years previous. Then he had been only Old Hickory's crown prince, now he was ruler in his own right and by powers few Americans had ever supposed were in him. Martin Van Buren had virtually refounded the Party of Jefferson as it was to last down to its crash upon the rock of the Slavery Question twenty years later, and as it was to reform afterwards. At this Convention the name "Democratic Party" was definitely adopted for the first time, signifying a break with the Jackson Era, when the official title had always been Republican.

The assembled delegates meant no aspersion on Old Hickory, but the distinction was nevertheless complete. In 1836 the Party had been no more than Mr. Calhoun had scornfully called it: "A powerful faction (party it cannot be called) held together by the hopes of public plunder." That was not true of it now. The Spoils System was not abandoned, but it was submerged. Naught but the idealism of their principles bound the Democrats of 1840. The fainthearted had been driven away by the President's assault upon popular fallacies. The professional scavenger saw more hope of loot in the other camp. Only one—Amos Kendall—of the original Kitchen Cabinet was actively behind Little Van. Eaton had gone over to the enemy. Lewis was being roundly scolded by Andrew Jackson for his indifference. Ike Hill was lukewarm. Duff Green was cold. New recruits, men attracted solely by the principles at stake, had joined in to replace the deserters. Among the leaders now were John C. Calhoun, Hannibal Hamlin, John A. Dix—every one of whom would pass from the Party when its idealism vanished.

Four years ago no platform was adopted. This time the Convention nailed its colors to the mast with a brief and explicit declaration of its faith. The Democratic Party was against all manner of monopoly banks, soft money and subsidized business; it was for State sovereignty as applied specifically to slavery, internal improvements and federal loans; it favored a strict interpretation of the Constitution as concerning the rights, duties, and functions of a simplified, economical government. Nowhere in the statement was there a shadow of non-committalism or a breath of demagoguery. It bears testimony of the Eighth President's leadership to see how exactly the Party platform corresponded to his opinions, practiced and preached, throughout the past three years.

A solemn gathering were the delegates to the Convention, but not a despairing one. Their fight, they knew, would be uphill but not hopeless. The Whigs were armed to the teeth with organization, but the Spoils System reared a bulwark which had never been smashed. Thurlow Weed was a resourceful strategist, but he had yet to prove himself better than their veteran of three successful campaigns, Amos Kendall, whom the President relieved of the Post Office so that he might legally take charge of the field forces. And if Little Van himself chose to stoop, even slightly, to conquer, a trick or two from his inimitable repertoire might easily save the day.

While the Convention was still in session the Little Magician showed a flash of his one-time adroitness. Vice President Dick Johnson had been more hindrance than help in '36. He had led rather a spectacular sex life in which a weakness for negro mistresses and the ability to produce an unnumbered mulatto offspring had told heavily on his vote-getting prowess. On the other hand he had served well enough in his proctorship over the Senate, had shared the glories of Thames with Harrison and was therefore useful. To drop him entirely seemed unwise, while to rely on him exclusively seemed inadvisable. So Little Van caused the Convention to forego naming his running-mate and instead to recommend that States offer their own choice for a Second Citizen. By this means three favorite sons were harnessed to speed the Democratic chariot toward its visioned goal. Besides Johnson of Kentucky was Tazewell of Virginia, who might save the Old Dominion from Tyler; and James K. Polk of Tennessee, who bore Old Hickory's invaluable blessing.

This plan, though, was Mr. Van Buren's one contribution to the cause. Henceforth, all he could do would be to sit in the White House and write letters reiterating his stand on various questions. The management was left to Kendall; the propaganda, to his well-schooled Press. The latter it was that blundered and gave the enemy an opening which proved to be fatal. It is not possible to say what would have happened if the Baltimore *American* had never printed the following sentence, but certainly when it did, Martin Van Buren was doomed to the limbo of one-termed, discredited Presidents. Shortly after Harrison's nomination, the *American* commented thus upon the Clod-hopper:

"Give him a barrel of hard cider and settle a pension of two thousand a year on him, and my word for it, he will sit the remainder of his days in a log cabin."

For a while the Democrats made merry over the quip. Administration papers copied and elaborated upon the theme of Old Tippecanoe's dingy poverty. That it was untrue made no difference. The Clod-hopper was, indeed, a trifle needy, but hardly the down-at-the-heels pauper here depicted. He drew about $6000 a year from his clerkship; his farm, cultivated by sons and in-laws, was sufficient if not bountiful. One wing of the manor at North Bend was, to be sure, a log cabin which had been preserved as an antique curiosity, but the General had never lived there, much less

370 ]

been born in one. As for hard cider, it was considered the
most plebian of beverages, and if the Clod-hopper had
treated his guests to it, his home would scarcely have had the
far-flung reputation it did for hospitality.

The Opposition assembled these arguments in defense of
their candidate when suddenly the wave of indignation
against Democratic snobbery convinced them that, all unknowing, they had happened upon a wind-fall. Instead of
concealing the old man's shiftlessness, they began glorifying
his poverty; instead of explaining away the log cabin and
hard cider, they began flaunting them. At a rally in New
York the idea was tested of erecting a cabin for an audience
hall and serving cider for free refreshment. So instantaneous
was the success that the plan was repeated elsewhere with
most gratifying results. By May the device was becoming a
central theme of the Whig campaign; by June they had abandoned all pretense of featuring anything else. Came then the
deluge.

What happened in America during the summer and autumn of 1840 far transcended anything so mundane and
ordinary as a political canvass. It was, in all truth, a religious
awakening with every one of the time-honored embellishments. Old Tippecanoe was the Messiah come to deliver the
chosen People into the Promised Land. As inducement to
follow him there was the usual system of rewards and punishments, hawked hither and yon by himself and his disciples.
Instead of milk and honey, the People were promised "$2 a
day and roastbeef"; instead of fire and brimstone they were
threatened with "Matty's policy, 50¢ a day and French soup."
The Clod-hopper's heroism and his homely habits at once
upheaved him into godhead and made him, not the Son, but
the Brother of Man. Did the People travail and were heavy-
laden with debts? Then they were invited to come to his
Cabin where, he said, "the latch-string would never be in."
Were they low of heart and poor in worldly possessions?
Then they were exhorted to seek refuge in his bosom, unless, of course, "you *wish* to be poor and downtrodden, to see

your wife starve and your children in ignorance." The Log Cabin became symbol of the new awakening; Hard Cider, its sacrament; campaign songs, its litany; rallies, its revival meetings.

Primarily it was a religion of joy, fraternity and emotionalism. The truth had to be blindly and uncritically accepted. Fairly it might have been said that unless the voter's faith became as a little child's, Old Tippecanoe would never enter into his kingdom. To bring about this happy state of grace and reduce the electorate into a spirit of childish simplicity became the mission of the Clod-hopper's disciples. They wisely deduced that men are seldom more childish than in the presence of wine, women and song. Hitherto political rallies had been exclusively male. Now voters were urged to bring along their wives and sweethearts. The Sons of Tammany had long ago discovered the satisfactory plan of serving beer and light wine at public demonstrations, but cider proved to be both sacerdotal and stimulating. The use of songs and ballads was not new, but never before had the plan of mass singing been effectively tried.

The ritual of a Harrison rally was almost invariable. First the multitude drank its fill of the cider, listened to a few speeches and then were lead in song by men generally engaged for the purpose. Mounted on a platform, the songster gave the key, rehearsed the words, if necessary, and then whipped his audience into harmony. A few original tunes were written and used, but usually words were simply adapted to familiar melodies. Yankee Doodle, The Star Spangled Banner, negro spirituals, rag-time and local folksongs all saw service. When American talent was exhausted, there was no hesitation in paraphrasing foreign selections such as: La Marseillaise, Scots Wha Hae Wham Wallace Bled, Bonnets of Blue, Paddy Carey, Old King Cole. It was a rare meeting that did not sing Alexander Ross's popular parody of "The Little Pig's Tail," always accompanied by the rolling about of a huge ball, the diameter of a man's height and plastered over with Whig mottoes.

## The Crown

What has caused the great commotion,
                                    motion,
                                        motion
Our country through?
It is the ball a-rolling on
For Tippecanoe and Tyler, too
Tippecanoe and Tyler too.
And with 'em we'll beat Little Van,
                                Van,
                                    Van.

Van is a used-up man,
And with 'em we'll beat Little Van.


Or the adaptation of well-known lyrics by Robert Burns or
Walter Scott.

O Matty Van, my jo, Mat
When we were first acquaint
'Tis true you were not slow,
    Mat
With sinner or with saint.
But you have grown ould,
    Mat,
You never seem to know
How fast you're going 'bock
    agen'
O Matty Van, my jo.

O, Van Bur'en, my jo, Van
You've clomb the hill o' State
And monie a cunnin trick,
    mon,
Was feathered in your pate;
But now you're tottering down,
    Van
How rapidly you go!
You'll soon be sprawling at a
    fit,
O Matty Van, my jo.

One touch of Blair's hand, one
    word in his ear,
As Van reached the door, his
    carriage was near.
"We are gone, we are gone, by
    hook or by crook,
I must wend my way back to
    my own Kinderhook.
My light English carriage,
    though often it flew,
Couldn't match the hard gray
    of Old Tippecanoe.

There was mounting and
    tramping of Cabinet Clan,
And the Kitchen concern, some
    rode and some ran.
There was racing and chasing
    o'er Capitol lea
But the Little Magician no
    more could they see.
So dauntless in War, to his
    country so true,
Who could clear the Kitchen
    but Tippecanoe?

Or this parody of the old Scotch ballad "Sir Patrick Spens":

King Matty he sat in his big White House,
A-curling his whiskers fine,
And the *Globe* man Blair sat by his side,
A-drinking his champagne wine.

Then awful shook King Matty's locks
And fearful glanced his eye
And he stamped his foot upon the floor,
And he heaved a monstrous sigh.

O, what's the matter, King Matty, said Blair
O, what's the matter said he
I'm a-gwyine to go to Kinderhook
My family for to see.

Said Blair you are a good-hearted man
And love your family dear
I'd thought that you'd not go back
Till after another four year.

Nor would I go back, my dearest Blair,
But what the deuce can I do
The People say I must make room
For the Hero of Tippecanoe.

Then the *Globe* man's chin sank on his breast
And his eyes fell to the floor.
And his nether lip hung to the ground
And it couldn't drag any lower.

Alack and Alas, said the *Globe* man Blair
We're deep in the mud and mire.
Alack and alas, said Matty the King
The Sub-treasury fat's in the fire.

Now Matty and Blair they raised their eyes
Each other's face to see
And they placed their thumbs upon their nose
And their fingers twirled twiddle-dee-dee.

Or this one where the stanzas were chanted by the songleader, and the audience crashed in on the refrain:

Who while but yet a little boy
Was counted cunning, crafty, sly?
Who with the wily fox could vie?
Van Buren!

Who when an urchin young at school
Would of each classmate make a tool?
In cheating who the roost did rule?
Van Buren!

Who was faithless from his
youth?
Who hates the light and scorns
the truth?
And worst of sophists is, for-
sooth?
VAN BUREN!

When Madison for War de-
clared,
And foreign tyrants bravely
dared,
Against him who was loudest
heard?
VAN BUREN!

Yet when our country's gifted
son
All opposition over-run,
Who cried "Hurrah for Madi-
son?"
VAN BUREN!

Who made of Jackson a cat's
paw?
Caused him to violate all law?
And on the Banks made ruth-
less war?
VAN BUREN!

By scheming who to England
went?
By intrigue who is President?
By proxie who had millions
spent?
VAN BUREN!

Ask who the pen of scandal
plies
To blind an honest People's
eyes,

Then ask who fathers Ken-
dall's lies.
VAN BUREN!

Who holds the Purse, who
wields the Sword?
Who would be master, who be
Lord?
And make our Law his sov-
ereign word?
VAN BUREN!

Who never had an honest
thought?
Who to their senses others
brought?
And was himself a Tartar
caught?
VAN BUREN!

Who never did a noble deed?
Who of the People took no
heed?
Who followed worst of tyrant's
creed?
VAN BUREN!

Who like the wily serpent
clings?
Who like the poisonous adder
stings?
Who is more base than basest
Kings?
VAN BUREN!

Who rules us with an iron rod?
Who moves at Satan's beck and
nod?
Who heeds not man? Who
heeds not God?
VAN BUREN!

Who feigns to be sincere and
civil?
Is prone to every kind of evil?
And has less conscience than
the Devil?
VAN BUREN!

Who would his friends, his
country sell?
Do other deeds too base to tell?
Deserves the lowest place in
Hell?
VAN BUREN!

When November shall come
round
Shall hear reverberate the
sound

Magician, thou art wanting
found?
VAN BUREN!

Who then shall take his final
look
At toys in which such pride
he took
Next March—shall march to
Kinderhook?
VAN BUREN!

Now rally to the ballot box!
And vote the Patriot Farmer's
prox!
So shall obsquatulate the Fox!
VAN BUREN!

Their success went beyond even the fondest Whig imag-
inings. At first there was some copying of the Bucktail trick
for inflating the rallies by itinerant troupes of rooters, but
it soon became unnecessary. The size of the meetings was
incredible enough without exaggeration. In the beginning attendance was measured and announced in digits of thousands.
Three at Martinsburg, five at Auburn, seven at Niagara,
twenty at Utica, seventy-five at Bunker Hill and so on. But
after Dayton, where there were "one hundred thousand
strong," a new system was conceived. Surveyors were hired
who measured off a quarter of an acre and counted the persons able to stand thereon. After that rallies were computed
in "acres of men."

But no standard of measurement could calculate the enthusiasm. When the People were not singing in unison they
were chanting catchy doggerels over their work. Children,
dogs and steamboats were known to have been christened for
Old Tippecanoe. A common name for a span of horses became "Ty and Tip." The disciples began to be converted by
their own evangelism. Horace Greeley changed the name of
his paper from *The Jeffersonian* to *The Log Cabin*. Daniel

376 ]

Webster suddenly discovered a log cabin in his own family, boasting that his brothers and sisters had been born in one. Authors, poets, musicians and artists found ecstasy and redemption in the new faith. Scriptures in the form of Old Hero biographies gushed from the press. Epics were written to out-Homer Homer in description of the Clod-hopper's battles. A "Tippecanoe Waltz" by Charles Gayer made dreamy melody in many a dance-hall. Art found an undreamt-of circulation and remuneration in cartoons. Well-heeled in 1840 was the genius whose inspiration could express itself in symbolisms of the Faith. Here was the General, clad as a trapper, catching the Red Fox in a miniature log cabin; here he was again, as an Indian, paddling to the White House, whence the Flying Dutchman was making an escape; or yet again, here he was receiving guests before the cabin door (its latch-string invariably out) while Little Van, as an intruder, tampered with the cider keg nearby.

The incidental matter of issues scarcely survived the first month. When Henry Clay sought to put in a good word for the American System he diplomatically prefaced his remarks with the admission that he "spoke only for himself" and "did not pretend to announce the intentions of the new President." The aged and enfeebled Clod-hopper was dragged from rally to rally where he had only to show his face and open his jaws to endear himself to the audience. For the most part he was held unflinchingly to Mr. Biddle's advice about non-committalism, never varying from it save on the safest of grounds. His most erudite discussion of any subject came at Dayton, where he elucidated his opinions on national finance.

"Methinks, I hear a soft voice asking, Are you in favor of paper money? I am."

And there were "shouts of applause."

Home at the White House, Martin Van Buren must have been having most sarcastic thoughts on the rewards of Right and Wrong. So long as he had practiced chicanery and sham, he had succeeded; immediately he strove for something higher, he faced the disgruntling prospect of defeat. He was the Greek tragedy hero whose downfall is self-inflicted by his own strength. If the country was being rent by political machinery, duped by an old warrior and seduced by non-committalism, then it was because the Little Magician had made it all possible. He had taught the sword-play with which the Whigs were severing him from his dearest possession. He was the Red Fox, helplessly tangled in his own snares.

The best he could do was moil daily through the hundreds of letters that poured in upon him. All that had any bearing on the campaign he answered. Came one from an anonymous enemy jeering at his nearing destruction. Another from an anonymous friend warning against an attempt on his life. One writer feared a popish plot, one a negro insurrection, a third told how Weed, by certain canards, had turned the Catholic and Mormon votes against him. An astrologer offered to read the heavens—for a price; a blackmailer wanted $100,000 to disclose a plan that would save him; a prohibitionist asked his signature for the temperance league.

The Palace walls were no sanctuary from the storm that raged without. Through the windows he could hear street urchins chanting the incessant refrain: "Van, Van, he's a used-up man!" Over at the Capitol Congressman Ogle had made the famous Gold Spoon Speech which, printed in pamphlet form, out-shone Davy Crockett's biography as an extravaganza on the President's life, loves and habits. Twenty years ago some tableware, including a set of gold spoons, had been bought for use at the White House. Three preceding Presidents had used them, but according to Ogle, Little Van was the original purchaser. That, however, was only the departing point of Ogle's oration, which occupied him nearly a full day on the floor. Sparing neither imagination nor delicacy, the law-giver traced the First Citizen from his beginnings in the "cabbage patch at Kinderhook" to his present grandeur as a "lily-fingered aristocrat," making due reference to his alleged use of perfume for his whiskers, to his flirtation with the Countess of Westmoreland, to the "six cream-colored chambers" which the inventory under discussion showed were in service at the White House.

Both as speech and pamphlet Ogle's address achieved wide popularity and necessitated the publication of two more authorized biographies. Beyond this mild rebuttal Mr. Van Buren gave no evidence that he was at all disturbed. He continued his Saturday night dinners and attended the balls at Carusi's, bowing to the strains of "Hail to the Chief" as if totally oblivious to Ogle's taunt "I wonder where he fought his battles?"

To the end, if his private letters reveal the mind, he continued to hope that some miracle might save him. But long before November the writing was on the wall. In the spring, Connecticut, Rhode Island, and Virginia—Democratic States all in '36—went Whig. In August North Carolina joined them; in September Maine left the fold to go "Hell Bent for Governor Kent." That was the end of all hoping. Harrison was sure to carry the West; without the South and New England the Administration was doomed.

The news, when it came, was worse than the anticipation. Mr. Van Buren carried only seven of the twenty-seven States, and none of them of much importance either for sentimental value or electoral votes. Little New Hampshire was all he salvaged out of the East. Tazewell had saved him Virginia, and Calhoun had delivered South Carolina but, except for unimportant Alabama, that was all in the Jeffersonian South, while Arkansas, Illinois and Missouri constituted his total in the West. Pennsylvania, which he had rescued from Old Nick, turned against him. So did Dick Johnson's Kentucky and Old Hickory's Tennessee. But most galling of all, the Empire State, once his very oyster, was gone. Just one comforting ray of light came through the gloom. The Regency was vanquished, but the Wigwam stood firm. By a prodigious effort the Braves had won him the City with 982 votes to spare.

Only the first coming of Andrew Jackson witnessed such an orgy of joy among the victors. Not content with having trapped him, the Whigs must finish their sport with the

Red Fox. The New York *American* rubbed salt of vengeance into his wounds with an editorial beginning "The Empire State casts out her recreant son," and several weeks after election it was printing post-mortem doggerel to taunt him. The *Courier and Enquirer* insisted that "The history of the United States can furnish no such instance of an unworthy public citizen being thus severely rebuked . . ." When Congress assembled, Mr. Adams noted how "Clay crows too much over a fallen foe." The Mill Boy went into an exuberant rampage against the Divorce Bill, likening it and its author to "a convicted criminal with a rope around his neck." Silas Wright interposed that perhaps it would be a good idea to tear down the White House and erect a log cabin decorated with coon skins. Other Senators joined in the fun and once more Little Van's reputation was being raked over the coals of hate.

No position in American public life is quite so unenviable as that of a defeated President in his last months of office. Anything he does is almost certain to be undone by his successor; any ill-temper he shows among his associates will be ascribed to spleen for his passing glories. But Martin Van Buren sailed through this unhappy period with the same debonair detachment that had marked his whole term. Philip Hone, arriving in Washington, found him "fat and jolly." In his farewell message to Congress he rejoiced to find the country in a state of "health, plenty and peace," and he delivered to the lawgivers a fatherly lecture on how to keep it so. At New Year he gave his usual reception; in February, when Old Tippecanoe came to town, trailed by what Horace Greeley called "large and numerous swarms of office-hunting locusts," the President shattered all precedent by calling on his victor, bringing him to one of the exclusive Saturday Nights, and even offering to vacate the White House ahead of time so that the tottering Hero could have a place to sleep.

The closer approached the Fourth of March, the more raucous became the Capital City. Joe Hoxie, best known of the campaign singing-masters, came and conducted victory jubilees. The ditties of "Van, Van, he's a used-up man!" re-echoed from a score of barrooms and from celebrating marchers. So crowded was the City that Gadsby's erected a shed in the coach yard to feed the guests, and turned the dining room into a sleeping hall. The two Adamses, being the only previous examples of the humiliation, had set the style for defeated Presidents. The one had left town, the other gone into hiding on his successor's Inauguration Day. Not being invited to the ceremonies, Little Van was expected to save his face by one of the same methods. What then was the wonderment of the Capital City on the morning of March Fourth to behold him "walking placidly down the Avenue as unconcerned as any private citizen in the crowd."

Doubtless it was a departing gesture, for Martin Van Buren was not naive enough to suppose that he would go unnoticed or unremembered. Who but he could be more conscious of the contrast between this Ides of March and the last one? To the world, he had been everything then, and now he was nothing. But in his heart he knew better than that. He knew that his present state was much better than the first. Four years ago he had been an adventurer, a political pirate come to take possession of the booty. Now he was a leader of men, a champion of causes. He had come through the ordeal of defeat with a dignity that had never been his in victory. He had won, if not the election, the esteem and admiration of all thinking men. Pridefully and in honor could he walk the Avenue, turning his steps away from the Palace. He had served well there, and he knew it.

What was more—he knew that he'd be back.

*BOOK IV*

# CHAPTER I

*Exile*

(1841–1844)

D RY-EYED and with dignity, Martin Van Buren stood
again on the balcony of Stranahan's Hotel, looking
down at a throng that packed the village square. Two years
ago the same scene had reduced him to tears, yet of the
occasions, certainly this one rather than that was more befitting for emotional display. Then he had been a victor
seeking new laurels; now he was the vanquished come home
on his shield. Even in defeat the townfolk had turned out
to receive him, meeting his steamboat with "brass band . . .
the firing of cannon and ringing of bells." And but that he
knew how much arrangement had been necessary to accomplish it all, the returning native might indeed have succumbed.

For sixty-five days Mr. Van Buren had been ex-President,
during which time he had worn the mantle of a wise and
just ruler, dastardly dethroned. Ardently his managers had
worked to facilitate the rôle. The welcome at Stranahan's
made only one of the several which had masked his retreat
from the Capital City as a triumphal procession. Ere his departure from Washington, the Missouri Legislature, at
Thomas Benton's behest, put him in nomination for 1844.
In Maryland, in Pennsylvania, in New Jersey—none of
which States he had carried—the celebrations at his coming
almost made up in efficiency what they lacked in spontaneity.

[ 385

Reaching Manhattan he found that the Sachems had marched out the Tribe to parade him up Broadway to the Wigwam, there to hail him with speechmaking and cheers. During April Little Van had remained in the City, living the gay life, directing the Braves through their mayoralty campaign, and now on May 8th he was in Kinderhook, hearing the village orator wish him "thrice welcome home . . . and happy years under the shade of your own vine and fig tree—unless called again by the Voice of the People into public life."

The orator's final clause proved him a man of high diplomatic tact, for to be "called again" was an experience which Mr. Van Buren fully intended to court, and with all of his one-time cunning. The dignity of office had hampered his talents during the past engagement, but that need not happen again. Responding to the Missouri nomination he had made it perfectly clear that, while bashful to discuss so premature a subject, he would be neither deaf nor indifferent to the proposal at the proper time. That long-practiced coyness had been the gist of his every speech from Baltimore, the first stop, to Kinderhook, the last.

Playing the injured patriot was a task not fraught with much difficulty. The further the Election of 1840 receded into memory, the more evident it became, even to the People, that Little Van had been ignobly undone. Yet the ex-President could have understood a truer and more personal interpretation of his defeat. He could have seen in it the stern retribution of an all-knowing Destiny. Considering only his four years in the chief magistracy, he unquestionably deserved re-election, but prior to that were the accumulated sins of two decades for which he would be called upon to settle. His humiliation at the hands of the Boss and the Clod-hopper cancelled a part of his debt—but not all. It had chastened and subdued him; interrupted his progress toward honorable retirement and snapped off his career at the very moment when one more election would have made his life an artistic and unqualified success. Grievously had the Little Magician paid. And the end was not yet.

Whatever may have been his inner thoughts on the sub-

386 ]

ject, Little Van was too gifted a poseur to exhibit them, and too determined a careerist to accept his defeat as final. He was, as yet, neither old nor an outcast. His fifty-nine years rested as lightly upon him as the snowy-white side-burns upon his cheeks, as the confidential smile upon his lips. Losing the election, he had not relinquished his hold upon the Party. There was positive indication that he would receive a third unanimous nomination in '44, and if Old Tippecanoe did as badly in office as he was widely expected to do, the Democrats would surely return to power. No one need tell Martin Van Buren that, without a second term, his first was but a mocking reminder. The old Urge churned again within him. Once more he was the aspiring candidate; once more the Red Fox.

At first, it seemed that luck was with him. He had scarcely reached New York City when General Harrison performed more obligingly than the devoutest Democrat could wish. His health depleted by the rigors of the campaign, his final strength crushed under the onslaught of office-seekers, the old Clod-hopper passed to his heavenly reward a month after his Inauguration, and into his place went John Tyler, Virginian Jeffersonian, a man without a Party. Driven into the Opposition by his contempt for the Jackson policies, Tyler had never become a legitimate Whig, but Thurlow Weed, seeking to snare the Southern votes, had not averaged the hand of fate into his calculations. There now existed in Washington the impotent spectacle of a President without a Party and an Administration Party without a President. Nothing but confusion could come out of such a situation, and the more confusion, the merrier for Little Van. Time was on his side. He would wait until the iron was hot, then strike back for the restoration of his crown.

Meanwhile there were several months of waiting. In the interim the ex-President busied himself rebuilding his home and his Regency. He had finally decided upon "Lindenwald" as the new name for Kleirood, but much more than a change of title would be required to turn his purchase into the patriarchal estate that would, he hoped, rank with Monticello and the Hermitage as an American shrine. As the place stood now it was no more than an ordinary red brick farmhouse, unprepossessing from within and without. It must undergo a complete rebirth. To give it a change of face with which to begin life anew, Mr. Van Buren had the red bricks encrusted in a bright coat of yellow. To set it back from the highway and give it the éclat of a mansion, he caused a semi-circular driveway to be built with baronial gate-houses at each entrance. To insure its eminence above all neighbors, he added a conspicuous, if somewhat unsightly, pagoda, the Italian summit of which could be seen for miles, and from which one could look down upon the Hudson. In expectation of the many pilgrimages which he contemplated coming to his door, he erected an additional set of stables, two more kitchens and dug a new well. That his tables might groan with plenty, he stocked his cellars with wine, expanded his accommodation for beef-and-milk-giving cattle, for egg-laying and eatable fowl.

Outwardly and substantially Lindenwald was now ready to take its stand before the world, but there remained something to be done in the way of suggestion. For a man who confessedly read only "for amusement" and then chiefly in political journalism, extra book-space would hardly seem necessary. Nevertheless Mr. Van Buren built an annex off his parlor to serve as a library, and was soon ordering sets of the classics from New York. That his intimacy with his two illustrious predecessors might never be forgotten, he procured portraits of Thomas Jefferson and Andrew Jackson, and hung them in the dining room.

Then came other matters. The house, having belonged to the Van Nesses since 1780, and dating earlier than that, was unpretentiously colonial with panelled walls, wide brick fireplaces and beamed ceilings. Such provincialism was well enough for the average Columbia County squire, but for one who had been Ambassador as well as President, there seemed to be needed a certain exotic touch of the foreign. This idea may have accounted for the pagoda with its Italian summit, and, if so, Mr. Van Buren did not stint his inspiration. The

*Exile*

panelled walls were plastered over with a gaudy, but indisputably French hunting-scene; the brick mantlepieces were knocked out and marble slabs installed, ostensibly for the dubious beauty of the Neo-Grecian designs there carved.

By autumn most of the renovations were finished, but so far the only pilgrimages to arrive were neighboring gentry, curious to look over the changes. And the only guests seem to have been young Abraham, his wife and baby. Abraham, too, had suffered in the calamity of 1840. He had resigned a West Point commission to become presidential secretary and then, losing the latter job, he was having trouble to find work. He found at least a happy reception at Lindenwald. Not since the death of Hannah, twenty-two years past, had Martin Van Buren known a home. Until his four-year lease on the White House he had lived as a nomad in hotels and lodgings, seeing little of his boys. At the Palace two or three of them had usually been with him, but there was scant privacy behind the glass walls of publicity. Now he was living again in his children's children. Riding each morning before breakfast in a belated attempt to reduce his waistline, the squire of Lindenwald received congratulations from the Dutch yeomanry on his new eminence as a grandfather. As round, as jolly, as bewhiskered as a Santa Claus he responded to their salutes in the only foreign language he ever knew, and scattered jingling coins among them with a munificence that spoke a universal tongue.

In November he was receiving other congratulations. While the work was going forward on Lindenwald, he had kept up a heavy correspondence with his lieutenants—Marcy, Dix, Croswell, Butler and others—and they rejoiced with him over a turn of their fortune. It seemed that the only thing needed to revive the Regency was the presence and counsel of Matty Van. In the Assembly the Bucktails regained sixty seats, winning control there, and heavily cut Weed's advantage in the State Senate. All signs indicated that in another year, they would recapture the upper chamber along with the governorship. Matty Van had met his Nemesis on the home ground and laid him low.

From Washington came news still more encouraging. In the special session which Tyler called for June, Henry Clay introduced his entire American System: a repealer of the Sub Treasury Law, a new distribution act, a protective tariff and a re-charter for a National Bank. All of them swept handily through Congress, but the last two met with an emphatic veto at the White House.

"Tyler dares not resist me!" cried the Mill Boy. "I will drive him before me!"

Again he pressed through the Bank Bill, and again the President sent it back. Then there was havoc to pay. The entire Cabinet, save Mr. Webster of the State Department, resigned in a body. Angered Whigs held wild demonstrations at the White House gate. A scattering of grateful but bewildered Democrats waited on the President to render him thanks, and Mr. Clay on the floor next day turned mountebank to mimic their speeches. Almost overnight the attending confusion destroyed the confidence and equilibrium of Little Van's last year. Within a twelvemonth the national debt was more than doubled. Government credit sank so low that an emergency bond issue by the Treasury barely sold its quota. Ready funds were so scarce that the Army, Navy and civil service officers had to be left unpaid. An epidemic known as Tyler Grippe seized upon business; prosperity chuted downward toward despair.

Now, if ever, was the time to strike. Little Van sharpened his weapons. During the summer and early autumn he had appeared to be engrossed in nothing more exciting than his potato crop and his grandchild, giving every semblance of the retired Cincinnatus. But November, 1841, being the first anniversary of his defeat, seemed an apt occasion for reminding the electorate how ill-advised had been its decision against him. Therefore he began to issue statements with broad reference to the "apparent success of last year's buffoonery," and to express his faith in what he called "the sober second-thought of the People." The first probed the country's remorse, the second suggested that 1844 might not be too late for amends. The Little Magician's boom was on.

# Exile

In December he caused the first trumpet to be blown. The Albany *Argus* appeared early that month with an article saying that, for the salvation of the country, Mr. Van Buren must be renominated and reinstated no matter how reluctant he might be. Thurlow Weed pounced upon it, declaring the article "written by Dix, revised by Butler, approved by Van Buren." Doubtless it was, but the Regencymen hailed it as a clear call from the People. From all parts of the country came letters to Lindenwald urging its master to announce himself. But the Little Magician could bide his time. Let the Call rise until it reverberated throughout the land. Then he would answer. For the time being, the disintegration of the Whig Party spoke louder than any words he could utter. Its President was dead. Its Boss was disgraced for having carelessly put a Democrat in office. Its patron, Nicholas Biddle, was under indictment for a $400,000 fraud. Its two great leaders had both given notice of their resignation—Mr. Clay from the Senate; Mr. Webster from the Cabinet as soon as he should complete an important negotiation with Great Britain. Little Van said nothing about his candidacy, but he did give out that in February he would make another sentimental journey, this time professedly to visit the dying old Hero of the Hermitage.

Mr. Van Buren's trip to the bedside of his ailing friend was a remarkable expedition. The most direct route from Kinderhook to Nashville was, of course, diagonally across the Ohio valley. By the usual relay of steamboat, railway and stagecoach he could have made the round trip, plus the few days he actually spent at the Hermitage, in less than a month, and have returned to Lindenwald in time for the spring plowing. But instead of choosing the shortest distance, Little Van managed a U-shaped loop that included the seaboard States, the South and the West, making public appearances at the important cities, conferring with henchmen in every sector and spending not one month away from home, but nearly six. Without any barefaced unveiling of his purpose, he showed himself to an eager country, reviewed his army of petty managers, and knelt for the indispensable blessing of

Andrew Jackson. In addition to all this he exhibited the Little Magician's master touch for making the most of every opportunity. Not content with marshalling the forces and preparing himself for the fray, he moved to establish a treaty of mutual benefit with the enemy.

Journeying through South Carolina he had received a letter from Mr. Clay, inviting him to pay a visit to Ashland. Five days later the Mill Boy dramatised his withdrawal from the Senate in a speech which one of its hearers declared was "like the soul's quitting the body." In one superb effort the incomparable man renounced all Whig leadership save his own, utterly isolated Tyler and established himself as the only Whig candidate for '44. Mr. Van Buren had hesitated to accept the invitation until he heard of the speech. Visiting Henry Clay was daring a breach of friendship with Old Hickory, who had never forgiven the Corrupt Bargain. Still the chance for an understanding with his opponent seemed worth the risk, and Little Van decided to take it—after his call at the Hermitage.

The theory of what happened at Ashland is largely guesswork, but strongly supported by later happenings. There was one subject—the annexation of Texas—which guest and host were anxious to eliminate. Politically and personally both were against the project. In the first place, Tyler was using it as a bid for reëlection; in the second, annexation would entail an imperialistic war with Mexico, as well as the danger of alienating the industrial North, which could not countenance the acquisition of more slave territory. According to common supposition Little Van and the Mill Boy agreed to hush up the matter by refusing, if possible, to discuss it. And if non-committalism did not work, they would publish (as they later did) a simultaneous stand against annexation, thus removing that bothersome question from the campaign.

Whether or not the agreement was made, Mr. Van Buren is known to have left Ashland in exceedingly high spirits and, travelling onward by easy stages, he came at length to the small town of Rochester, Illinois, where bad roads forced him to spend the night instead of pushing on, as planned, to Springfield, the State capital. Informed of this change in itinerary, the lieutenants at Springfield loaded several wagons with Democrats and refreshments and hastened to Rochester, bringing with them a huge, awkward fellow who, though a Whig, had been included, they said, for the ex-President's entertainment.

Wondering, perhaps, if the man were some sort of a clown, Little Van soon became aware that Abe Lincoln's talent was for story-telling. When the rail-splitter had obliged with several tall tales, the Little Magician matched them with some of his own, "going back," the audience marvelled, "to the days of Hamilton and Burr." After an informal beginning, the sport quickly graduated into a contest with one story "following another in rapid succession, each more irresistible than its predecessor." It was well after midnight when Little Van, crying that "his sides were sore from laughing," called a halt, and bade the company good-night with the assurance that Abe Lincoln was a man he would never forget.

Home again at the end of July, the traveller set his mind to the manifold tasks of a candidate and Party Director. He must take care of the avalanche of letters which the trip had brought to his desk, and he must oversee the autumn elections. November saw the complete restoration of the Regency, at home and abroad. The Bucktails won the governorship, all but one contested seat in the State Senate, several additional places in the Assembly and in the House of Representatives. The country elected an overwhelming majority of Democrats to Congress, and to distinguish them as anti-Tyler as well as anti-Whig, the faction became known to friend and foe alike as the Van Buren Party.

The Van Buren Party! Never in his life had the Little Magician bowed to such a compliment. A leader and a Director he had been before, but to have the dominant national party bearing his name was something that Mr. Jefferson might have envied. Blithely Mr. Van Buren laid plans for the Convention. Ben Butler would be his floor leader; Polk, his running-mate; "The sober second thought of the People," his campaign slogan. Eager to ride at the crest of the wave, he set an early date for the Convention: August, 1843. The delegates, he indicated, would be picked as usual by the State Central Committees, that being the Kitchen Cabinet's method for packing in a majority of professional job-holders.

On these last two propositions he heard the first murmur of sedition. Mr. Calhoun, hoping to blaze the trail for his own nomination, protested against holding a Convention fifteen months before the election. The candidate, whoever he was, must come fresh from the People. And the use of handpicked delegates was viciously undemocratic. Let them, he urged, be chosen in open primary elections.

Little Van, for all his professed faith in the People's "sober second thought," was not so impractical as to trust it to such an extent. By his scheme he would control fully three-fourths of the Convention. For the sake of appearances he complied with Mr. Calhoun's first request, moving the Convention up to May of the presidential year. But on the method of picking delegates, he was adamant. Gaining his point, Little Van lost an ally. Mr. Calhoun signified his withdrawal from the Van Buren Party by going over to Tyler, from whom he soon accepted the State Department, but the loss failed to disturb the man now known to his country as the Sage of Lindenwald. The Great Nullifier's habit of embracing lost causes made him, at best, a doubtful asset, and besides, favoring annexation, he could do less harm from the outside.

Serenely at Lindenwald the ex-President passed the early months of 1843, remembering, perhaps, how ancient and impotent an enemy was this same Mr. Calhoun, how often and how handily he had been cozened. From Indiana came a letter inquiring his views on Texas; he ignored it. From Cincinnati came another attempting to trap him as Weed had trapped the Mill Boy. Would Mr. Van Buren agree to abide by the Convention's nomination, no matter who the candidate might be? He did not ignore this one:

"My name and pretentions, however subordinate in importance, shall never be at the disposal of any person whatever, for the purpose of creating distractions or divisions in the Democratic Party."

It was not an answer. It was an ultimatum. He, Martin Van Buren, *was* the Democratic Party.

In the garnering of delegates he saw that opinion widely upheld. Mr. Calhoun managed to collect some support in South Carolina, but elsewhere neither he nor the other serious candidates—Lewis Cass, Dick Johnson and James Buchanan—made any headway. State after State fell in behind the Regency. In September New York had pledged her votes to the Little Magician; in December it was Alabama; in January it was Louisiana, and so it went. The horizon indeed was bright, but Little Van would have done well to put his ear to the ground, where he might have heard ominous rumblings. Down in the Capital City a plot was hatching that would settle Martin Van Buren's score with Destiny—and with John Caldwell Calhoun.

Duff Green sat at his desk, writing himself a letter and signing another man's name. The other man, Congressman Gilmer of Virginia, looked on approvingly, and when the rhetoric had been polished in Duff Green's best style, mailed the epistle to a Baltimore paper for publication. There and in reprint the country read it, and stirred in alarm. Great Britain (said the letter) was secretly planning to seize the Republic of Texas, so long denied admission to the Union. Once she secured a foothold, England would proceed to expand, and then woe betide the South and West. He only hoped, was the writer's conclusion, that the American Government would act "soon or not at all."

The warning, coming from so authoritative a source as a Congressman, created the expected amount of sensation, but no marching redcoats coming to view, it soon subsided. A formal apology to the British Embassy quieted trouble from that quarter, but when Gilmer and Green caused a Tennessee Representative to send Andrew Jackson a clipping of the letter and ask his advice, a flame was kindled that would not be quenched till Appomattox. To Old Hickory the name of Great Britain was as a trumpet to a war-horse. He sent back a reply that fairly smelt of gunpowder. The Government, he said, had but one duty—immediate annexation. Gilmer secured the letter from his Tennessee accomplice and filed it away for future reference. Produced at the proper moment, he opined, it would "blow Van out of the water."

And it did. Thirteen months later, on the eve of the Convention, the letter was published under a forged date line. Frank Blair filched an advance copy and sent it to Lindenwald, but, even forewarned, the Red Fox was helpless. Spread before him that March day of 1844 was the artistic irony of his life's pattern. The debt of atonement he owed to John Quincy Adams had been paid in kind when a Boss and Old Tippecanoe did to him what a Director and Old Hickory had done to the Puritan. In kind, too, was the debt to his other major victim about to be collected. Just as the Crawford Letter of '30 had ruined Mr. Calhoun, so this Jackson Letter of '43 would ruin Little Van.

Still he did not submit without a struggle. For over three years he had contrived to avoid the subject of Texas. He could avoid it no longer. His mail and the editorial columns were choked with demands for his opinion. If he pronounced for annexation, he would betray his native North and renege on his presidential record. If he pronounced against it, he would defy Old Hickory, the South and West. Here was an excruciating dilemma, but the Red Fox had eased out of such fixes before. Bravely and with cunning he strove. He must have notified Henry Clay to prepare to make good their bargain. He sent Ben Butler flying to Nashville seeking the General's renunciation of the letter. Old Hickory could not deny that he had written it, but he raged incoherently that he had never intended it for such purposes and that he was for Van no matter what happened to the Lone Star Republic.

The statement did not hush the conspirators. Mr. Calhoun was working in the State Department on a treaty for accepting Texas, but negotiations were not expected to go through before Election Day. Annexation, therefore, was the paramount issue. What did "the Northern man with Southern principles" have to say?

Among many other such inquiries was one from Congressman Hammett of Mississippi. This one the ex-President selected to reply. It took him three weeks to concoct his answer, and what he produced was the Little Magician's last fling at vanburenism. Though eclipsed, in this commentator's opinion, by that previous masterpiece, the resolution on the Nullification Proclamation, the Texas Letter has a sound claim to stand first among the Eighth President's feats of evasion. It befuddled not only his contemporary audience, but posterity as well. His best biographer was pleased to call it "one of the finest and bravest pieces of political courage," and a majority of the historians ever since, being too lazy to consult the original document, have made that opinion their own.

This chronicler finds it hard to blame them. Reading the Texas Letter *in toto* is a task he would wish upon no fellow mortal. In sheer verboseness and elaborate circumlocutions it is both a literary monstrosity and a political treasure. So long as to discourage the average newspaper reader and so deliberately intricate in its wording as to confuse even those who plowed through it, the document almost accomplished its author's purpose. It covered six and a half colums of fine print in the *Globe*, and was said by living persons to be ambiguous enough "as to proclude 96 out of 100 electors from ever acquiring a knowledge of its contents, except at second hand." Had Little Van aimed at coherence, he could have expressed the whole context of the Letter in a single sentence. This, briefly, was the sum of his conclusions:

Unless Texas could be acquired without War, he was against confiscation; but if Congress voted for her admission, "I would consider it to be my further duty to employ the Executive power toward annexation."

In other words he attempted to transfer the burden of decision to other shoulders, and, failing, he fell prostrate beneath it. For when the Convention met at Baltimore, it appeared that the ex-President's Southern and Western support was shaken. Many delegations pledged to him were anxious to be free and needed only an excuse to bolt. Mr.

Calhoun's floor-leader supplied it. He moved, Mr. Chairman, that this Convention adopt the rules of that victorious year, 1836, including, of course, the Two-Thirds Clause, which was of Mr. Van Buren's own authorship but which had been carelessly abandoned in 1840.

That was the end of Little Van's chances. The motion was fought for two days and finally carried. On the first ballot, the ex-President was 13 votes over a majority, but 32 short of the necessary two-thirds. Until the fifth he held his lead, yielding it then to Lewis Cass with Buchanan and Johnson still within striking distance. Ben Butler "wept like a child" when, quitting the hopeless fight on the ninth, he withdrew his candidate's name, and swung the support to a man whose name had not appeared until the previous ballot. James K. Polk, tail of the Van Buren ticket, was nominated by acclaim on the assurance that, having few known opinions, he would certainly beat Henry Clay who had many.

Deserted by the Party of his own creation, tricked by a strategem of his own making, set aside for a man who had never been more than his subordinate, Martin Van Buren drank to the dregs of his retribution. But the end was not yet. Before the Convention adjourned, it passed a resolution that politely read him into exile:

"We hereby tender to him in his honorable retirement, the assurance of the deeply-seated confidence, affection and respect of the American Democracy."

They had bid him good-bye before he sought it.

And still the end was not yet. . . .

2

(1848)

Having sped the last of his departing guests, Mr. Van Buren turned from the doorway and came back upon a scene that was a deserted battlefield of gayety. On the sideboards of his dining room stood disarranged half-emptied decanters of whiskey, brandy and schiedam. In the hall remained a large glass bowl which had been filled with lemonade punch, ruddily spiked with Burgundy. In the drawing-room were leveled-off platters that were recently heaped with figs, raisins, cakes, cookies and candies. Everywhere on the lower floor existed the genteel disorder that a visiting throng leaves behind it. Except for his servants he was alone in the house. His sons were scattered. Abraham was off at the Mexican War; Martin, Jr. was in Washington on his father's business; Prince John and Smith Thompson were with their own families in New York and Albany.

From noon until nightfall of this New Year's Day, 1848, Martin Van Buren had been playing host to a chattering, ever changing crowd of neighbors who had come to his reception, had been gliding as graciously and jauntily among them as if they were a White House company. But though Lindenwald by the seventh year of his residence had become the social center of the countryside and mecca of a polished and plentiful hospitality, its owner was anything but the blissful, contented squire he liked to appear. The dream that his home might become a sentimental replica of Monticello was still only a dream, and he himself but a phantom of his own desires. Yet with the coming of another presidential year, old hopes awoke within him. He was only sixty-six; still there was time.

The past four years had not been an experience to mellow Martin Van Buren into a benign and beautiful old age. The death in '45 of General Jackson, and in February, '48, of Mr. Adams made Little Van the one living ex-President, but even that venerable distinction could not soothe the canker in his soul. Content to do so, he might have accepted at least the nominal title to patron sainthood to the Democracy. The ignominy of his defeat at Baltimore could have been glossed over by a proper show of detachment, for James K. Polk, after all, was as much his presidential creation as he himself had been Old Hickory's, as Jemmy Madison had been Mr. Jefferson's. Moreover, the Eleventh President had displayed a willingness to accept the Sage of Lindenwald as his sponsor. Two months before Inauguration he had written to acknowledge his debt of gratitude and to give devout thanks for Little Van's successful efforts "to reconcile the Party to . . . my nomination and . . . election." He had decided, said Mr. Polk, to donate the War or Treasury Departments to any New Yorker of Mr. Van Buren's picking and he also begged "any suggestions you may think it proper to make in reference to the *whole* Cabinet."

But the Sage of Lindenwald was too worldly a saint to believe it more blessed to give than to receive in politics. Mr. Polk, in asking for "suggestions," had meant just that, and when Little Van aspired to become Director again as well as patron, their relations strained tautly and then snapped. The War and Treasury Departments were only minor portfolios. Little Van demanded that one of the Regencymen be made Prime Minister; he demanded in addition the sole control over New York's share of federal plunder.

This was further than the President cared to go. As Speaker of the House he had been only a patient wheelhorse, but as First Citizen he objected to being ordered about. Outraged at such insubordination, Little Van let it be understood that he would have all or nothing. He instructed Wright, Butler and Cambreleng to decline appointments and, to set an example, he himself turned down a tempting ministership to England. By these actions he meant to isolate Polk, but he only succeeded in isolating himself. The Party's politely-worded sentence to "honorable retirement" became one of harsh and unmitigated exile.

There seemed no mercy from the furies that haunted the Little Magician for his past transgressions. By plunder he had built up his Regency; by the same token it must be wrenched from his ownership. Their Matty Van's renunciation of spoils was too much for the Bucktails. They had stuck by him through many dark days of defeat and when, there were no plums to be plucked, had cheerfully done without them. But for the Director to scorn the fruits of a Democratic victory after four lean years was a policy impossible to understand or to tolerate. Big Bill Marcy ac-

400 ]

cepted the War Department, loyally declined by Ben Butler, and thereby became New York's patronage dispenser and the Regency's new chief. Matty Van, toast of the Bucktails, ruled his province no more.

There remained a faithful few. The rank and file followed Marcy into the greener pastures, but others stood firm. Besides the Old Guard of Wright, Dix, Croswell, Butler and Cambreleng, was the Young Guard led by Samuel Jones Tilden, and by the brilliant, handsome, dissolute Prince John, who spent one term in Congress and another in jail for raucous behavior, before Governor Wright appointed him Attorney General. At the head of this resolute band the little adventurer laid plans to escape from his Elba. He would need, he knew, to recruit an army as he went along. Without patronage there was only one way to do it; he must find himself a moral issue.

That was not difficult. In the mid-Forties there was one ready-made for any man with the hardihood to seize it. The Mexican War and a treaty with Great Britain widened American borders to the Rio Grande and the Pacific Ocean, a territorial expansion larger than France and Germany combined. The problem of dividing this vast domain into States brought a renewal in Congress of the Slavery Question and, in 1846-7, it caused a loggerhead over the Wilmot Proviso, which advocated a prohibition of slavery in the new lands. The squabbling of North and South over the West eventually gave America the Republican Party, but meanwhile it gave Little Van his issue. Since the President was against the Proviso, the ex-President was for it. Here was the spark that put life into his hitherto synthetic following. A schism in name and nature cleft the Democrats of New York. Their opponents called the Van Buren men "Barnburners," likening them to the improvident farmer who will burn down his barn (the Union) to get rid of the rats (the institution of Slavery). And the Barnburners reciprocated by calling the Marcy men "Hunkers," saying that they *hankered* after federal plunder.

The spectacle of Martin Van Buren, even vicariously,

crying shame upon political hunger for spoils is merely comical, but his attempt to ride the Barnburner band-wagon indicates how piteously he craved transportation out of his banishment. As President, one of his proudest acts had been his stand against the Abolition fanatics. Now he became their darling. If his statecraft contained one element of staunchness and consistency, it was in his regard for Jeffersonian State Rights. Now he became involved in the downfall of that very principle. Had he turned renegade whole-heartedly and with the ringing conviction of a zealot, it were possible to believe him horrified at Slavery on humanitarian grounds. Had he stood hip and thigh beside the Abolitionists, going with them to their extremes, he might have ended his career in a glorious burst of idealism and hostaged his name to history as a fallen martyr of freedom.

But the sublime recklessness that drives statesmen into unchartered regions of reform was no part of the Little Magician's make-up. At his best, as in the presidency, he could be a stubborn and doughty defender of stable doctrines. He was no pathfinder. Becoming a Barnburner, he attempted the ungainly straddle of keeping one foot on familiar ground. Jefferson, Madison and Patrick Henry, he informed the country in writings during this period, had all frowned upon Slavery. That they had nevertheless practiced and condoned it did not lessen their ardor nor prevent him from being their disciple. He was, he insisted, the true voice of the Democratic Party.

Actually his position would be hard to classify. He was neither fish nor fowl. He had enlisted the Abolitionist to his banner, much as he had the Loco Focos a few years back, accepting their huzzas without wearing their livery. He was almost, but not quite, the Northern man with Southern principles. To the North he offered the proposition of free soil in the West; to the South, the guarantee of continued Slavery. In a word, he would apply the Wilmot Proviso to new States; the Jeffersonian principles to the old. He favored dictatorship through Congress for one part of the country; home rule through local legislatures to another. This was compromise, though certainly not reform, but it pleased all anti-Slavocrats, both radical and conservative. The Abolitionists, overjoyed to have the use of his name, hailed him as a deliverer; the milder elements drifted into his camp to swell the ranks. Many papers, there were fifty in New York State alone, began carrying his name at their flagstaffs. Asked by the Wilkes-Barre *Farmer* if he would consider the Democratic nomination, he was "sincerely and heartily desirous to wear the honors and enjoyment of private life," but would not shun the "sacrifice" if called by the unanimous voice of the Party. It was the Little Magician's well known preamble to a candidacy. Restlessly at Lindenwald, he awaited the Call and when, by the end of January, it did not come, he put off for New York in search of it.

Setting himself up in Julien's Hotel, just off Washington Square, he made his lodgings the Barnburner headquarters. Mr. Polk, whose diary noted "I have now passed through two-thirds of my presidential term and most heartily wish the remaining third was over," surprised one and all by refusing to consider renomination. It meant another open season on the Glittering Prize, and increased the possibility that the Democracy might landslide to the Little Magician, especially if he could count on support from New York. Daily Prince John and Sammy Tilden dropped into Julien's to discuss the prospects, and one day Little Van handed Tilden a manuscript.

"If you wish to be immortal, take this home with you, complete it, revise it, put it into proper shape and give it to the public."

The document, when published as an Address to the People, turned out to be a constitutional defense of the Wilmot Proviso, an attack upon Slavery, but in the main an argument intended to prove that the Barnburners were the "regular" Democrats of New York and thus entitled to represent the State at the National Convention. The Hunkers had already selected their 42 delegates, and the best the Barnburners could do was hold a rump session and choose as many more. With Prince John in the van they departed in May for Baltimore. But they soon came back.

For the Democratic Convention, fashioned along lines drawn by the Kitchen Cabinet, was no place for an anti-Administration delegation. The Committee on Rules at first objected to receiving them, but finally agreed that, as a Barnburner explained it, "the regular delegates might occupy half a seat a piece, provided each would let a Hunker sit in his lap." There was no advantage to the Barnburners in halving their votes and then being bound by the Convention decision, so Prince John dramatically marched his cohorts out of town; reassembled them at Utica to declare his father the choice of the Empire State, and then called a Convention of the national Free Soil Party to make the nomination binding.

As strange a collection of political bedfellows ever to gather under a single name, the Free Soilers met at Buffalo in August. Appropriately enough they held their Convention in a church, supplemented by a circus tent. Here were religious zealots arm in arm with disgruntled spoilsmen; wild-eyed Abolitionists rubbing elbows with long-haired Loco Focos; a Negro delegate from the North holding conference with gentlemen from Maryland, Virginia and Kentucky, the only Southern States represented. Here mingled the ragged edges of both major parties; Whigs, disgusted that Henry Clay had been set aside for another old Hero, Zachary Taylor; Democrats, reviling the Party for having nominated the vanburenish Lewis Cass, another General. Out of the melting pot rose a seething geyser of enthusiasm. Fifty thousand strong, the Free Soilers sweated and sang; prayed and paraded under a broiling summer sun. Night fell, but the multitude stayed on by torchlight to hear orator after orator expound upon the Little Magician. Frothed one of them:

"When I saw this man that I had formerly believed to be timid and calculating; this man enjoying the universal confidence and affection of the Great Democratic Party, willingly sacrifice all this public confidence and esteem, and plant himself upon the spot where freedom dwelt and bid defiance to the South—it was a sublime spectacle—it was the poetry of politics—it was the religion of patriotism!"

In a screaming frenzy of ecstasy and admiration, the Convention gave Martin Van Buren his third unanimous nomination for the chief magistracy, and in the heat of inspiration named Charles Francis Adams, son of the Puritan, for his team-mate. "We the People here assembled . . . putting our faith in God . . . inscribe on our banner;

" 'Free Soil, Free Speech, Free Labor and Free Men.' "

A nation gasped at the news. Martin Van Buren defying the Democratic Party, consorting with outcasts and fanatics, sunk so low in political fortunes as to be running on a hopeless third ticket! Even at that the nation could not know the full extent of the incongruity. Little Van, Democrat, had accidentally founded the Republican Party, founded a great vehicle of idealism by a sordid quarrel over patronage, by a none-too-noble attempt to harness an otherwise sacred cause to his own promotion. Whatever the deed was worth, he received small credit for it at the time. Mr. Polk thought it was "selfish, unpatriotic and wholly inexcusable." Mr. Webster rumbled "that the leader of the Free Spoils Party should become leader of the Free Soil Party, is a joke to shake my sides and his."

But to Little Van it was no joke now. He had caught a lion by the tail and dared not let loose. In all probability he never intended to carry the affair to this conclusion, but his attempts to decline the unwelcome honor were both humorous and unavailing. Too often he had cried "Wolf Wolf" for anyone to take him seriously about "my unchangeable determination never again to be a candidate." For once in his life he was sincerely reluctant. In later years a friend begged him for a confidential opinion on it all, and the Sage replied with this parable. A man, walking along a country lane, beheld an overturned load of hay into which a lad was digging with frenzied vigor. Asked the reason for his vim, the boy responded:

"Stranger, Dad's under there!"

Like the hay-load, the Little Magician's last band-wagon

proved top-heavy, and Prince John was left to dig him out of the débris. John did his best. He swung through the West on a prolonged speaking tour while his father, too old for such work, stayed home writing letters and posing as the big-hearted patriarch, willing, though regretfully, to leave his beloved acres for the country's salvation. The myth of his bucolic contentment was a constant note among his can-vassers. Once Ben Butler was telling an audience how the gallant old squire would vault over fences in his eagerness to exhibit the Lindenwald turnip patch.

"Damn his turnips," yelled someone in the crowd. "What are his present opinions about the abolition of slavery?"

Canvassers and candidate could have held scant optimism that autumn. Little Van's one hope was to throw the election into the House where Cass and Taylor might prefer him to each other. But presently he saw that he was fighting not only two rivals but all the assembled ghosts of his past. Nothing he had taught was lacking from the campaign strategy of the enemy. Both parties had ignored the Slavery issue; both were heavily armed with organization; both relied largely on the outdoor popularity of their heroes. Not even the Little Magician could better his own works. He was beaten before the first ballot was cast, but only the final tabulation showed the fullness of humiliation. His elec-toral count was zero. In only one State south of the Potomac was he credited with a single vote. In Virginia he polled an embarrassing total of nine, and when the Free Soilers raised a cry of "Fraud," a Virginian is said to have answered:

"Yes, fraud! And we're still looking for that son-of-a-bitch who voted nine times."

CHAPTER II

## *Escape*

(1849–1855)

ONCE more from the balcony of Stranahan's Hotel Martin Van Buren looked down upon an assembled throng, but this time there were neither tears in his eyes nor ambition in his heart. Arm in arm beside him stood that marvellous bag of bones who was Henry Clay at seventy-two. A guest at Lindenwald, he had consented to this appearance in town, though with no thought save to please his host. To the cheers he bent his crackling old body in a courtly bow and spoke briefly out of a throat that barely had strength to push up the words. A few days later he departed. The two old cronies, friends and enemies for almost thirty years, said their final farewell.

It was a great emptiness which the magnetic Mill Boy left behind him at Lindenwald, an emptiness that found its center in Mr. Van Buren's heart. Faded long ago was the hope that his home might become the end of pilgrimages, and it was difficult to persuade even his friends to a visit. In his files were many notes declining invitations on one pretext or another. Kinderhook was too far off the beaten path, and Little Van's comrades not as young as they used to be. Some of them came: Sammy Tilden, Winfield Scott, David Wilmott, Frank Blair and Thomas Benton, the last particularly nonplussed at the elegance of the manorial estate. Especially Little Van's fingerbowls fascinated the Senator from Missouri.

"I am a little chary of new customs," he confided later, "but when I saw Mr. Van Buren dip the tips of his fingers in the bowl and wipe them daintily on a napkin, I just raked back my sleeves and took a good plain Republican wash."

But except for these visits, few and far between, life was a lonesomeness for Martin Van Buren, behind the fir and pine trees that shaded his lawn. Lindenwald was indeed the end of a pilgrimage, but the pilgrimage was his own. In his solitude he had ample time to contemplate how inglorious had been his passing from public life, compared to the passing of the men whom he had repeatedly vanquished. Adams, Webster, Clay and Calhoun—his victims all, yet at the end they, not he, were the winners. Theirs already were names immortalized in a nation's history; his, he knew, would scarcely outlive his body. John Quincy Adams—Old Man Eloquent they had come to call him in the House—had literally died in harness, swooning over his desk as he rose to address the chair. And that matchless trio—Clay, Webster, Calhoun—did their finale on the same stage together.

All had been in retirement when the furore over Slavery threatened a Civil War. Their ages, in 1850, totally 209 years, they had returned to the Senate for a dying effort in defense of their causes. The day for each speech was announced in advance and the Capital City packed as if for an Inauguration. On February 5th crowds at the Senate Chamber extended clear through the corridors into the street, when the Mill Boy rose to offer his famous Compromise that would postpone Civil War for another decade. So feeble that he had to be helped up the front steps, he rose like a ghost from its ashes and flung off such eloquence that all rules were broken and men rushed from the galleries to wring his hand and to kiss his cheek. Mr. Calhoun's turn came next. Stark and gaunt as a derelict ship, half-paralyzed, his throat closed with a tubercular growth, he sat like a grim statue of death while a colleague read off the address, a mortal challenge to all enemies of his menaced Southland. And last, Mr. Webster, as if holding the balance, thumped off the booming magnificence of his Seventh of March Oration—"I speak today for the preservation of the Union."

Yes, they were the winners, Martin Van Buren was sure to have known, as he read the reports of their exit from the stage they had long dominated. Shallow triumph that he alone had gained the Glittering Prize which those three had craved so intently. Sour victory that he would outlive them when, in the only sense that mattered, he was already dead and they would live on forever. He could understand that the defeat of 1848 was his decease as an historical character. He would not be buried for 14 years thereafter but, remaining above ground, it was only to know the appalling experience of viewing his own remains, of seeing himself as posterity would see him.

Martin Van Buren could have gone straight home from the polls in '48 and written his own biography without so much as waiting to learn the authentic date of his death. That, in fact, was what he attempted to do, but so melancholy the task that there is small wonder he never finished it. Gathering the material, summing up the story, he found it would have been difficult to imagine the outline of a tale more shot with comic irony and baleful paradox than his own. . . .

He was 17 when he tried for his first public trust and 66 when he tried for his last one. Over that half-century there had been several times when he was not holding a political office, but none when he was not a candidate for one. Until beaten by Harrison, he never experienced a major setback; except for the Supreme Court, he never attempted an office he did not achieve. As Surrogate, Attorney General, Senator, Governor, Ambassador, Prime Minister and President, he had touched upon every department of government—the disciplinary, the judiciary, the parliamentary, the diplomatic, the advisory, the administrative. He had re-founded one of the two national parties and founded the other, taking up where Jefferson had left off, beginning before Lincoln had started. With his Classification Bill in 1814 and his Sub Treasury Act in 1837, he gave America her two most effective measures for the propagation of War and Peace—the compulsory enlistment of man-power, the governmental control of money. Thus, superficially but not without truth, it may be argued that his military contribution was more practical than Washington's, his fiscal plan more permanent than Hamilton's, his party-building more durable than Jefferson's, his foresight more penetrating than Lincoln's. By all laws of logic and arithmetic, Martin Van Buren knew that he *should* rank with the greatest of statesmen, but the irrefutable fact stared him in the face that he did not.

As a politician his claim was more distinct, but here again he saw himself faring little better with posterity. He had lived to behold his two innovations—the Spoils System and non-committalism—become characteristic features of American statecraft, but already they were so taken for granted that no one thought to remember who was accountable. Three political organizations for whose destinies he had been signally responsible—the Regency, the Kitchen Cabinet, the Wigwam—had all been supreme in their day, but only the third was still in existence, and the mention of its name was no reminder of the Little Magician. To historians of the Nineteenth Century, Tammany Hall meant Fernando Wood, Boss Tweed and, further back, Aaron Burr. Martin Van Buren had only to think over the list of Presidents during his lifetime to see how emphatically his term had divided, so to speak, the sheep from the goats. He could feel that he had drastically changed the course of American history, but in no way to endear his memory.

Of himself as a man, Little Van might perceive a more galling neglect. Up to 1850 he had been the subject of nine biographies and the hero of a popular novel called *The Partisan Leader*. America knew he had risen from potboy to President, but the story of his success found no place in the hearts of his countrymen. The careers of Jackson, Harrison and Taylor were being held up to the Younger Generation as shining examples of achievement, but none of these had started at lower beginnings than the Boy Lawyer, none ever set his eye more resolutely on the goal of all American

Boys or won it by a more unaided application of industry. Without taking another man's blood, without touching a dishonest penny, without being cheapened by scandal, without any assistance from luck, the man from Kinderhook had ascended from penury and bondage to prominence and independence. He had walked with Kings and been honored by the People. He had served in the Palace and come back to the farm. In brief, the high points of his life had all the raw materials for the American Success Story. But no uplifter would ever tell Youth to remember Matty Van. And Matty Van knew it full well.

Indeed, if the Eighth President had any hope that time would be more generous to him, it is well that he lived no longer than he did. Happy for him that he never knew how his family, his village, his State, his country would neglect not only his fame but his memory. Yearning to perpetuate himself as an ancestor, Mr. Van Buren deeded Lindenwald over to his youngest son on the understanding that the latter would live there permanently, making the place a family estate. But hardly was he dead than Lindenwald was sold on to strangers. Scarcely a stick or stone in the vicinity of Kinderhook remained in the family, and even the grave where they finally laid Little Van beside Hannah would have to be cared for out of the church funds. A town in Arkansas, a county in Michigan, and a street in Washington were named after him, but Kinderhook, having celebrated his seventy-second birthday, lazily abandoned the custom, and not till 1933 remembered to put his name on the High School. His State, from which he was the first President, recalled the fact only in 1910, when Governor Charles Evans Hughes vetoed a bill to build him a monument. And as for his countrymen—when in 1934 a batch of presidential signatures went up for auction, his brought $2.25—which was (let it be whispered) $1.75 less than Polk's. . . .

A knowledge of these latter indignities Martin Van Buren was mercifully spared, but they might never had happened had his knack as an opportunist stayed with him in old age. Apparently he never realized that the fame he so earnestly desired was his for the taking. Letting the world know how little he really cared for the cause of humanity was a tactical blunder that doomed him to eternal obscurity. After '48 he bolted the Free Soilers and began making overtures to his estranged Democrats, continuing half-heartedly to the end of his days. The Free Soil mission had not changed, but Little Van's ideas of expediency had. He simply could not abide defeat, much less isolation. In '52 the Free Soilers nominated another ticket, begging his support, but he wrote a letter to Tammany endorsing the preposterous Franklin Pierce, Democrat. In '56 the reformers, their ranks swollen by new recruits, changed their name to Republicans, but retained the identical slogan of '48. It was "Free Soil, Free Speech and Fremont," but again Little Van clung to the skirts of another victor, writing to Tammany in behalf of James Buchanan. And in '60 he pillaged his own citadel by voting against Abraham Lincoln.

Had he, having hoisted the Anti-Slavery banner, stuck to it; had he, having fired the first important gun, remained, even passively, in the fight, Martin Van Buren might have gone down in history as the pathfinder for the Great Emancipator. But he lacked either the courage or the convictions to follow through a difficult cause, and quitting it, he quitted his main chance for immortality. . . .

By the autumn of 1852 he had collected enough data to make a beginning on the *Autobiography* with which he told Ben Butler's son "I must vindicate my Administration." The lonesomeness of his banishment ate in cruelly upon him. The idea of becoming a country squire had seemed entrancing enough in '41 when he anticipated another four years in the White House, and the potboy's dream of becoming ancestor to a landed aristocracy was one that never left him. But the game of playing the patriarch seemed hardly worth the candle. Old Hickory and Mr. Jefferson had been true ruralists; had gone from their homes to the Palace and returned to a life they preferred. Little Van's preferences had always been for the social world, and there was none of that at Lindenwald. Visitors were ever more difficult to entice;

his favorite son, Prince John, would have nothing of the country; and when the old man tried to dilute the solitude by proposing marriage to a Kinderhook spinster (a daughter of Francis Sylvester) she turned him down.

More and more he came to resent the life he was leading; more and more to long for the diversions of town and travel. Even while affecting a love of the soil for presidential purposes, he had spent remarkable little time on his acres, and after 1848 he spent less. His letters show him constantly making plans to get away, which he did as often as his pocketbook and his newly-acquired gout would permit. His best biographer recalls, without stressing the significance, how frequently the ex-President was to be seen strolling with Prince John along Wall and Nassau streets, when he was supposed to be home peering over his crops.

Sojourns to New York and other resorts were sedatives for his restlessness; they were not cures. He knew he could find no sanctuary in America. His friends, save Washington Irving, had been nearly all political, and he was at odds with most of them now. Reminding the public that he was still alive was likely to produce remarks such as appeared one day in a Richmond paper: "If there is a man within the limits of the Republic who is cordially abhorred and detested . . . that man is Martin Van Buren." These were not pleasant serenades for the evening of one's life, and one could not feign deafness forever.

So once more he contemplated escape. Remembering where his most congenial and carefree moments had been spent, he decided, passing his seventieth birthday, to return to Europe. There, among the bright capitals and watering places, he was content to live out his declining years. Bearing some notes for the neglected manuscript and many letters of introduction, including one to the Pope and another to the King of the Belgians, he sailed in the spring of '53, accompanied by his son Martin, Jr. The unprecedented arrival of an ex-President somewhat perplexed the formulators of trans-Atlantic etiquette, but the wise little courtier sent word ahead that he expected to be treated only as a private citizen. Nevertheless he was gorgeously received. Europe opened the royal portals of drawing room and dining salon to the man whose reputation for polished gentility had spanned an absence of twenty years. France and Great Britain; Belgium and Holland, Switzerland and Italy. For two years he meandered about the continent, meeting with equal pleasure and ease the great and the fashionable, the royal and the holy.

No inhibitions restrained him now. Before, being a candidate, he had had to protect his democratic chastity, had had to fear what the People might think and his rivals might say. James Buchanan, as Ambassador to Great Britain, had strained international relations by abandoning the wear of kneebreeches, but Citizen Van Buren's initial move was to order full court regalia from a London tailor. On his first visit to Holland he had denied, tongue in cheek, that he might be of aristocratic descent; this time he petitioned His Dutch Majesty for a knightly coat-of-arms, which he shipped home to grace the walls of Lindenwald. In America ex-President Fillmore was dickering for reëlection with the anti-Catholic Know-Nothing Party; in Rome ex-President Van Buren was calling on Pope Pius IX, whose Holiness (so went the rumor) almost converted him to the true faith. In America Mr. Stephen A. Douglas was causing Kansas to "bleed" for freedom; in Turin Mr. Martin Van Buren was hobnobbing with that fearsome dictator, Count Camillo Benso di Cavour. In America as many as thirteen States were trying the noble experiment of liquor prohibition; in Aix-les-Bains, Little Van was nursing an annoying case of gout, brought on by his indulgent taste for delectable wines.

Having wandered to his heart's content, the happy expatriate, rounding out his seventy-second year, settled down in a villa at Sorrento and began work on his memoirs. Evidently he was more than satisfied that death should find him on foreign soil but, as fate would have it, the son instead of the father died abroad. Martin, Jr. had never been healthy. He left his parent to consult physicians in London, and the

Escape

coffin which arrived at Kinderhook in the summer of '55 contained his body.

Again, as from his rejected ambassadorship, Mr. Van Buren sailed sorrowfully westward. Tragedy had cut short his last vacation. He was coming back to a life he prepared himself to hate. What was there for him at Lindenwald? Or in all America? He was only returning to an exile.

And yet in his very exile he found the final escape.

2

(1856–1862)

"I, Martin Van Buren, of the town of Kinderhook . . . heretofore Governor of the State and more recently President of the United States, but for the last and happiest years of my life a Farmer in my native town. . . ."

It was the last will and testament of the Little Magician, and in it he revealed the abiding miracle of his existence. There were six years of life remaining for him after his return from Europe, but the quota was half spent before he seems to have perceived the inner happiness they brought him. So long had he feigned at Jeffersonian serenity in retirement that, meeting at last the genuine fact himself, he hardly recognized it. With the bridges of strife burned behind him, with old age forbidding any more flight from himself, he looked about and Lo! the peace and satisfaction he had sailed an ocean to find were here at his own doorstep. He who had loathed the boredom of rural life, discovered in it the healing balm for his bruised vanity. He who had burlesqued a love of the soil and of the things that sprang from it, learned for himself the poet's simple truism:

> "Nor less I deem that there are Powers
> Which of themselves our minds impress;
> That we can feed this mind of ours
> In a wise passiveness."

Lindenwald, as it happened, was no shrine, but it was a

[ 415

home and that was still better. In his new daughter-in-law
(for Smith Thompson had married Harriet Irving) he found
a congenial spirit. Together they planned and supervised
small changes about the house: a sun-parlor off the living
room, a refurnishing of the upstairs. He even, in faithful
idolatry of Mr. Jefferson, tried his hand as a household inventor, designing a revolving bookcase and a queer-looking
implement which may be optimistically identified as a coffee
percolator. But chief among his pastimes was the management of his farm. To sit on his pony directing the laborers
in the field became his substitute for directing the Regency.
He took as boastful a pride in the size of his potato crop as
he had in the size of his election majorities. Between himself
and Frank Blair, now a farmer at Silver Springs, Maryland,
went an animated correspondence over agricultural matters.
He pridefully sent Blair the prize specimen of Lindenwald
potato seeds and received in return the juiciest specimen of
Silver Spring peaches, while Blair wondered over the Red
Fox's "old age of sweetness out of a youth of acrimonious
bitterness."

He was, Little Van had become willing to admit, no national saint. Even the prestige of being the sole living ex-
President had not lasted long. At Lincoln's election in '60
Mr. Van Buren shared the title with four deposed First
Citizens. Still, if the distinction was gone, so was the stigma
that went with it, for no President since Andrew Jackson had
been reëlected. Mr. Van Buren found sublimation for his
missing sainthood in being the village patriarch with prerog-
atives and idiosyncrasies that none would dare question or
attempt to rival. When he cantered into town of a holiday
there was always a crowd of boys about Stranahan's, scuffling
with one another for the honor of holding his bridle, while
he sat in the taproom chatting for hours. When he drove to
church of a Sunday it was in the gilded English coach, the
wonder of the neighborhood. When he sat in the pew reserved for him by common consent, there was a special foot-
stove for his comfort and, if chilly, he had no hesitancy in

using one of his fur gloves as a skull-cap—a violation of all sacred decorum, but who would think to criticize Mr. Matty Van?

More than a privileged character, he was an institution. Kinderhook built him no monument in her market place, but the tree under which he frequently rested his pony became known throughout Columbia County as the Van Buren Elm. No pilgrims or protégés thronged for his blessing, but he seldom passed a certain house on the Stuyvesant Falls road, save a venerable negro would hobble out and recite a charm to ward off evil spirits:

> "Injun' flea
> Bit mah knee,
> Hurrah for Marty Van Buren
> He lose it."

Less and less the contented old squire came to care or to notice what was going on outside the narrow circumference of his existence. He was seventy-five: everyone was debating the Dred Scott decision, reading or re-reading *Uncle Tom's Cabin*. He was seventy-seven: John Brown was condemned to the gallows for insisting that negroes were human; Charles Darwin was condemned to hell-fire for insisting that human beings were monkeys. None of it interested the Sage of Lindenwald as much as marketing his crops and hearing news about his two grandchildren at school. An autograph hunter wanted his signature; someone in Van Buren, Arkansas, wanted a contribution for the church there; James Parton wanted some inside information for his *Life of Jackson*, but little else reminded the squire of his past glories. Now and then he dictated a few pages of his book. He had long since lost the energy to complete it. He came across a letter from Thomas Jefferson which inspired him to begin *A History of Political Parties*. His sons had to finish it after he was gone. The pleasant drowsiness of his dotage closed in about. He snoozed in the sun and before his fireplace. A touch of asthma, twinges of gout, disturbed him but spasmodically.

In December of '60 he would be seventy-eight. The end could not be far; he was reconciled that it should be so.

Meanwhile men and events were moving forward to make a drama whose end he would not see. Familiar happenings probed at his memory. Another Cabinet dissolved when Southern Democrats deserted Buchanan. Another triumvirate—Douglas, Davis and Seward—held command in the Senate. Another Log Cabin Slogan was making a man First Citizen. But the march of history meant less to Martin Van Buren than the change of seasons. December snows covered his furrows, and South Carolina seceded from the Union. March thaws loosened the turf for plowing, and Abraham Lincoln was inaugurated in the Capital City. April showers fermented his seedlings, and the rebels fired on Fort Sumter.

Came then a letter dated April 16, 1861, from Franklin Pierce at Concord, New Hampshire. We are, said Mr. Pierce, five ex-Presidents. Let us meet in Philadelphia, cradle of the Union, and offer some plan which will save the nation from War and destruction. You, Mr. Van Buren, as senior ex-President must call us together.

It was Little Van's last chance for the fame he so dearly had coveted. A gesture, if nothing else. An encore to that famous toast which had doomed Nullification once before: "Our Union—it must be preserved!" Then, at least, a forgetful country would be reminded who was Eighth President. Then, at least, the public press would ring a requiem of praise or damnation to the Little Magician.

But things that had been so important once, seemed not to matter now. Politics and Patriotism—they had a distant sound. Tyler and Fillmore; Pierce and Buchanan—two Democrats, a Whig and an independent—what a deal of wrangling there would be. He replied to Pierce that he would not call the meeting. Came other letters begging him to change his mind, but he heeded them not. The year wore on while blood dripped from the moon and from bayonets. Another spring brought the War's first anniversary and with it another opportunity for the ex-Presidents to arbitrate.

## Escape

Little Van looked lovingly over his meadows. Philadelphia was a long way off, and his gout was bothering him. The Union must be preserved, but it was time to be planting potatoes.

He would not be there for the harvest.

**THE END**

# The Author's Confessions

WORK on this volume led me over the trail of Little Van's own footsteps: from Kinderhook to Washington via Albany and New York. In these four places the bulk of the information was found. At the New York Public Library were most of the necessary books; at the Congressional Library in Washington, the manuscript material, innumerable pamphlets and the newspaper files; at the State Library in Albany, several volumes not to be found either in New York or Washington, and at Kinderhook was information which no book contained. At Lindenwald, for instance, I found the coffee percolator which none of the Van Buren biographers seem to have noticed, and at the town bank I met Mr. James Reynolds, one of the few living persons who knew the Eighth President in the flesh. Mr. Reynolds, as a boy, attended Little Van's funeral and, as a man, inherited from his father the revolving book-case which once stood in Lindenwald. To Mr. Reynolds I owe my thanks for a kindly reception and for several facts included in the last chapter.

A few miles from Kinderhook, at Chatham, I was fortunate in locating Mr. Albert S. Callan, whose intimate knowledge of the Eighth President caused this biographer to blush in ignorance. Mr. Callan gave me the negro jingle, passed down to him by one of Little Van's neighbors; told me of offering the bill which Governor Hughes vetoed, and told me with what difficulty he finally managed to effect the Martin Van Buren High School. Also he gave me several homely touches which I might have done well to include in the text. One, for instance, tells how Matty, before he loved Hannah, had another sweetheart whose grave in the Valatia cemetery, a mile or so from Kinderhook, he was wont to visit in secret. Another relates how, in exile at Lindenwald, the ex-President used to be seen of an evening pacing his lawn, arm in arm with his two Irish maids.

## The Author's Confessions

By far the biggest surprise I encountered while writing the book was to discover what a fandom the Little Magician has left behind him. Obscure as he is historically, there remains a cult which continues to worship and to wonder at his ways. Not only in and about the Dutch counties, but everywhere did I come across these disciples. I discovered one at a wedding; my wife met another at a cocktail party; my mother met a third at a tea-party, and my cousin, still another on a pullman car. In all but one case the disciple was a total stranger who accidentally mentioned Van Buren of his own volition, and then enthusiastically offered information and especially anecdotes about him. Here again, I have excluded from the text some pleasant tales. One person told me that Little Van and Old Hickory arranged a semaphore code through which to communicate by hanging lamps in their windows at night. Another recited the usual "ghost story," telling how apparitions of Little Van often appeared to frighten the caretaker at Lindenwald.

It seems necessary here to say a word about my sources. The appended list includes everything on Van Buren except the verbal information I picked up in my travels. I have made no account of the pamphlets concerning other characters, such as Cheetham's attack on Burr which I was forced to read in the original. And I have not listed the newspapers consulted such as the New York *Times*, from which I took the description of the funeral. But otherwise the bibliography will explain whence came the information. For the reader's sake and my own I have dispensed with footnotes, and can only offer my word that all quotations here are genuine, to the best of my knowledge. I will preserve my own notes and stand ready to produce my facts for any statement under dispute. In no case have I invented a quotation, though in three places I have allowed myself to edit them. The Sunrise and the Nice Day anecdotes appear in several versions, contemporary and modern, direct and indirect quotations. I have given them here in their most convenient form. The same applies to the Virginian's quip about the so-and-so who voted nine times. I have put the story into what I thought was its best wording, using single quotation marks as an indication. Again: in citing authority I have kept strictly to contemporary sources, except in four places where for comparative purposes I quote modern writers. These places are indicated in the text.

Except for his speeches, there are only three main sources on

Van Buren; I shall consider them briefly. The Autobiography: Van Buren undertook it, as he admits to "justify my administration," which is to say himself. He carries it only up to his vice presidency, giving little or nothing of his childhood, marriage or home life. His purpose being one of justification, Little Van makes full use of his talent for glib explanations. Now and then he is amazingly frank and pleasantly chatty, but for the most part he is laboriously building himself up as a martyr and a statesman. The book is verbosely, unskillfully written and never revised. He thinks nothing of running one sentence the length of a page, a habit which made it necessary for me to cut up so many of my quotations into broken sentences. Very decidedly the Autobiography is no pleasure to read and, in many cases, is not even reliable.

The Van Buren Papers: These letters were carefully selected, first by Van Buren, later by his heirs before they went to the Congressional Library. They are another branch of his justification program. Planning the Autobiography, Van Buren wrote to many of his friends asking for the return of old letters he had sent them. Andrew Jackson, among others, sent him a large number, asking that they be returned when copied. They never were returned, much to the displeasure of Old Hickory's biographers. Probably Van Buren burned whatever he found incriminating, both in the Jackson batch and in any other collection upon which he could lay hands.

The Mackenzie Collection: One assortment, however, he had no chance to burn. One day in 1845 William L. Mackenzie, a New York customs officer, broke open a trunk belonging to Jesse Hoyt, one of Van Buren's lieutenants, and discovered about two hundred letters by Van Buren and various members of the Regency. Linking these together to form a running story, Mackenzie published what he misleadingly called a biography of the ex-President, then preparing for his last campaign. In this collection are almost all of the quotations in which Little Van speaks openly of such matters as the Spoils System, betting and other subjects which do not exalt his fame.

No one, I suppose, ever wrote a biography single-handed. Certainly I did not, though mine was the only hand to beat the typewriter keys. In addition to the several persons mentioned above, there are eight others to whom I owe much gratitude. My wife, my father, my mother have suffered with me, chapter for chapter. They have read and re-read for criticism and advice; have done everything possible to speed and improve the work. Dorsey Alexander, a Princeton Sophomore, has been my outpost in that seat of learning; Dr. W. Stull Holt of Johns Hopkins and Dr. Henry Steele Commanger of New York University read the script for historical accuracy, though neither must be held liable for any mistakes that may appear. Finally, I would mention two whose help was no less valuable, although it was indirectly given: Captain Louis Wardlaw Miles and the late Gordon Huntington Harper. To all these, and to anyone accidentally omitted, go my heartiest thanks.

# Bibliography

---

## 1

## SOURCES ON MARTIN VAN BUREN

ORIGINAL:

*Autobiography* (Covers roughly 1800-1834). Edited by John C. Fitzpatrick. Printed by Gov't Printing Office, 1920

*The Van Buren Papers* (61 volumes of letters and notes in original handwriting). Library of Congress, Washington, D. C.

*The Mackenzie Collection* (about 200 letters by Van Buren and his friends). See "Author's Confessions" for details

Speeches and Official Papers at N. Y. Public Library and Library of Congress, Washington, D. C.

GENEALOGICAL:

Frank J. Conklin—*The N. Y. Genealogy Record*, July and October 1879

Harriet C. W. Van Buren Peckham—*History of Cornelius Maessen Van Buren*, New York, 1913

BIOGRAPHICAL:

George Bancroft—*Martin Van Buren to the End of His Public Career*, New York, 1889

Samuel Flagg Bemis—*The American Secretaries of State and Their Diplomacy*, New York, 1928

Montgomery Blair—*Martin Van Buren, Diplomat*, Harper's Magazine, 11/09

William Allen Butler—*Martin Van Buren: Lawyer, Statesman and Man*, New York, 1862

Davy Crockett—*The Life of Martin Van Buren*, Philadelphia, 1835

Moses Dawson—*Sketches in the Life of Martin Van Buren*, Cincinnati, 1840

# Bibliography

William Emmons—*Biography of Martin Van Buren*. (Really a selection of his writings and speeches.) Washington, 1835

William M. Holland—*The Life and Political Opinions of Martin Van Buren*, Hartford, 1835

John Robert Irelan—*The Republic* (vol. 8th of the 18 volumes is life of Eighth President). Chicago, 1887

John S. Jenkins—*Lives of the Governors of State of New York*, Auburn, 1851

Adrien Hoffman Joline—*Martin Van Buren, the Lawyer*, Chicago, 1907

Denis Tilden Lynch—*An Epic and a Man*, New York, 1929

William L. Mackenzie—*The Life and Times of Martin Van Buren*, Boston, 1846

Cora Miley—*A Forgotten President*, Americana, 1929

Peyton F. Miller—*A Group of Great Lawyers of Columbia County, New York*, Hudson, N. Y., 1904

Samuel P. Orth—*Five American Politicians*, Cleveland

Edward M. Shepard—*Martin Van Buren*, Boston, 1888

William O. Stoddard—*Lives of the Presidents*, New York, 1887

PAMPHLETS (mostly anonymous and often dateless):

Albany Argus Extra: *Life of Martin Van Buren*, 1837

Washington Globe Extra: *Life of Martin Van Buren*, 1840

Van Buren Executive Committee: *Life of Martin Van Buren*, 1844

*A Word in Season*—Washington, 1840

*A Brief Account of the Life and Public Opinion of Martin Van Buren*, Washington, 1840

*How the Wand of the Magician May be Broken*, Washington, 1840

*The Claims of Martin Van Buren to be President*, Washington, 1840

*Martin Van Buren and the War*, Albany, 1840

*The Inconsistency and Hypocrisy of Martin Van Buren*, Washington, 1840

*Sketches in the Life and Public Services of Martin Van Buren*—A. J. Brady, no date

*The Crisis*, Richmond, 1840

*A Looking Glass at the Worthies of the Buffalo Convention*, Washington, 1848

*Letters Addressed to Martin Van Buren by Corrector*, 1830

*The Van Buren Platform,* Washington, 1848
*On Anti-Vanburenism,* Boston, 1836
*Martin Van Buren*—Gilpin Henry Dilwood, Washington, 1836

2

## WRITINGS OF CONTEMPORARIES

GENERAL MATERIAL (nearly all of these offer some first-hand anecdotes on Van Buren) :
John Quincy Adams—*Diary.* (Edited Allan Nevins) New York, 1929
Levi Beardsley—*Reminiscences,* New York, 1852
Thomas Hart Benton—*Thirty Years' View,* New York, 1856
Mrs. Catherine Bonney—*Legacy of Historical Gleanings,* 1875
William Allen Butler—*A Retrospect of Forty Years,* New York, 1911
William H. Crawford—*Journal,* Northampton, Mass., 1925
David Crockett—*Autobiography,* New York, 1923 (reprint)
Oliver Dyer—*Proceedings of the Free Soil Commission,* Buffalo, 1848
E. F. Ellet—*Court Circles of the Republic,* Hartford, 1869
Franklin Ellis—*History of Columbia County, New York,* Philadelphia, 1878
Henry S. Foote—*A Casket of Reminiscences,* Washington, 1874
O. C. Gardener—*The Great Issue,* New York, 1848
Jabez D. Hammond—*History of Political Parties in the State of New York,* Albany, 1842
Philip Hone—*Diary,* New York, 1889
Gaillord Hunt (Editor)—*First Forty Years of Washington Society,* New York, 1906 (Letters of Mrs. Samuel H. Smith)
Harriett Martineau—*Society in America,* New York, 1838
Reginald C. McGrane (Editor)—*The Correspondence of Nicholas Biddle,* Boston, 1919
James K. Polk—*Diary.* (Edited by Allan Nevins) New York, 1929
Perley Benjamin Poore—*Perley's Reminiscences,* Philadelphia, 1886
Nathan Sargent—*Public Men and Events,* Philadelphia, 1875
Winfield Scott—*Memoirs,* New York, 1864

426 ]

# Bibliography

William Henry Seward—*Autobiography*, New York, 1891

Henry Tilden—*Clippings from Newspapers of 1840*

Martin Van Buren—*An Inquiry into the Origin and Course of Political Parties in the U. S.*, New York, 1867

Thurlow Weed—*Autobiography*. (Edited by Harriet A. Weed) New York, 1870

Henry Wilson—*The Rise and Fall of the Slave Power in U. S.*, Boston, 1874

Henry A. Wise—*Seven Decades of the Union*, Philadelphia, 1876

## 3

## BOOKS ON CONTEMPORARIES

*John Quincy Adams*—John T. Morse, Jr., Boston, 1882

*Mr. & Mrs. John Quincy Adams*—Dorothie Bobbé, New York, 1930

*The True Aaron Burr*—Charles Burr Todd, New York, 1902

*Aaron Burr*—Samuel H. Wandell and Meade Minnegerode, New York, 1925

*Life & Times of Aaron Burr*—James Parton, New York, 1860

*Thomas Hart Benton*—Joseph M. Rogers, Philadelphia, 1905

*John C. Calhoun*—H. von Holst, Boston, 1888

*John C. Calhoun*—William H. Meigs, New York, 1917

*Louis Cass*—Andrew C. McLaughlin, Boston, 1891

*Henry Clay*—Carl S. Schurz, Boston, 1888

*The True Henry Clay*—Joseph M. Rogers, Philadelphia, 1912

*Life and Character of William H. Crawford*—Thomas Cooper, Albany, 1824

*Life of William H. Crawford*—J. E. D. Shipp, Americanus, Georgia, 1908

*De Witt Clinton*—Dorothie Bobbé, New York, 1933

*De Witt Clinton and the Origin of the Spoils System in New York*—Howard E. McBain, New York, 1907

*Peggy Eaton*—Autobiography, New York, 1932

*Peggy Eaton*—Queena Pollack, New York, 1931

*Life of William Henry Harrison*—H. Montgomery, Cleveland, 1852

*William Henry Harrison*—Dorothy Burne Goebel, Indianapolis, 1926

*Alexander Hamilton as Promoter*—Charles H. Schrieber, Americana, 1921

*Alexander Hamilton*—Henry Jones Ford, New York, 1920

*Alexander Hamilton*—Frederick Scott Oliver, New York, 1907

*Washington Irving*—Henry Boynton, Boston, 1901

*Washington Irving, Esq.*—George S. Hellman, New York, 1925

*Andrew Jackson: The Border Captain*—Marquis James, New York, 1933

*Andrew Jackson*—Gerald W. Johnson, New York, 1927

*Andrew Jackson*—James Parton, New York, 1860

*Andrew Jackson*—William Graham Sumner, New York, 1916

*Andrew Jackson*—John Spencer Bassett, New York, 1916

*Thomas Jefferson*—Alfred Jay Nock, New York, 1926

*Thomas Jefferson*—John T. Morse, Jr., Boston, 1883

*Jefferson & Hamilton*—Claude G. Bowers, Boston, 1925

*Rufus King and His Times*—Edward Hale Brush, New York, 1926

*Abraham Lincoln*—William H. Herndon, New York, 1892

*Dolly Madison*—Maud Wilder Goodwin, New York, 1896

*Dolly Madison in "Wives"*—Gamaliel Bradford, New York, 1925

*James Madison*—Sidney Howard Gay, New York, 1909

*James Monroe*—Daniel C. Gilman, Boston, 1899

*The Strange Disappearance of William Morgan*—Thomas A. Knight, New York, 1932

*James K. Polk*—E. I. McCormac, Berkeley, California, 1922

*Randolph of Roanoke*—Gerald W. Johnson, New York, 1929

*John Randolph*—Henry Adams, Boston, 1882

*John Randolph of Roanoke*—William Cabel Bruce, New York, 1922

*Memorial of Ambrose Spencer*—Horatio Potter, Albany, 1849

*Life, Character and Public Service of Ambrose Spencer*—Daniel D. Barnard

*William Henry Seward*—Thornton K. Lothrop, Boston, 1898

*The Prince of Darkness—Talleyrand*—Gamaliel Bradford, New York, 1932

*Life of Daniel Webster*—George T. Curtis, New York, 1870

*Daniel Webster*—Henry Cabot Lodge, Boston, 1883

# 4

## GENERAL BIOGRAPHY

Library Editions:
*Biographical Dictionary of American Congress* (1774-1927)
*Dictionary of American Biography*
*Appleton's Cyclopedia of American Biography*
*National Cyclopedia of Biography*
*Biographical Sketches of Preeminent Americans*
*National Portrait Gallery of Americans*
*New York State's Preeminent Men*
Collective Biography:
Gamaliel Bradford: *As God Made Them,* Boston, 1929
Gamaliel Bradford: *Damaged Souls,* Boston, 1923
Gamaliel Bradford: *Wives,* New York, 1925

# 5

## GENERAL

James Truslow Adams—*The March of Democracy,* New York, 1933
Herbert Agar—*The People's Choice,* Boston, 1933
D. S. Alexander—*Political History of New York,* New York, 1906
Claude G. Bowers—*The Party Battles of the Jackson Period,* New York, 1923
E. Douglas Branch—*The Sentimental Years,* New York, 1934
Ralph C. H. Catterall—*The Second Bank of the U. S.,* Chicago, 1903
Edward A. Collier—*History of Old Kinderhook,* New York, 1914
Mary C. Crawford—*Romantic Days of the Early Republic,* Boston, 1912
Charles Hemstreet—*Nooks and Corners of Old New York,* New York, 1899
Charles Hemstreet—*Literary New York,* New York, 1903

Frank R. Kent—*The Democratic Party—A History*, New York, 1928

William S. Kline—*The Village Beautiful*, Kinderhook, 1911

Sarah M. Lockwood—*New York*, New York, 1926

William MacDonald—*Jeffersonian Democracy*, New York, 1906

Gustavus Meyers—*A History of Tammany Hall*

Meade Minnegerode—*Presidential Years*, New York, 1921

Meade Minnegerode—*The Fabulous Forties*, New York, 1934

Frederick Austin Ogg—*The Reign of Andrew Jackson*, New Haven, 1919

George H. Payne—*History of Journalism in the U. S.*, New York, 1920

Esther Singleton—*The Story of the White House*, New York, 1907

Edward Stanwood—*A History of Presidential Elections*, Boston, 1884

Charles Burr Todd—*A History of the City of New York*, 1899

M. R. Werner—*Tammany Hall*, New York, 1928

Paul Wilstach—*Hudson River Landings*, New York, 1932

1. BIRTHPLACE OF MARTIN VAN BUREN
KINDERHOOK, COLUMBIA CO., N. Y.

2. EARLIEST LIKENESS OF MARTIN VAN BUREN

3. THE FIRST TAMMANY WIGWAM—THE PIG PEN

4. DEBTORS' PRISON

5. A. HAMILTON                    6. A. BURR

7. OLD DUELLING GROUND
WEEHAWKEN, 1804

8. MR. AND MRS. MARTIN VAN BUREN

9. DE WITT CLINTON

10. CAPTURE OF THE CITY OF WASHINGTON

11. BATTLE OF NEW ORLEANS

12. A SENATORIAL ENCOUNTER

13. THE EATON QUICKSTEP

14. THE REJECTED MINISTER

15. THE PRESIDENT'S HOUSE IN 1831

16. MARTIN VAN BUREN IN HIS MIDDLE YEARS

17. THE LITTLE MAGICIAN INVOKED

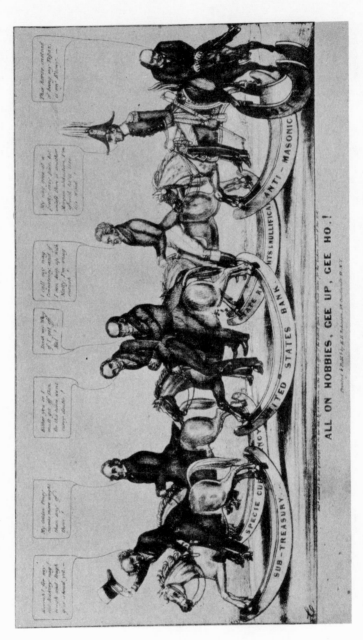

18. ALL ON HOBBIES, GEE UP, GEE UP, GEE HO!

19. THE CUT DIRECT

20. THE MEETING AT SARATOGA

21. THE NORTH BEND FARMER AND HIS VISITORS

22. O. K.
(OFF TO KINDERHOOK)

23. SETTIN' ON A RAIL

24. MATTY MEETING THE TEXAS QUESTION

25. MATTY TAKING HIS SECOND BATH IN SALT RIVER

26. A VIEW OF THE POLITICAL WORLD FROM KINDERHOOK

27. MARTIN VAN BUREN'S TOMB     28. THE VAN BUREN COAT OF ARMS

29. LINDENWALD